Ladies of the Ironhorse

Ladies of the Ironhorse

The Voices of Those Who Wait at Home

Task Force Ironhorse in Iraq
April 2003 to April 2004

Rhonda Eggleston

St. John's Press
Tuscaloosa, AL

All proceeds from the sale of this book will go to the 4th Infantry Division Layette fund and the 4th Infantry Division Museum. The Layette program is administered by the Division Family Readiness Group and provides gifts to the families of newborn babies. Recipients must hold the rank of E-1 through E-4. The Museum is dedicated to preserving and telling the story of the 4th Infantry Division from World War I to present day.

Author's photo by Susanna Bunker—by permission

Cover art by SGT Rudy Gomez, 4ID—by permission
Cover art manufactured and distributed by KPE, Inc., Kim Federici and Peter Florczak
http://www.flowersinglass.com—by permission

Printed in the United States of America
Published by St. John's Press, Tuscaloosa, AL
Cover design by Charles J. Boyle:

First Edition, 2005
ISBN 0-9710551-9-X

Ladies of the Ironhorse/Eggleston, Rhonda—1963
Ladies of the Ironhorse, The Voices of Those Who Wait at Home, Task Force Ironhorse in Iraq, April 2003 to April 2004

10 9 8 7 6 5 4 3 2 1

For the Soldiers and families who made the choice to serve their country proudly and with honor.

Contents

Introduction

*T*he idea for this project first came as I was driving home from the 4th Infantry Division's reunion at Ft. Hood in September of 2003. Because my husband was deployed with Task Force Ironhorse for Operation Iraqi Freedom from March of 2003 through March of 2004, we officially became part of a very large army family. I had met some of my new kin that morning, and it encouraged me to talk with other wives who have been through wartime deployments. Our community support had been outstanding. Our family had rallied around us, but there is just something about talking to another army wife that helps you keep your feet on the ground and know that your Soldier's deployment to a war zone can be tolerated, even accepted, for we too, play a large and important role in our Soldiers lives.

I also met Bob Babcock that morning; a Vietnam veteran, who was e-mailing daily updates to three thousand friends and family of Task Force Ironhorse. Bob estimated that by the time his e-mails were sent on to other contacts, around fifty thousand people received these updates each day. There were four sections in the updates that included articles from the press with anything pertaining to 4ID(4th Infantry Division).

Additionally, Bob provided casualty reports as they became available, a little bit about the 4ID history, and letters from family members of what they were hearing from their Soldiers.

I thought about the advantages in communication that we have now, compared to those who experienced previous wars. I thought about the press and the two-edged sword of twenty-four hour information. Using Bob's updates I decided to put this question out to wives: "What inspires or encourages you to be strong during your Soldier's deployment?" and see what responses I would receive. Not only did I receive replies from wives, but also from mothers, sisters, aunts, grandmothers and other extended family, so, I decided to include them as well.

In the following pages are the answers I received to that initial inquiry and also the highlights from Bob's family letters in his daily update. This is the story of a year in the life of families who have Soldiers deployed to a war.

Our Soldiers have made the choice to serve their country, defend freedom, and oppose tyranny. Good soldiers know that the consequences of war are separation from loved ones, disability, or death. They know they might be called upon to make these sacrifices. They face those sacrifices squarely and do their duty; that is what makes them heroes. Family members also know the consequences of war. They must face how the war changes the Soldier they love and they must choose to stay positive when they want to weep or be angry.

Good family members choose to give the support their Soldier needs, and that is what makes them special. This tenacity of spirit and moral clarity are what makes America a great nation.

So many different people from so many different places are represented in these pages, but the one thing that is common in the responses of all are love: love of God, love of family, and love of country.

As a relatively young nation we are still learning to deal with our wealth, power, and freedoms, but what Operation Iraqi Freedom and the War on Terror have shown is that we, the American people, as diverse as we are, will take care of our own. We learned our lesson after Vietnam. We do not like cowardly bullies, and we can still rise to the challenges that are before us. I think you will see that represented in the following pages, ingenuity, compassion, and steadfastness, are all still within us.

The excerpts from Bob's update are meant to give an understanding of what family members faced each day—the drudgery and disappointment of no news, the fear of bad news, and the pride of good news. If you would like Bob's complete updates, you can send a donation to American's Remembered at **American's Remembered, Inc., PO Box 68222, Marietta, GA 30068 or via e-mail at babcock224@aol.com** and receive them on CDs. American's Remembered is a non-profit organization dedicated to preserving the memories and experiences of Soldiers and civilians who have served our country. A shameless plug, but anything for Bob; you see he is the papa of our 4ID Iraqi Freedom family.

We have faced many challenges during this year. We have formed many friendships. We have waited at home watching the news and seeing history unfold with anxious and triumphant moments. Troop manifests, yellow ribbons, Family Readiness Group meetings, collecting school supplies for the Iraqi children, memorial services, and welcome home celebrations were ways that the War for Iraqi Freedom was lived out at home.

These pages reflect the pride we felt while we waited for our Soldiers to return home.

Foreword

I am pleased to comment on *Ladies of The Ironhorse*. This collection of correspondence between familes, and between the Soldiers of Task Force Ironhorse while they were deployed in Iraq, demonstrates how vitally important family support is to everyone involved. Through these messages the reader will come to fully appreciate the love, the sacrifice, and the patriotism of our military families who remained behind. Preserving these day-to-day messages, written spontaneously and from the heart, is an important piece of the history of Task Force Ironhorse. The authors will know that they are deeply appreciated, and families who face similar separations can find hope, encouragement and strength in their words.

Not long ago, I wrote a special message of appreciation to the Family Readiness Group community of Fort Hood. I believe this is an appropriate opportunity to share with you some of that message, thereby revealing how special and important these ladies are to me and to my husband, LTG Raymond T. Odierno, the commander of Task Force Ironhorse.

"It was a great honor and privilege to be part of such a wonderful group of spouses in the 4th Infantry Division and Task Force Ironhorse. They showed great dignity, grace and strength throughout the deployment. When we learned how long the deployment would last, it brought us closer together and these incredible spouses carried on without complaint.

"The Casing of the Colors ceremony on 27 March 2003 was a day we will never forget. Our Soldiers marched onto the field and the families encircled them, showing their love and support for them and for their mission. From that day on we became one team in support of the War on Terror. I have never been part of a finer, more dedicated and loyal group of Spouses. Like their Soldier, they are true American heroes who made incredible sacrifices and served their country proudly.

"We were so proud of The Task Force—the hard work they performed each day, and the professional manner in which they went about their business. We will never forget the feelings we felt when we heard that Task Force Ironhorse had captured Saddam Hussein. Whenever we saw an American flag, it had even more meaning to us, knowing our husbands/wives were there protecting our freedom and making great sacrifices. You couldn't get through the National Anthem without becoming emotional and feeling pride for our spouses and all our troops.

"We missed our best friends; they were on our minds all the time. As spouses, we were always there for each other and we stuck together as a team. They were a truly special group who lifted each other when necessary and inspired each other with their strength. We worked hard together, but we had fun together, too. We counted on each other for support during the tough times, lending a helping hand or a word of encouragement whenever needed. We learned how important Faith is, and most importantly, we learned how to laugh and cry together.

"Our Family Readiness Group Leaders shouldered incredible responsibilities and did so with sincerity, strength and compassion. It was out of their love of army families, the troops and their love for the 4ID that caused them to give so generously. Especially hard were the loss and injuries of our Soldiers. The FRGs and Care Teams gave so much to ease the pain and the entire Division mourned and felt each loss.

"The Welcome Home Ceremonies in the gym and all the sounds and feelings among the spouses and families waiting for their Soldier was an incredible feeling. As they marched in, we felt such great pride and love and we waved our flags and cheered in tribute and appreciation for their bravery. We felt the presence of the Soldiers who paid the ultimate sacrifice and also the presence of our injured Soldiers.

"We were very lucky to have the great support of our rear detachment Soldiers and chaplains. We will never forget waking up each morning to the 'Daily Updates' from Mr. Bob Babcock. It was a great morale booster for all family members and Soldiers. We received superb support from the agencies on post and from the surrounding communities. We will never forget their generosity during the deployment.

"The uncasing of the flags ceremony and the welcome home celebration on April 22 was a great way to celebrate the sacrifice and accomplishments of our Soldiers and their families.

"I'll cherish forever the great bond we shared throughout the deployment. The spouses and troops of the 4ID and Task Force Ironhorse will always have a special place in my heart. God Bless our troops and their families, and, God Bless the USA."
Steadfast and Loyal.
Linda Odierno

ONE

MARCH - APRIL 2003
The Battle Begins

*T*he time our Soldiers had trained for had arrived. The most lethal division in the army was going over to Iraq to be tested. Troop manifests were occurring around the clock. The assemblies were a time for families to say their final good-byes. As you can imagine, tears and fears of the unknown were common in gyms at Ft. Hood and other posts around the country. As our Soldiers' buses pulled away from the gyms to go to the airport, we waved our flags—some of us tried to smile, and we cried. The battle of the home front had now begun.

Our Soldiers landed in Kuwait, unloaded ships, and pushed into Iraq. They were able to see for themselves how Saddam Hussein had plundered his own people. We learned why the phrase urban warfare was such an ugly reality for our Soldiers in Iraq. It did not take long for that reality to set in. We read of the first Task Force KIA (Killed in Action) and several similar articles.

To aptly portray the flavor of this anthology, our story begins with the reflections of several wives and mothers as they recall the heartache of separation, extreme pride in their Soldier husbands and an understanding of their mutual sacrifice.

22-29 March - Task Force Ironhorse Deploys
We finally received word that the Pentagon had abandoned the plan of using Turkey, and now the Task Force would enter Iraq through Kuwait. All the ships were redirected from Turkey to the Persian Gulf.

The 27th of March was the flag casing ceremony for the division. The day was a beautiful spring day such as only Texas can produce. Every brigade of Task Force Ironhorse was

1

represented by soldiers and flags on the parade field in front of the 4th Infantry Division Headquarters. All of our soldiers were in new desert camouflage uniforms (DCUs). The pageantry of this ceremony made me proud to be an army wife, and General Odierno's speech was one of the most inspiring I have ever heard.

27 March - Commanding General's Remarks - Colors Casing Ceremony

Ladies and Gentlemen, Leaders of Central Texas, Friends and Family of the 4th Infantry Division, and soldiers, non-commissioned officers, and officers of the Ironhorse Team —thank you for joining us on this brilliant spring morning deep in the heart of Central Texas. I want to welcome you all to this morning's ceremony. We have cased the colors of Task Force Ironhorse, for deployment to the Central Command Area of Operations as we join the fight to replace an unethical, immoral, tyrannical regime.

Our nation has been engaged in a global war against terrorism since the tragic events of 9/11. A little over a week ago, the most powerful coalition ever assembled initiated combat operations against an evil and oppressive regime as part of Operation Iraqi Freedom. The coalition is performing magnificently in a just, but dangerous mission. Right now as I speak, our comrades are engaged in battle over 7000 miles from here. Our brothers and sisters from the 3rd Infantry Division, 101st Air Assault Division, the 82nd Airborne Division, the 1st United Kingdom Armored Division, the 1st Marine Division, the 173rd Airborne Brigade, as well as many other soldiers, marines, sailors, airmen, and coast guardsmen from several nations are selflessly risking their lives for our common defense. Some have already made the ultimate sacrifice and we owe our freedom to them. Others are in the captivity of a brutal and oppressive regime. Please remember them and their families in your thoughts and prayers. They will never be forgotten.

I want to read to you a very recent quote from our Commander in Chief that is particularly appropriate as Task Force Ironhorse deploys: "In every generation, the enemy has produced enemies of human freedom. They have attacked America because we are freedom's home and defender. The commitment of our fathers is now the calling of our time."

The Ironhorse has been summoned, and we will answer that calling. It is not a calling that we answer for money, easy work, or glory—rather, it is a calling from deep within our hearts to protect you, our families, and each other. It is a calling for the love of our country, defending our way of life for the next generation of Americans. It is important for all Americans to support our soldiers. I want to recite an e-mail I received recently: "It is the soldier, not the press, who has given freedom of the press. It is the soldier, not the poet, who has given us freedom of speech. It is the soldier, not the campus organizer, who has given us the right to demonstrate. It is the soldier, not the lawyer, who has given us the right to a fair trial. It is the soldier who salutes the flag, who serves under the flag, whose coffin is draped by the flag, and who allows the protester to burn the flag."

Out on Cameron Field today with our colors is a small slice of Task Force Ironhorse. The Commander of Troops is our Chief of Staff, COL Jim Barclay. I also want to recognize the salute battery from Bravo Battery, 2nd Battalion, 20th Field Artillery led by 1LT Luis Cruz and SSG Chad Reynolds, the Division color guard led by SSG Kenneth Traynum, and the 4th Infantry Division Band, led by CWO Jesse Pascua. They represent the exacting standards and discipline of this Task Force.

These colors and soldiers standing before you today represent over 33,000 teammates in Task Force Ironhorse. Many have already deployed and are in harm's way. Each and every soldier has voluntarily raised his or her right hand and has taken an oath to 'support and defend the Constitution of the United States against all enemies, foreign and domestic.' I admire them for their bravery and courage, and I am humbled to serve in their ranks. It is because of them that we enjoy life, liberty, and happiness today. Please join me in a round of applause for these magnificent warriors.

This task force began taking form several months ago and was built upon the nucleus of the 4th Infantry Division. It was the intent of Central Command to build a lethal, self-contained force available to conduct decisive, war winning operations anywhere in Southwest Asia, and that's what we have done. On a Saturday evening in mid-January, we were given the order to immediately deploy our equipment. We doubled in size and swelled to over fourteen thousand pieces of equipment. Within five days, trains were leaving our installations to load ships. Within eight days, ships were ready to sail. Within a month, our equipment was ready to unload and conduct combat operations. It was a team effort that we are all proud of, and it would not have been so swift and agile without the help of our fantastic teammates that include: every major subordinate command on Ft. Hood—the First Team, 13th Corps Support Command, 3rd Signal Brigade, 504th Military Intelligence Brigade, 89th Military Police Brigade, 21st Air Cavalry Brigade, MEDDAC, and DENTAC—the Phantom Corps HQ's and the Joint Movement Operations Center, going 24/7, our dedicated garrison agencies—DOL, DCA, DPW, AG, ACS, Red Cross, Lane Volunteer Center, and many more—and most importantly, the unwavering support of our families and the local community.

In short order, we will link-up with our equipment in the sands of Southwest Asia, and the full combat power of the task force will come to bear, quickly and decisively, upon an enemy that has no idea of the combined arms hammer that is getting ready to strike him. I guarantee you that every soldier in the task force is highly trained, motivated, and absolutely prepared to deal with any mission that lies ahead. We have dedicated, technically competent, and moral soldiers, the best non-commissioned officer corps, all led by the finest officer corps in the world. Our leaders have complete confidence in the competence of our soldiers, and our soldiers believe in, and have complete trust in their leaders. That is what sets us apart from any foreign army. A lot is made of the 4th Infantry Division's modern equipment and capabilities, but what it comes down to is our soldiers. The Army is about soldiers who have integrity, moral values, and dedication to the mission ahead. The soldiers of this Task Force are the epitome of these values.

This task force casing ceremony is both a hallmark of history and a beacon for the future. Since 1917, the 4th

Infantry Division has defended liberty and freedom in combat: first in the two world wars on the bloody battlefields of Europe, and again in the sweltering jungles of Vietnam. The names are a never-ending drum roll of honor and commitment: St. Mihiehl, Meuse-Argonne, Utah Beach, the Huertgen Forest, the Battle of the Bulge, Plieku, Dak To, and Central Highlands. Almost sixty years ago our colors liberated Paris from the grip of vile and tyrannical rule. Over five hundred thousand soldiers have worn this patch. Once again we have been called upon, and I assure you that the magnificent soldiers of this powerful task force will continue the long, proud, legacy of the Ironhorse Division.

To the soldiers of Task Force Ironhorse, I am confident that we are trained and ready. We have the most modern and lethal equipment in the world, but it is each and every one of you that makes us the most formidable force in the world today. We will see him before he sees us; we will act before he acts; we will engage and destroy before he can move; and it will NOT be a fair fight. He does not have a chance. Our brothers and sisters from the Phantom Corps, including the 1st Cavalry Division and 3rd Armored Cavalry Regiment, are also coming to join us in this just and noble cause. Trust your leaders, rely on your training, maintain your exacting standards, press the initiative, take care of your buddies, and know that the world is counting on us. This is war, not a game. Coming in second place doesn't count. We will win decisively, we will make our nation proud, and we will make the world a better place for our sons and daughters.

Ladies and Gentlemen, we have a non-negotiable contract with the people of America to fight and win our nation's wars. Our purpose is just, our mission is clear, and this great task force is ready. This is not a war about religion; it is not a war about oil; it is not a war about politics. It is a war about ensuring our freedom and maintaining our way of life for future generations of America's sons and daughters, and it is a war to ensure freedom for the oppressed Iraqi people. Freedom is not free—it never has been, and it never will be. We pray for peace and do not wish for war, but we train to fight in order to protect our families, each other, and our country. Our cause is right and our resolve is unwavering. The proud soldiers of Task Force Ironhorse will join our brave comrades to ensure our freedom.

To all the families of Task Force Ironhorse, your sacrifices are a great testament to your patriotism and support for your country. Please take comfort that your husband, wife, father, mother, son, or daughter is part of the best-trained organization is the world today. They are experts who know their business. They know their job. The support for Task Force Ironhorse over the past months has been phenomenal, and I thank you in advance for your continued support. Central Texas is a cradle of patriotism, and it gives me great pride to be in the midst of such loyal and devoted citizens. Ft. Hood, as well as our other installations, recognizes that our Army is about people and families. They are dedicated to ensuring that our families are taken care of while we are deployed.

It gives me great comfort to know that our families are safe and have first class family readiness groups and rear detachments that they can go to for support and assistance. We do not know how long we will be gone, but we do know that we will accomplish the mission as quickly and efficiently as possible. The enemy has no chance for success. The colors of Task Force Ironhorse will be unfurled in a matter of days, and we will not let you down. We stand by our motto, "Steadfast and Loyal."

God Bless America
Ray T. Odierno
MG, Task Force Ironhorse
Commanding

Brittany West - Wife of SPC Logan West - A Co 5th EN BN

My husband has been deployed since April 2nd, 2003. The life of a military wife is not easy, but it has its rewards. I have been around the military my whole life; it's all I know. And so it was not surprising when I married a military man. I did not think it was going to be too bad because my dad has been deployed many times, but it is different when you love someone, than when you are *in* love with someone.

I have known my husband since August of 2002. Soon after setting our wedding date, we found out our lives were going to change in just 9 months. Since we knew he was getting deployed, we moved our wedding date to December 2002. We had no clue when he was leaving, but I knew it could be any day. Luckily we got to spend three and a half great months together as a married couple before he deployed for Operation Iraqi Freedom. I think the hardest part of this deployment was deployment day. It was hard for me knowing my soul mate was going to be half a world away. I think the hardest part for him was getting on that bus saying good-bye to his nine-month pregnant wife.

That night was the hardest; I sat in my car for hours after leaving the Company. I just could not walk into the empty house. For some reason, sitting in the car listening to the last CD we listened to together, made me feel like he was still here. I called my mother-in-law and she talked me into the house. Then I cried a few hours and went to bed. When I woke up I felt empty, but I went on with my day like it was okay until bedtime, then it was hard again. A few days later I was just fine; I knew I had to do this; I had to stay positive for my unborn child. On May 21st, 2003, I had our beautiful baby boy.

My husband could not make it back for the birth. In fact, the day Ethan was born the alert went back up to high. If it were not for friends and family, there was no way I would have made it; they kept my head on straight. My mother was my coach, and my friend, Cristy, videotaped the birth so my husband would not miss a thing. Still, to this day my son has never met his father, but one day really soon he will. He will someday tell his child he was not there when he was born because he was fighting for the freedom of Iraq. My experience as a teen mother and wife is hard and no one can say differently. But I always keep in mind they're doing this to make our children's lives and our grandchildren's lives better, keeping our country safe and free. That is the best reward of this deployment. My husband is a hero and may not have his own holiday or memorial, but to our son and me, he will always be a hero.

Tina French - Wife of SGT Richard French - B BTRY 4-42 FA

My husband has been deployed to Iraq since 5 April 2003 with the rest of his Battery. I miss him dearly and love him very much.

We have two wonderful kids, Victoria (five years old) and Richard Jr. (two years old). Victoria and Richard have kept me going. You see, both of them are in speech therapy a couple of times each week. Our daughter is also in pre-kindergarten. I walk her to school so it gives me some exercise, and I love doing it. She is doing great, one of the smartest in her class. After I take her to school, I go to ladies aerobics three days a week at my church, the First Baptist Church of Copperas Cove.

Also, what keeps me going are all the friends and family that we have, especially family.

Well, even though today is Saturday, we are off to our church for a Women's Conference.

Black Dragons, HOOAH!

Cindy Rankin - Mother of SPC Matthew Rankin - A Co 1-22 IN

My son called to tell us the Fourth Infantry Division was being deployed to Iraq. He wanted us to come and get his car rather than store it on post. We knew that he was going, but definite dates had not been set. We drove to Killeen, Texas and started searching for a motel room. We hadn't stopped to think that other fathers and mothers would also be meeting with their sons and daughters.

I hugged my son when it was time to leave him. We had taken pictures and spent time just being together. I asked him if he had any regrets about joining the Army. He was only seventeen when he enlisted and his daddy and I had to sign for him to get into the service. He was very unhappy with school and had done all kinds of research on enlisting. He told me that this is what he wanted and he was ready to make a difference. He wanted to put his training to good use. I waited until after he left us before I cried. His unit deployed on April 2, 2003. We had his address and began writing him every week. I sent him packages of items that, by surfing the Internet, I found were needed by our Soldiers. I located websites dedicated to our military personnel and I joined their newsletters. I watched CNN, MSNBC, and FOX news. I accessed the Fort Hood website and added it to my "favorites" list along with the Killeen Daily Herald, Operation Military Pride, Operation Sandbox, and this wonderful Internet newsletter.

I started a scrapbook, and with my Mom's help, clipped news articles and printed out information from the Internet. Whenever anyone asked about putting him on their church's prayer list, I thanked them and said, "of course." Everyone commented about how well I was holding up. I told them that my son was doing his duty, and that I was so proud of him. I put up yellow ribbons at home and at the public library where I work. I wore a small yellow ribbon and a red, white, and blue pin that says "Support Our Troops." I worried.

I am on my fourth notebook, and someday when my son is ready, I will give all four to him. He's not ready to keep them now. His experiences are too new. He has matured so much. He has seen a different world. He is looking forward to being back in the States. He is contemplating his future. He doesn't want a fuss made over him. He was just doing his job. He has become a MAN, and he will always be my HERO!

16 March - "Momma, We Have the License."

The engagement came in August 2002. The wedding date was set for July 2003. The War in Iraq changed everything but the love and devotion of one South Dakota Army National Guardsman and our daughter.

December, 2002: Concern and wondering if he'd be activated and how they would respond with their pending wedding plans. Most of the discussion came from him; he didn't want to get married just to make her a widow.

Early January 2003: he turned twenty-one, no news on activation.

January 20, 2003: The kids had talked on the phone; he had just been told they wouldn't be activated. Three hours later he called with the news, they'd just been activated. Our daughter came to our room crying and pleading for advice. She loves this man; she'd marry him in a heartbeat. Even if the worst could happen, she needed to be his wife.

Through the cold South Dakota night she drove, calling home on her cell phone to keep awake, to share her fears and to cry with her momma. Three hours later, well past midnight, she's walking down the hallway toward his door and the future they need to decide.

The call came into my classroom on January 21, 2003, at 9:10 a.m. she said, "Momma, can you get here by 6:00? We're getting married."

Two calls go out, his Security Guard radio calls him to the Principal's office, "Our daughter is getting married tonight at 6:00." The second call goes to the florist to request bridal bouquets to be ready in two hours.

Emotions abound, no wedding dress... maybe I'll take mine. No family and friends to surround her with love... make some calls.

Her cousin, four-hundred miles away, pulls children out of school, a husband out of college classes, and plans to head west to meet us at the church.

Brothers get called at their job sites, shovels are dropped, delivery trucks head out with replacement workers, and the boys plan to travel east thirty minutes behind us to their only sister's wedding.

And so we go, over the same cold highway she traveled in the night, flowers and champagne securely tucked in the back seat. I stitch together the wedding ring pillow while the cell phone intermittently rings. "Momma, we have the license." "Momma, we meet the pastor at noon." "Momma, I'm walking through Wal-Mart trying to find something to wear to my wedding and buying gold bands."

No tears, no concerns that her wedding attire would be a white sweater and black dress pants, she was marrying the man she loves and that was enough.

Much is thought about when a momma is driving to her only daughter's wedding, but usually it isn't about the war, and if he'll ever come back. "Oh God, he must come back... Please, God, bring him back," is the heart wrenching prayer I first said on her wedding day.

It's amazing what can be accomplished in a mere ten-hour window of time. His family and friends purchase a cake, green and gold decorations, and food fit for the celebration. The Lutheran church was beautiful, stained glass windows and all. His family had done it out of love and devotion and our family will forever be grateful for the wedding they pulled together with a moment's notice because of the war. That evening our beautiful daughter becomes an Army bride.

Four days later, her much loved groom drove off to face an unknown foe. His unit was attached to the 4th ID. They sat at Ft. Leonard Wood until April 4, 2003, and then the true waiting began.

20 March - They Are Always Our Little Boys

I just read the memory of a year ago from the mother of the newlywed. Tears were really streaming down my face. I am the wife of a brave Soldier waiting in Kuwait to come home and start our lives again with our three children. This has been such an emotional roller coaster for me. I have to be strong for everyone around me, his parents, siblings and especially my children. I assure them that Daddy was coming home soon. In the back of my mind thinking, what would I possibly say to them if, God forbid, he were never to come home.

With everything that I have gone through as a wife, I can't imagine having one of my little boys deployed to war, because they are always our little boys whether they are five, like mine, or twenty-five. As mothers and fathers, it is natural to always want to protect our children, but I can't imagine how all you parents have felt having their protection out of your hands. My hats are off to all of you. There is no need competing over who has it harder, or who misses their Soldier more, but as spouses, let's not forget their sacrifices and don't exclude them. It's their babies out there fighting so our babies are safe! God bless all of us and especially our troops all around the world!

Trisha Jackson - 4th MP CO - Wife of PV2 Joshua Jackson - Co C 588 EN BN

Joshua and I were married February 10, 2003, and found out he would be deploying to Iraq later that month, and I the following month. Neither one of us knew the next time we would see each other, nor if we would even be able to write letters to one another because of the fact that neither one of us knew our overseas address. About a month and a half before I was to load up with my company, I discovered I was pregnant. It came as a shock to Joshua and me. We were both happy but also saddened by the news. We knew that I would be able to stay in the States, but he would still have to go.

11

Joshua left April 10, 2003. We had just bought a house and had only lived there together for those ten days before he left. I began receiving letters from him shortly after mid May. Well, to make a long story short, our son Dellic Joel Jackson was born Sep 11, 2003. He weighed eight-pounds, one-ounce, and was twenty inches long. He is my inspiration to keep my head up and my hopes high. I know I must be strong, not only Joshua, but for my son as well. Although his daddy couldn't be here for Dellic's birth, I know that in his dreams he was right there beside me.

Sometimes it's not easy being the wife of a Soldier; there are many lonely nights and sleepless hours wondering how your husband is doing. Is he safe? Is he warm? Is he hungry? But knowing that my husband is fighting for peace for his family and families all over the world fills me with pride and a feeling of security that nothing I've ever felt before can compare to.

Jo A. Johnson-Price - Wife of SGT Jerry A. Price II - HHC 1-22 IN
My son and I carry on as if Jerry is still here. Occasionally we take three deep breaths; with each in-breath we feel his love and safety entering us; with each out-breath we felt tension leave us.

Leann Martin - Wife of LTC Joe Martin - 1-67 AR
I'll never forget this deployment. I know that our husbands have made friendships that will last a lifetime. We've always heard that Soldiers form incredibly special bonds with their brothers in arms. The situation they find themselves in leads them to depend on each other and take care of each other. Well, I know that this deployment has given me the opportunity to make friendships that will also last a lifetime. As wives we have been thrown into a situation that is actually building incredible friendships for us. All of us in the Fourth Infantry Division will have a special bond with each other. When we all go our separate ways and meet up again in a few years, we'll be able to say, "Remember when..."

No one else will quite understand what we share—but we'll know. Words won't have to be spoken; it'll be that look of understanding that true friends share. The love of my Soldier, his commitment to our nation and the love and friendship of other wives with husbands that have the same commitment—that's what makes this crazy life we lead all worthwhile.

The other night my eight-year-old son asked, "If Daddy gets Osama and Saddam, will he be able to come home?" Life for a child is so simple. I had the fun task of trying to explain that Dad would come home in April, even if he caught Saddam or Osama. I tried to explain to him that Dad can't leave his Soldiers behind. It's interesting explaining to an eight year old that his daddy loves him and wants to be with him, but that the job he has right now is so important he has to finish it.

Renee' Bryant - Wife of COL Al Bryant, Assistant Division Commander (Support) - 4ID

This has been on my fridge for nearly a year now. My husband, son, and brother-in-law are currently serving in Iraq.

I am a small and precious child, my dad's been sent to fight,
The only place I'll see his face is in my dreams at night.
He'll be gone too many days for my young mind to keep track,
I may be sad, but I am proud—
My daddy's got your back.
I am a caring mother; my son has gone to war,
My mind is full of worry that I have never known before.
Every day I try to keep my thoughts from turning black, I may
be scared, but I am proud—my son has got your back.
I am a strong and loving wife, with a husband soon to go,
There are times I'm terrified in a way most never know.
I bite my lip, and force a smile as I watch my husband pack,
My heart may break, but I am proud—
My husband's got your back.
And I am a Soldier, serving proudly, standing tall.
I fight for freedom, yours and mine, by answering this call.
I do my job while knowing the thanks it sometimes lacks—
Say a prayer that I'll come home.
It's me who's got your back.
Author unknown

17 April - Bob Babcock

This is from a from a letter to the editor of the *Marietta Daily Journal*, written by one of our readers who is a Marine widow and the fiancée of another Marine with twenty-seven years' service. She is the daughter of an Army chopper pilot who fought with 1st Cavalry Division in the Ia Drang Valley in 1965.

"The Marines, Sailors and Soldiers I know are proud to be fighting this War on Terror. Of course, they don't want to die, and of course, they'd rather be home mowing the lawn or watching a ball game or drinking a marguerite with friends. The reason they go, and the reason they gladly serve their Commander In Chief (and they do) is because they love us and know our freedom and way of life was attacked on 9/11. As one crusty old marine told me, 'They knocked down my blanking trade centers, and that's why we fight. It's as simple as that.'

"Our Marines and Soldiers haven't forgotten, so why have we? These men and women are not victims. They serve gladly. Enlistments are high. Many wounded are anxious to get back to their posts."

Vickey Kiraly - Wife of 2LT John Kiraly - HHC 3-66 AR

There are a few times in the life of a military wife that camaraderie is formed with other spouses. A moment shared and etched in time. This is a story of one such time in which three women shared the moment their husbands left for war. They did not know each other before this moment, but they were feeling just the same.

There we were...on top of a hill.
Just behind us was a brightly lit flashing bank sign. ...Looked like a good place to go if you wanted free checking. They spared no expense on the sign. Those bulbs were almost blinding. But there we were.
Three women...on top of a hill.
We all had the same story. Our husbands were leaving. Not on a business trip, we should be so lucky, but off to war, the war in Iraq. On that day there was no celebration, there was no pomp and circumstance and hardly any noise to speak of. There was just the dark starry night, the sight of a military airplane taxiing off to the runway and three shadows watching closely. There we stood, broken hearted, fearful of the future, lonely and non-the-less proud of our husbands. This was the moment we all dreaded, together, on top of that hill.

Two of us were not new to the life of a military spouse. Nineteen years of servitude combined. Experience had taught us not to wallow in our deeply rooted fear, but to grab hold of it and not to let it go, at least until our husbands came back home. This was a time "for accepting all challenges, so that you may feel the exhilaration of victory." These sorts of statements are the things experienced military spouses live by. But spiritual readings tend to soothe the soul even more.

The third was the spouse was of a new Soldier. Her husband had just completed AIT, then received orders to Fort Hood and within weeks was off to begin his life as a Soldier in Iraq. Of the three women on that hill, she was the most vulnerable.

The life of a military spouse is hard. It has been said that the military life will either break or make your marriage—and that is the truth. For the two seasoned wives on that hill, chances are slim that the military will break these marriages. But what of this third spouse who was leaving the area the very next day. She was new to the area, had no friends to speak of, she had no children to keep her busy or a place she could make into a home. She did not want to tackle loneliness by herself, and who can blame her.

So there we were together, on top of that hill.

The day began just like any other with the sun bright in the sky. But this was the day he would leave for war. By two-thirty in the afternoon first roll call formation began. It was a sight to see hundreds of men and women, brothers and sisters, husbands and wives, boyfriends and girlfriends, mothers and fathers; all gathered in one general location, all slowly saying good-bye to their Soldier. Tears were everywhere, but neither of us had tears to shed. We did not want our husbands to see tears.

After roll call, all of the Soldiers were required to go to a holding area. The holding area is nothing more than a gym. Here Soldiers are placed on lock down, all in an effort to desensitize them from their civilian lives. Many family members followed their Soldier to this place and had to say their final good-byes. All family members left within a small span of time, especially after a captain told everyone to leave the general area. Tears were everywhere, but none of *us* had tears to shed. We didn't know each other before that moment, but afterward, we became friends.

We stood outside the gym for hours hoping to get a glimpse of our husbands. Even through a small stint of pouring rain, we did not falter. That brought the three of us even closer. Eventually, the Soldiers were given a 'smoke break' and we all got to see that final glimpse of our husbands. There was even an opportunity for a small kiss and hug. We did not want our husbands to be desensitized of us yet. There was plenty of time for that, one year, to be exact.

Another hour had passed since the final glimpse, when we saw a chaplain move into place outside the gym. Soldiers slowly shuffled out of the gym and the chaplain shook their hands one by one and gave some words of comfort. It was then that we truly received our last glimpse of our husbands. Each one of the husbands was surprised to see his spouse still there. Each husband boarded his bus knowing his spouse was with him all the way.

Eventually the four buses, with military police escorts, started their trek toward the airport, and without falter, the three of us caravanned right behind. The six or seven mile drive seemed to move in slow motion. Again, there was no noise to speak of.

At the airport gate, we all parked our vehicles and walked toward the gate. We knew we could not enter, but again, we just wanted to get one last glimpse. Unfortunately, the military police hindered our notion. One police officer actually said, "Just let go." And another said, "They could be waiting for hours." But this is what they do not realize—at that moment, we were three women who 'let go' hours ago, and we were three women with nothing but time on our hands. One last time with our husbands was taken away.

We moved to our cars quietly when one of us had an idea. We would just go somewhere else where the military police could not tell us anything. The parking lot of the bank on top of the hill was perfect. It had a direct view of the airport and runway.

So there we were...on top of that hill.

Not because we wanted to be there, but because we all just wanted to see our husbands one last time. War is interesting; it makes the most unlikely people become friends. That one moment of seeing our husbands' plane takes off into the southern sky will always be remembered.

Three women, same story, battle to see their husbands for one last time. *...on top of that hill.*

Special Letter to Our Ladies of the Ironhorse

Dear Ladies of the Ironhorse, I am delighted to send my thanks and admiration to the spouses who take care of the home front and make military service possible for thousands of deployed

Soldiers. You are asked to be everything to yourself, your children, and your community during a difficult time, and you manage it all with courage and grace. I especially admire the way you help and support each other.

As wife of the Commander in Chief, I am privileged to meet Soldiers and their families at posts across the country. Each of these meetings reinforces for me the real meaning of America's freedom. It produces people like you and families like yours.

President Bush and I are unceasingly grateful for your devotion to your family and to America. He joins me in sending best wishes.

With Warm Regards,
Laura Bush

Linda Odierno - Wife of MG Raymond T. Odierno - Commander, 4th ID and Task Force Ironhorse

Dear God,

I am proud to be wed to one who defends freedom and peace. My challenges are many and I pray for your love and guidance to meet them. Special to me are the symbols representing my religion, country, community, and home. I pray for the wisdom and grace to be true to their meaning.

You, Lord, are the symbol of my religious beliefs and the source of my strength. Because my life is full of change, I cherish the solid and constant spiritual foundation you provide. Help me, Lord, to be an example of your teachings.

My national flag represents freedom. Let me never forget, or take for granted, the hope it shows to the world. Bless those who have made sacrifices for freedom. As I enter the gateway to a military community, guide me to reach out to others and keep it a wholesome place. May my charity be given without thought of personal gain.

My wedding ring represents eternal and never-ending love. Let me celebrate all of the joys of togetherness and find comfort in them during times of separation. I pray also we are spared the ultimate sacrifice of duty to country.

My house is a symbol of our family and its unity. It is the place where we share memories of the past and build dreams of the future. Make my heart and hands willing to do even the smallest tasks that will make our house a better home.

Thank you, God, for daily being with us as we live in the Army. Please grant us your continued blessings, increased strength and infinite guidance, as we live to your honor and glory. Amen

Task Force Ironhorse - April 2003 Casualties

1LT Osbaldo Orozco, 26, was killed in action on 25 April 2003 when his vehicle rolled over due to response to enemy fire. He was assigned to Company C, 1-22 Infantry, Fort Hood, Texas. Lieutenant Orozco was the first casualty of Task Force Ironhorse.

LTC Joe and Leann Martin, and Children

Leann Gives A Farewell Hug to LTC Joe Martin

Children of LTC Joe and Leann Martin in Front of Battalion Headquarters

LTC Joe Martin's Children Welcome Him Home

TWO

MAY - 2003
Waiting For News From Our Soldiers

*A*t this point our Soldiers were in Iraq. Headquarters was based out of Tikrit. They were beginning patrols, finding weapon caches, and winning the hearts and minds of the Iraqi people. Communication was still rare or even nonexistent. Family members watched TV, surfed the Internet, and listened to the radio for any news they might be able to pick up. Unless it is about your own Soldier, though, it is never enough. Fortunately, Bob Babcock opened his e-mail update series to family members of the 4th Infantry Division and Task Force Ironhorse in May 2003, beginning with the 1st Battalion, 22nd Infantry Regiment, 1BCT. (1st Brigade Combat Team).

27 May - Bob Babcock
Here is the response from readers to the question about items to send a Soldier. Some of the things our guys have requested are powdered drink mixes such as Crystal Lite, Gatorade, etc. Also, bug spray and sunscreen is important. They would like any snack foods such as chips, beef jerky, Chex Mix, Oreos, and Chips Ahoy. They say that any food you can add hot water to, such as Cup of Soup or Ramen would be appreciated.

Further, they ask for foot powder, single load laundry soap, toilet paper, baby wipes (Lever 2000 makes a great wipe and not always necessarily for babies.) They could use waterless shampoo and wash. (It can be purchased at a sporting goods store.) They'd like local newspapers or at least some interesting clippings of local new. They request trash bags, batteries, envelopes, writing paper, and lots of pictures!!!

28 May - Snail Mail

We finally heard from our son in Ba'quabah. He is with B Co, 2-8 IN, 4ID. He made a five-minute phone call to us from Iraq. So far he has written fifteen letters home of which we have still only received the first one, dated six weeks ago. He said he has gotten a total of seven letters from us but no packages. We have sent probably about fifteen letters and two packages. So the mail is still not getting there as much as is sent. But the mail coming out of there is not moving at all. Anyway he said the 2-8th is doing well. They are on patrol and garrison duty for the area in case other parents or families of the 2-8 want to know.

29 May - Feels Like Their Missions are Useless

It saddens me that the media is no longer following our troops still out there. It feels as though they are being abandoned. In the last letter I received from my son, dated 4/16/03, he states that they got there too late and they missed all the fighting action. 4ID was the last to deploy from Fort Carson; I think they feel like their missions are useless and thankless. So the media goes home, and the Soldiers who got there a little late stay behind cleaning up the mess. Hopefully the US does not forget about them.

What it Means to Love a Soldier - By Jamie Reese - Special to American Forces Press Service

She stands in line at the post office waiting to send a package to her husband, a U.S. Army Soldier serving in Kuwait. Envelops, pens, paper, stamps, sunscreen, eye-drops, gum, batteries, powdered Gatorade, baby wipes and Twizzlers. He said he needed the sunscreen and baby wipes. She threw in the Twizzlers.

There's a common bond at the post office in this military town. People aren't just sending letters and packages; they are sending smiles, hope, love and just a touch of home. People look around at the others, sharing their concern, fear and pride. They take comfort knowing they are not alone.

Passing through the gate leaving the Army post, she enters another world. A world filled with pawnshops, surplus stores, barbershops, fast food galore and, of course, "Loans, Loans, Loans." This is a life that includes grocery shopping at a place called the Commissary. A life that has her venturing to the Post Exchange, referred to as the PX, instead of heading to Wal-Mart.

This is where you come to learn, appreciate and respect the ceremonious traditions of Reveille and Retreat, and of course, the national anthem from a completely different perspective.

At 6 a.m., or as the Soldiers call it, "0600 hours," Reveille can be heard across post. The bugle call officially begins the military workday. At 1700 hours, Retreat sounds, signaling the day's end. Soldiers render salutes, chatter fades and all eyes are drawn to the nearest flag. At 2300 hours, the bugle sounds Taps, denoting not only the "final hour" of the day, but also honoring those we have lost.

When the national anthem plays in a military town, a special aura fills the air. Men, women, and even children stop to pay their respects. Civilians place their hands over their hearts. Soldiers salute. In this world, the national anthem isn't just a prequel to the echo of "Play Ball."

Since she married her Soldier and experienced the Star Spangled Banner from this perspective, she's noticed how people in civilian towns react to the national anthem. She notices the people who continue to talk, the hats that stay on, the beer that doesn't get put down, and even the jeers at the person singing the anthem. The meaning seems to be lost to a majority of people. But if she looks closely, she can see who has been blessed enough to learn this lesson. Some are grandparents, some are parents, and some are young children.

At first glance, children growing up in this world of artillery, tanks and uniforms are the same as any other kids from any other town. They do the things that kids do. They play sports, go to school, and play with their friends. The difference is that their group of friends may change once a year, or more, due to a change of duty station.

They don't have any say in this. They could be two years old and not remember a thing about it, or they may be sixteen years old getting ready for prom and having to uproot and move again. They're known as "military brats," a harsh misnomer for those who learn a lifestyle of sacrifice at such a young age. Yet, it makes them strong.

The little boys become the men of the house and the little girls become the ladies. They adapt to these different situations. They live with the reality that one, or even both parents, may not be around to celebrate birthdays and holidays. They know there will be times when they look into the stands during Little League games and see only an empty space in the bleachers. At the same time, these kids have a sense of overwhelming pride. They brag about their daddies and their mommies being the best of the best. They know their Mom's been through deployments, changes of duty stations, and the ever-changing schedules Army life brings. While Dad is away, she takes care of the house, the bills, the cars, the dogs, and the baby.

To cope with it all, she learns military families communicate via the Internet so he doesn't miss out on what's happening back home. But he does miss out. He won't be there for the baby's first steps, and he may have to hear his son or daughter's first words through a time delay across a static-filled telephone line.

She remembers what it was like before he left, when everything seemed "normal." Normal except for the pressed uniform, the nightly ritual of shining boots, the thunder-like sound of the Apache helicopters flying overhead, and the artillery shells heard off in the distance. Okay, relatively normal—when they occasionally went to the park, spent holidays together and even enjoyed four-day weekends when he could get a pass. But, the real challenge began with the phone call.

She relives the moments before she kissed him good-bye. A phone ringing at 0400 hours is enough to make her heart end up in her throat. They've been expecting the call, but they weren't sure when it would come. She waits to hear the words, "Don't worry, it's just a practice run." But instead she hears, "Here we go."

So, off he goes to pack, though most of the packing is finished because as a Soldier, he is "always ready to roll." She gets the baby, but leaves his pajamas on because it is just as well that he sleeps. She takes the dogs out, she gets dressed, all the while trying to catch glimpses of her husband. She wants to cherish his presence because she doesn't know when she'll see him again. She knows that in other homes nearby, other families are enacting exactly the same scene.

Within fifteen minutes, the family is in the car heading to the "rally point." As they pull up, they see Soldiers everywhere, hugging their loved ones. While people love to see tearful, joyous homecomings, fearful, anxious, farewells are another story. Too soon, with his gear over his shoulder, he walks away. She is left behind, straining to keep an eye on her Soldier. As the camouflage starts to blend, only his walk distinguishes him from the others.

She takes one last look and takes a deep breath. She reminds herself she must stay strong; no tears, or, as few tears as possible, just words of encouragement to the children, to her friends, and to herself. Then she turns, walks back to the car, and makes her way home to a house that is now eerily quiet.

She mentally prepares for the days, weeks, even months ahead. She needs to focus on taking care of her love while he is overseas. Her main priorities will be the care packages, phone calls, e-mails, and letters sprayed with perfume. And she can't forget to turn the stamp upside down to say, "I love you."

Taking care of her family, her friends, even strangers—it is her mission as an Army wife to do these things without a second thought. At the ripe old age of twenty-two, she knows the younger wives will turn to her for advice. "How do you balance a checkbook? How do you change a tire? When are they coming home?" Only when she knows everyone else is OKAY, the bills are paid, the cars maintained, the lawn cut, the kids asleep, the pets calmed down, and the lights are off, does she take any time for herself.

Alone at night, she runs the next day's events over in her mind to make sure it will all get finished. She reviews her checklist of things to do, things to buy for his care package. Once again, she checks the calendar to count down the days. Before turning in, she checks to make sure the ringer is on for the late night phone call that might come in from overseas.

Before she falls asleep, a few tears hit the pillow. But even as the tears escape, strength enters her mind, body, spirit and soul. She remembers why she is here. She remembers the pride and the love that brought her here in the first place, and a sense of peace comes over her, replacing, if only for a second, the loneliness, the fear and the lingering heartache she feels while her soul mate is away.

This is what it means to love a Soldier. She wouldn't have it any other way

30 May - Hang Tight

I just wanted to give an update. My husband is with the 3/29 FA out of Fort Carson. He called me yesterday at 4:00 p.m. our time, which was 2:00 a.m. his time. He sounded in great spirits. He said he is getting my letters slowly. He has gotten four packages out of the eight I have sent. He told me to just hang tight on the mail situation. He said he has mailed ten letters, and that the commanders there are working to get the mail problems solved.

31 May - Soldiers Were Really Upset

I finally heard from my son for the first time today. He is in HHC (Headquarters and Headquarters Company) 3rd BCT. He sounds extremely upbeat, proud, and doesn't seem real bothered by the fact that they have had no showers since Kuwait. The flies are terrible, as is the heat. They are somewhat short on rations and the sandstorms keep blowing.

He and all the Soldiers were really upset when they went into one small town and saw children with no shoes, ragged clothing, all dirty, living in mud and clay huts just 'looking at them with blank looks'. So most of the Soldiers threw them MRE's (Meals, Ready to Eat) and even water, 'even though we, ourselves, were running low...'

My son even requested that I send small American bills he can give to the children. He is only twenty and has not been even a year in the Army and he is seeing so many things most of us will never see in our life times.

31 May - Stand Firm in Your Faith - Spiritual Reflection from Chaplain (LTC) Brewer

I would like to take a moment of your time to greet each of you in the name of the God of peace and love. I have been attached to the 4th Infantry Division to serve as your Rear Detachment Chaplain to provide religious support to you and your families during this time of war. I am a part of your unit ministry team that works out of the 25th Street Memorial Chapel, and I want to encourage you to make use of us in pursuing your faith journey and supporting your spiritual and physical needs. Come and join us as we work together as God's fellow workers in worship, fellowship, and in duty to our country. It is my hope to be able to encourage each of you in fulfilling this vital work, a work I believe that our Lord established for us long ago in His providential care.

Last night, the evening of the 29th, I witnessed several of our fellow Soldiers prepare themselves to fulfill their duty to our country at the manifest site at Starker Gym. They carried big loads. Each one of them was burdened down with prescribed equipment, weapons, and carry-on luggage for the flight. Each one of them was also burdened with their own thoughts and feelings as they worked together in fulfilling the mission. I am not really sure but I think that the heaviest loads they were carrying were the loads they carried in their hearts and minds, and not the ones on their backs and in their hands. These courageous Soldiers and those helping them fulfill the job at hand were all taking a stand for the freedoms we love and cherish in our lives and for our families. They are about to join our teammates in southwest Asia in this same honored service and in helping them complete the mission we have been given to defend our freedoms.

I believe we can best support each of those who have taken the same journey by standing firm in our own faith and in our willingness to do our jobs in fulfilling the mission. I want to encourage you to be strong and courageous as you face today and tomorrow. The Bible tells us in Psalm 37, verses 3–4, to "Trust in the Lord and do good... and He will give you the desires of your heart." Listen to the Word of the Lord and His Holy Spirit speaking to your hearts as He seeks to give you strength and to help you stand firm in your faith—and all of His peace will comfort you and your loved ones. *Look at God.*

My prayer for you is that you will stand firm in your faith and receive the blessings of God as He desires to fill your hearts with more and more of His peace and joy. May God bless you and keep you strong. These things I pray for you in the Name of Jesus Christ, my Lord and Savior.

Tammy Day - Wife of SFC Larry V. Day - 64 CSG

My husband wrote one of the following poems before he left for Iraq; then his mother wrote a poem to him before he left; and finally my daughter wrote a poem about him after he left. The poems are below in the order as mentioned above.

No, Don't Pray for Me
No, don't pray for me
I have done nothing worthy of your prayer
I serve our country simply to repay a debt to those who served
before me

No, don't pray for me
Pray for the starving children of the world
That they may find peace and a scrap of food to eat
No, don't pray for me
Pray for the abducted child and the runaway
That they may find their way home
No, don't pray for me
Pray for the abused and neglected child
That they may find a safe place to lay their weary head
No, don't pray for me
Pray for the child who lost a parent to the service of their country
That they may find solace in the knowledge that their parent
sacrificed so that they may continue to live free
No, don't pray for me
Pray for those who served in the Revolutionary War, the Civil
War, WW I, WW II, the Korean War, the Vietnam War, and
Desert Storm
That their deeds and sacrifice will not be forgotten
No, don't pray for me
I have done nothing worthy of your prayer
I serve our country simply to repay a debt to those who served
before me
No, don't pray for me

To My Son

I may not have carried you for 9 months, or saw your first step,
your first tooth, or kissed your boo-boos
and wiped away your tears,
In fact I didn't know you existed for 14 years,
I didn't want to get close or try to get near,
For that would mean loving you and that would mean fear,
So I stayed in the background let you be your father's son,
Oh yes there was laughter and even lots of fun,
But you have a mother and I didn't want to seem like I was
trying to interfere or come in between,
But no matter how hard I tried not to let you in,
Over time there was no question about it, you win.
Maybe it was the sadness in your laughter, or in your eyes,
Maybe it was the weekends, the move to Connecticut,
all those good byes,

I don't know when I knew I loved you it just happened one day,
I knew that there was nothing or anyone
who could take it away,
You always thought I compared you to Steven ...this is not true,
You are as different as night and day
and I love you because, you are you,
You helped fill part of that hole that I didn't think would heal,
You filled it with love stamped it and put on your seal,
As I sit and type my heart is breaking in two,
God knows how scared I am of loosing you,
I love you my son, it is important for you to know,
For it is never said enough and you are not here for me to show,
But my arms are around you hugging you tight,
Kisses of love will surround you each night,
So go my son, do what you have to do,
Just remember now and forever,
I will always love you.

Daddy's Angels
Angels are above you to keep you alive
God is there to help you stay strong and healthy
No one can kill you because you are so strong and very brave
So I don't worry about Daddy very much.
With All My Love
Daddy's Girl

Jaime Springman - Wife of SPC Shawnne Springman - 3rd BCT 1-8th INF

I am a 24 year old mother of three. My husband is currently serving in Iraq. I am very, very proud of him. I am new to deployment ways. The longest we have been apart was when he was in basic training. It has been hard on all of us. I never send bad news to him in letters or talk about stuff that may effect him while he is there. We all miss him very much. What gets me through the days and nights is my family, friends and my FRG group from Fort Carson. They have been a huge help. I just would like to thank everyone for being there for me, him and our kids. I would also like to thank other troops and their families. It is hard on everyone. THANK YOU FOR MAKING IT EASIER ON US ALL.

Task Force Ironhorse - May 2003 Casualties

SGT Sean C. Reynolds, 25, died at on 3 May 2003, in Kirkuk, from a gunshot wound after an apparent accident involving his personal weapon. He was assigned to the 74th Long Range Surveillance, 173rd ABN.

CW3 Brian K. Van Dusen, 39, of Columbus, Ohio; **CW2 Hans N. Gukeisen**, 31, of Lead, South Dakota; and **SGT Richard P. Carl**, 26, of King Hill, Idaho, were killed in a non-hostile incident on May 9, 2003, near Samarrah, Iraq. The Soldiers were on board a UH-60 air medical helicopter that crashed in the Tigris River. All were assigned to the 571st Air Medical Company, Fort Carson, Colorado.

PVT Rasheed Sahib, 22, of Brooklyn, New York, was killed on May 18 in Balad, Iraq. Sahib and another Soldier were cleaning their weapons when the other Soldier's weapon discharged striking Sahib in the chest. Sahib was assigned to HHB, 20th Field Artillery Regiment, 4th Infantry Division, Fort Hood, Texas.

SPC Nathaniel A. Caldwell, Jr., 27, of Company B, 404th Air Support Battalion was killed Wednesday in Baghdad, Iraq, the Department of the Defense announced. According to the 404th Family Support Group, Caldwell and two others were in a Humvee responding to a perimeter breach when they rolled the vehicle.

SGT Keman L. Mitchell, 24, of Hilliard, Florida, died on May 26, 2003, in Kirkuk, Iraq. Sgt Mitchell jumped into a seven-foot deep body of water. When he failed to resurface, members of his squad retrieved him. Medical personnel went to the scene and started cardiopulmonary resuscitation. Mitchell was evacuated to a forward surgical team and was pronounced dead on arrival. He was assigned to Company C, 4th Engineer Battalion, Fort Carson, Colorado.

SSG Kenneth R. Bradley, 39, died of an apparent heart attack while serving with Task Force Ironhorse in Iraq. He was assigned to Company B, 588 Engineer Battalion.

THREE

JUNE - 2003
Concerns

By June 2003 our Task Force Ironhorse community was spread across the country and a few places outside the continent. Part of Webster's definition of community is "a smaller group of people within a larger on having interests, work, etc., in common." Another part of the definition is "friendly association and fellowship".

By the end of May, Bob Babcock added to his updates, a "What Our Families Members Are Hearing" section. We exchanged information about units and what the Soldiers needed; we vented, encouraged, and became a community. Many people in that community have never met, but if by any chance I get to meet them, we will be able to reminisce as old friends.

The big concerns at this time for family members were mail, phone calls home, and when our Soldiers would be returning. We also wanted to know what we needed to send that would make their lives more comfortable. One of our big frustrations was the media—their lack of attention, and when the division got their attention—their lack of attention to detail.

Lachelle Huron - Wife of Mark Huron - 299 EN BN

My children and I moved ourselves from Germany to Ft. Hood, Texas in June. Mark took command of the 299th Engineer Battalion with 4ID on June 13th in the Iraqi desert. I know that many have been praying for our family, and I asked God how I could encourage them for being so faithful in their praying for us. The following is what He gave me to share:

To Respond as a Child: Matthew 18:1-5

Every challenge that comes into my life is an opportunity for God to be glorified—for His love to be demonstrated to me, in me, and through me. And when I respond to Him, as a child who trusts her Father completely, He is able to care for me, as He desires, and His love is seen and witnessed by those around me.

If I respond as the self-focused child, sitting in one place, having a tantrum (a pity party) then I can't experience Him and His care to the fullest. However, as soon as I get up and move towards Him in obedience, He swoops me up into His arms and raises me above my circumstances and I enjoy His care from a position very close to His beating heart (the center of His life and love). A position in which I can see the power and strength in His caring and protective arms; so close, He only has to whisper and I can feel His breath on my face and I hear His voice in my ear; so close His scent surrounds me and I am continually aware of His presence; so close, I can look into His eyes undistracted by what goes on around me; so close, the challenge, the adversity that had me sitting in a rebellious heap, has achieved its purpose, drawing me close to Him.

I send many thanks and kindest regards to those who are praying for Mark, Courtney, Cameron, and me. Your prayers turn our heads from our circumstances and toward our loving Father, and then propel us towards Him and into His loving arms.

2 June - Exploding Ammo
We were a little down last week when we received a letter from our son that took almost a month to get here. In the letter he described a fire that occurred on his tank. No one was injured as they completed an emergency evacuation due to the ammo exploding, but all their gear and personal items were destroyed as well.

3 June - I'm So Proud
I received my first phone call from my husband on May 27, around 11:30 p.m. Colorado time. He is A Co, 1-8 IN, 3BCT, 4ID. I also received my second letter from him on May 28, and in it he spoke of a raid that they completed in twelve minutes. Everyone, all the way up to the Division Commander said it was very well done, and the people who had seen the video taken from above said it looked picture perfect. Just another example of how well trained our guys are. I'm so proud!

3 June - Situation Looking Hopeless

I just wanted you to be aware that I received three letters from my son in yesterday's mail. He is in Co A, 1-68 AR, 3BCT, 4ID out of Fort Carson. He started off his first letter with: "So there we were, surrounded by Iraqis and taking fire from all sides. Our situation was looking hopeless... Naw, just kidding." It sounded like the start of a good story though, didn't it!

He talked about traveling through Iraq, through the outskirts of Baghdad, how the country was very poor, and that the things he saw were worse than any slum or ghetto he had ever seen, how some cheered them, and some gave them the finger or shoe, how the further north they went the more hostile it was. He described an April 27th mission in which they attacked a suspected Special Republican Guard compound where several hundred paramilitary forces were expected to be: two Iraqis killed, one wounded, and four to five prisoners. No Americans were killed.

Some humor in his letters: "I do know for a fact that Iraq is a pretty miserable place, and if you ever had plans to come here, you should probably reconsider. Antarctica is probably better than here, as is Death Valley or the Sahara Desert."

"A little lizard just crawled next to my foot, glad it was not a snake. I had a can of cold spaghettios for dinner last night. In any normal situation, that would be disgusting, but for me right now it was all right. The craziest thing I saw, though, is how the Iraqi people drive. New York City drivers have nothing on these people. One van actually hit our vehicle along the side as it swerved back into the right lane before hitting a bus, head on, in the left lane. I am fairly certain you don't need a driver's license in this country."

3 June - A Rustle Behind Me

My husband is with the 299th Engineer Battalion, Co A. The one funny story my husband wrote about, and I'd love it if you'd share it on your site, is this: "Yesterday I was standing in line for the outhouse and heard a rustle behind me. I quickly looked to see what it was, and lo and behold, it was a familiar sight: A blue Wal-Mart bag stuck on a bush, flapping around. I laughed as I thought to myself, no matter where you are, there is always a Wal-Mart nearby!"

The mail I received ranged from April 26th thru May 7. So I guess the mail system is getting better.

4 June - Prepare For the Worst

On Friday I got eight letters at one time from my husband. He is with 1/10 CAV, A troop, 4ID. He says they are not getting a lot of information, but that they are still being told to be prepared for the worst as far as when they will be home. He said they are being told there is no time line, but to expect January; so when I see that some people are saying it could be sooner, I am hopeful.

Stacey Shreve - Wife of SSG Douglas Shreve - Co B 4th FSB

I did not write this, but it says what every Soldier's spouse feels.

"If you're not in love with a Soldier, you can't know adventure. You don't know smelly gray PT uniforms that require a daily washing. You can't understand green and brown camouflage bags flooding your bedroom floor.

"If you're not in love with a Soldier, you can't understand the meaning of the phrase 'going to the field' and the weeks you spend away from each other.

"If you're not in love with a Soldier, you can never imagine the hole in your heart when that phone call comes. 'Honey, I am leaving tomorrow to go overseas. I don't know how long I will be gone or exactly where I am going, but I want you to know that I love you—always!'

"If you're not in love with a Soldier, you don't know what it's like to say that final good-bye. You don't know what it really means to be glued to the television. You don't understand fear and you can't possibly understand the sleepless nights of endless crying wondering if you will ever see the love of your life again.

"If you're not in love with a Soldier, you can't know the immense joy, the uncontrollable smile, or the butterflies in your stomach when you see your Soldier march into the family waiting area upon redeployment. You can't understand the self-control it takes to stand on the other side of the room as some higher-up gives a seemingly endless welcome home speech while all the Soldiers stand in formation. You don't know what it's like to have that second first kiss or what it's like to experience puppy love all over.

"If you're not in love with a Soldier, you can't truly understand how to make every moment count because you never know when that phone call may come again.

"If you're not in love with a Soldier, you can never really understand how very delicate life is!"

4 June - Media Seems to Forget
My son is with HHC, 1-22 INF BN, 4ID. I got an e-mail the other day and he seems to be doing okay. He is helping to rebuild the hospital in Tikrit. The media seems to forget our Soldiers. This is my son's second time over there; he was in the Gulf War. I hope they will all be home soon. God Bless America.

5 June - Keep Sending Goodies
My son is with A CO, 104th Military Intelligence (MI). We just received word from the rear detachment through our Family Readiness Group (FRG) person that they have been receiving lots of calls from family members because word had it that our Soldiers were still having to ration water and food.

The 'LT' says that they are now each getting two bottles of water (one and a half liters) a day, and they have tanks of purified water available. The purified water is okay to drink but has a funny processed taste, and the guys prefer the bottled stuff. (Of course!) She said that bottled water is a luxury on the battlefield. She further stated that our Soldiers are getting three Meals, Ready to Eat (MRE's) a day and some have the capacity to have one hot meal each day. She encouraged us to keep sending goodies to supplement the MRE's. I wanted to write and let those folks who have been worried about the water situation that it seems to be under control now.

Ellen Moericke - Wife of SFC David J. Moericke - Co A 704th DSB
One experience that I have had during this deployment is my toddler son thinks his daddy lives in our telephone. He picks up the phone, holds it up to his ear and says, "Daddy." He hugs our phone and sometimes cries when there is no answer.

When my husband does call, and they get to talk, he is so excited he cannot stop talking about it afterward.

Submitted by Linda Odierno - Wife of MG Raymond T. Odierno - Cmdr.,TF Ironhorse, and Ann Campbell - Wife of COL Don Campbell - Chief of Staff, 4ID

At Walter Reed Medical Center in Washington DC recently the Sergeant Major of the Army (SMA), Jack Tilley, was with a group of people visiting the wounded Soldiers. He saw a Special Forces Soldier who had lost his right hand and suffered severe wounds of his face and side of his body. The SMA wanted to honor him and show him respect without offending, but what can you say or do in such a situation that will encourage and uplift? How do you shake the right hand of a Soldier who has none? He decided to act as though the hand was not missing and gripped the Soldier's wrist while speaking words of comfort and encouragement to him.

But there was another man in that group of visitors who had even brought his wife with him to visit the wounded who knew exactly what to do. This man reverently took the Soldier's stump of a hand in both of his hands, bowed at the bedside and prayed for him. When he finished the prayer he stood up, bent over the Soldier and kissed him on the head and told him that he loved him. What a powerful expression of love for one of our wounded heroes! And what a beautiful Christ-like example! What kind of a man would do such a thing?

It was the wounded man's Commander in Chief, George W Bush, President of the United States.

This story was told by the SMA at a Soldiers Breakfast held at Red Arsenal, AL, and recorded by Chaplain James Henderson, stationed there.

6 June - Appreciate the Little Things

My nephew is in 1-22 IN, 4ID. Some of the other guys got seven dollars together, went to a local ranch and bought a goat, turkey and chickens. They killed, skinned, feathered, gutted, dug a hole, and had a BBQ. He said they had a great time. I guess they are learning to appreciate the little things, including having salt.

7 June - Bob Babcock

I received a note yesterday from the best possible source of information on the 4th Infantry Division, Major General Ray Odierno, the 4th Infantry Division commanding general. Here is the message that he asked me to pass on to our family members:

"Bob: I wanted you to know that today we had a moment of silence prior to our morning update remembering all the great Americans who gave their lives fifty-nine years ago. I wish I could cover every unit assigned or attached to 4th Infantry Division, but that would be impossible. We are over thirty thousand strong. What I can tell you is that every unit is working extremely hard and making a true difference. We are making it better for future generations of Iraqis. There are still significant pockets of resistance in some areas, but overall it is a safe and secure environment.

"In reference to our e-mail and phones: This country's telecommunication infrastructure is nonexistence; therefore we must rely on military communications. Since the Division is spread over a 400 X 400 kilometer area, we need every bit of communications to conduct tactical operations. We have provided one worldwide cell phone per battalion for morale calls. Every one should be getting a call soon. Outgoing mail has been improved, and you should begin seeing the benefits soon.

"I can't tell you how proud I am to serve with all of the great Soldiers in this division. Their dedication and professionalism are incredible. I also want to thank all of the families at home for all their sacrifices and support. We couldn't do it without you."
Steadfast and Loyal
MG Ray T. Odierno
CG, 4ID

Stella Jason - Wife of SSG Richard Jason - HHC 588th EN BN
I never thought that being an Army wife would help me so much. My husband is a Staff Sergeant E-6 with fifteen years of service to our nation under his belt. Together, we have shared eleven years of marriage, two wonderful children and (thank God) only three Permanent Change of Station (PCS) moves. When preparation for this deployment began, it was the hurry up and wait game from hell. It took its toll on us, and quite honestly, I was relieved to see him go. Not because I wanted him gone, but because "the game" was over, and I finally had some solid ground to stand on.

I decided to devote my time to embarking on a career path, and I chose nursing. And then, about a week into school, my dad was diagnosed with inoperable lung cancer. So, up to Illinois we went, my children and I. We uprooted and just left, to be what support we could to grandma and grandpa. We stayed with them from September to January. My dad is still alive, but I know that day draws ever nearer, and I thank God for the time we have.

My children and I are back home now, and all back in school. I am still pursuing a career in nursing. Even though I know that I may lose the two most important men in my life, there has been an unwavering strength that has carried me through the teary nights and anxious days. I realize now, more than ever that it takes a special kind of woman to be an army wife, a diamond in the rough. It takes a strength that goes above and beyond the call of duty; it takes courage and grit, and just plain determination that you will not be beaten by your circumstances. I am so proud to be a diamond in the rough. I am strong, I am able, I am an Army wife.

8 June - He Hasn't Written

Richard is with the 2nd Brigade, 1-67 AR, HHC (Go Dealers!) I spoke to Richard this morning! He sounds GREAT, thank God. He was in excellent spirits. The connection was very bad, so we had to say everything twice, but it was beautiful to hear his voice.

He said the Army has resolved the mail-out problems, but it was still an issue for him, as he hasn't written any letters.

I cursed him roundly. He blamed dyslexia, and his work schedule, and a traumatic childhood. (where does he come up with this...?) He said that things are starting to settle down a little, so he's not working as many hours. I told him that I was going to enclose a pre-addressed envelope with a checklist for him to put marks next to and then just sign it and return it.

He said he thought that was probably a good idea...

Sigh...

9 June - Precious Minutes

Got an e-mail from my husband in the Mississippi Army National Guard, 223rd EN BN assigned to the 4ID, Tikrit. They have received the hospital and busted up some old regime people who were charging folks for admission to the hospital. He has negotiated runway repairs for the airstrip, and they finally have phone access.

I spoke to him for the first time in nine weeks and it was the greatest one-minute yet. Hooah! Coming from a military family, I know communications can be scarce, but those minutes were precious. Thanks for your updates on the whole division; it makes the picture complete.

10 June - A Proud Mom of an American Soldier With the 4ID

My son, who is with the 588th EN BN, A Co, called yesterday. I missed the call. I was in church, but my husband was able to intercept it. My son said he is doing fine, but hot. He is receiving his mail and packages. I know this because I have sent letters saying that if I don't hear from you, I am not sending cigarettes.

My son asked if we had received his letters. We have not.

He told his dad, "Tell Mom to send cigarettes." He said the letters and packages are keeping him going. He is glad to be hearing from home. When my husband asked him where he was, his reply was, "Iraq." That's my boy.

I have waited for this call for a long time, and it finally came. I want to tell everyone out there: be patient, it will happen. My son said he may be calling back in two weeks. God bless our troops and may they return home soon.

Submitted by Tanisha Perkins - Wife of CPT Curtis Perkins - 404 HSC

Dear Sydne,

How is everything going on your special day? It is a special day in that you are happy, healthy, and blessed the lives of your mother and me with one complete year of joy and surprises. It is truly a blessing to have you as a daughter! There are many things I wish I could say in person, but I have an obligation to assist in keeping this world of ours safe and free. I hope that I get to see you and your mother soon! Until I see you I want you to accept this poem in my absence as I sit, think, and dream of you:

Dreams and pictures are all I have of you
This is to say a lot and I guess it will do
But often I wonder do you think of me
Do you need me there; to be all you can be?
So strong as a baby, independent it seems
Observant and patient; what does this really mean?

This means that you were sent to us with a purpose
A reason deeper than represented by the surface
You've shown us the true meaning of life
Through all the mistakes, hardships, and strife
It is true that my job is stressful at times
But knowing you are safe gives me the "peace of mind"
And yes it is true your "FATHER" is not perfect
But the stories and drama makes it all worth it
Your mother is the foundation of what we have
Through sickness and health; the good and the bad
But that is not what this poem is about
Although it lays the foundation without a doubt!

A Second Poem to Sydne
Sydne! This poem is about the joy that you bring to my life
Making this all possible, I have to thank my wife
It is you Sydne; I wish to hold in my arms
To look into your eyes and protect you from harm
To smell your fresh neck and play with your ears
To be there for you throughout the years
When I left home you we're considerably small
Three weeks later, you began to crawl
And now I hear that you are trying to walk
Before long I expect to hear you talk
My point is that your life is passing me by
To miss all these things makes me cry
You see, family to me is much more important
But this job that I have makes things uncertain
Now that your first birthday is finally here
There is one thing I would like to make perfectly clear
I may leave sometimes, but my love will stay
I love you Sydne and HAPPY BIRTHDAY!!
From Daddy with Love!

11 June - From the Mother of a Wounded Co B 1-22 IN Soldier

My daughter-in-law called me today after she spoke with my son this afternoon. He will be transferring to Walter Reed Army Medical Center in DC sometime the end of the week. He has had three surgeries on his arm; there is major damage there, and the doctor told him his eardrum was blown, that the most he could hope for was partial hearing, if that, in his right ear. The doctor also told him he probably would end up being medically discharged from the Army, as his injuries are permanent.

Like I said many times, I'm thankful he's alive and coming home. We can deal with the injuries. I'll keep you posted.

11 June - He Could Hear Me

I hit the jackpot yesterday! We received a total of ten letters from my son who is in Co A, 1-22 IN, 4ID. My son told me he has done a lot of thinking the past month. He said for the first time, he can actually say he is proud of himself, and that he feels like a man. He said between me and the Army, we have raised "one hell" of a guy.

He went on to tell me how I have made him strong through all of this. When things got bad and he put his head down, he could hear me telling him to pick it back up. When he thought he couldn't accomplish something, he heard me telling him he could accomplish anything he wanted to. He told me how he felt bad the last three years for not being home for me when things got hard, but, he also said he realized it was okay when he remembered how strong I was, and how I always held my head up high.

I will take a lot of credit for my son's strength, but I have the Army to thank for helping my son become a man!

13 June - Update From the Mother of Wounded Co B 1-22 IN Soldier

Just wanted to let you know that my son left Spain today. He is supposed to be arriving about nine p.m. tonight. I think he is going to Walter Reed. That's what they told my son anyway. But who knows. I told him to try and call when he gets in.

Thanks for forwarding his sergeant's wife's e-mail. I answered her back, and she ended up giving me a phone call. We had a good conversation about what happened. Her husband (God bless him) was injured also, but he wouldn't leave his troops. He was bandaged up and went back to his unit.

I told her to thank her husband for me, for taking good care of my son. I wish all of them would come home now. That's the latest. I'll let you know when I hear more.

He was told he would be at Walter Reed no more than seventy-

41

two hours. He was based in Ft. Hood, so they will probably send him to the hospital there. We'll see.

13 June - Rose Petals
We received three letters from our son in Tikrit; he's with the 74th MRBC out of Fort Hood, Texas. In the first letter, dated May 2, he sent rose petals from one of Saddam's rose gardens... said it was the closest he could get to sending flowers for Mother's Day! He is staying at one of the palaces there.

In his letters he says all are doing fine, keep the mail coming. Can't tell you how proud we are of him and all of our troops. Our prayers are with them.

14 June - From the Wife of a 1-8 IN Soldier
Be safe, and continue to spread every American's story, serving proudly in our Armed Services, (especially Army). Whoever the Soldier, past or present, there is a story and something to learn. With each service member, there is also a family back home. Each day that goes by, we will not forget! Not about our present service members or our past service members.

Let it be known that, we, the Army family have come a long way in supporting each other. The Soldiers of today have peace of mind knowing that we have learned from the past and that our communities and neighbors support us through the families left behind. They are doing what they can for the Soldiers fighting for what we stand for.

I am a proud American, raised by a proud American Marine. He was a little surprised when his oldest daughter (of three girls) joined the Army. I believe that 'shocked' was a better word for it. But he raised me to stand for our freedom and know what our 'Old Soldiers' have been through. I really had no other place I wanted to be. Now I am a veteran of the Armed Services and married to a career U.S. Army enlisted Soldier. It was written in the stars—I was meant to serve the Armed Services one way or another. God Bless Us All! Happy Birthday.

14 June - Seeing a Kid's Face Light Up
Yesterday I received a seven-minute phone call from my son, and he sounded great. He is a platoon leader with Charlie Company, 1-68 AR, 4ID, now spending time in Tuz. He said, "You should

see the kids' faces when we roll through an urban area. They've never really been able to see a real tank before, so they get all excited. We go slow enough to make some sort of eye contact. I love seeing a kid's face light up when I wave to them. They get all excited. That's why I feel we're justified in being here. As Americans, we really don't know how good we have it."

He also said that he saw a dad whack his son with a belt for waving to my son and his platoon. I think that's terrible. He said the days go by a little quicker now that he is a platoon leader. That's a good thing for him, believe me! We have been saving all of the 4ID updates for him when he returns as well as all letters. I've told him this is part of his history, another chapter in his book.

15 June - Going For a Swim
My husband is a Civil Affairs officer with 2BCT in Ba'qubah. During his last phone call, he used a calling card and had a lot of minutes to talk. He put his Iraqi translator on the phone who couldn't believe he was speaking to someone in the U.S.

My husband's team bought and butchered a lamb and had a kabob feast. They found one of Saddam's many palaces with a beautiful lake surrounding it. They all jumped in for a swim. They were probably the first to do so because no one dared to do such a thing during the previous regime.

I enjoy receiving ideas from others on what to send in care packages. Since CA interacts with the people, I also send things to give to the children: tennis balls, flashlights with batteries, yo-yos, lollipops, matchbox cars, and appropriate little dolls.

16 June - Wearing the Ivy Leaf
This isn't necessarily newsworthy for others, but I wanted you to be aware of something that is happening in Omaha. The College World Series (CWS) has kicked off with its usual fun and flair. The CWS is close to my family's heart. It was probably most important to my father-in-law, Dennie Poppe, NCAA Director of Championships.

This e-mail is to let you know that on opening day, the head groundskeeper called Dennie out on the field and each grounds crew member was, and still is, proudly wearing a 4ID patch on their uniform, not just for my husband Carl, but for all 4ID Soldiers. They are thought about, prayed over, missed every day.

17 June - Ah... Pictures!

After a very long mail drought, I received two letters from my son last Monday. He also called last Monday night. We talked for about ten minutes.

On Saturday, I received a letter with a camera inside (and film) to be developed. The letter was dated 21 April 2003. We had given up on any hopes of receiving this, but it arrived. The envelope was very torn up, but I got the pictures developed and right at the counter began to cry when I saw his picture in front of a palace. Somehow, it made every emotion I have had since the beginning come to the surface all at once. One of the pictures I had made into a 5x7 for my dad for Father's day. I mounted it with 'I've got your back' as a title at the top, and his name, unit, 'Operation Iraqi Freedom' and the words 'Proudly continuing the service legacy' at the bottom.

During the week I also received two letters from my younger son who is with the 248 Engineer Company, attached, I think, to the 130th Engineers. I have no idea of even a general location for him, but just to hear from him so soon after he arrived was awesome.

He graduated from high school last spring, and as I drive past his high school every day, I can't help but reflect on how life has changed in only one year. Last year I was worried about what I would wear to graduation, would he trip and fall walking up to get his diploma, would we find a place to park, etc. Now, I realize that none of those things matter as much as knowing he is okay.

In closing, please know that your reports are a very big part of what is keeping me going right now. I have printed up nearly everything to save in a scrapbook for when my Soldiers return. Thanks so much.

20 June - Flea Collars

One of the postings on your website indicated that a Soldier has asked his family send him flea collars. This is a bad idea! Flea collars for dogs and cats will not fight the sand fleas the Soldiers are exposed to in Iraq. They work against canine and feline fleas. In addition, the pesticides in the collars can cause chemical burns, even when worn outside the uniform, as the sweat from your body lets the pesticide flow to the skin. With enough exposure, there is even the possibility of a systemic chemical poisoning.

44

20 June - Stamp or No Stamp

My husband told me on his last call that his buddy who runs the mail decided to test the stamp or no stamp theory and sent out two letters on the same day to the same address-one with a stamp and one without. Both letters arrived on the exact same day. So I plan to save my stamps and let him send those letters free!

20 June - Camel Spiders? Humm...

We received a letter from our son with HHC, 3-66 AR on June 14. He told of going before the promotion board and passing (so they are trying to keep up with things even though they are in such conditions). He had received packages and some letters and all were appreciated, and he would be glad to come home. Also, he had killed a camel spider the size of his hand.

He learned they are called camel spiders because their bites are lethal enough to kill a camel and they can leap six feet at a time. He found it difficult to sleep that night!

Bob Babcock added this caution: To wives and parents, don't get concerned about this. In Vietnam we had "One Step Vipers." Supposedly, you took one step after being bitten and that was it. We never heard of a person killed by a snakebite. The same will be true of spiders. Soldiers love to tell tall tales like this.

21 June - Update on Our Wounded Co B 1-22 IN Soldier

I just wanted you to know my son is home. He arrived last night. He's on a thirty-day convalescent leave from the Army. His arm looks nasty, but he's in good spirits. We don't know what the future holds for him, but he's here, and that's all that matters.

Thanks for the continued updates. Even though my son is home, I pray for and support our Soldiers still deployed. My yellow ribbon won't come down until they are all home.

21 June - Birthday Present

On Thursday, June 4, I heard from my son who is with the 46th CHEM CO, 2nd CML BN out of Fort Hood, supporting the 4ID. I must thank the Army for the man my son has become. Although this is the most frightening thing a mother can experience, I am so very proud of what he is doing and the person he has become.

We had only fifteen minutes, and he was only allowed the

one call; it felt like fifteen seconds, and there was so much I wanted to say and ask. This all occurred the day before my birthday, and I could not have received a better present than hearing his voice for that short time. My thoughts and prayers are with all the Soldiers. God bless.

23 June - Low Morale?
My phone rang at 5:17 this morning. I answered and heard the most beautiful thing in the world. He said, "Hi Baby!" I have waited to hear his voice since April 23. He's with Co A, 2-8 IN (Mechanized) and he's in a small town called Mogdadiyah. I was surprised after hearing how low morale is to find him laughing and joking for a little more than ten minutes!

23 June - Brothers at War
We received a call from our son in Co A, 3-29 FA out of Ft. Carson. He said he can call home once a week for ten minutes. He is doing guard duty, etc., north of Baghdad. A few hours later we received another call from our other Army son in Afghanistan. He is with Co A, 4-31 IN, 10th Mountain Division. So you can imagine our joy hearing from both our sons on the same day!

I agree with Bob's advice about not counting on exactly when the Soldiers are coming home. One of my sons described orders like this, "Anything is possible—don't count on your destination and arrival time until you arrive."

23 June - Pretty Scary
We got a call from our son, Support Platoon, HHC, 1-68 AR, 3BCT last night at ten minutes of midnight. He asked us to send him the APO address of his friend in the 101st Airborne who's been in the thick of it from the start.

We received a letter from this 101st friend who described how much he had learned about Iraqi tanks (Russian T72s and, I think, T80s) from Bud before he joined the 101st. He said what he learned from Bud helped save lives even though Bud wasn't there. He was the only one in his unit who had detailed knowledge of the weaknesses of the Iraqi tanks and it changed the way they attacked the tanks.

He said it was pretty scary attacking tanks with a Humvee. But he couldn't say enough about how Bud had helped them. You can just imagine how proud I was to read the letter. Bud loves our Abrams tanks. You can also imagine how disappointed Bud was when he learned he would be driving a supply truck in Iraq, instead of being on an M1A2 tank. All of the tank crews were full when he arrived at Fort Carson.

24 June - Link to the Infamous Camel Spider
My brother called us on Saturday, but we missed it! He sounded disappointed, but said he would try to call again next week. He is a medic in E Co, 4th FSB, 4ID out of Fort Hood. We talked to him the week before for only a minute or two because the connection was lost.

A quick side note—I searched for the infamous camel spider and found a link off the Air Force page. They're pretty scary looking, but they're not as bad as the stories that I've been hearing.

24 June - Doing Fine, Just Hot!
We received our first call from our son in Iraq who is with HHC, 1-12 IN, 3rd BCT, 4ID. His father and I were both at work, so neither of us got to speak with him. His sister was home. He told her he's doing fine; it's just very hot. He hoped to speak with his father because we're here at Ft. Drum, NY, and his dad is leaving shortly for Afghanistan.

I pray constantly that God will pull the two most important men in my life through this as well as all other service men and women. It was a great day in my house even though I wasn't the one to hear that voice I'd been longing to hear say "Hi Mom!"

Please continue to pray for our service members serving throughout the world.

25 June - Send Pillows
After missing two calls from our son, it was a shock when around 7:30 p.m. last night, which I think is around 2:30 am there, he was on the phone. He is with the 3-66 AR from Ft. Hood. Oh, one last thing, send pillows. I did, and it is a treasured item, so get one out in the mail, everyone.

26 June - Stranger From Iraq
I am writing, not with news from my Soldier, but with a personal experience that may interest anyone who has Soldiers in Iraq.

I live in an apartment in Houston, Texas. I went to the mailroom the other day to check my mail and struck up a conversation with a man there, who was obviously from the Middle East. I asked him where he was from, and almost with shame, eyes moving toward the floor, he said he was from Iraq. I told him I have a son over there who is a Soldier.

This man said he thanks God every day for the US and for the Soldiers who are over there ridding his country of Saddam's evil regime. He told of the horrors he witnessed and also of the atrocities he endured at the hands of this regime. He is a Shiite Muslim. He further stated he fled his country, secretly, twelve years ago while in his early twenties. He said, even with its nasty climate and desert land, he loves his country and would like to return to be with his family someday. He thought that was a dream he would never realize, but that with the brave actions of our Soldiers and our country's heroic invasion, this dream may be realized sooner than he had ever imagined.

Talking with this man, hearing his experiences, and seeing the longing in his face to return to a peaceful Iraq made me even more proud of my Soldier in A Co, 104 MI. It only reinforces in my heart that my son and all the troops over there are making a huge difference in the lives of the Iraqi people! If God leads you to it, He will bring you through it!

27 June - Forced to Look at Himself
I got my first letter from my son with the 1-22 IN, A Co, 2nd Platoon. I got one quick five minute call on June 1, and he said that he was healthy, starting to receive some mail and for us not to worry about him. It is easier said than done.

Today's letter said he felt this deployment might be one of the best things that has happened to him because it has forced him to look at himself and his future. He has befriended a seven-year-old Iraqi boy that he would like to bring home to give him a future. This is from a twenty-two year old newly married young man. The letter was dated May 30, and was such a wonderful gift to his Dad and me. God Bless the 4th ID.

27 June - Donations
My husband, HHC, 1-12 IN, called on Monday for the first time in about three weeks. The connection was terrible; it sounded

like a tornado was in the phone. But it's better to hear "WHAT!" a hundred times than nothing at all.

I read about someone getting a donation from a Hacky Sack company. I thought I would include what I did for my husband. I called a radio station and got one of the DJs to donate some mixed CDs to my husband's platoon. He made over forty CDs for me with all different types of music on them. All I had to do was get a CD player out to him. They all loved it even if they didn't like the music. May God bless all of our Soldiers. HOOAH!

28 June - Birthday Love

Yesterday was my nineteenth birthday. I was very happy when I was with my friends celebrating and I find that my husband, Alpha Co, 1-44 ADA out of Fort Hood, TX calls on the phone! It was good to hear his voice although I hated hanging up when it was necessary. There wasn't much time to say anything else but that we loved each other and that I hoped he would be here in time to see our next child be born.

He said the only real reason they let him talk today was because he told them it was my birthday.

28 June - Take My Kids, Please...

June 25th was a great day! I heard my husband's voice for the first time since our 18th anniversary in April. "Hi, Sunshine!" What a way to start the day at 2:38 am. He is a Sergeant in A Co, 3-66 AR, 4th ID. His letters, which are more precious than gold, have been flowing more frequently now. Some of his letters are filled with humorous stories and his spin on different situations. In a letter to our teenage daughter, one story involved an Iraqi couple that asked if he wanted to buy their children.

He writes: "I looked in the back seat, and there's these two kids, a boy and a girl probably six or eight years old, looking scared to death! How bad do you have to act for that?"

I can hear the car ride. "That's it, one more word... If I have to say it one more time... okay, that's it, I'm pulling over and selling you to the Americans. Let's see if you act like that for them!"

It gives a whole new twist to the old "don't make me pull over" line.

29 June - Anniversary Cigar

I wanted to share this special anniversary message my husband sent on our fourth wedding anniversary, which was June twenty-sixth. He is in South Tikrit, with 4ID, 1BDE, 4FSB, E CO, and a Soldier to the core. Here is the 'Op Order' he e-mailed me:

Happy Anniversary, Hon. Four wonderful years. Wish I could be there to celebrate it with you. I have ordered a cigar social to celebrate it the best I can:

RAIDER ANNIVERSARY
Who: Everybody is invited
What: Cigar Social
Where: Tikrit South, under the camo net
When: 261930DJUN03- UTC
Why: To celebrate my wife's and my fourth anniversary.

Coordinating Instructions: Bring your own chair and bring your own cigar (coordinate with me if you are short a cigar). RSVP to 'Echo Mike' on.... *Radio frequencies and e-mail address censored for security purposes.*

Task Force Ironhorse - June 2003 Casualties

SGT Atanacio Haro-marin, 27, of Baldwin Park, California, was killed on June 3, south of Balad, Iraq. Sgt Haro-marin was manning a checkpoint when his unit came under enemy fire from rocket propelled grenades and small arms. He was assigned to Battery C, 3rd Battalion, 16th Field Artillery Regiment, Fort Hood, Texas.

PVT Jessie M. Halling, 19, of Indianapolis, Indiana, was killed on June 7, 2003, in Tikrit, Iraq. PVT Halling was at a military police station when his section received rifle propelled grenade and small arms fire. The Soldier received a fatal gunshot wound. He was assigned to 401st Military Police Company, Fort Hood, Texas.

CPT Curtis Perkins Says 'Happy Birthday to His Daughter Sydne

CPT Curtis and Tenisha Perkins, with Daughter Sydne

MAJ Tony Garza (Left) - LTC Kirk Eggleston, Division Surgeon, (Right) Distribute Medical Books to Iraqi Hospitals. Dr. Hamid (Center)

FOUR

JULY - 2003
The Heat of Summer

*T*he Fourth of July is usually hot, but our Soldiers were in even hotter weather. We celebrated our country's independence at home; our Soldiers celebrated in Saddam's home. We sat in our yards, shot off fireworks, and oohed and aahed. Our Soldiers shot off fireworks that the press liked to call "shock and awe." We watched the news and read newspapers, paying close attention to anything regarding Operations Desert Scorpion and Sidewinder. Task Force Ironhorse was now in the thick of it. Messages from the field confirmed that battlefield actions were frequent and violent. Seven Task Force Soldiers were killed and many more wounded.

In Bob's Updates we exchanged recipes, planned long-distance birthday parties, and learned from an extension agent at Iowa State University that the temperature does not get hot enough to safely 'can' brownies. Patrols, raids, RPG's, weapon caches, AK-47's, and 'high value targets' were words and phrases that expanded our vocabularies and our topics of conversations. Normal life for the family of a deployed Soldier also includes coming up with ways to keep the absent Soldier in touch with the family. Babies born without fathers present, birthdays, anniversaries, and deaths in the families still occurred. We also needed to learn to deal with injuries and deaths of soldiers. Life went on at home but we never forgot our soldiers and in Bob's Updates we encouraged each other to find ways to support them.

Some of our Soldiers in the Sunni Triangle had access to Clear Creek II PX. Air conditioners trickled into the country. Dining facilities, along with recreational facilities were opened in many of Saddam's palaces. Our Soldiers would need these comforts.

We received word on July twenty-fourth that Task Force Ironhorse would be in Iraq a full year. While that was not the news we wanted to hear, good family members settled in for the long haul. We strove to live up to the 4ID motto, "Steadfast and Loyal."

1 July - Wounded Soldier Loves His Country

My nephew just got back from Iraq. He was wounded in action around thirty days ago. He was checking boats on the Tigris River when opposition forces opened fire on them. He was one of the first Soldiers wounded in the attack. His wound isn't anything life threatening, but it took him out of action. He's doing well and continues to have surgery on his wound. It's very good to have him back, but I know he still thinks about all of his brothers and sisters in action, as are we.

He is Bravo Company of the 4 Engineers and part of the 1-8 IN Task Force. One of his first comments when he returned was, "I LOVE THIS COUNTRY!"

1 July - Sees Son on TV

Today, my heart jumped into my throat as I watched the Sidewinder video clip shown on CNN several times. Our son was part of a group of Soldiers searching a home for weapons. I watched transfixed as our son entered the home, pointed to an area to be searched, opened an oven door, and looked into a cupboard and crib. We have heard from him sporadically by phone, and although he has written every day, the mail delivery is poor. If this country is key to the Middle East, then our news should have more clips on our Soldiers at work trying to make it happen. We have no idea when he will return to American soil, but we grasp at any information of his whereabouts and condition, as countless families do!

2 July - Mother and Baby are Fine

My son is in B CO, 299 Engineers currently in Tikrit. On Sunday morning his wife gave birth to a beautiful eight pound thirteen ounce boy. We contacted the Red Cross, they got to him, and he called his wife at the hospital within twelve hours! She said he sounded great, and he was relieved that mother and baby were fine. He was still a little shaken because he was escorted from working on a tank by two guards with no explanation as to what was going on. They just told him to come with them. Then they gave him the phone and congratulated him on the birth of his new son! Having this new baby boy here is such a blessing as it's a piece of our son to hold onto. I wrote a letter to him yesterday and told him I would spoil the baby rotten for him. My cup runneth over.

2 July - Oh, The Stories He'll Tell
We finally received a phone call from our son at 12:30 a.m. Monday. It was so good to hear his voice! He is a Cavalry Scout with HHC, 1-22 IN, located in the Tikrit area. He asked us if we had heard about the money and jewels being found during a raid a while back. He was there!

It has been very rewarding for us to read his letters as he grows more confident and mature. He had written us a good-bye letter before his first mission in case he didn't make it back. It was very emotional. Although the danger is obviously still there, his confidence has certainly grown. This is a real testament to the quality of our Soldiers, and the leadership there. I just harp on him in every letter, to remain constantly vigilant. (I'm sure the commanders do the same).

Our son had a very unique request in one of his letters. He asked us to send a five iron and golf balls! Our son is a very good golfer and wants to play college golf when he returns. I was surprised at first, but then knowing our son, I can see him pounding golf balls when he is not chasing "bad guys." We sent a large package the next day, which included a five iron (maybe we should have sent a sand wedge?) and golf balls. We also sent two cameras. I told him we want lots of pictures. Can you imagine the stories he will be able to tell his children and grandchildren?

Hooah for every one of our Soldiers! May they all make the absolute best of this and every situation, and stay safe!

3 July - Thanks, Mon
My son is at this time attached to HHB 3-29 FA. He is out of Fort Carson, Colorado—usually with A CO, 1-8 IN, 3BCT. I received a telephone call from him at 4:45 a.m. (Pacific Time) on Sunday. He said he is at an airfield but did not disclose the exact location. He said he is used to the heat (thank goodness). He also said they are able to shower and are eating hot meals now. He thanked me

profusely for the three cartons of cigarettes I sent. Also for the pictures of his new baby that he has yet to see.

3 July - A Caring Commander Steps In
My husband is with A CO, 588th EN BN. He was in Camp Normandy, North of AL Ba'qubah. On Father's Day, my mother (the Soldier's mother-in-law), who was staying with us, was rushed to a local hospital in the Fort Hood area. She had pneumonia and kidney failure and landed at Scott and White in Temple in critical condition. She was placed on a ventilator and the ICU prognosis was grim. I called The Red Cross the following day and they sent an emergency message for him to come home. The Red Cross followed up with me daily until I confirmed that he had received the message.

Over there, a very concerned captain really stepped up and helped convince the others to let my husband come home to help with the situation. He arrived almost two weeks later and is here now. It does go to show that there are commanders who really do care about our families and will try to help us when we are in need. A big round of thanks goes to him. Also, after a harried couple of weeks, Mom is pulling through and surprising everyone. She is not out of the woods, but has made amazing progress. Having my husband here has really eased the stress on the family. Best Wishes to all out there.

Stand Firm in Your Faith - Spiritual Reflection from CH Brewer - 4 July 2003
Happy Fourth of July to all of you and your loved ones, we want to honor those who are providing us the time to celebrate our cherished freedoms: your spouses, friends, our fellow Soldiers and Armed Forces throughout the world. It is their faithfulness to these ideals of freedom and democracy that places each of them in the "shoes" of all those who have gone before in winning this God-given right for all of us—the right to be free and to pursue the lives God has so graciously given us. These are the truths we hold to be self-evident as the framers of the Constitution put it so eloquently in words that we honor today by our lives, both in words and deeds of selfless-service.

Today is the day we celebrate the meaning of freedom by sharing together with those we love and with those we live beside in community. It is a day truly meant for joy and happiness. It is a day when we remember our nation's founding history won by the blood of those who served long ago, kept by the blood of those who have served since that beginning. It is a day unique in such celebrations worldwide. Our uniqueness comes from the fact that this day does not celebrate a military victory but a victory of an idea. The ideals of freedom and happiness mark the fullness of what this day means to each of us.

We know that such ideals, established long ago through the gift of those who faithfully served this nation and those who serve today, put meaning behind the ideas of equality, freedom and the pursuit of happiness in living our lives today. We know from our nation's history when the meanings of these words and ideals were fulfilled by lives of integrity, by people who did what they said they would do and lived according to the principles of our nation's founders. We also know from our nation's history when the meanings of these words and ideals were not fulfilled and the pain wrought upon us all because of a lack of integrity. Each of us has the power to fulfill these ideals today by seeking to live lives of integrity, doing what we know to be right, and doing what we say we will do. Our lives can demonstrate the same courage that our founders demonstrated long ago and that our fellow countrymen and women who serve today demonstrate by their actions. I believe this is what integrity means according to our Army values, the same values that supported the framework of our Constitution and nation then and today.

I believe you face hardships each day of your lives. You demonstrate it when you stand up for what you believe in. Each of you demonstrate integrity and courage in the face of many trials and lend your voice to those who are not as strong. You demonstrate it when you stand up against compromising your values and ideals when those forces that oppose such values tempt you to "just look the other way", saying "it won't really matter this one time", or "nobody will know, so just go ahead and do it". You demonstrate it when you do not give in to the fear and anxiety of the moment, when you seek to reach out, with the help of others and your combined strength, to continue to build upon the ideals this nation was built upon—equality, freedom, and the pursuit of opportunity.

4 July - He is a Patriot

We got a call from our son last night. He is with C CO 1-8 IN, in Balad. They move around a lot. He has been to Samara, Tuz, Falujah, Tikrit, and more in just a few weeks. He says they have not enjoyed the comforts we hear about, but his spirits are very high. He has become a patriot; he loves the USA and thanks all who pray for the Soldiers and take care of their families in their absence. Write to them often. They can't get too much mail. God bless these young men and women. We sleep better at night because they are willing to battle with evil men who would do harm to us and destroy our freedom.

4 July - This Bad News Didn't Matter

I just wanted to let you know I heard from my husband yesterday, 2 July. He's in 1-44 ADA, and has moved to Tikrit. He is doing well. He said, "Hon, I have some bad news..."

I got scared, but it was just that he lost his wedding band. He had it on his dog tags so he wouldn't scratch it up, and the chain broke. He was really upset, but I told him it didn't matter; it can be replaced. All I care about is his safety. More rumors on coming home dates, but I don't pay attention anymore.

4 July - They Know How to Cook

I just wanted to let you know that I got a call this morning from my brother who is in 1-68 AR from Ft. Carson, Colorado. I was so happy to hear from him. He does sound in good spirits and said that Iraqi people know how to cook. My brother said the food is wonderful over there. We only had ten minutes to talk, and it was the shortest ten minutes that I have ever had. But it was worth it all. My brother said that they have done a few raids but nothing dramatic. I am glad that God is keeping His hand on my brother and the rest of the 4ID. Thanks for everyone's prayers and support. I will not stop praying until my brother is back on American soil.

Twila Christman - Wife of LTC Conrad Christman - BN Commander 104th MI

Initially it was very difficult for my two daughters, ages five and seven years, to be separated from their father, and they each responded in their own unique style. I think one of the most important things as we all go through this deployment is to not lose sight of our children, their fears, concerns and struggles. It is also important to keep a sense of humor and to see the incredible sweet and naive side of childhood. With that said, these are my stories of inspiration.

One night while I was lying with my five year old daughter, she asked me, "What if Daddy meets a really pretty girl with long, straight hair, falls in love and gets married; then he won't be our Daddy anymore."

After responding to her and adding that I was the prettiest girl for her Daddy, she said, "Yeah, but what if she is really hot." After recovering my composure, I asked her what "hot" meant, and she responded, "fancy." Upon hearing this story, my shocked husband assured me that I did indeed meet this criterion for him and our daughter had no worries. Glad to know my husband still thinks I'm hot!

My seven-year-old daughter has wanted a dog since she could talk. My husband and I decided that it was time to take the plunge and get her a puppy. After much deliberation and dog hunting, we ended up with a precious little Shih-tzu named Jewels. My daughter told me about a week after bringing our puppy home that Jewels had "taken away all of the sadness I feel about Daddy being gone." Ah, this helps take away my sadness as well, and has been so worth the extra work and responsibility.

6 July - He'll Always Be an Infantryman

An update from one of our wounded B Co, 1-22 IN Soldier's mom. He was wounded in early June.

My son and his wife left this morning to go back to Texas. It has been a wonderful two weeks getting to visit with them. My son has made a remarkable recovery in the two weeks he has been here. He is starting to regain some movement in his right hand, although he still can't coordinate his fingers unless he moves them with his other hand. He has a lot of scars to his face, legs, arms and hands, but they will fade over time. He calls them his 'battle scars'. He begins aggressive therapy when he gets back to Ft. Hood. He can hear ringing in his right ear, so we are hoping that's a good sign.

He is very grateful, as am I, to the fine Medical team the military has for our Soldiers. We spoke a great deal about what happened in Iraq, and why he and one other Soldier were the only ones sent back to the states. He is very grateful to be here, but like a true Soldier, he feels bad that he is not back with his unit. We don't know if his injuries will allow him to remain in the Army, but like he said, 'I'll always be an Infantryman, 4th ID, 1-22 IN, B CO.' (According to him, "Best damn unit in the Army", I know he's biased.)

Thanks again for the daily updates. My son read your updates daily while he was home. When he is settled, he is going to give you a call.

God Bless our Troops.

6 July - He Shows His Colors
On July Fourth, we received our fifth wonderful, but all too brief, e-mail from our son, a 1LT with the 204th FSB with the 2BCT, in Ba'qubah. Besides just knowing that he was safe, the best part of his e-mail was that he sent a picture of himself in his 'home sweet home' tent that had been taken just an hour before! I just can't ever get over our technology. It is unbelievable that we could see and hear him instantaneously from so far around the world! He looked remarkably well, which is the most wonderful thing for a mother to see!

I suppose the thing that Jamie wanted us to see in the picture of him in his 'home' was the American flag hanging above his bed (sleeping bag over crates). We hadn't known that he had brought it with him. It first hung over our front porch, then it hung over his bed during his high school years, his bunk bed in his college dorms, his apartment at Fort Knox during his Armor training, and in his house in Killeen. The same flag is now in Iraq with him. Isn't it amazing what a powerful symbol it is? What comfort it gives him and us, knowing that he has it with him! God bless all our troops and God Bless the USA!

7 July - Who Are You?
Many memories will come from this time of separation from our loved ones serving overseas. A few we'll want to forget, but some we'll remember as quite humorous. For instance, a memory we have is of our first satellite phone call from my husband serving in Ba'qubah with HHC of the 588th Engineering Battalion of the 2BCT, 4ID.

I had my cell phone and received the first call from an

'unknown' number, 899-something. They left a message of 'strange' voices I couldn't make out. Then the call came again; this time I answered and heard, "Hi, Birdie."

Not recognizing the voice or number, I questioned, "Who is this?" The caller replied, "It's me, your husband. Hey, what's our home phone number?"

That's when I paused, very suspicious of this man claiming to be my husband and asking for our home phone number! We are to be somewhat on alert as wives home alone, no yellow ribbons on the door, etc., so I cleverly asked, "What's your father's middle name?"

He replied, "Joseph."

Then I realized I had no idea what his father's middle name was. So next I interrogated, "What's your brother's middle name?" since I knew that one. Needless to say, he passed the test, and we laughed that I spent about twenty percent of our limited ten-minute phone call trying to verify his identity. (By the way, we had just moved before he left, so that's why he didn't know the home phone number.) Anyway, it was a blessing he got through, and fortunately I now receive a call about once a week and no further interrogations!

Denise Whaley - Grandmother of PV2 Brian Craycraft - B Troop 1-10 CAV

I would like to tell you about how much I love and support my grandson while he is in Iraq. Brian is my oldest grandson and he stayed at our house a lot when he was growing up. Actually, I thought of him as another one of my kids. That is why he is so special, and why I have kept in contact with him during his army duty and deployment. I send him letters every week. I also send him copies of the sports section of the weekly paper, so that he can keep an eye on his favorite team, the 49ers, and all the other sports teams. I feel it keeps him close to what he really likes and take his mind off of what is going on over there for a minute or two. He has seemed to really enjoy it.

His mom sends him boxes of things he likes. Unfortunately, I cheat and send him gifts from Fiji's. They have all the snacks that he likes, and I feel like it gives him something different. It's also very easy to order online, and they do ship over there. It took me three months to get signed up for him to be able to e-mail me, but I finally succeeded. This way, he can call his mom more often and e-mail too. Sometimes, I get a couple of e-mails a week, where she only gets a phone call. I feel it is important to stay in touch, and this is really a personal way, and then I print it and share it with the rest of the family. My other grandkids take his letters and e-mails and pictures to school for show and tell. That made Brian very happy and proud to be someone they could look up to.

I also signed up with Mr. Babcock, which took a while, but I finally found your site. I also look at army.com daily to look at the pictures from all over and try to catch a picture of him. I can keep up with where he is approximately and know that he is safe. It's all very interesting. This helps me deal with him being so far away and helps me feel close to him while reading all of this information.

I strongly urge wives and other family members to sign up for these sites. They are free and very easy to look up. The hardest problem is getting signed up for e-mail and finding the right family readiness person to contact. In the long run, it is so very well worth it and will make them feel close to their Soldier, as I have. I worry constantly, but this has made it a lot easier for me. I wish the best to the new wives who will have to do this. Hopefully, this information will help them to cope more easily and stay strong, as I have. I can't wait for my Soldier, my precious grandson, to return to the states safe and sound, along with all the other troops. God Bless America. Thank you to all our Troops.

8 July - They have Bathrooms!

Our daughter-in-law had been spending a few days with us last week while our son is in Iraq with the 4ID, 3rd BCT, HHC 1-8 (MECH). He called our home on Thursday and said they had gone to a base and for the first time in three months they had air-conditioning, bathrooms, phones, and hamburgers and fries for lunch! We were so happy because he sounded so good and we wrote down where he was, Balad. Imagine our shock when we heard the next morning that there had been mortar fire there and many were injured! He called us at 10:30 that evening and told us all were doing well, and he had not been injured, though he had been close to where the shells exploded. We are thankful no one was killed. He said they will be moving on again soon, but seemed in really good spirits.

8 July 2003 - Bob Babcock – The Cost of Freedom

I received the following note Sunday from the wife of one of our deployed Soldiers with 418th Civil Affairs - a Reservist who is now part of Task Force Ironhorse:

To celebrate the Fourth of July weekend, this morning I had the opportunity to stand before more than three thousand people at church at all three morning services and speak on my experience in coming to the U.S. as a war refugee (from Vietnam) and becoming a citizen. I also shared my perspective of what the word, 'freedom,' means to me from the perspective of a Soldier's wife. Here is a brief excerpt if you want to share:

We just celebrated the Fourth of July. We tend to think a lot about the word, 'Freedom,' and its meaning around this time. Lately, I've been thinking a lot about the words, 'Freedom and Separation.' You all have heard the saying, that freedom is not free, right? For me personally, the cost of freedom is separation. I was separated from my father for ten years when I came to the United States as a child because of a war. I grew up without him, and when we were reunited, we had lost so much time in between that I viewed him as a father figure but not as a dad, if you can understand that. My mother and I are just now realizing this fact. She was separated from her husband for ten years! She survived in a new country and a new culture without knowing the language and raised seven children on her own. What an amazing woman!"

Presently, I am going through another period of separation in my life as my husband is in Iraq to assist in rebuilding that country and provide for the Iraqi people their liberation. The people of Iraq are now enjoying some of the privileges that we take for granted: freedom of speech, freedom to vote, and freedom of belief. My husband, I think, has a little bit more compassion in his interaction with the Iraqi people than most Soldiers over there because he realizes that many of them are like his wife at one time. They are victims of war.

I hurt for my husband when I think of him missing out on precious time with our children. We have a thirteen year old, a four year old, and a three year old. He is not able to experience the joy of physically watching them grow and participate in their lives as a father during this time. In my humble opinion, that is the sacrifice that our military men and women are giving—that is, time away from their loved ones, especially if they are a parent.

8 July - A Dollar for Those Flowers

This was written by my husband on May 1, (my birthday) who at the time was part of 4ID, 3BCT, 1-68 AR, Alpha Company. He is still in the same unit, but with HHC now.

"Our company was the Quick Reaction Force (QRF) and there was a mission to secure a site that an AH-64 Apache attack helicopters shot last night. So me, and two other tanks, and three scouts moved north about thirty kilometers. The site was right on the Tigris River, and it was nice to be by the water.

"We checked on the site and talked to the locals, and as we were pulling security, one of our tanks saw what looked like an enemy compound, so we called up the grid and in an hour or two, elements from another brigade were assaulting the area. We could not help with the assault because it was across the river, but it was neat to see. We've been looking for people loyal to Saddam, and for our battalion, it is the biggest find so far. Nothing is confirmed, but it's neat that we could have made something happen.

"Then on the way back, we had a tank break down at an intersection, and tons of kids came up trying to sell things and asking for food. They were all boys. I paid some kid one dollar for Iraqi money, and of course when I did that they all started going wild. Off in the back some girl (probably thirteen or fourteen) had picked some flowers and stood quietly behind the fifteen to twenty boys. I pointed to her and showed her a dollar trying to tell her I would give her the dollar for the flowers. Well, everyone saw what I was doing, and the girl tried to get close to the tank, but the boys would not let her, so the dad pushed his way through, picked up the girl and lifted her so we could exchange the money for the flowers. It was so cool because everyone watching cheered.

"Men think they are superior to women here, and to have me point out the girl and give her the dollar was a huge victory for her. Hard to believe they really never experience something like that—men being nice to women. That fact made it even more powerful. Of course, the girl looked like she fell in love with me. Pretty funny. I pressed the flowers she gave me and am sending them to you. I am not sure they will make it, but I wanted to share the event with you..."

The flowers made it back perfectly and are in a special picture frame now.

Susan Almaguer - Wife of LT Almaguer - A Troop 1- 10 CAV

I don't know if it's too late for the stories, I hope not. My little one is in the bath right now, so I pulled our computer desk over by the bathroom door. This has been the only chance I have had lately, as my little girl has been sick. I had received an e-mail that you were doing this, and right away I thought of the night (three days after my husband left) that my little two year old realized that daddy was not here.

We have a routine for everything. I was trying extremely hard to keep things that way for our little girl, and of course daddy played a very big part in the daily routine. The day started off pretty normally, and I was doing my best to do things for her that daddy usually did. I tried to keep up the same little games they would play, and tried to do things the way he did them. She just was not interested and said so time after time.

I figured I was trying too hard and decided to back off a little. It was bedtime, and she went down as she usually did without any argument. I left the room and tried to get some of the few hundred things done, things I was not able to finish during the daylight hours. Out of nowhere I heard a great big thump, and of course thinking that she had fallen out of her bed, I ran into the room. She had been standing on one of her chairs and had lost her balance and had fallen. She was in the process of pulling down all the pictures of daddy that I had put in her bedroom. Some of them she had already pulled down and had put in her bed. Her little eyes were red and tears were falling.

She pointed to her bed and said "Night, Night." I laid her down again and watched her as she fell asleep clutching all of her daddy's pictures to her chest. I cannot say I got very much sleep that night. It was by far the hardest night I have had since my husband left seven months ago. She woke up the next morning, handed me the pictures and said "daddy work-daddy okay", she gave me the biggest smile and hug, told me she loved me, then turned around and went to play with her toys. She said it in a matter-of-fact way, like she knew without a doubt that he was in fact, okay.

So now, when I don't get the phone calls or the letters, I think of that morning and I know that he will be okay. I believe that children have a way of knowing things that we as adults cannot explain, and they seem to be the ones that give the most comfort in the most trying of times. My baby girl is truly my little angel sent from heaven, and we both miss her daddy more than words can possible express.

9 July - She Reenlisted!
Got a call from our daughter this morning. She is with Charlie CO, 4FSC, 4th ID. They are in Samarra in support of the 1-66 AR. She reenlisted on July 4th. She said they took pictures and she will be sending them to us. She also said she will be going before the E-5 board (promotion to sergeant) next month.

Needless to say, we are very proud of her. She's doing what she needs to, and when we talk to her, she seems very upbeat and never complains about anything. We pray for her and all of our Soldiers. May God bless them all and return them safely to us.

9 July - A Stark Reminder
I received a cell-phone call from my son, HSB, 3-16 FA from Doha, on July seventh, while in my hotel room. We were visiting the site of Flight 93 crash in Shanksville, Pennsylvania, home of my wife. The Flight 93 Memorial Chapel for the victims has photos posted of each person who died, with a personal summary of their life and mission while on the flight. It is a stark and humble reminder of why our Soldiers are on their mission in Iraq! A 'must see' for military families!

9 July - He Made Our Weekend
I heard from my son early Sunday morning. He is with 3BCT, 4ID, 4th Engineers out of Fort Carson. It was the second time he has called since he left April 2nd! What made it extra special was that our whole family was in town for the holiday weekend. He only had seven minutes to talk, but we passed the phone around so everyone could say, "Hi, I love you and miss you."

Before he left, his grandfather had requested that he pee on Saddam's palace walls like he used to do on Pa's fence when he was a little boy. My father asked if he had, and he answered 'Many times!'

He made sure to tell me not to worry. (Right!) He did say he was getting our packages and mail. That call sure made our weekend!

11 July - A Bunch of Us Who Care
Just wanted to tell you that I heard from my Soldier, Co B, 2-20 FA, this morning at 1:00 a.m. I was so excited I started crying. His parents came in for the weekend and we thought for sure he would call but he didn't. Imagine their disappointment. I felt awful. No one has been able to talk to him with the exception of me since he left in March. My son did get to talk to him this morning for a bit before the phone cut out but he was so excited!

Thanks again for all the information you give out. It's the highlight of my day. I go to work knowing when I open my e-mail, your update is always there. This is my first experience with the military life, and it's been...? (I don't even know what word to use.) But my family has been one of my biggest supporters! They love him as much as I do, and they have even adopted his parents into our family as well. Thanks again! Thanks to everyone as well—they are my constant reminder that there are a bunch of us who still care!

11 July – Doing His Job Well
I have been worried about my son, who is with C Troop, 1-10 CAV, from Fort Hood. He finally got to call after three weeks of us not hearing from him. I didn't get a chance to tell him about hearing The Star Spangled Banner before his brother's baseball game, and how this year is the first time it had true meaning because of him joining the military.

I am so proud of him and all of our Soldiers who willingly wanted to serve our country. He has not once whined about being in Iraq. He sees it as going there to do a job and do it well. Thank you for putting together the 4ID updates. I have started making a copy and sending it to him so that he would get mail, and it is easier to jot a note at the end than trying to find the time to write a letter. Things are too trivial here compared to where he is and their living conditions. I know they are all ready to come home to the United States.

12 July - Memories are What We Have
I received a letter from my husband today; 3-66 AR in Bayji. He said he was well and can't wait to come home and meet his daughter for the first time. She is due in three weeks. He wrote something I want to share with you; it really warmed my heart.

"When you have nothing, all you have are memories; they keep you alive and keep you going. They drive you to do what you have to do. I know back home I have everything I need, but when you are so far from home you feel like you have nothing but memories and hopes for the future and for a brighter day where instead of getting up and seeing the dirty faces of the men around me, I see my wife and daughter. Till then I have the memories we've made and the thought of our future together."

I'm so glad he's keeping his spirits up and knows I'm waiting here for him.

12 July - Rocket Propelled Grenade Attack

I received a call last night from our son. He's with 1-22 IN, 3BCT, 4th ID. One of the companies was just hit with RPG's and he wanted to let us know he was fine. My heart and prayers go out to the families who have lost loved ones or has had anyone injured.

My husband will be deploying in about one and a half weeks for Afghanistan with the 10th Mountain Division. I was at Wal-Mart getting some photos developed today and I ran into a Soldier here at Ft Drum who just returned from Iraq yesterday. Of course I shook his hand and welcomed him home. He was in the same location that our son is right now. He talked to us about the RPG incident that just happened. I also received three letters this week from our son, and he sounds well, considering.

Thank you, Bob, for your updates. This is the second stop every morning—coffee first!

Medic Mom and Spouse.

Submitted by Donna Saine - Mother of SPC Sean M. Lewis - HHC 588 EN BN

I am a PAM (Proud Army Mom, www.proudarmymoms.org). The group of ladies I met on line, and some in person, have been my saviors. If other mothers of the 1st CAV or any other unit want to join they can go to this web site. These ladies have been my inspiration. If you're not hearing from your Soldier, you are hearing about theirs.

There are many things I will cherish from this learning experience, but most of all: Be there for each other. You are not in this alone. Don't listen to the news as they only tell you the bad things going on, not the good things. The Fourth Infantry Division has accomplished many good things for the Iraqi people; you just don't hear about them unless you go to your unit's website and read their updates. Task Force Ironhorse puts out a weekly to bi-weekly update of things going on over there, and it has the good and the bad. This is where you should get your information.

Then there is Bob Babcock. If you are part of Fourth Infantry Division, and you weren't getting his updates, you have missed a lot. There are no words to thank him. He has made it easy for us not to watch the news. He kept us all informed and made it easier to go on with the rest of our day. I pray the units going over there now have someone like him. I commend the wives of the Soldiers, for holding their families together while their husbands are away.

First, I just want to say to the wives of the Soldiers that if there is any way at all that you can get along with your mother-in-law during this time, it is wonderful. I happen to have a wonderful daughter-in-law, and she always lets me know if she had heard from my son, her husband. We always kept each other up to date if one of us heard from him. This helps tremendously!

Second, find someone you can talk to. Yes, you must be strong in front of the children, but find a time out for yourself. Find someone that you can tell your innermost fears to, so you don't hold them in. If you let it out, it will not sit on your heart as bad.

And third, continue to pray for the families who have lost loved ones, but be grateful that yours is okay. This is not a sin, it is human nature. We never want to see anyone hurt or killed, but this is war, and it will happen. My son happened to lose his right leg during this deployment. He is currently at Walter Reed, and he continues to be strong. He is so positive he inspires me! He is grateful that GOD spared him! But he is also thankful that it is only a leg, (His words, not mine.) And, he is so grateful for his buddies that saved his life!

15 July - It's a Girl!

Just a little happy news. My little brother and his wife had their baby on July 11. It's a girl, six pounds, eighteen inches long. She is so cute! My brother couldn't be there of course, since he's in Iraq, but he has been able to call her a lot, and they have let him talk for a long time. Let's hope he gets home to his little girl soon! I got to be there through the whole labor and delivery, and it was so awesome! I can't wait for him to see her!

15 July - He Got Stung in the Butt!

My husband is with A CO, 1-22 IN. Last Thursday I received six letters from him ranging in dates from June 20-June 26. They were all very interesting, explaining what he does over there. One of his stories in the letter stated that he had been stung by a scorpion, but after a night at the hospital and several days on medicine, he was feeling better. That was very scary to hear, although when he wrote, he thought I would find the story funny since he got stung in the butt! He is living in Tikrit, and said it is just really hot. He has gone on several raids and pulls guard duty a lot. The letters were great, but then on Friday morning at 7:30, I received a call from him!

16 July - God Listens

Just wanted to let you know that today I heard from my daughter who is in Company A, 704 DSB. I hadn't heard from her in about three weeks and I've been a little worried. I was just praying, "God, please, I need to hear something from her," and just then, the phone rang, and it was her!

Wow, God certainly answered my prayer quickly! She sounded good, but tired. She had been on night watch and was anxious to get to sleep. It was about 8:00 a.m. Iraq time when she called. We got cut off two times, but it was so great to hear her voice.

17 July - His Lucky Cards

I heard from my son; he's a medic, 4ID 1-22 IN. I sent him some playing cards in one of the packages I mailed to him. Some of the guys were using his cards one day. Well, I guess he went outside to have a cigarette, and just then, one of the guys called him over to give him his cards back. Just as he walked away from that spot, a grenade was thrown right where he had been standing. He said everyone hit the ground. He now calls them his 'lucky' cards. If not for them, he might not be so lucky! He now thanks me very much for sending them.

Of course, I asked him to tell me what was going on with him, so he had to say, "This is why I don't like to tell you things, Mom; I know right now you're going crazy!"

He's right, I am! It seems to be all about luck over there now, and that has me VERY worried about all of them.

17 July - Does it Get any Better?

My husband is in 978th MP from Ft. Bliss, TX. Our daughter received a letter from him last week, which perfectly illustrates the need for our troops in Iraq.

He wrote, "Yesterday an Iraqi kid about sixteen walked up to me. He was pretty brave because my weapon was basically pointed right in his face (I was not sure if he was a good guy or not.) While I was pointing it at him, he handed me an Iraqi coin, grabbed my hand and shook it and said to me, "'Thank you and the Americans for everything. We like free.'"

Does it get any better than that?

17 July - She's Got Real Patients, Now

My daughter is a medic with HHT 1-10 CAV. She can't tell me where they are, but said northern Iraq. In her latest letter (postmarked June 20, received July 11), she mentioned they treated what she termed 'her first real patients' (not scrapes and bruises this time). She called a couple of times and unfortunately, I missed her calls. However, she is a good letter writer, so I hear from her about every two weeks and I get a couple of letters at a time.

17 July - Mushy Stuff

On Sunday July 6, I got a phone call from my husband. He is with HHC 1-8 IN, 3BCT, 4ID. He said that they were doing good. Thursday, July 10, was my twenty-first birthday. I was so hoping for a phone call. Well, I did not get one of those, but I got a dozen red roses. My card said, 'Near or far, I will always love you.'

Of course, I cried then. I tried to put the pieces together on how he had them sent to me. He has no credit card over there. I asked his mom and she swore to me that she had nothing to do with it. I was still confused, although very happy. Well, on Saturday the twelfth, I received my third phone call. I said, "thank you for the roses, but how did you do it?"

He played it off by saying, "What are you talking about?" Then he tried to tell me that the Iraqis must have sent them to me. I did let him talk to his mom, and she asked him how he did it. He used his phone time instead of calling me to call the flower shop, and he told him that he would pay for them when he returned. I am still amazed. That is enough of the mushy stuff. He seemed to be doing pretty well. He is in a location where there is an air conditioner and also a gym. All he requested was more bug spray and Copenhagen snuff.

18 July - Bob Babcock - Accepting the Sacrifices
This was sent by one of our readers to the AP. It most likely will never be printed, but it impressed me so much and conveys my feelings as well. I wanted to include it here for all our 4ID family members and friends to benefit from.

To Whom it May Concern:

I am quite disgusted with the amount of negative time and energy your office spends writing articles about the 'poor families' and the 'poor service members.' I am a Soldier, a mother and an Army wife, as well as a Family Readiness Group leader. I try to focus my wives on the positive aspects of being a military family. Our family members who are in the military are warriors. They accept the sacrifices and dangers that accompany such a career. The families accept this as well.

This is a time of renewal for Iraq, and renewal does not come without conflict. Our mission there is as critical as ever. Does the logic of that make me feel good about family separation? No. But I will not subscribe to, nor propagate the negative, melancholy, and depressive attitude the media forces on Americans. The media should be the tool to uplift and inspire the American people and its military families through this time of separation.

Where are the human-interest stories? Where are the reports of the positive things the troops have done, i.e., fixing a generator at an orphanage or bringing medical care to Iraqi families. Where are the stories of inspiring personal interactions between service members and Iraqi citizens? They exist, my husband tells me. Other wives tell of interactions of their husbands with Iraqi citizens. The Army reports, through military channels, of school playgrounds being built and fire station communication systems being updated.

As a Soldier and an Army spouse, I'm tired of hearing about those Soldiers who 'fought the war so they should be able to come home.' That is crap. My husband came back from Korea in August for five days, went to school for two months, and is now in Iraq. That is military life. Deployments depend on the mission, not on whether it is convenient for the service member to be gone.

The media should express the positives. Despite complaints

about the military postal system, communication between the service member and the family has never been better.

Honor those who serve their country and their families. Separation would be a lot easier if society didn't propagate the negative. The media should find ways to support the military rather than use it as a line of gossip.

19 July - After Three Wars

Today was my seventeenth anniversary with my 10th Mountain Division Soldier, who will be leaving soon. Twice this week we received letters from our HHC 1-12 IN, 4ID medic son. He sounds really good considering he's still living in his '577' (mechanized vehicle) the last I heard. However, I just read a message from another mom who said her son is in the same exact unit, and she spoke about an air conditioner. Before these two letters, I hadn't heard from my son since before the Fourth of July. He said he tried to call us on the third but couldn't get a good line, just kept getting disconnected. No news is GREAT news. I've learned this after three wars and two peacekeeping missions.

19 July - A Card Shower

We are new to this 4ID news and have enjoyed getting the e-mails about what is really going on in Iraq. We also enjoy reading e-mails from families telling how their loved ones are getting along and sharing hints on what to send over. Our son is with HHC, 1BCT, and is living in a palace in Tikrit. He gets to call every Wednesday around noon for ten minutes. My husband, my daughter, and I always make sure we are here at that time. He sounds strong and is always upbeat.

Here is a hint I would like to pass along. Last week was his twentieth birthday. Early in June, I got this idea to have a card shower for him. I put an ad in our local paper, in our church bulletin, and had it announced on our local radio station. I had people send the cards to us by a certain date, and then we mailed them in a big box to our son.

Along with the cards, we sent snacks, a prepackaged cake with icing and candles, gifts like a Nurf football, Nurf basketball, Frisbee, water balloons, etc, etc. We sent everything out to him three weeks before his birthday and told him to have a BIG party. The package arrived two days before his birthday, and they did have a party, and he said the guys had a good time. He said it took him three days to open all the cards. I think the whole thing was very special for him. Since then, two other local families of Soldiers have done a card shower. We continue to pray for the Soldiers in the 4ID as well as the rest of the Soldiers in Iraq.

20 July - Planning Ahead
Today is my thirty-second birthday and my husband was able to call; it was pretty cool. I was on the phone with him about five minutes and my front door bell rang. When I answered it, there was a lady standing there holding twelve long stem yellow roses from my husband. (He had his grandmother order them before he left.) I couldn't believe it—talk about good timing. That was the best present I could have ever dreamed of, well, except him coming home. Anyway, he said that they are all doing good waiting on their next mission.

20 July - Crackhead and Elvis
My husband is with HHS, 2-20 FA 4ID. As many of you have experienced, when you have such limited time on the phone, it's often spent taking care of 'business': "How are you? Do you need anything? How is the family?"

We don't have time to just talk and laugh together. This phone call was different. It was full of funny stories and laughter.

My husband was telling me about the numerous stray dogs in Iraq. The unit has befriended a couple. 'Crackhead' guards the motor pool and barks when anyone comes near. If our armed forces weren't enough, they now have a guard dog!

Then, there is Elvis. He appears to have had his ears and tail cut off and needs to be cleaned up, but otherwise looks a lot like our own dog, Lady. My husband has even made good use of the flea collars sent to him. He has been putting them on the dogs!

I know this story doesn't seem like much, but it meant a lot just to hear my husband laughing and having a 'normal' conversation. A great feeling that I'm sure you all miss as much as I do. I also found it somehow comforting knowing the Soldiers have these dogs to care for. Not quite the same as their own pets (or children), but it is fun to know they are finding enjoyment in just having the dogs around.

20 July - Chicken and Watermelon

I got another letter from my son today who is with Bravo Company, 1-22 IN, 4ID. I am receiving about three letters a week now. This last letter was dated July 4. He started out by saying "Happy Independence Day."

He said his day started out pretty rough as he was just starting back to camp after a night of raids when he was dispatched to provide security because another of the platoon's Bradleys got hit by a land mine. He said, thankfully, there were no serious injuries from the explosion.

He had to do road checks and stopped a truck hauling frozen chicken leg quarters, so he and some of his buddies bought some. He said that they roasted the chicken parts, cooked some potatoes and even got a watermelon, so the day ended up pretty good. He said not to worry, that he was fine and was starting to adjust really well. He said "Remember, Mom, I was born to be a Soldier and do this."

Talk about a proud mother....

20 July - Professionals

Thank you for including the letter concerning troop morale. The author stated eloquently the thoughts I have had about the negative media since my husband served in Vietnam in the late 60s. Daily comments from you and the readers give me courage and support, as my son and his wife are now serving in Iraq. I receive the most positive and uplifting communications from them, and that is what they receive from me as well.

They deployed to Iraq knowing that this would be a life-altering situation for them and determined that, as professionals, they would do their best to make the most of the situation in a positive manner. We had many discussions, difficult as it was, about the negative side of war. No one can go through a situation like this and be unchanged for life. It is surely the positives on which we must concentrate.

The military does deserve the support of the American public, no matter what political opinions an individual may have, and the media does have the power to influence. Hooray to all Soldiers serving in the military, and to those dedicated family members who serve as a support team to those Soldiers!

My day begins with a cup of coffee and this website. My son

is with Company A, 1-12 IN, 3BCT, out of Ft. Carson, and his wife is with HHT, 3 ACR, also from Ft. Carson.

21 July - Don't Pity Me
No recent word from my husband, but I have two suggestions. Use them (or not) as you feel fit. In today's update, one mother of a 4ID Soldier said her son would be disappointed in her 'whining' about him being there. I am often pitied when people hear my husband is over there, and I am alone with our fourteen-month old children. My response every time is: "This is all part of the military life. I knew what my husband would have to do as a Soldier way before I married him. I have the easy part; I'm here with my children, safe. I thank you for your concern. Please just keep up the support for our troops."

It upsets me when people pity me; I'm damn proud of my husband and his fellow troops. They are the ones who have it hard, and we, as families of Soldiers, need to make others aware that we do not need pity, just support. That's a pet peeve of mine, and I figure it may help families to know how to respond to such comments.

21 July - A Proud Army Mom, Navy Sister, and Coast Guard Daughter.
My grandfathers were WWI and WWII vets. My dad and uncles are Korean and Vietnam war vets. My brother who is still active duty in the Navy is a vet of the first Gulf War. Now my son is in Baghdad, and he will tell you, he's doing what he signed up to do. I've raised all my children to stick to their commitments and we will stand beside them. All of our Soldiers, our sons and daughters, brothers and sisters, husbands and wives, need our unconditional support right now.

Am I afraid? You bet I am. Some days my fear is unspeakable, and it's the support of family and friends that I lean on while being strong and supportive for my son. Someday, he may know the myriad of emotions we go through day by day and week by week. But for now, our letters and packages are newsy, upbeat, and even trivial at times—and full of love and prayers. History will let us know if we should be angry or proud of our nation, but for today our Soldiers have nothing from me but love, pride and prayers.

23 July - We'll Have a Big Breakfast

I received 3 letters from my grandson yesterday. He is with the 1-17 FA from Ft Sill, Oklahoma. He said he was fine; it's just hot over there. He is in Balad now; said it was pretty quiet right now. He said he had been to the PX the day before and able to get some things he wanted there. He said he would sure be glad to get home when we could all go to Golden Corral and have our big breakfast on Saturday mornings. It's a routine thing: All the family that can gets together every Saturday morning for breakfast. We sure miss him but will make up for it when he gets home.

Kim Bedford - Wife of SPC James K. Bedford - C Co 5th ENG BN

You asked for submissions on how one gets through this and this is how I am getting through the deployment. Once you think that you have yourself composed and ready for the deployment date, the morning comes. You drive to the meeting place and act as though nothing is about to happen, just another day. Then your husband is called away to get into formation for boarding a bus. That was when the tears started for me.

When they drive away, you become a river of tears. You can't see straight and you think your world has ended or just left on a bus. Back to your house that you shared and the home you made, to think what to do now, go home to your parents or stay here and stick it out. You are so stuck on 'poor' you. Then something in your mind clicks, and you become proud. Proud because it is your husband who is going to make this world a better place. Proud because he cares enough and is selfless enough to put his life on the line for millions of strangers. You walk with your head held high and realize that "this too shall pass." Don't get me wrong, the tears keep coming, but now I think, "Wow, we've gotten through forty-two weeks and only ten are left." Before you know it, they will be home.

I wrote to my husband every day. Sometimes the letters were five pages, and sometimes they were only five words. It was my way of pretending that he was here. By telling him my day, he didn't miss too much. I did leave out details of what I had for dinner because I knew that there was no comparison and I didn't want to make him hungry. I sent him pictures once a month. I would shoot a roll of film and send him the pictures, my way of keeping him informed. There are a couple rules to live by, at least in my opinion:

1. Believe and have faith. God didn't do this to punish you. I have yet to figure out what the purpose for this is, but I know He knows that I can handle it even if I doubt myself.

2. Be proud.

3. When you get to talk to your loved one, don't forget the "I love you!" It means the most.

4. Don't watch the news, they never tell you anything good that we are doing or have done.

5. Don't feel sorry for yourself—you have family and friends; our Soldiers are alone in a strange country.

James missed out on his daughter's birth. When he gets home she will be almost eight months old. I had a piece of him with me the entire time. He only has pictures. Deployments are hard on everyone, but they are the hardest on the Soldiers. To get through it, lean on your friends and family. That is why we have them.

23 July - He Knows Why He is There

Our son is with 4ID, C troop, 1-10 CAV, from Fort Hood, Texas. We received two letters from him on Saturday. Says he has gotten about eighteen of the forty-two letters we have sent. We have them addressed, stamped and numbered on the back so he knows in what order we wrote them. They are going on night raids but not finding all of what they hoped for. He's had a couple of close calls with the Iraqi 'Soldiers.' He is on the Iran-Iraq border. Says it is 130–140 degrees and very hot. He is learning some Kurdish from the people. They are friendly towards us and very thankful we are there.

He's adopted a little dog he's named Mad Max, after the movie. He loves that little dog and has been sharing some of the food we've been sending him. I've got a bag of dog food to send him now. He says that he has needed some time by himself and has been going off by his Bradley and playing Solitaire or Yahtzee alone, pretending he is playing with Mom. We played a lot of that when he was growing up and when he was home on leave.

He is still saying we are there for a good reason, as you wouldn't believe the living conditions of the people. They've been involved in digging up the mass graves. What they are finding has really upset him. He has two nieces, ages five and two, and they have found remains of small children around their ages. It makes him think of 'his girls.' It also makes him angry that we didn't go in there sooner and rid the country of Saddam and his party. In the time he has been there he has never mentioned we are there because of weapons of mass destruction (WMDs). Their main goal is to free those people as far as he is concerned. I have to agree with him.

All of us here just pray for a safe return, and that we find Saddam and rid the world of his kind. We all want our loved ones home safe, sound, and soon, but they have an important job to do.

At twenty-four, he feels for the first time a sense of pride and purpose in his life. He's grown up a lot since being there. The biggest thing I have watched for is whether he is keeping his sense of humor, and he is. Thank you so much for the updates and for including what other families are hearing. I have gotten several ideas from them and am using them.

23 July - The Silver Necklace

This is the first time that I have responded to these updates. Mostly because until now I guess I felt that I really didn't have anything newsworthy to share. I wanted to share this experience with the rest of you because I find that what is being reported in the media doesn't portray all that is being accomplished in Iraq.

Yesterday I received a camera from my husband who is currently living outside of Baghdad in a gutted-out hospital. He belongs to C BTRY, 3-16 FA, 4ID, from Fort Hood, Texas. I had the film developed. As I looked at the pictures on the way home (I couldn't even wait to get home,) I saw several pictures that my husband had taken where he is standing or kneeling next to Iraqi children. There was one in particular where he is kneeling down next to a beautiful Iraqi girl that couldn't be much older than our daughter. She is smiling, and the look on his face is no longer cold and hard, but young and innocent.

A few weeks ago he sent me a letter in which he enclosed a silver necklace with a silver heart pendant. In his letter he explained that as they drive through downtown Baghdad, the children run alongside the convoy throwing peace signs and waving. Oftentimes my husband and his unit throw candy to them. One day as they rode through, a little girl caught my husband's eye and he got down from his vehicle to see if she wanted anything.

She gave him this silver necklace. He sent it to me with strict instructions to keep it close to our hearts.

I just wanted to share this experience with you all. It helps me to think that even out of all the violence and frustration, that our Soldiers are having these moments with the Iraqi people. Not only to boost their morale, but to help them remember why it is they are there and to help them focus on their overall mission.

24 July - Bob Babcock - 251 Days and a Wake-up

I've wondered what I can say when the news that we got today came out. I've suspected all along that next April would be when our Soldiers will come home. After we all let out our collective 'DAMNs!' let's settle in and continue to support our troops and each other.

Raising hell with the press or your congressman just makes you look bad—we are in a war on terror, and we have to see it through to the end. I hope that all our 4ID Soldiers and families rise above their disappointment and accept what has to be done to preserve our freedom.

Once again I'll go back to history and point out that our 4ID Soldiers in WWI were overseas from April 1918 to August 1919 (seventeen months), our WWII 4ID Soldiers were overseas from January 1944 to July 1945 (nineteen months), and had been drafted for the duration of the war. Our Cold War Soldiers in Germany in the early 1950s served twenty-four month tours, and our 4ID Soldiers in Vietnam had the same twelve month tour as our current Soldiers will have. And these were, for the most part, draftees.

Bottom line... We're all in this together with our troops in Iraq and we'll support them and each other in any way that we can. We need to get creative, as we now know that we have longer than many of us had hoped it would be. Our predecessor's families made it through previous wars and we'll make it through this one. Maybe it's time to start a "short timer" calendar like we all had in Vietnam. Assuming an April 1 return, that means we now have '251 days and a wake-up...'

24 July - Extract from a letter by a 2nd Platoon, Alpha 1-44 ADA officer to his wife:

Sounds like you are still curious about exactly what goes on over here, so I'll try to give you a synopsis of what the average day is like.

0130: Woke up to get ready to go on patrol at 0300.

0130-0230: Got my tracks ready to go on patrol.

0300-0700: Patrol my little corner of Iraq. (I am basically the sheriff of the area I am in, so it's a lot of fun. Although it's pretty easy to enforce the law when you have five thirty-three ton tracked vehicles with multiple gun systems.)

0730-1100: Slept after a long night driving around Iraq.

1100-1400: Did some paper work and some other officer stuff.

1400-1600: Watched one of the DVDs you sent with some of the guys from the Battery.

1700-Now: Got on the computer to write you a letter and do some other paperwork.

Rest of the Night: Eat dinner, maybe watch another movie, and get ready to go out on patrol again.

Most of the days over here tend to be the same and tend to run together when I am pulling long hours, but working a lot does make the time pass by a lot faster. Next week will be spent pretty much working on all my Bradleys, so I'll be getting my hands dirty a lot.

Michelle Wass - Wife of SSG Bradley Wass - 299 EN BN

I wrote this to my husband, shortly after we were told the deployment would last a year.

April fifteenth, two thousand and three-
The day you left to help Iraq be free.
April nineteenth, the day you left Kuwait-
I longed to talk to you, but had a long wait.
April twenty-first, my first letter from you-
My first mailbox dance, I looked like a fool.
Five weeks with no calls, didn't know what to do-
Every time the phone rang, I prayed it was you.
It was a Wednesday, May twenty-first to be exact-
I answered the phone and almost had a heart attack.
I remember I cried at hearing your voice-
'I Love You' never sounded so nice.
You said you were fine and missed me too-

Just doing what you had to do.
July twenty-third a news story I read-
4ID would be deployed for a year it said.
I could not believe it and called to find out-
No one knew anything, what was that all about.
My heart sank so low I thought it would break.
Another phone call to tell a spouse,
It was news no one could take.
I am so lonely, I long for your touch, a hug or a kiss-
So many days together we will miss.
I tell you goodnight, before I go to sleep-
I try to be brave for you and not weep.
I love you so much; I hope that you know-
Do I do a good enough job, does it show.
You think I'm insane, poems I don't write-
With you gone so long, you may well be right.
I am very proud to be your wife-
Thank you for asking me to share your life.
These last eight months must go fast and be over-
I miss you, I love you, best friend and lover.

25 July - Mom OK?

My husband is a Sergeant in B CO 1-22 IN, in Bayji. I got a phone call from him this week and he sounded pretty good. I was worried at first because he had been calling every three days or so, and I hadn't heard from him in two weeks. He said he went to town to pull guard. His shoulder came out of place again. He said they almost sent him home but decided to keep him and let it heal up again. I'm very proud of him and all of the other Soldiers that are working so hard. My son is only two, but he is great support. When I start to cry he gives me a big hug and says, 'Mom okay?' and then yells, 'Daddy, come home.' It's so cute that he makes me start laughing.

25 July - Bob Babcock - A Message From the Commanding General

What better way to start an update than with a message to our Ironhorse Family from the Commanding General, MG Ray Odierno. He sent this within an hour after the update came out on Wednesday night announcing the redeployment date.

To the Ironhorse Family,

Your husbands and wives are working tirelessly every day to improve the lives of Iraqi citizens and set the conditions that will allow us, and other U.S. forces to redeploy. They have fought fiercely against the remaining Saddam loyalists, while at the same time compassionately helping the Iraqi people move to a free, democratic society. I am impressed daily by the magnificent performance and attitude of every Ironhorse Soldier. I Know some of our Soldiers and their families have already sacrificed much, and we will never forget them.

As the CENTCOM Commander, General Abizaid said recently while visiting Task Force Ironhorse, our mission is critical to fighting the global war on terrorism, and we must defeat terrorists here so that we don't have to defeat them in the U.S. We will complete our mission no matter how long it takes. Undoing thirty-five years of repression and tyranny will not be quick or easy; our Soldiers have performed brilliantly and will continue to do so. The United States will leave Iraq only after the mission is complete and free Iraqi people enjoy a safe, secure, healthy, and prosperous society.

As we said prior to deployment, we are committed to completing the mission the president has given us, and we are proud to see this task through to completion.

In support of this long term effort I believe the division will be here about a year. If conditions are met that allow withdrawal of forces sooner it may not be that long, but we need to plan for a year. Our Soldiers are professionals; they will persevere and complete this continuing mission with the same motivation and dedication they've displayed from the beginning of this operation.

Our Soldiers are focused on the mission at hand. But I have personally been proud of the unwavering support we have received from all the friends and family members of the Task Force Ironhorse. You are true heroes and your continuing support allows us to maintain this focus. The exceptional way that the Ironhorse family has rallied from the moment we deployed is as important to the division's success as the combat performance of our units. Our Soldiers will not let up the relentless pressure on the enemy; we need the same level of effort from the Ironhorse Family.

The challenges of combat will continue; the challenges at home caused by separation and anxiety will endure as well. Through your continuing support we will complete the mission and return to celebrate our success in Iraq, as well as the success of each family member who sacrifices daily as loved ones are deployed. We all look forward to reuniting with our families again.

Our mission is difficult and I greatly appreciate all you do for your Soldiers and for each other. Thank you all for your kindness, prayers and sacrifices, while you continue to support us. God bless all the Ironhorse families and God bless our Soldiers. We will get through this together showing everyone what I already know—We have the best Soldiers and families in the Army.

Steadfast and loyal
MG Ray Odierno
CG 4ID

July (Undated) - The Top Twenty Reasons Why it is Good for My Husband to be Deployed Until April

20. No cereal bowls left on the computer desk.

19. I can put up flower pictures all over the house and take down the ones he likes (Bud Lite neon).

18. Unlimited shopping on E-Bay, no questions asked.

17. Unlimited Internet time, no sharing required.

16. I haven't had to spend money on beer in months.

15. I don't have to put the toilet seat down.

14. I can have a chick flick marathon any time I want.

13. I am going to look like one of those 'Baywatch' babes when he gets home.

12. There are no dirty brown t-shirts and black socks lying all over the house.

11. I can watch 'The Wedding Story', 'The Baby Story', and 'Trading Spaces' as many times as I want.

10. The TV will stay on a channel for more than five seconds.

9. I don't have to hear him tell me what a good driver he is.

8. I don't have to shave my legs.

7. It will take me until April to clean up the mess I've made out of 'his' garage.

6. I can't hear him snore from Iraq.

5. I have my king size bed all to myself—that is, until my two girls moved in.

4. I don't have to explain why my trip to Target for a new frying pan cost $100. (You know—along with the frying pan I also needed new utensils, plates, burner covers for the stove, a new cookie jar, laundry detergent was on sale, and toilet paper, and Ziploc bags, and...)

3. A thirty-day NTC Rotation will be a minor inconvenience.

2. There are twenty-one Sundays and so many Mondays that I don't have to watch football this year.

And the number one reason why it is good our husbands are deployed until April is...

The 'Honey-Do' list has turned into the 'Honey-I-Did' list.

25 July - Eager to Do His Part

My husband is new to the 4ID as of June. He had just graduated from flight school when he found out what unit he had been assigned to in Ft. Hood. He was excited to learn he would become a member of the 4ID aviation. When he called ahead to speak to his new commander to introduce himself, he learned that his unit had been in Iraq for nearly two months. There wasn't a second thought in his mind, but to catch the next plane to Kuwait even though he was told he didn't have to go. He's been so eager to do his part in this war and finally he has his chance, and I fully support it! He arrived in Tikrit yesterday, so this is all beginning for me.

I am so grateful that I found this site. I love getting these updates; it makes me feel connected. I am staying with family ,along with my three children, and look forward to April with all my heart and am grateful that my wait is only nine months instead of twelve. I am so happy to be a part of the 4 ID family. Thank you again for such a warm welcome!

25 July - Short Marriage, Long Separation

I heard from my husband again a few days ago. He is with the 204th FSB (Forward Support Battalion) 2nd Brigade, 3-67 Armor out of Ft. Hood. We actually were able to talk for almost twelve whole minutes. This is the longest we have talked since he has been there. He sounded upbeat. He really wanted to hear all of the current news from home and discuss plans for whenever he will come back. He said all he can think about is coming home and finally being able to live together. He was on a year tour in South Korea, returning only three weeks prior to deployment; so in our two years of marriage we have yet to live in the same country, state, or house.

He was able to call again briefly later that night. He said that he is getting his mail and packages and to keep them coming because he really looks forward to getting any mail. I try to write him a letter every day. I have turned it into my journal that I mail off each day just discussing everyday thoughts and events going on here. This has really helped me to be at peace, and when he receives them, it brings him peace and comfort as well.

26 July – Soldiers are Optimistic

I just wanted to let you know that I heard from my brother who is a Sergeant in Company C, 3-29 FA. He called my mom and me this morning at 3:00 a.m. our time. He is doing great, and it was wonderful to hear from him especially with the recent announcement that they would not be coming home till April of 2004. He says it's really hot there, but that the Soldiers are optimistic and believe in what they are fighting for.

26 July - Proud Granddaddy Looks Down From Heaven

Well, talk about a Christmas present in July... Our son, who is in the Support Platoon, HHC, 1-68 AR, 4ID called from Balad last night at 10:40 p.m.! He was in good spirits, which always picks our spirits up too. His little sister answered the phone and you could tell instantly who she was talking to by the thrill in her voice. We asked how things were going, and he said okay. He's still driving a truck. I told him I bet his Granddaddy was looking down from Heaven with pride. His Granddaddy drove a truck in Patton's 3rd Army during WWII.

We had seen on the news that Balad was taking mortar fire regularly since their arrival. We asked if the bunkers we heard about had been completed, and he said yes, but they hadn't needed them since their completion.

I told him how many of the guys at work stop me weekly, and some daily, asking if we've heard from him, and how's he doing. I also told him the instructor I had last weekend for a pilot seminar

I attended noticed the yellow ribbon I wore. During class the instructor stopped between topics and said he had noticed the ribbon and wanted to know who I had in the military. I told the instructor and classmates my son was in the 4ID in Balad, Iraq.

The instructor said he was glad to see I was wearing the ribbon and to tell my son he was proud of him and appreciated what he was doing for all of us. I said I certainly will—and I did last night. I get teary-eyed just recalling the exchange.

27 July - An Amazing Story
I am writing to you tonight because something amazing happened to me while at work today. My husband is serving in Iraq with the 4th EN BN, 4ID out of Fort Carson. I have struggled over the past few days with the news of our Soldiers redeployment. That is, until today! I met an Iraqi family while they were shopping in my store, and they noticed the dog tag I wear with my husband's picture on it. The father came up to me and asked me if my husband was in Iraq. I nervously told him yes, not sure what to expect.

He told me he was half Iraqi and half Kuwaiti; he was a father of three the same ages as my three children at home. His wife stood at his side, and we began to talk. He first began with stories of how he and his family got out of Iraq and into Kuwait twelve years ago. He went on to tell me how he traveled to the US (Denver) five years ago to go to school. He now works in Kuwait in the oil fields. He had decided to bring his family to the US on vacation to show them where he went to school. They will be here for the next month. I got the nerve up to ask him if we are wanted in Iraq, and he quickly answered my question and said, "Yes, your husband is wanted and needed in Iraq."

He went on to tell me how the Iraqi people have lived under the rule of Saddam. He referred to Saddam as 'The Living Devil'. I cannot tell you how many times he and his family thanked me for my sacrifice. He promised me every day from here on out until he gets word from me that my husband is home safely that he will include him in his daily prayers. At one point while talking to the family, they began to speak in their language to one another, and the next thing I knew, all three children left.

While the children were gone, the father told me he had something for me and that I must take it. He told me it was just a very small way of saying thank you for sacrificing so his children can have the same kind of lives as mine. He said it's our way of saying thank you for our freedom. His children then returned with a sack; inside was a Barbie Doll for my seven-year-old daughter. He said, "From my daughter to yours."

They all thanked me again for the sacrifices that my family has made. It was by far the most touching moment I have ever had in my life. He asked me if I would please keep in contact with them over the years as our children grow. I promised him I would. They invited my family and me to visit them in Kuwait. They told me they would teach me to cook; I told them I would teach them how to make meatloaf. I was kidding of course, but they didn't quite understand the joke or even what a meatloaf was.

I wanted to share this with you because today I found out why my husband is in Iraq. I came to an understanding of why it may take longer than expected to finish the mission at hand. I looked at these children and thought of my own and how different things have been for them. One story he told was of his oldest, at 5 years old, throwing a pebble at an Iraqi Soldier, and then the Soldier put a gun to his head, threatening to kill him. The grandfather begged for the child's life, but what ended up being the child's savior was that he had the same name as the son of the Iraqi Soldier. I talked to this family for what seemed to be five minutes but was actually an hour and a half. Tomorrow my letter to my husband will be quite different; it will include a lot more of 'Way to go', 'You're doing an amazing job', 'Keep up the great work' but more importantly, 'I am so very proud of you.'

My husband also served in Desert Storm with the Marine Corp, and now has been a part of Operation Iraqi Freedom with the Army. I just thought this to be an amazing story worth sharing. Include it in your daily e-mails if you would like. Maybe it will help some of the families understand why our loved ones are needed and maybe it will help them to know our Soldiers are very much needed in Iraq and appreciated by most of the Iraqi people

29 July - Getting Creative

My stepson is in the 204th Forward Support Battalion, attached to 1-67 AR, 4ID in Camp Scunion. I am writing in regards to getting creative. I sent out an e-mail to a bunch of people that I know at work (be sure to check on the soliciting policy) telling them that he was going to be there until April-May time frame, and that there were several Soldiers in his unit that weren't receiving packages, and that I would like to send a 'unit care package.' I also included the Women's Ministry leader at my church in the e-mail.

You would not believe the response I've received. I truly believe people want to help, they just don't know how. Within twenty minutes I received five e-mails stating that they would adopt the Soldiers that weren't receiving any letters or packages and probably fifteen to twenty more e-mails from people who want to help with a 'unit care package.' I was so touched because most of the e-mails started out with, "I would be honored to help" and ended with "thank you so much for thinking of me."

One woman from my church took her three kids shopping over the weekend (I just did this Friday) and created a box for a Soldier from each of her children and had them write a generic letter to the Soldier. I was so amazed and thrilled.

29 July - Neat Story
I went to the local CVS pharmacy today wearing my 'I Support My Son—Operation Iraqi Freedom—Fort Hood, Texas,' T-Shirt. The gentleman behind the counter inquired if my son was in the army. I replied that he is deployed to Iraq. It turns out that he is a 4ID veteran out of Fort Hood. I mentioned that my goal is to continue to collect donated items from my school, church, and community so that every Soldier where my son is located gets something from home. He said that next time I'm ready to ship out a box to come by and mention his name, and he'd give me supplies for our troops.

The moral of this story is to keep mentioning our troops so that our communities don't forget that there is still a war going on and that our troops need their support. You never know who will be touched by your efforts and give of themselves!

29 July - A Stranger's Support
I just wanted to share something with everyone that really warmed our hearts. Our son is in 3BCT, 4ID, out of Fort Carson. Since he has been in Iraq, our local paper has had two stories about him. One was when he first went to Iraq; the other was when we had a big party for his twenty-second birthday. That was back in June.

Yesterday we got a call from a woman who lives in our town

and has seen the articles and has been thinking of our son and wanted to send him a care package. She called to find out if that would be okay with us and what he needs!

All my family and my friends have been so kind to send care packages, letters and e-mails to our son, but to have a stranger call us and want to support our son (and us) like this really made our day. Sometimes the days get hard with him being over there, but when something like this happens it makes it a little bit easier.

29 July - They Want Us to Stay

My husband is in Ba'quabah, attached to the unit that suffered the loss of three of its Soldiers this past Saturday while guarding a children's hospital. This past Sunday, he asked his translator if he wanted to come to service with him. This young Muslim man readily agreed.

The chaplain spoke of the three Soldiers who were killed guarding the children's hospital. Afterwards, my husband's translator went up to the chaplain, shook his hand, and expressed his apologies for his people. He said that the incident was not a reflection of the majority of their thinking. They do want Americans to stay and help in rebuilding. My husband thinks this is the translator he is going to keep.

30 July - Operation Pillow Fight

Back in June, I found out that my son, a field medic with 3-16 FA did not have a pillow with him. So being a mom, I promptly sent two pillows with thirty pillowcases for any of his buddies that might need one. When Bradley finally called us, he said most politely that the Army does not issue pillows, let alone pillowcases to Soldiers out in the field for practical reasons. They are bulky and there is no space to keep them, which makes sense. Pillows are not a necessity, but a luxury.

I did some checking with Fort Hood and was told to go ahead with it—no problem—great idea. Well, Operation 'Pillow Fight' was started. My goal is to send at least two-hundred and fifty pillows (large travel size) with pillowcases to my son and his group (approximately one-hundred fifty, give or take a few on any given day). A friend, who has a son who is a pilot with the Air Force Reserve, will be taking the pillows directly to Baghdad for them to be forwarded on to the boys.

Our community has been great, with the large department stores gladly pitching in to help. People want to do anything that helps our boys and girls overseas, all you have to do is ask them. So as long as they are over there, we need to keep those ideas flowing to make their lives just a little bit more comfortable.

30 July - Magazines for the Troops

I asked at my dentist office a while back if I could have the used magazines when they were ready to cycle them out for the new ones. I told them if they would save them for me, I would gladly pick them up monthly and send them to our guys. So far, I have picked up three big stacks from two different dentist offices. (Sports Illustrated, Golf Digest, Time, Newsweek, and more) Have a great day.

30 July - Getting Close to Saddam

I heard from my husband who is in Company A, 1-22 IN last night. He called around 3:30 a.m. He is doing well, and I was the one who broke the news to him of them leaving in April. They hadn't been told yet.

He also said they were on a raid to capture Saddam's bodyguard, and when I woke up this morning, he was on TV. He was holding the bodyguard's arm and leading him out of the house. It was very exciting to see him.

I have been on the Internet all morning looking for him, and I have seen several pictures of him. When I asked how he was doing, all he said is he is hot, sweaty, and ready to come home. I don't blame him, but he said he is doing his job and will be home as soon as he can. So if your man is in A Company, 1-22 Infantry, watch Fox News; that is the best channel to watch to see your husband.

30 July - Great Tank!

My son called yesterday to tell me that his tank ran over a land mine and that I would see in the Washington Post the article with a quote from him. He said that he and his crew are fine but it was quite a shock. There was a lot of damage to the tank. He said all they saw was red (fire) and then smoke. He continues to reassure me that he's safe.

30 July - A Fine Person
I heard from my son who is in HHC, 1-67 AR. I can't imagine the grief of the families who lost their loved ones on Saturday. I had the privilege of meeting PFC Perez, who was my son's buddy. He was such a fine person who was full of life. During the minute phone call, I asked my son if it was his buddy Perez who had died. He said it was. He was in the back, and he had to identify the bodies. I can't imagine what they are all going through. My thoughts and prayers are with all the families who have lost their loved ones.

31 July - Taking Care of a Friend
I was at work today when my receptionist paged me to tell me my brother was on the phone! He just got moved from Company A, 3-29 FA to HHB, 3-29 FA, so he is now in the desert. That kind of bummed him out because he had been in a place with lots of trees and shade.

He has made new friends and says they have been really nice and welcoming to him. He was able to use the satellite phone for about ten minutes, and even though we were disconnected twice, I was able to find out that he's getting his packages now within two weeks.

He has asked me to start sending packages and writing to one of his best friends because he does not have much family and barely gets any mail. I told my brother I adopted a Soldier so he knew I would not mind doing this for his friend. He told him that I would, and his buddy got pretty excited to know he'll soon be getting stuff from us. My brother said he will be able to call us on his birthday, too. Their birthdays are an exception for them to make extra calls.

He also said, "They caught the #3 guy on the backlist yesterday." I told him I thought number three was one of the Hussein brothers, but he says since they are dead, it's now Saddam, Chemical Ali, then this other guy they got. I'm assuming he was talking about the bodyguard, but I'm not sure if HHB, 3-29 FA is attached to the guys we saw on TV. No matter, because I told him we are proud of each and every one of them and that all of their jobs are important and dangerous. He did say keep the mail coming, that's what he looks forward to the most!

93

Task Force Ironhorse - July 2003 Casualties

SFC Dan H. Gabrielson, 39, Spooner, Wisconsin, died on 9 July in Ba'quabah, Iraq. SFC Gabrielson was assigned to the 652nd Engineer Company, Ellsworth, Wis. He was traveling in a convoy that came under attack and was killed by the hostile fire. He was assigned to the 652 Engineer Company, 588th Engineers.

SGT Melissa N. Valles, 26, Eagle Pass, Texas, died on 9 July in Balad, Iraq. Sgt Valles was assigned to B Company, 64th Forward Support Battalion, Fort Carson, CO. She died as a result of non-combat injuries.

SPC Christian C. Schulz, 20, died on 11 July as a result of a non-hostile weapons discharge. He was assigned to Company C, 3rd Battalion, 67 Armor, Ft. Hood, Texas.

SGT Daniel K. Methvin, 22, Belton, Texas; **SPC Jonathan Barnes**, 21, Anderson, Missouri, and **PFC Wilfredo Perez Jr.**, 24, Norwalk, Connecticut, were killed on 26 July in Baghdad, Iraq, while supporting Operation Iraqi Freedom. The Soldiers were killed as a result of a grenade being thrown from a window of an Iraqi civilian hospital that they were guarding. The Soldiers were assigned to Headquarters and Headquarters Company, 1st Battalion, 67th Armor Regiment, 4th Infantry Division, Fort Hood, Texas.

CPT Leif E. Nott, 24, of Cheyenne, Wyoming, was killed on July 30 in Belaruz, Iraq, while supporting Operation Iraqi Freedom. LT Nott died of wounds received in a small-arms attack on a tactical operations center. He was assigned to A Troop, 1st Squadron, 10th Cavalry, 4th Aviation Brigade, 4th Infantry Division, Fort Hood, Texas.

FIVE

AUGUST - 2003
Families Dig In Their Heels

243 days and a wake-up until April 1, 2004....

*I*n August we settled in for the long haul of a full year deployment. How did that play out in day-to-day life? Our Soldiers were busy with Operation Ivy Lightning, confiscating weapons and protecting the pipeline. Offensives were intensified, with our Soldiers daring the bad guys to battle, by driving down 'RPG Alley.' Instead of raids on houses, the raids included streets and neighborhoods for weapon confiscation. Chemical Ali was captured. Saddam's sons, Uday and Qusay, and his grandson were buried after a battle. Saddam's daughters fled to Jordan for refuge. But Saddam was still free and on the run.

The terrorists were busy also. They switched to using IEDs (Improvised Explosive Devices) as convoys traveled down roads. They also bombed the Jordanian Embassy and United Nations' Headquarters.

For us at home, settling in for the long haul meant we continued to send packages and letters. We lived to hear from our Soldiers. We sent hundreds of neck coolers; we organized book drives and golf equipment drives. We wished every one of our Soldiers would be granted one of those four day passes for R and R. (Rest and Recuperation) One of the Family Readiness Groups started the 'Top 20' lists that Bob Babcock included in his updates and helped us keep our sense of humor through all of what we are reading and watching on TV. We did not always get good news of the Task Force. Our families also received tragic news. Pride, hope, patience, and love were what helped us through the final days of summer.

1 August - A Little Relaxation Goes a Long Way

My husband is with 2-20 FA out of Ft Hood and he was one of the fortunate ones with time in Qatar this past weekend for some R&R. I was so relieved that he was getting a chance to 'escape' for a little while. He did say that he got a massage each day, and it was nice to shop in a real PX. And, it was nice to have a real bed and a hot shower (as opposed to the warm ones he normally gets). He spent most of his time on the Internet and making calls to family. I know the family enjoyed hearing from him. I got numerous calls from him and we enjoyed every minute of it. No lag time, and no time limits. He sounded great and well rested by the time he was headed back. I'm so glad this is an option for the guys. Stay strong, everyone. If they can do it, we can do it!

1 August - Soldier Takes it Hard

I received a phone call from my grandson last evening. He is with the 1-67 AR in Ba'quabah. He was in, I guess, a form of shock from witnessing the three Soldiers that died at the hospital, as he was only fifteen meters from the site. We talked about five or six minutes and by the time he stated that he wanted to turn the phone over to others, he was in better spirits.

He informed us that he had received all of our packages so far, and the latest one he received was mailed on the eighteenth of July. He asked us not to send so many packages but we told him to just share with others that are not so fortunate. Also sent him a copy of the request you made for our troops to get the names, etc., from all of their buddies for future reference. Grandma said that she really appreciates the updates, otherwise she would go nuts.

1 August - Does Anybody Care?

Our son is a 'dismount' (foot Soldier) with Company B, 2-8 IN, in Ba'quabah. We received a long awaited letter from him today and would like to share with you a few of his thoughts:

"First let me say thanks! Thank you for sending me such great packages and letters. It really helps. I am sorry I haven't written a lot lately, but we've been so busy. We have missions every day, and most nights as well. Last night I finally slept eight hours! That's a first! Every week someone gets killed. I wonder, does the media even cover them? Does anyone besides our family and friends even care that we are still here?

"I don't think people care as much now that Baghdad was taken. In the event that I don't make it out, which is a reality that we live with daily, just know I love you all and that I would consider nothing a greater honor than to die defending my brothers and my nation, so that others won't have to. Hopefully by me being here, no one else in our family will see the price we pay for freedom, and never see the things I have."

The letter was signed '240B gunner extraordinaire.' We're very proud of our son and look forward to seeing him next April.

2 August - Bob Babcock

Last night I heard from one of our mothers who told me her daughter, a medic with 1-10 CAV, had been wounded and was headed for Germany. I sent her a note back asking if she had been involved in the incident where LT Nott was killed. Here is her answer (used with her permission).

"Yes, that was the incident. It happened July 30, late evening, Iraq time. She is still in the hospital near Tikrit—had a five-hour surgery since the wound was in her thigh and hit an artery. They had to graft a vein from her other leg for repairs. I was notified by Ft. Hood personnel about six to seven hours after the incident. She called after surgery, about fourteen hours after the incident, and was surprised I already knew of her condition. Ah... modern communication. We were only able to talk for about four minutes before the phone cut out.

"She is stable and will be airlifted to Germany and then stateside. I spoke to her again last night around noon Iraq time for about twenty minutes. She sounded good, although she was groggy from meds. She said she is okay. She said she was trying to help them help her while she was lying on the ground. That's my Soldier."

2 August - How to Pack a Box

One of the postal workers let me know yesterday that the post office had problems with families shipping over liquid boxed drinks, like those that go in children's lunchboxes. If they are not packed properly, the little boxes of juice burst inside the shipping boxes. It's important to pack large boxes with a good distribution of the supplies, taking into consideration the weight, size and nature of these supplies.

I often use singly wrapped toilet paper rolls, individual packets of tissues, candy bags, etc. to separate items and lighten the load if I'm sending drink mixes, which tend to be heavy items. However, if you do send little juice boxes, you could seal them inside zip-baggies, which your Soldier can recycle for personal use or putting food in to keep bugs away. So far, I've sent ten huge boxes of donated supplies to my son's unit. And thanks for the tip from another reader about using extra tape on boxes because they get a beating during the delivery process. I'm much more careful now.

I pray for all of our Soldiers and their families daily. I told my son before he left, "Be strong and of good courage—for God is with you wherever you go."

2 August - Just Your Usual Mortar Attacks

On Wednesday morning at 8:30 am CDT my daughter got a phone call from her fiancé (B CO 2-8 IN), and they got to talk for ten minutes. His spirits were pretty good, considering they had had the memorial service the day before for the three HHC, 1-67 AR guys killed Saturday. God bless their families. His biggest complaint was that he wouldn't be going to watch UT play this next season. He said everything was back to normal, just your usual mortar attacks. The thought of mortar attacks being common is a little unnerving! God bless our troops....

Alicia Horne - Wife of SSG David Horne - Co A FSC 204 FSB

David and I got married in 1991; he was a PVT E-1 or an E-2, I'm really not sure of his rank. I do know he made six-hundred dollars a month. That seems like so long ago when life seemed simpler.

We had our first son in 1992 and our second son in 1993. Then, in 1994 we were sent to Ft. Sill, Oklahoma. In 1995 we had our little girl and David was sent to Korea, a short six months later. It was that one-year tour that everyone has to do away from their families. In 1996 my husband came home, and we made our new home right here at Ft Hood, Texas. We talked about getting out, but decided David most likely would not be happy doing any other job than the one he was doing.

We celebrated our tenth year of marriage on September 11, 2001. We had this big deal planned for weeks before the day, but when the towers were hit, we decided staying home was a better idea. I have seen David angry before, but he told me then he was glad he reenlisted for nine years because he was going to make certain his family was safe.

David went to Drill Sergeant School, and had eleven days to completion. The kids and I were planning a trip to go watch him walk across the stage, with all the pride we could ever have for one man (or at least we thought). He called and said he was coming home early because of the war. I knew sooner or later we would go to war, and a part of me was scared to death (I am still scared— so many times).

Our kids were so happy Daddy was finally coming home. Since David and I had gotten married, I have pinned every rank on his chest, and I have always been proud of him for the man he is. David made the E-7 list. Since that time, he has been in Iraq. I could not be more proud of him. David has always made me feel safe and has always been there when he is needed, even if he is thousands of miles away. When we sat down and told the kids he was going to Iraq, it tore our hearts out seeing them with that hurt look. But they said to him, "Daddy, just get the bad guys and come home so the kids in Iraq will have a good life."

Army life is not always easy, but it's not always hard either. Since David has been gone to Iraq, I have found out I'm glad I have him in my life, and that I certainly don't want to ever be a single parent.

As I look around my house, I think to myself, "I can't wait for him to be home so he can fix this or that." I can't wait for him to hold me in his arms and say, "See, I told you I would be okay." Mostly, though, I cannot wait for him to come home, so I can have a Saturday night to run to the store and let Daddy spend time with the brat pack, so all of their fears will disappear for just a little while.

If I could go back in time and relive my life knowing what I know now, I honestly would not change a thing. If by some chance, I never get to see David again, I know he made my life complete, and I did the same for him. For the people who are joining the army and just starting out, yes, army life can be hard, but love conquers all, and as long as you love each other, you will make it through all the bad things and enjoy all the wonderful things; you just have to have faith in each other.

3 August - I Got Your Back

I just wanted to share something from a letter I received from a buddy of my son. It was postmarked July 14, and I got it the 31st. They are in Battery C, 3-16 FA. We met him when they graduated from boot camp together at Ft. Sill, and he became an instant part of the family then. He writes, "Don't worry about your son; he's a high speed Soldier, and I got his back."

It made me feel good reading that. To know that despite the hardships, my son continues to concentrate on doing his job. And it was nice of his friend to take the time out to write me and let me know that.

3 August - Taking it Hard

Our son, HHC, 1-67 AR, Ba'quabah, called last night about 7:30 a.m. Pacific Time. This was the first we had heard from him since July 1st. We only spoke for about three minutes and then lost the connection. He was allowed to call because of the incident at the hospital in Ba'quabah. The men were from his patrol. They had split up. Some were guarding the hospital and some were guarding the radio tower. They had been switching off. This just happened to be his turn at the tower. He said the guys were taking it hard, but they have been kept busy to keep their minds off of it.

It has been pretty 'hot' over there with gunfire every day. They are not fighting an organized military force. It is just civilians doing stupid things.

They have a small room set up with a TV and a DVD player. So my next care package will be filled with DVDs and maybe some popcorn! He hasn't had any R&R yet, but has talked to a couple guys who have. He sounded tired, so I hope he gets some soon. God bless all our troops, guard them and protect them and bring them home safe and sound.

3 August - Things are Getting Better

I received a call from my husband in B CO, 1-8 IN, last night. It was not his night to call just yet, but he was brought in especially to call me to ask me the information to send paper work to him for his promotion. Talk about a command who cares about their Soldiers!! That was uplifting.

He said that the condition of life is improving for them. They have air-conditioning in the building they stay in, and one of the sergeants has a laptop and they can watch DVDs on it. Someone sent them the Sopranos series and they are hooked!

Things are getting better for our men, ladies! He said it feels like it might start to cool off. Now with the cool air-conditioning, the heat feels like a brick wall when they walk out into it. They come in and out of camp about once a week or every other week, so they get phone calls and sometimes a trip to the PX. There is a satellite phone traveling around and they get a free ten-minute phone call on that when it comes around.

He sounded well—very 'bummed' considering all the things he will miss, but proud of who he is and of what he is doing. Our second baby will be born the end of September; our son will be two the first of November; my birthday and his, etc., all of that. He bought a huge American flag and it hangs on the door of their building now. That lifted all their spirits too! Keep praying, writing and sending packages. They all wait impatiently every day he said.

5 August - Watch for the New Iraqi Army

We got a phone call this morning, Monday, August 4, from our son-in-law who is with 1-17 FA attached to 1-10 CAV. He sounded good and said that he was safe. He told us he was able to watch the first group of Soldiers from the new Iraqi Army who had finished boot camp get on the bus for AIT. He was impressed. He said there was "bus after bus of Iraqis headed out." His only regret was he didn't have his camera with him to film the event.

He liked some of the new things my daughter sent him last month. He asked for more Gordita Meal Mix from Taco Bell, canned chicken and instant mashed potatoes and green beans. He is 'cooking.' He also wanted his favorite cereal and powered milk.

5 August - The Iraqi's Have Taken to Shooting at Us

After missing two phone calls in a row and not hearing from my son for three weeks, I went out and bought a cell phone, then called my phone company and requested call forwarding and it has already paid for itself. I do not leave the house unless I have switched on the call forwarding. We heard from him on Saturday, August 2, while at our family reunion. He is with Charlie Company, 2-8 Infantry, 4th ID.

My husband said to me, "How does he know when we are

101

not home? If we didn't have the call forwarding we would have missed his call again!"

My son said he used to use a phone in town to call in between the satellite phone calls, but the Iraqis have taken to shooting at them so they no longer go into town to use the phone. I thank the Lord daily for our wonderful Soldiers and pray for their safe return. GOD BLESS AMERICA!

6 August - Reenlisted Somewhere North of Tikrit

Although I haven't talked to my son in a couple of weeks, I know through his wife that he is okay. The most wonderful news is that he reenlisted on Sunday for three more years, while located somewhere north of TIKRIT. He is a Staff Sergeant with the 404th DASB, 4ID.

It's simply amazing that although the Soldiers are over there living in such conditions, they still want to reenlist and continue to serve our wonderful country. I never thought that one of our sons would follow in his Dad's footsteps. He is a Vietnam veteran and a retiree with twenty-four years of service. Our hats are off to them, and they are truly 'our heroes.'

My husband and I are so very proud of him, and just pray for his safe return home when the time comes, as well as all the other Soldiers over there. God bless America, God bless our Soldiers and their families, and God bless President Bush.

6 August - She Looks Just Like Him

Yesterday, my husband called me for the first time in five weeks. I recently had our first child on the 30th and thought he was calling from the Red Cross message I sent. To my surprise he hadn't gotten the message yet and was so happy to hear that I had her.

He was a little mad that it had been five days and he still hadn't gotten the message, but he got over that fast. He was so happy and sounded like he was going to cry while he was on the phone. He can't wait to get home and see her for the first time. She looks exactly like him and nothing like me. He thought that was pretty funny. He will be home the end of this month and can't wait to hold his little girl, and I can't wait to hold him.

6 August - His Awards Will Be Right Alongside Mine

We received a long handwritten letter from my son last week, including a copy of the Bronze Star award and the Combat Medical Badge. What was more poignant in this is that he related this to my having been awarded the Bronze Star and the Combat Infantryman's Badge in 1944 with the 44th Infantry Division. I was a grunt. He had my awards shadow box framed; now his will be proudly displayed alongside mine, to pass on to his son. If you're looking at the arithmetic, I am a much older dad. I think there aren't too many proud dads of Soldiers in Iraq who served in World War II.

7 August - Thanks for Including It
I'm the wife of the Physician Assistant who just received the Bronze Star and Combat Medic Badge. Thank you for including that in your update, as I know you made my father-in-law even more proud of both his and his son's service to our country!

7 August - Lifesavers
My nephew is with HHC, 3BCT, 4ID out of Fort Carson. There are eight families from my nephew's maternal branch that are sending packages to him. I'm not keeping track of his paternal side or what his wife's family is doing, but it is a sure thing that we have been keeping the post office busy and making the stock holders of various merchandisers richer. From the beginning we wanted to send plenty for him to share and he has been doing so. Some of us have sent other packages directed to specific Soldiers that have sent thank you notes to one of us.

I received a letter from one of those Soldiers August 4th. It was post marked July 20. He was very humble and genuinely happy to be receiving support from our families. He spoke of having respect and love for us even though he does not know us. He said, "It's a great pleasure to work with a man with such a loving family."

He also said the packages were a 'lifesaver.' This is also what we had hoped for. It was my thinking that if we could boost morale and make them more comfortable due to the items we sent, that it could possibly make them more alert and in a better frame of mind to do their job and get home alive.

7 August - Don't Stop Now
I got a letter from my husband today! He's doing well, missing

home of course. He mentioned (which is why I'm writing) that the wife of one of his Soldiers has refused to write to her husband until she gets a letter back from him.

He told her he hadn't been writing because there's nothing to write about (Thank God!!) He showed the letter to the other guys because he was so upset by it. For anyone getting discouraged because their Soldier's not writing, please write anyway! I know how much my husband looks forward to our letters from home. We've got e-mail, phones, and cars to go visit; all they've got is each other. Please don't stop writing!!

8 August - Former Cop Trains New Iraqi Police Force

My husband is in HHSB, 2-20 FA, attached to alpha troop 1-10 CAV out of FT. HOOD Texas. He has been to Khanaquin with Charlie CO and near Mandela with Bravo CO, both of 1-10 CAV. He has been training the Iraq people to be police officers and to be able to keep law and order in their country. He is a former police officer and is enjoying the work he is doing.

His first graduating class was sixty-four people and his second class was one hundred five people. He also said that has been on the Iraq news and in the paper and he feels like a celebrity, everyone is asking for his picture. He is getting homesick but says that time is starting to move faster now that he is moving around more.

8 August - Norman E. (Gene) Tinnin, President, 17th Airborne Division Association

Dear Warriors of the fighting 4th (IVY) Division:

On behalf of the 17th Airborne Division Assn (WWII) 'Thunder from Heaven,' I send heartfelt love and respect to the fighting Soldiers in Iraq. We of the WW II era realize that the Soldiers on the ground in that God forsaken land are in harms way big time. It would be great if only one could readily recognize the foe from friends and have time to respond appropriately.

We 'Old Timers' appreciate what you heroes are doing to preserve the liberties we have in this great USA. We send our thoughts and prayers for your safety and victory in battle AND the policing and peacekeeping as you toil under trying conditions. May you return safely to your families and loved ones SOON! We salute you!

9 August - Count Your Blessings

I have not received a phone call from my husband with the 588 EN BN in Ba'quabah for over two weeks now. Despite making that cell phone my closest friend, still no calls. I understand I am not the only one, however, and was informed by a recently redeployed Soldier that satellite phones really are hard to come by over in Iraq, especially when things get busy. If a satellite phone is down, that's even more of a challenge.

I was blessed with weekly phone calls for three weeks in a row, but now they just aren't coming. It's tempting to get discouraged, but tonight after talking with my grandparents who endured three years of separation during WWII with only the snail-mail of written letters, I was reminded how fortunate we are to hear that voice, even if it's just once!

So for those of you getting down because you haven't heard his/her voice... just count your blessings and remember those letters are just as important as phone calls if not more so! And there's always prayer!

As my Pop-pop says, "Your grandma went through some rough times, but she's one tough cookie and has been by my side ever since!"

They celebrated their 60th Anniversary last fall and I think that says it all. In the meantime, my list of things to talk about grows longer and longer, and I can always have hope he'll call again soon!

9 August - Aching to Hear His Voice

We finally got a call from our son, Saber Platoon, G Troop (Fort Hood) in Tikrit. We keep up with him through his wife whom he calls about twice a week. They are getting hot meals, a little more rest this week, and he asked us not to send any more 'junk' food because, "I'll eat it."

He did ask for canned ravioli and more books to read. He said he's read about 30 books since he's been there. I sent a camera especially for photos of himself and his platoon and his housing. He said he would take pictures and send it right back. It was so good to hear his voice.

When he left in March, we told him to always call his wife first because we did not know how often he could make the calls. But the past three weeks we have been aching to hear his voice.

When friends asked how they could pray for Eric and us, I would tell them, "I just need to hear his voice again."

Since April 15th, we had only heard his voice on a sound bite on a national public radio interview with his platoon. Praise God,; He does answer prayers. My middle son even knew about the expected call through Eric's wife and kept me home all day so I would not miss it. The letters and phone calls are so important for the Soldiers and the families!!

Nicole Rummer - Wife of SPC Travis Rummer

After receiving an e-mail from me, this is what my husband wrote:

You just hit it on the head, which sums up the way I have been trying to live life since I've been here. I have things to make up for and I have expectations to live up to. I have not been the best person I could have been, so I will make sure to do it right, for I won't have the chance to do it again.

I have hurt those that love me in many ways, but through it all, by my side they have stayed.

To their love I owe everything, and promise to give them the love they deserve, and show them how much I have changed.

I did not write this to make you cry, Nicole my love. You inspired me to express these feelings, so dry your eyes.

Without your love I would be the same, still uncaring, still having no shame.

Not knowing what it was to be loved was punishment enough. I thank God for my gift from above. That's you, my angel. I love you and always will.

P.S. I hope I didn't make you cry; I just had to find another way to explain my feelings for you and how I think. I love you so much, baby.

Later My Love,
SPC RUMMER

11 August - A Memorable Evening

We went to an Aaron Tippin concert last night at our county fair, and luck was with us. We were able to meet Mr. Tippin, not once, but twice, and he and each of his band members kindly sent a message by video to the troops. They told us that they are trying very hard to get a concert together to perform in Iraq for the troops.

We were able to videotape the entire concert and Mr. Tippin

constantly reminded the audience of who was fighting for their freedom. I am sending the tape along with signed pictures. The pictures are of our son Bradley and his best friend Luke, that they sent from Iraq. I'm also sending a pillowcase that the entire band put their well wishes on. It was truly a memorable evening. Keep the good thoughts.

11 August - Flag Means a Lot

Received a sweet letter from our son, B Co, 1-8 IN, 3BCT. He told of a heart-stirring incident that occurred during their recent Assumption of Command Ceremony. He spoke of the man whom he referred to as 'our new Hoohah-Hoohah CO.'

Our son said, "During his assumption of command ceremony, he pulled a folded US flag from under his arm and explained that it had been given to him by a Ranger who had hoisted the flag on Omaha Beach, June 6, 1944." Our Soldier said that even though that "flag is sixty-years old (maybe older than that), it is still beautiful as ever, so red, so white, and so blue. Some of the corners are fringing away, but it's the most beautiful flag I've ever seen. I love that flag that the Captain has. I've never seen one that had so much meaning to it. That flag means a lot to me. A lot."

He went on to tell us that they'd had a tremendously bright day that day, which included a company run (the first in three months) and an awards ceremony in which his squad was awarded the Army Achievement Medal for discovering some enemy mortars and mortar rounds. He said after that, "The Company formed up with the mortar tubes in the middle and that beautiful flag flying overhead for Company photos. What a day!" He ended by saying that though, "the flies land on our lips, the fleas are horrible, the mosquitoes are worse than Alaska, Iraq is a (non complimentary) hole, I don't know if we're ever coming back, but days like these are pick-me-ups."

God love them all. And thank God for days such as these, sprinkled amongst the stormier ones.

11 August - Rather be Walking

We received a letter from our son on Saturday. He is with Company C, 2-8 IN, 4ID, from Fort Hood, Texas. He says they have been busy lately. They are teaching him to drive the Bradley. He says it's fun, but he would much rather go back to being a dismount. Twice, while he has been driving, they have had RPG's fired at them.

He tells his dad and me not to worry because he is well trained and will take care of himself. We are so proud of him. He will be twenty-one on the 21st of this month. I wish he could be home to celebrate this milestone in his life, but he has a job to do and will not come home until it's done. April seems like forever, but with good friends and co-workers (and last, but not least) your newsletters, it will be here before we know it.

12 August - Modern Communications

Just wanted to let you know that I heard from my husband last night. He is in HHC 1/12 IN out of Ft Carson Colorado. He is still up north around Kirkuk, says the heat is tolerable, but they have air conditioners that work about half the time. He carries a laptop with him, and we have been able to communicate that way; it's a wonderful alternative to letters that take a while. I still write every other day though.

He has made friends with an Iraqi boy who comes to the gate often to chat with the guys. They have started a softball league. He has never played and is now getting pretty good he says. Anyhow, life is good; he has no major complaints other than the obvious—coming home.

12 August - A Great Army Plan

I received eighteen photos and an audiotape from my son who is in Al Muqadidayah, Company A, FSC, 204 FSB, 2-8 IN, which only took two weeks to get here! The mail is improving.

One of the photos was of him reenlisting on July 4th as they cooked steaks! It will be his last round for twenty years. He will be thirty-eight when he retires! What a good plan!

12 August - My Two Favorite Men

Today when I arrived home from work, I had a thank you letter from my son's First Sergeant. He wrote to let us know the forward aid station and main aid station with HHC, 1-12 IN, 3BCT, 4ID all enjoyed the sixteen boxes of morale goodies my employer, my husband and I had sent them. Said the instant tea and Jello pudding sticks were the biggest hits.

Some also enjoyed the cigars my husband insisted on sending.

He mentioned that our son is his mobile aid station driver and is doing an exceptional job, like everyone else, just as he knew they all would and that we should be very proud, because he surely is. This really touched my heart and brought tears to my eyes. I am an extremely proud American mom.

Just another note: My husband has arrived safely in Afghanistan from 10th FSB, 10th MTN DIV, for his eight to twelve month rotation assignment. It is a double dose, but I'm hanging in there for my two favorite men (my son and husband) because they've got my back. God bless all our troops, everywhere and bring them home safely.

12 August - She Made My Day

I was in the bank drive-through and a lady got out of her car behind me and came to my window and told me she saw the stickers I have on my car. One is a yellow ribbon with, 'I support the troops,' and the other is an 'I love my Soldier' decal. She had tears in her eyes, and she thanked me for the sacrifices that I must make because my husband is deployed; then she asked how my husband was, and how I was, and if I needed anything. It was the most touching experience I have had.

I told her thank you so much and that my husband is doing fine. She wanted me to tell my husband when I talked to him next how grateful she is to him and proud of the job he is doing. I took her hand and thanked her again.

Needless to say, I cried all the way to work. What a wonderful and caring lady. I don't hear stories of people doing things like that in this huge town (Colorado Springs), so this made my day.

Hooah! - Bob Babcock

Many of you probably wonder about what "Hooah!" means. I recently received a note forwarded by a 4ID vet that I served with in Vietnam, (former C Company, 1-22 IN Commander and aide to MG Peers, a former CG). Here are the definitions:

Hooah (who-ah), Adjective. US Army Slang. Referring to, or meaning anything and everything except 'no.' Generally used when at a loss for words. Also:

1. Good copy, solid copy, roger, good or great, message received, understood.

2. Glad to meet you, welcome.

3. I do not know, but will check on it. I haven't even a vague idea.

4. I am not listening.

5. That is enough of your drivel. Sit down.

6. Stop sniveling.

7. You've got to be kidding.

8. Yes.

9. Thank you

10. Go to the next [briefing] slide.

11. You have taken the correct action.

12. I don't know what that means, but am too embarrassed to ask for clarification.

13. That is really neat, I want one too.

14. Amen.

13 August - Words of Wisdom

As always, I check my e-mail as soon as I get up. I love reading the letters from other family members of the Army's 4ID. I wanted to share something that happened to me. I work in a doctor's office and proudly wear a picture of my son each day. People will comment, but sadly, don't really show much interest. Today a WW II veteran come in; he was a member of the 29th Field Artillery, and when he saw the picture of my son in his Infantry uniform, he stood as straight and tall as he could and snapped a salute that was as crisp and clean as a newly taught private. Of course, he asked all about my son and where he was, what he was doing and what we hear from him. He passed along this message:

"No matter where you go, who you become in civilian life, how the world treats you—in your heart of hearts you will always be a United States Army Soldier."

He told me to tell 'my hero' thank you for all that he is doing and that there will never be another thing in his life that will change him like his time in the military, "but that he will have to choose for it to be a change for the better or the worse."

Those were words of wisdom. I told him about this website and promised to bring in all of the information that I could. Just want you to know, Bob, that you are appreciated by all of us out here in the civilian world.

HOOAH, and God bless the 4th ID.

13 August - I'll Fatten Him Up...

Just wanted to give an update on my husband with Company A, 1-10 CAV. He called me this morning at 0800. He sounded tired and said he was miserable since it is hot over there. He was upset about the RPG explosion that killed LT Nott. He was involved in it, but he didn't want to talk about it until he gets home.

He was the acting First Sergeant, but is now back on his tanks where he is at the traffic control points. They don't see much, but in town there is more going on. So I am glad he is back on his tank now and hope they will all be okay after the recent tragedy.

I sent him a Polaroid about a month and a half ago and have received several pictures. He looks good although he has gotten skinny. But I will fatten him up when he gets home. I pray this is over soon and our troops return safe. God bless!

14 August - Send the Teddy Bear

This is to the lady whose fiancé asked for a teddy bear. Around Easter, I sent my fiancé a small stuffed bunny. I told him if he didn't want to keep it, I understood, and he could use it for target practice or whatever else he could come up with. He decided to sleep with it. When he told me that, I cried. Anyway, tell her to send the bear, apparently they don't get teased, or if they do, it doesn't seem to faze them.

14 August – You Get Back More Than You Give

I got a letter dated August 2nd from my adopted Soldier in Co A, 3-29 FA. In his letter they had just found out that they will be in Iraq for a year, and everyone is a little heartbroken about that. He said that they have been busy, so that helps out a lot.

He thought it was pretty cool that my nephew is in the 1-8 infantry, and said that they were supposed to come over and support them but when they got there their mission totally changed. He also said that they were near Baghdad where a lot of the attacks are still occurring, so they have to stay on their feet and stay alert.

He thanked me for the care package I sent and all the support that I am giving. It warmed my heart receiving his letter and I just had to share it with you. If anyone out there knows of a Soldier that doesn't get much or any mail, please write to them. You get back so much more than you give. Take care, and God Bless Our men and women in uniform.

15 August - Looks Good in Full Gear
I finally received a postcard (handmade) from my son who is in C Company, 2-8 IN, 4ID, out of Fort Hood. The postcard had a picture of him in the middle of a street in a town with people and shops along both sides of the street. He is in his full gear. He looked really good. I have also received a lot of 8 x 10s made from negatives he sent to my brother, who printed them up and mailed some back to him to give to his friends and to me so I can give them to his brother and sisters.

16 August - Send Pizza
My husband, B Co 404 DASB, was able to call me last week, and then this past Thursday at 3:30 a.m. We talked for almost forty-five minutes. Every now and then when I'm on my computer at work, he e-mails me, and we are able to talk back and forth for a few minutes. His attitude and spirits have been exceptional!

I could hear his fellow Soldiers in the background kidding around and laughing with him. One of them asked me to send him a supreme pizza! He has not complained about anything. I did not ask him where he was or what he was doing because I don't want any pressure on him. The last time he told me anything, he said he was in Tikrit, so I assume he's still there. Have a great weekend. ...nineteenth care package going out tomorrow! HOOAH!

18 August – Send a Barney Card
My four-year-old daughter got a postcard from her Daddy yesterday and my two-year-old son a birthday card the day before. Where he got a 'Barney' card for a two-year-old in Iraq, I don't know. I assume AAFES, and so I say, "Way to go AAFES."

My husband is with A CO, 104 MI out of Fort Hood. He called this morning at 1:00 a.m., which of course doesn't bother me, but he is losing track of what time it is here because he said he waited to call so as not to wake me up. He seems in good spirits, but e-mail is down. .He is talking of reenlistment...

18 August - Think Before You Speak
I received a phone call from my husband Friday. He is in 1BCT, 299th Engineers, A CO. ('Proven Pioneers. 1st on Omaha!') He was very down when he first called, but I managed to get him

112

laughing by the end of the ten-minute call.

He said they had read a recent news article where people were saying we shouldn't be in Iraq. I wish people would think before they talk to a reporter. All of our Soldiers would much rather be home with their families. Instead they are putting their family life on hold and their lives on the line to help the Iraqi people. I wish I could be interviewed. I'd tell the world how proud I am of my husband and all our Soldiers for all they do every day!

On another note: My husband has repeatedly told me his day hinges on the mail. If he gets some, it's a great day; if he doesn't, it's a bad day. So to all, keep writing, even if it's just about your trip to the store or how well the garden is growing. One page or ten pages, just write to your Soldier!

18 August - His Sergeant is His Friend

We talked to our son Friday night. It was a sad call. He is with G Troop 1-10 CAV, Fort Hood. His home is with 4-42 FA, Fort Hood. He told us that he lost a good friend, SGT Steven W. White. He said it is hard, but he needs to keep going on.

I thought it was special that he called him his friend and not his Sergeant. When he was at Fort Hood our son would tell us all the time he was going to his Sgt's home to have dinner. We think it was Sergeant White. Our thoughts and prayers go out to SGT White's family.

18 August - Superstars!

After two long months of not hearing from our son, we finally received a call from him. He is in the 1-10 CAV on the Iran/Iraq border. The day he called it was HOT. He said the normal temperature is 120 degrees. Although conditions are rough, he said he believes in what they are doing, and he is glad he is there. He says our military has helped the Iraqis in many ways and continues to do so.

Also, we were pleasantly surprised and very proud to get a forwarded letter from the Commander of the 1-10 CAV in which he applauded three men for their efforts. One was our son because he and one other Soldier are keeping the generators running in very adverse conditions. He called them superstars. We are very proud of his hard work and perseverance. I'm sure the same can be said for all our Soldiers. We are proud of all of them.

18 August - Save Money, Cut 'Em Loose

I just wanted to share a tip with all of the spouses. A way to save even more money while the Soldiers are deployed is to have them taken off of your car insurance. There is no penalty or fee for doing this and in my case, I cut my bill in half. A friend of mine did the same. All it takes is a phone call to put them back on a week or so before their return. If anything, it gives us more money to spend on our care packages! Take care and God bless!
An HHC, 1-12 IN Wife

19 August - Red Cross Comes Through

I just wanted to let you know that the Army isn't all bad. My ex-husband passed away at age forty-six on August 3. We were divorced, but still really close and Frank has been both my sons' father since 1988. I contacted the Red Cross so they could inform my son. I knew he was going to take it hard and explained to the Red Cross about their close relationship and to please ask that the news be broken to him gently. I also requested that he come home. I thought they never would since Frank was not his biological father and because we were now divorced.

To my surprise, they let my son come home. It took from a Sunday night to Friday night to get him home, but he was able to say good-bye to his dad. I cannot tell you what comfort this brought to me and of course to his younger brother. Sad to say, I must send him back to Iraq this Wednesday. It will break my heart, but I'm so thankful that they let him come home. I'm also grateful for the Red Cross. The people who assisted me were so helpful and caring.

19 August - Ambush!

We found out yesterday that my nephew who is with the 1-8 IN (MECH) out of Fort Carson was involved in the convoy ambush. He is in the Kuwait Hospital and had surgery to remove shrapnel from his back. I thank God that he is going to be okay. There were others involved and I just want to let the families of those brave Soldiers to know that my thoughts and prayers are with them at this time. No updates on him as of this morning since they only have one satellite phone I was told.
God Bless Our Troops.

19 August - He Fought Honorably

We received a call Sunday morning that our son's (of the 4th MP company) convoy came under attack, and he was wounded by shrapnel near Ba'quabah, forty-five miles northeast of Baghdad. The attackers detonated a roadside bomb and then opened fire with RPG's and automatic weapons. Most of the shrapnel hit his face and ear. He is expected to recover fully. His Sergeant called, informing us that he is being transported to Kuwait for surgery. He said that our son fought very honorably, protecting other Soldiers while he himself was wounded.

19 August - Condolences

My husband is the wounded Soldier who was traveling with Sergeant White who was killed when the vehicle hit the mine. He is with HHB, 4-42 FA. I just wanted to let you know he is doing okay. He suffered from a broken tailbone and minor burns. He is now in Germany at Ramstein hospital. As of now, we do not know what the next step of his journey is. He has been in touch with me quite frequently with his updates.

My son and I would like for Sergeant White's family to know that they are in our thoughts and prayers. I would also like to say how proud I am of the Soldiers in Iraq. Keep up the good work, guys! Thank so much for the updates. They have really kept me going. Once again, our condolences to Sergeant White's family.

19 August – Medic Tries His Best

On Saturday I heard from my son, HHB, 4-42 FA. It was not a very easy phone call for him or me. He is a medical specialist and was there when the mine exploded under the carrier that SGT White was in, and he, with the help of another Soldier, got him out of the carrier, and then my son attended to him medically. My son is having a hard time right now dealing with this; he is having nightmares. I know this has to be so hard for everyone in the unit. I send my prayers that they all are able to handle this. My prayers and sympathies especially go out to the family of SGT White.

19 August - Never Take Anything for Granted

My husband is with 46th Chemical Company, 2nd Chemical BN, and I am fortunate that I get to hear from him often. He reports that it is extremely hot there, and that they are doing their best to keep their spirits up. He misses us very much. He cannot wait to be back home. He has told me numerous times that he will never take anything for granted again.

He has befriended some of the Iraqis. He said that one Iraqi man in particular is trying to convince him that he needs more than one wife. I don't think so! It is still funny to listen to what this man has said to try and convince my husband to marry again and again and again.

God bless all the troops that are still over there. I pray for a safe stay there, and a safe and soon return to your loved ones.

19 August - Three Soldier Sons
Does life get any better than this for the mother of three deployed Soldiers? I got a phone call from son number two of B Company, 299 EN BN, 4ID. He sounded exhausted, but says he is fine. He has no complaints. He talked about registering his vehicle and insurance stuff. Said that only thing he could use is LEVER 2000 body wash and that he is very spoiled with all of the goodies I send. Nice conversation, a little taken aback at how serious and grown up he has become. He apologized all over himself for not writing. Assured him that it was okay, and that I understand they have some pretty rough days, and I would rather he get an extra ten minutes of sleep than write to me.

Son number three called yesterday and again this morning, central time (National Guard, 248 EN CO). He also sounds tired, but seems to be doing well. Told me to stop sending so much junk food; he is starting to gain weight. He's a Communications guy and doesn't get as much activity as the other guys. Anyway, he said to send more gum. I will be in search of some lower calorie snacks. They head out and will be 'on the road' again for a while.

Son number one was able to e-mail from Korea. He is doing well and says that for now, they are housed in the building assigned to the US Army Band. He said that after living in tents, it is like being in a four star hotel. As always, thank you for the updates. They keep me going in between communications with the kids.

19 August - Military Sacrifices
Today was our grandson's first day of kindergarten. As his mom was walking him into school in Killeen, two Kiowas flew over. She told him, "See, Daddy must be thinking about you right now."

He's a pilot in E Troop, 1-10 CAV and our grandson said, "Yep, and I'm thinking of Daddy, too."

It brought tears to my eyes that his daddy wasn't there for his big day. Do people really understand the sacrifices of our military? I am so proud and thankful of all those serving our country.

20 August - Little Things Mean a Lot

I heard from my husband this morning. He is with the 3rd Platoon, B Company, 1-22 IN, in Bayji. I did get to tell him about our son learning to walk last week. He was overjoyed to hear that. It all puts things in perspective seeing our little boy walking because when he left our son wasn't even crawling yet. So, needless to say, my husband is heartbroken that he is missing so much, but he is handling things well. Just like a true Soldier should. He didn't say much about what is going on since we had very little time to talk, but his spirits were high.

20 August - Phone Card Drive

I started a phone card drive at my church a couple of weeks ago for our Guardsmen from south Mississippi, most of who are with the 890th EN BN. Those precious few minutes on the phone make all the difference in the world. I know many families across the U.S. are having a hard time scraping by because the Guard pay is much less than their civilian pay. I know of some here that can't afford to get a phone card to their Soldier.

My church, Bayou View Baptist, (I have to brag!) collected enough phone cards and money to send nearly 200 cards over to the CSM (Command Sergeant Major) who will see to it that they are distributed to those who need cards. I hope this sparks some ideas to other churches and organizations. So many folks want to help, they just don't always know what to do. I am going to start another phone card drive in September or October for the holidays.

20 August - Ah, Those British

I have a son and daughter-in-law in the 3ID and a son in 1-8 Infantry of 4ID. While I was visiting England, I wrote my sons a post card and some letters. When I went to the post office in England, they were a bit confused as to how to send these letters to our boys in Iraq. What they finally decided on was to send them to their own military and put in red ink on the letters and

117

post card, 'U.S. Armed Forces Mail - please forward.'

I wasn't sure if this would even reach the kids, but lo and behold, they reported to me that they did receive these letters; it took twenty-five days to reach them. Now that's a great effort by the English postal system as well as the English Military.

Great Allies, those Brits...!

20 August - To Bob Babcock From his Daughter:

Daddy, our country is truly blessed to have the men and women who make incredible sacrifices to protect us each and every day. I cannot imagine any greater sacrifice than those of parents who are separated from their children. I was blessed to witness Annabeth's first day of kindergarten, and Annabeth was blessed to have me there. Please relay that Annabeth prays for our Soldiers every night, and mentions very specific concerns in her prayers. For example, "Dear God please make sure the Soldier men are not hungry."

Tonight we will include in our prayers the Soldiers and their children, and extra special blessings to the 'kindergartners' that miss their Mommy or Daddy.

21 August - The Look in His Eyes

My husband, a 2LT with HHC, 1-67 AR, Ba'quabah) wrote me a letter postmarked August 5, 2003, that I received yesterday. I would like to share a piece from this letter. It reads:

"I was talking to an Iraqi man who does contract work for us; we call him Mr. Mohammed. He heard the rumor that Saddam Hussein was surrounded, and he wished he was there to see him get caught because he could not believe how a man so evil could rule a country for thirty years and no one do anything about it.

"You should have seen the look in his eyes; he was so happy to be free. I'll never forget it. I know some people here don't like us, but just to see one of the Iraqi people experience what we as Americans sometimes take for granted, is more than enough to make me love what I am doing. Never in my life have I been so proud to be an American as I did today. I'll never forget the look and smile of Mr. Mohammed for as long as I live."

Hearing this makes our separation worth it. I am so proud of him and all of our guys!

Cherice Morgan - Wife of SSG Kime W. Morgan Jr.- Co B 1-68 AR - 3RD BCT

What has kept me strong through this deployment? What an interesting question and my answer involves so many things and people. First and foremost, my faith in God has kept me strong, has kept me focused, and has kept me grounded. Second, my husband is my rock and my best friend. He has been in Iraq all this time, loving me, wanting to be home with me and our kids, but doing his job for this country, for us, and his family has made every day easier to get through.

Knowing what we share is rare and special, and knowing our love surpasses all distances and time has made me strong. I have been married to my angel for nine years, and no matter where he has to go in his military duties to this country, I will always be here waiting, praying for his safety, and loving him for being a man, my husband, a father to our children, and a Soldier. His love, loyalty, and faith in me as his wife keeps me strong.

My two girls, who are only five and six, have kept me strong. They are bright and intelligent, they have seen me cry in loneliness and have cried with me, they have seen me jump and smile in joy when my hubby got online or sent me a letter. They have shared in my joy. They have wiped my tears away, and I have wiped theirs, and when it was very hard, our arms were there to hold each other and soothe the pain away. They have shared their own pain and accomplishments in making it through without their father here. They love him and respect him even in his absence; they say he is their hero. My husband, my children, and my family are my heroes.

Not only has my family kept me strong, but my extended family, which includes my brothers, my sisters, my moms and my dads. My friends who have given me so much strength, I thank God for my support group; they are an awesome group of ladies who I will remember forever. All of these, my friends and family, have kept me strong and encouraged me to go on another day, have told me how strong I am to be without him for so long. I am like every other wife who has a great man to call her own, and knows he is worth everything to her. I am just a wife in love with her Soldier, making it through with the hope of one day soon holding him in my arms, seeing him smile, listening to him breathe while he sleeps, hearing him laugh at my stupid jokes, or chase

119

after the kids in fun, and feeling safe again in his arms. My hope of seeing him again keeps me strong. And his love keeps me going.

Proud Army Wife and Proud Mommy

22 August - He'll Stay as Long as It Takes
Bob, tell your granddaughter that my husband, HHC 3-67 AR, Ba'quabah, is really touched by her prayers. Our son started kindergarten on Monday without his daddy. We took lots of pictures, but it was a little heartbreaking. We are all toughing it out well, though. My husband's philosophy is that he will gladly stay there as long as it takes, so our sons will only ever go there as visiting tourists.

23 August - Feeling the Heat
I received a letter from my son who is with the 404th DASB, 4ID, somewhere in Northern Iraq. He sent a picture of himself in front of a thermometer. The thermometer had the state of Texas on it. (Their unit is based in Fort Hood). A computer sign under it printed HELL, and the thermometer was registering just under 140 degrees. Can you imagine! He said in the letter that a little earlier it had registered just over 140, but he was too busy to get the picture taken then. He says that you should never let anyone tell you that you don't feel the heat when it's dry heat because you definitely do.

23 August - Get Their Names
Your advice to have our Soldiers get names and addresses of 'war buddies' just gave me an idea that you might want to share. I am going to send my husband a notebook with the appropriate questions on each page, or maybe just a phone book kind of booklet. As you said, if he gets it on loose paper, he will more than likely lose it.

23 August - He'll Probably Stick Around
My son is a medic with A Company, 1-22 IN. During all of this going on over there, he has passed the promotion board and is waiting for his points to be promoted to Sergeant. His four years is up in eight short months. He was planning on leaving the Army for sure. Once in Iraq, however, he has reconsidered and is now thinking of reenlisting for three more years.

Speaking from a mother's point of view, a day will not go by without me worrying, yet I do believe he made the right choice by joining the Army, and there couldn't be another mother more proud of her son than I am today and always!

24 August - Two Sons Serving
To the mothers with two sons serving in Iraq. I also have two sons there. One is 1-10 CAV, E Troop, and the other is with the 101st in Mosul. They both arrived in Kuwait within two to three weeks of each other, have missed each other by two to three hours at Baghdad Airport and have still not seen each other. I know it would help both if they could actually visit by phone, or better yet, visit in person but so far that has not worked out.

They sent letters to each other but have only been successful once; it took two months for them to get them. I think they have e-mailed, when the 1-10 CAV pilot had limited access to a computer. These are great men, but I think of them as my 'boys.' Both will celebrate birthdays in October, two weeks apart.

I fret and stew about their safety but realize they are doing what they want and need to be doing for the protection of their families and all people worldwide. We have got to be positive and help them get through these tough times.

As someone at church said to me, "We have got to be prayer warriors and send those 'scud' prayers to the Middle East." An interesting way of putting it, but one that might just help get the job done! By the way, in every letter I send to them I include a self-addressed envelope. I just put my return address label in the middle of the envelope. All they have to do is write 'free mail' in the upper right hand side and their return in the left. I sometimes enclose a sheet or two of paper. I think they get the hint!

Tisha - Wife of a Sergeant - 16th Signal BN
I am a twenty-four year old Soldier's wife. This is my first duty station with a hubby who is a Sergeant with the 16th signal battalion out of Ft Hood. He was deployed April 5, 2003.

How can I forget that day? I never will. This deployment has brought me more strength and patience than I ever thought I would have. We had just bought a Ford Mustang the month before my hubby left. Not even two weeks after he left, I went through an automatic drive-through car wash (the same one hubby had used), and my antenna was ripped off the car. The hood was even bent. So I had that fixed on my own.

I've had to deal with dead puppies, killing bugs on my own, having to get the car door fixed when a buggy at Wal-Mart hit it and dented it (that cost me four hundred dollars). I got lost in Austin and San Antonio with friends, got the oil changed, took out the garbage, did the budget, fed the dogs, washed the dogs, watched the dogs destroy the storage shed outside, and picked the dogs up, way out at Sugarloaf range on Ft. Hood. Our two golden retrievers have escaped more than once.

And finally, the funny thing that happened tonight (it's been raining all day long,) I walk into my bedroom, and what do I see? Water on the floor! I walk into the back bedroom and see water on the floor! I look outside into the backyard and what do I see? A lake that is about to overtake the house at any minute.

Do I cry? Do I get angry? No, I laugh my butt off! What else can you do? I laugh the laugh of the Army wife that has been through it all without her husband to take care of it. I laugh the laugh of the Army wife that knows she can deal with it. I've had my moments, but I've realized life is short. So what if I have only one towel left to take a shower with? So what if I've used every other blanket, towel, and sheet in the house to dry up the water? So what if my dog thinks it's a puddle to play in? I'm alive, I'm happy, I'm strong, and I've made it through another day. Woohoo!

26 August - Cousins Serve

Our son went over with the 4ID, but is now supporting the 3rd ACR. However, something happened this weekend that I thought you might enjoy. Our son, HHC, 16th Signal BN, met his second cousin (181 Trans BN) for the first time! They are both near the Euphrates and Ar Ramadi. They shared war stories and kept looking for the 'family resemblance' in looks, mannerisms, etc. Our son reported that their meeting was 'weird, but cool!'

The reason that I say history repeats itself is because almost exactly sixty years ago, their grandfathers, who were brothers, met up in Bougainville in the middle of WWII. One brother had just become a father for the first time, and the second one went to congratulate him and ended up also being the first to inform him he was a dad: mail was delayed. We are excited to have some good family news!

26 August - Those First Cries

I have some bittersweet news for you! My first grandchild was born August 19, at 5:29 a.m., weighing seven pounds, twelve ounces. He is nineteen and one half inches long with a head full of brown hair like his daddy, my son! It was very sad at the same time as our Soldier serving with HHC, 299th EN BN, 1BCT was not there for the most important day of his life. He would have been so proud of his wife, Jessica!

I was there, as well as her mother, to help with the delivery. I audiotaped the last forty-five minutes of labor and the delivery so he could at least hear what went on. That for sure was a quick way for him to hear his son's first cries! I also taped messages from people who saw the baby so that dad can hear the reactions of family members. It's the next best thing to being here.

I must commend the Red Cross. I called them within an hour after the birth on Tuesday evening and he got word Wednesday evening. He was able to call on Thursday. It was so good to hear his voice, although he is very depressed about not being here with his wife for the birth of their firstborn. Even though that is one of the many sacrifices of being in the military, it still hurts.

28 August - A GI Birthday Cake

This is for the woman who wanted some ideas for her husband's birthday. I always make my son a birthday cake so I couldn't miss it this year. I got two metal cookie tins (white). I glued the top to the bottom of one to look like cake layers. I glued the bottom tin to a paper doily, so it looks like it's on a plate. I got cording and glued it on the top, around the middle and around the bottom to look like icing. I decorated with stickers and then glued candles to the top tin lid. Surprisingly, it looked like a cake. I also filled the tins with things he liked that would survive the trip.

28 August - Send Silly Things

I wanted to reply to the lady asking about what to do for a birthday. My husband turned twenty-one last week and his grandmother and I got together and asked our friends and family to send him twenty-one of something. He got twenty-one bags of chips, twenty-one lollipops, and twenty-one puzzle books—just silly things to make him laugh. My husband is in B Troop, 1-10 CAV, and he said that they are doing well but are ready to come home.

123

28 August - They Were Happy to See Them

I just got a letter from my hubby, 3rd Platoon, 4th MP Company. He said they went to Kirkuk, and that the people there were so happy to see them. He said most of them there are Christians, and they thanked them for coming to Iraq. He asked one of the families if they knew where he could get ice. They went into their house and brought him two bags and some flowers! He tried to pay them, but they wouldn't hear of it. It makes me tear up even writing this now. He said, "Honey, these people are so poor that they don't have running water or electricity."

He said that he is usually part of the Quick Reaction Team that goes into town to try and find gunmen when they shoot at the gates. He also asked for more film because he is taking pictures like crazy. The last thing he said is that he loves and misses us, and he loves getting my letters.

28 August - An Iraqi Says Thanks

Our son's unit, 3-16 FA, is living at the Hammad Shihab hospital north of Baghdad. The *Iraq Today* newspaper recently did an article on the Soldiers and the citizens who are working to rebuild this hospital. The editor, Hassan Fattah, was kind enough to e-mail a picture of our son, which was included in the paper. I don't have the article to send you, just a photocopy. Hassan Fattah wrote a nice note saying, "Thanks for your note. I have attached the picture of your son. You should be proud that he is one of the people making Iraqi lives just a bit better."

It's nice to know that some of the Iraqi people appreciate what we are doing for them, and we are always proud of our son, because he is a good person. He also just became a father for the first time; his baby girl was born August 15! Mom and baby are doing great and living with us.

29 August - Mandate to Freedom

My son is with B Company, 1-22 IN, 4ID in Iraq; most likely around Bayji. I've been visiting my wonderful daughter-in-law at Fort Hood, Texas for three weeks and have been helping out her sister who will be deployed in October and her husband in January. I helped baby-sit their twenty-month old boy and a seven-month-old baby girl, and I loved every minute of it! It's hard on families, especially the children, when both parents are deployed.

It is a unique perspective visiting an army town and seeing Soldiers in various parts of their daily life, whether in uniform at the local Wal-Mart, shopping at the PX, or on post going about their duties. Seeing Apache helicopters flying overhead with that distinctive rotary sound they make and the constant boom from weapons as troops train for future deployment is a constant reminder of our mandate to freedom. It fills me with pride to see our Soldiers and wish other people could have this experience.

29 August - Planning for Christmas

My brother called yesterday, HHB, 3-29 FA, from Samarra airfield. He says they finally have air conditioning, and that he actually has to cover up at night when he sleeps! He loves the packages we send. He said they have cooks now, so they get a hot meal for breakfast and a hot meal for dinner. I'm already planning Christmas for him. I'm sending him a battery operated fiber optic small tree, and I plan to mail him a present once a week starting in November, so he'll have small things to open on Christmas day. Also, I'll send small inexpensive gifts for him to give some of his buddies on Christmas Day, so hopefully this will make them feel like their Christmas won't be so bad this year.

Angela Chopper - Wife of SGT Robert Chopper - 1-68 AR

This is just an example of what my husband has been writing from the minute he left our house on 3 April 2003. This is from the card I took to the delivery room with me when I had our fourth and final son. He wasn't able to be there, but he was there in these words and in spirit. I also took a picture with me so our son could see his Daddy first thing. My husband's strength and his faith in me as a woman and a mother is what has kept me going so far. When I'm starting to fall somehow he knows it, and when I've been my lowest there has always been a letter or card in the mailbox to pick me up again.

"To My Sweetheart, The Love of My Life: I just wanted to take a moment to write a little note, and tell you that I am so very proud of you. Every day that we're apart, you amaze me! I know you're a very strong, independent woman, but the way you've handled this deployment is baffling to me, every time we talk, I get stronger just by hearing your voice. Many of these other guys'wives are talking about divorce, leaving their Soldiers, going home to mom, and assorted other things. But you just keep on 'keeping on', with spirits high.

"I know there have been days and nights when you've probably struggled, but somehow you always seem to be doing very well and simply handling it, regardless. In fact, I just hope you still need me when I do get home! Maybe it sounds a little silly, but I never expected this to be so tough on me, and I thought you would be the one struggling. It does my heart a ton of good to hear you doing so well! I just hope that someday you will be able to understand how proud you make me feel!

"I've said it before, but I feel it bears repeating: you are the rock that keeps me grounded! Thank you from the very bottom of my heart, for being you! I just hope with all my heart that you realize just how proud I am to be your husband!"

30 August - Where's My Golf Clubs?

I saw the article you posted about the mom in Illinois doing the book drive. I am the other lady in the article. I did indeed do the golf equipment drive, which was incredibly successful. We received several thousand dollars worth of equipment. We then got the equipment to Ft. Hood, where it was put on a cargo plane back in July. The problem is that the equipment never made it to my husband. It is somewhere in Iraq.

I am hoping that if everyone who reads your daily column asks their people in Iraq, perhaps we will make contact with someone has seen or heard something. I am talking about tons of equipment, not just a club or two. My concern is that my husband is going with unnecessary convoys trying to locate this equipment. No one wants their loved ones driving around Iraq any more than they have to. Please, anyone that can help me I would greatly appreciate it. My husband is with G-6, HHC, 4ID.

Michelle Epperson - Goodman, Mo

I do not have a husband or brother in Iraq this time, but I do want to tell the mothers, wives, sisters, and daughters thank you. Many people may not tell them that, but I do thank them for their family members fighting for our freedom and the freedom of others. I just want them to know that our thoughts and prayers are with them and their families.

Submitted by Myrt Catlett - Mother of SGT Mark A. Catlett – Co C 1-66 AR

We saw it coming early in his life. He preferred fatigues to blue jeans and T-shirts. He would rather be in the woods than in the safety of the yard; in a sleeping bag rather than a bed. We changed schools, from my husband and my Alma Mater to a school that offered ROTC. He followed Desert Storm with the intensity of an officer and his room carried pictures of all the planes and artillery that were used there. Those abilities to plan and execute back yard war games carried that child Soldier to command his ROTC Ranger unit in high school and then on to join the National Guard where he would earn scholarships to a nearby military college.

Two years into college, military aspirations became more profound and on a June afternoon the announcement came that he had joined the Army. After three tours of duty in the Middle East, including Iraq at this time, his Dad and I have learned that our once "want-to-be Soldier" had a dream that God has allowed him to fulfill while also affording us the opportunity to see that dream come true. Prayer and encouragement are the pains that allow dreams to be birthed. May we all realize how important it is for our sons and daughters, or husbands and wives to pursue their dreams even if it takes them into harm's way. We have learned that God is the God of the Universe, not just America, and wherever our son is deployed, God has already gone before; and yet, He is also present to care for the family he leaves behind.

Task Force Ironhorse - August 2003 Casualties

SPC Justin W. Hebert, 20, of Arlington, Washington, was killed on August 1, in Kirkuk, Iraq. SPC Hebert was on patrol when his vehicle was struck by a rocket-propelled grenade. SPC Hebert was assigned to the 319th Field Artillery, 173rd Airborne Brigade, Camp Ederle, Italy.

PVT Matthew D. Bush, 20, of East Alton, Illinois, died on 8 August in Camp Caldwell, Iraq. A fellow Soldier tried to wake Bush and noticed he was not breathing. Bush was assigned to F Troop, 1st Squadron, 10th Armored Cavalry Regiment, Fort Hood, Texas.

SSG David S. Perry, 36, of Bakersfield, California, was killed on August 10, in Ba'quabah, Iraq. SSG Perry was inspecting a suspicious package when it exploded and fatally injured him. Perry was assigned to 649th Military Police Company, U.S. Army National Guard, Camp San Luis Obispo, California.

SGT Steven W. White, 29, of Lawton, Oklahoma, was killed on August 13, in Tikrit, Iraq. SGT White died of injuries sustained when his M113 armored personnel carrier hit an antitank mine. SGT White was assigned to Headquarters and Headquarters Battery, 4th Battalion, 42nd Field Artillery Regiment, based at Fort Hood, Texas.

CPL Craig S. Ivory, 26, died on 17 Aug 2003 of a non-combat related injury. He was with the 501st Forward Support Co, 173rd Air Brigade, Southern European Task Force, Vicenza, Italy.

SPC Ronald D. Allen, Jr., 22, of Mitchell, Indiana, died on August 25, near Balad, Iraq. SPC Allen was conducting convoy operations when he was involved in a vehicular accident. SPC Allen died of his injuries. Allen was assigned to the 502nd Personnel Service Battalion, 43rd Area Support Group, Fort Carson, Colorado.

SGT Sean K. Cataudella, 28, of Tucson, Arizona, died on August 29, in Ba'quabah, Iraq. SGT Cataudella was driving a military vehicle when he hit an embankment and rolled into a canal. SGT Cataudella was assigned to the H Troop, 10th CAV, 2BCT, 4th Infantry Division, Fort Hood, Texas.

SSG Mark A. Lawton, 41, of Hayden, Colorado, was killed on August 29, north of As Suaydat, Iraq. SSG Lawton was in a convoy that was hit by a rocket-propelled grenade. He was assigned to the 244th Engineer Battalion, U.S. Army Reserve, Grand Junction, Colorado.

SSG Kime W. Morgan Jr. and Wife Cherice

SSG Kime W. Morgan Jr. and Children

SIX

SEPTEMBER - 2003
Staying the Course

212 days and a wake-up until April 1, 2004...

*T*he September 11th memorial service in Iraq and at home helped us keep our focus on what needed to be accomplished in Iraq. Families and Soldiers stayed the course in spite of politicians in Washington bickering about money and the media misrepresenting what was happening in Iraq.

Our Soldiers in Iraq continued to confiscate weapons, arrest bad guys, and hunt for Saddam. Iraqi Civil Defense started to go on raids and worked with our troops on the Iranian border. Civil Affairs teams opened schools, updated hospitals, and started immunization clinics. VIP visitors included Donald Rumsfeld, Bruce Willis, and Drew Carey. More dining facilities opened to provide hot meals for some Soldiers.

Families started to plan for the holidays. Chaplain Brewer initiated two operations in which families could participate. The first was Operation Pencil Box. Donations of school supplies were gathered to be sent to the Iraqi school children. The second was Operation Peace and Joy. Chaplain Brewer gave us a list of ideas and helped us to get packages sent over to Iraq.

The best news we received was the beginning of the Mid-Tour Leave program. While not all Soldiers would be allowed to participate in this program, there were many heart warming stories of Soldiers giving up spots so that some of their buddies could come home, family members who supported their Soldiers if they gave up their spots, and an outpouring of thanks from a grateful nation as Soldiers came home.

Reading these stories made me proud to be a part of this great country, part of the mighty 4th Infantry Division, and helped me face a holiday season without my Soldier.

3 September - Iraqi Policeman Wants Us...
I had a wonderful weekend. I got a phone call from my husband (401st MP CO, 720th MP BN), a letter, three postcards (one for each of my kids), an e-mail, and my husband's picture was in the newspaper for an article you had discussed in today's e-mail. My husband is a battalion commander's escort. He was very happy with the success of that raid and said they have had a lot of success with many of their missions.

He said he was speaking with a Colonel of the Iraqi Police and the man thanked them for being there. The majority of Iraqis do want us there and I couldn't be more proud of my husband. He says the Colonel 'promoted him' to a Major in the Iraqi Police Department. My husband got a kick out of that. God bless our troops and bring them home soon.

4 September - Tape Recordings
I have read about many families sending tape recorders to their Soldiers. I, too, did that but with a twist. I tape my son's favorite radio station here about once a month and send him the tape. He gets to keep up on the latest music and events in our area, but then he can tape a message for me and send it back. He says he even likes to listen to the commercials! Just trying to keep him in touch with the U.S. anyway I can.

5 September - On the Downhill Slide
I got a call from my fiancé last night. He's with HHC, 1-8 IN, 3BCT. He'd been on a mission the last few days that was supposed to be in the middle of four hundred or so supposed Fedayeen, but he said not much came of it. An interesting thing was that Dan Rather went with them on the mission, so he said to be watching for updates and news footage on that. He said it's still hot, but everyone at the TOC (Tactical Operations Center) is doing well. He said the homesickness is getting worse but I reminded him that this is his sixth month there, which means we're on the downhill slide. Looking at it that way cheered him up just a bit.

Kathy Sepanic - Wife of CPT Jason Sepanic - Echo Med 204th FSB

I have been a company-level FRG leader for the duration of the deployment. I was talking with some of the other spouses in the FRG recently and telling them how, in some respects, being the FRG leader has been easier with our Soldiers gone. Although we all are dealing with the stress of our spouses being gone, we have become much closer than we ever would have had the Soldiers been here. Just being with the other spouses is comforting to me because I know that their spouses are with my husband.

We do all sorts of things together. Of course we have our monthly meetings and any fundraisers that we do, but we also have had Sunday football gatherings (not a lot of football watching necessarily, but a good reason to get together), monthly adult dinners out (no children), and some activities for the kids (touring Pizza Hut, Easter Egg Hunt, making pillow cases for deployed parent, etc.) Besides scheduled FRG activities, there are a handful of us who call each other to get together on our own. I know this closeness would never have developed had our Soldiers been here. I feel so fortunate to have had the opportunity to know such wonderful friends.

5 September - Off With the Flak Jacket and Helmet

After quite a long time without hearing much from our son, we received an e-mail today. He is with C BTRY, 1-44 ADA and is still in Tikrit. He said thanks for sending him so many food packages but that we can scale back because they now have access to a dining hall. He still wants drink mix though. His birthday is coming up, and all he wants is a Drew Bledsoe jersey (Go Bills!).

We'd like to thank all the other families for sharing their good birthday ideas. They helped us to prepare. He will be going to Qatar next week for R&R so we are looking forward to a long phone call from him. He said it would be nice to go a few days without his helmet and flak jacket.

6 September - Support Each Other

I just wanted to let you know that I got to talk to my husband a couple of days ago (a SGT with B Co, 1-66 AR), for fifty minutes and four seconds. It was nice to hear his voice. He said they are getting plenty of food now, so stop sending Spam! I laughed at him, and told him there was some in the next box I was sending, and that he would have to just eat it! He laughed and said he would give it to some of the Iraqi kids.

After getting to talk to him for so long, I felt like a giant weight had been lifted off of my shoulders. I don't think the rest of the country realizes how hard things are on military families when Soldiers, Sailors, Marines, and the Air Force get deployed. But we're tough, as my husband has told me several times; this is our first big deployment since we've been together. As his CO says, 'Tough times never last, but tough people do.' For me, these longer phone calls are such a great morale booster. And they always seem to come at just the right moment.

I am going to end this on a sappy note to all of the spouses out there: keep holding onto hope; not everyone in the world could do our jobs. Who supports us and who doesn't is not important, because we all support each other!

9 September - Blessings

To the young mother whose husband serves with 46th Chemical Company in Ba'quabah: Your recent note praising the Red Cross certainly touched by heart. My son is with HHC, 3-67 AR also in Baqubah. We family members sacrifice so much of our lives in support of our Soldiers and we do so proudly. My prayers are with you and your family. May your baby receive God's blessings of perfect health and your husband arrive home safely to be with both of you. With love,
A Soldier's Mom

9 September - The Chosen Ones

Yesterday, September 8, I got a birthday card from my husband. He's part of the 1-10 CAV, 4ID. I'm going to be twenty-one on the tenth of this month. It broke my heart to realize he wouldn't be here for my birthday, our son's first birthday, or Thanksgiving, or Christmas. But that's what makes us, the families of Soldiers, who we are. We are strong and brave and are picked out by God to endure this kind of family sacrifice, so that others can have the same happiness. I love my freedom fighter, he means the world to me, and I miss him.

P.S. What are some of the other families doing to celebrate the holidays with their Soldiers? ...any ideas?

133

11 September - Bob Babcock

Every one of us reading this can tell you precisely what he or she was doing on September 11, 2001, a tragic day in world history that none of us will ever forget. Each of us, in our own way, should pause to remember those who lost their lives two years ago today. Never forget what was done to us, and know that we must remain resolute in our determination to win the War on Terror, of which our deployment to Iraq is the current key focus.

11 September - The American Way

I heard from my husband. He shared some of what life is like there for them. While they still have to be aware of the homemade bombs and occasional RPGs, the area that they patrol and work with is very much in order. The people are more than willing to, and I quote, 'drop information on a dime.' The children and adult males still run along side the vehicles and the troops as they move through, with shouts of, Hello Americans! Thank you Americans! Don't leave us Americans!'

My personal opinion on that is that 2-8 IN, C Company, is doing exactly what they've been trained to do and they are doing it in the compassionate American way. These people are being treated with respect and concern, and it's being reciprocated.

I am incredibly proud of my husband and his troops. He said that because of the relationship they have with these people, they were able to make a 'large haul' last week and that an Al Quaida member was snitched on immediately. It was a wonderful conversation. And I'm left feeling so much better about what is going on over there. I think I'm going to stop watching the news.

Wouldn't it be nice, if the media thought that good things were news too? My husband said that in his area, he would say that the support is no less than ninety-nine percent. There are only a smattering of Loyalists and Baath and Al Quaida support. He said that the other one percent supports the bad guys out of fear.

11 September - From a Soldier with the 21st Combat Support Hospital in Iraq:

The reason I write to you today, is to let you know that if the two Soldiers in the IED attack were from 3RD COSCOM, they are out of Germany, not Fort Hood. It is an easy slip, and I know you try to make sure that you get the information as accurate as possible, but I did not want families worrying about our Fort Hood families, when in fact it is our Germany families that we need to be praying for and worrying about with this particular situation.

We see the majority of the 4ID patients that are evacuated to the Level III hospitals in theater. There are four locations for these hospitals. Two of them are a part of the 21st CSH. One is in Balad, and the other hospital that we are operating is in Mosul, Iraq. It is very reassuring to read the responses from the family members in your last portion of the daily update. I know lots of Soldiers from 4ID who have access to your site and are reading your words everyday.

I know tomorrow will be a very emotional day for our nation, and for our Soldiers over here. There are numerous Patriot Day Ceremonies scheduled across Iraq. Please tell your readers that the US Soldiers will never forget or question why we are here and our remembrance of those we lost on 9/11 are three thousand more reasons why we freely chose to be here, representing our nation, in Iraq today. The time we are spending here is but a phase of our journey as Soldiers and it is a time that we will always remember in our lives.

11 September - He's in Michigan?

My son is with Charlie Company, 2-8 IN, 4ID out of Fort Hood, Texas. He was part of Operation Cliffhanger that took place on August 11. They were loaded in Blackhawks and dropped in the middle of a village of around forty houses. It took them about forty-five minutes to reach 'Objective Michigan' where they made their way to 'East Lansing'. At first I thought, why in the world did the Army send my son to East Lansing, Michigan and not let me know about it ahead of time. I was sure I could have gotten a police escort and could have been there within an hour. Then as he continued with the details of their effort, I figured out he was still in Iraq. I guess it was a hopeful mom wanting her son home. God Bless all of our Brave Soldiers!

11 September - School Kids Adopt Her

We received another e-mail from our daughter tonight (104 AVN, 4ID). She is doing okay. Said the mortars were still a regular thing. They had filled four-thousand sandbags and placed them around their tents the other day. She had received the latest package from us, and a letter and pictures from her boyfriend. She had also received a box of letters from 5th grade students who have adopted her. She has pictures of her family hanging on one side of her cot and drawings (sent by a 5th grader) of the Pledge of Allegiance and pictures from New York (taken by our other daughter this summer) hanging on the other side. She says she sees them every morning and remembers what she is over there fighting for. She says it is cooling down more and more, and now she has even had to put on her winter PTs to sleep in.

CPT Stacy Gerber - 212 FA BDE - Wife of MAJ Loyd Gerber, XO, 1-17 FA BN

During our last coffee, we all sat around and there were many complaints about what we were going through with our spouses not being around. I know the deployment is tough and I too, have missed my husband dearly. As the ladies were sharing their stories, I spoke up to say that I could not complain about my life with my husband gone. The replies were, "of course you can, we're going through the same thing, we understand," etc. I then said that I had nothing but good things to say because I've truly been blessed. My husband and I are active duty. We waited three long years to get pregnant; well, we finally did, two months before he left. I went to Korea on an exercise for seven weeks, late into my first trimester and had some moments of morning sickness, but all in all I had a wonderful pregnancy with no complications, only the threat of a ten-pound baby.

My husband's battalion commander saw an opportunity to send my husband home on R&R leave during the time our baby was due. Because the doctor was concerned with the size of our baby, she wanted to induce me at my fortieth week. Well, my husband arrived home in time to see me in my final week of pregnancy and to be in the room when our beautiful baby was born. She was eight-pounds, six-ounces. Of course, sending him back a week later broke my heart, but our baby got to bond with her daddy, and that meant more to me than anything.

I had childcare fall through at the last minute, so my retired dad moved out here to help me for a while. He not only helped me set up the nursery prior to the baby's arrival, he is currently her caregiver until he goes home when our Soldiers redeploy.

I am back at work and our baby and I have adjusted well.

I only suffered from some guilt because I felt as if I couldn't give my baby all she needs because I work, and I can't devote the time I used to give to my job because I have our little angel to care for.

Although my story may not be the norm, my husband and I have been married for six and a half years and we both have around fifteen years in the service and have never been deployed until he was deployed last spring. Of course, the first few months were rough, and I remember around the third, fourth, and fifth month, I would cry myself to sleep some nights because I missed him so much. After the baby was born and I said good-bye to him at the airport, I've had less emotional outbreaks. Our little girl helps keep me focused and positive.

We bought web cameras so we can visit once a week and he can see his daughter. I take digital photos of her, put them in folders on our computer each month and copy them to a disc to send to him so he can see his little girl grow. I shared my feelings with some close friends and other wives within our battalion; I found that they, too, shared the same feelings, and I think we all helped each other get through. I stay as active as I can in the FRG; it really does help!

12 September - We Stood at Attention
A Soldier in Alpha Co, 2-4 AVN, 4ID, e-mailed his wife:

Something neat happened today at dinner. The news was on the TV, and they were showing a memorial ceremony at Arlington National Cemetery. As a part of the ceremony, the national anthem started playing. Everyone stopped what they were doing, and stood at attention. It was really moving. Deep down, regardless of all the other stuff that breaks us down each day, we all still understand what it's all about.

12 September - A Great Box From Iraq

I was so surprised today. I received a box from my son, 1-12 IN, 4ID. He was able to mail something home for the first time while he was on a twenty-four hour R&R. The box contained four cameras and a gift for mom. I was so excited I took those poor battered cameras he had been hauling around for months to the local drug store that had a one-hour photo service. The clerk looked at them and said, "My goodness, they have really been through something!"

I said, "If you only knew." One was even broken, so she carefully took it apart and revealed its contents. I was so amazed to see how the people live there, the children were running alongside of the tanks, lugging a box, and holding Pepsies out to our military guys. Some of the pictures were of the pipeline fire. It was hard for us to understand a fire burning under ground.

Their cots were on the roof for cooler sleeping: no tents or frills. But I will tell you the one thing I did see over and over was a sense of pride on the faces of these fine young men. Their smiles radiated, "Yes, I am here, I am proud to fight for America's freedom, and for the world's peace."

What a wonderful box my children and I received today. I was beginning the day telling them about the reason we must never forget September 11, 2001. Thank you for keeping us all connected during this time.

16 September - Sou-eee!

Our son (E TRP, 1-10 CAV) called yesterday to talk about the good news! Silly me: I thought he was calling with good news about when he was coming home or something related to Iraq, when actually he was calling to say how good it was to hear that Arkansas had beaten Texas on Saturday! Our family is crazy about the Razorbacks, and we are always happy to hear when they beat Texas. We have taped the game for him, and he is anxious for us to send it. His brother (101 ABN in Mosul) sent an e-mail Saturday night and he had actually been fortunate enough to see the game on AFN. They both sounded 'high,' which is just great. It is so good to hear them happy. We need more "ups!"

Valerie Pugh - Written by her son, PVT Armando Rodriguez - Co A 1-67 AR

Written in the early morning hours of September 15, 2001

Protect Over Me
Well, Lord, what can I say?
It's happened once again.
In our wonderful country
Someone has committed sin.
We started the day as usual,
Not knowing what was to come.
We had no idea we'd lose so many,

Or where it would come from.
Most started out living their life
Just like a normal day.
They had no idea a beautiful day
Could end in such a way.
As for me, I'm sitting here
With this uniform on,
My hands silently folded together
Praying to You and Your Son.
I do not know what's going to happen
Or what we are going to do.
I hear them talking about war
And I know it must be true.
Many people have been put in
Situations just like this.
Unfortunately a lot of them are gone
And them we will continually miss.
They fought and died willingly for our country
So that I may have the right
To sit here at this desk on duty
And this poem I can continue to write.
So Lord I pray and ask You
With all of my heart—protect over me.
For I know that it's only a matter of time
Before the battlefield I will see.

17 September - A New Appreciation

I am the mother-in-law of a Soldier who is with HHC, 1-8 IN, 3BCT, 4ID out of Fort Carson. Your updates have given me insight into the life led by our Soldiers, and especially this incredible young man who is married to my beloved daughter. I am new to military family life, and I am amazed at the sacrifices made by our Soldiers and by their loved ones. I am both proud and fearful, and I have a whole new appreciation for our military. I have never relied on prayer like I do now. May God bless our Soldiers and all who support them.

18 September - From a Sergeant's/Soldier's Mom

My son who is with A Company, 1-67 AR, was scheduled to fly back to the States (to Ft. Hood, TX) September 11, completing his enlistment December 2003, which had originally been August 2003. Instead I received a phone call at work from him on September 10. He wanted to let me know that he had extended his tour of duty. He will not come home until the rest of the 4th Infantry does in April 2004.

At first I yelled, "no," and then asked if he was pulling my leg then I realized that he is staying in Iraq. He explained, "It would have eaten me alive if I left my guys!"

He told me he feels like he is leaving his family behind to be with his Army family to complete their mission. I told him we will always be here waiting for him, and I told him I wanted him home for my selfish reasons, but I understood that he has a path to follow. I have a true hero in my life, my son. My chest burst with pride, I shed a tear of joy. I love and respect the man he has become. Continuing to pray for all of our American heroes.

19 September - Shame on Them

I just wanted to mention that I think it is so sad that the stories such as 'Grand Opening of School in Al Asriya' don't make the nightly news. These types of stories not only serve to boost support for this war, but also morale for our troops. Shame on them! Makes you wonder what else we are missing.

19 September - Dinner, The Iraqi Way

My son called at 4:00 a.m. on September 4, with an interesting story. He is a 2LT with the 3rd Brigade, 1-44 ADA, Charlie Battery. He was in great spirits and told about the area in which he is stationed, an air base south of Mosul. He and his platoon have been protecting the families in this area from what he terms 'the bad guys' and doing things to help the farmers in the area.

One day they helped pull a pipe from the ground, which had been mistaken for a military target. One of his crewmembers gave 'blackened' cigars to the Iraqi patriarch of the group. He was so excited that he dragged the guys back to his house for dinner! They weren't allowed inside, as the women were there. They sat in front of the house and drank tea (chai). My son said he never dreamed there would be anything in Iraq worth drinking, but they have the best tea in the world! The youngest son brought out goat's milk, but the guys stuck with water!

Everything is very communal; everyone drinks from the

same cup. Then the boy brought out rice with unleavened bread and okra. That was eaten with the hands. The Iraqi people don't use utensils and don't spill a thing! The family laughed at my son and his driver and gunner for making such a mess! He said that the army gave them a list of Arab terms that he has found nearly useless during his stay. He tried out some of the phrases with the patriarch, and the guy understood very few of them! He said all communication was through gestures and facial expressions. They must have communicated well, though!

22 September - Just Doing My Job

I received four letters on Thursday, three on Friday, and a call at 12:09 Saturday morning, from my husband, A Company, 1-22 IN. I wanted to share a little of one of his letters with you. Just so you know, at my father's place of business they have a sign up, a flag and a yellow ribbon. I told my hubby about it, and this is what he said, "tell your dad that they don't need to have stuff up on a wall for me. I am only doing my job and helping out a group of people that need a lot of help. I am not a hero or someone special. I am only a man who chose to do a job and now only have to pay for it by missing his loved ones."

When he called on Saturday it had been twelve days since I had heard from him; he sounds homesick and is missing everyone.

23 September - Mid Tour Leave Approved - Letter From MG Odierno:

Families and Soldiers of Task Force Ironhorse,

We have an opportunity for many Task Force Ironhorse Soldiers to spend some time with their families in the middle of our deployment. The Secretary of Defense has approved a CENTCOM program that will allow Soldiers serving a 365-day tour of duty to take two weeks of mid-tour leave. Soldiers are eligible to take leave between their fourth and tenth month of deployment. This is an expensive, complex undertaking by the Department of Defense; our leadership is making this investment in the morale of troops and families to lessen the hardship endured by families every day we are deployed. We will begin sending Soldiers on leave immediately and will continue the program through January; we will prepare units for redeployment in February.

We are in battle daily throughout Iraq; ongoing missions and the program's enormous logistical requirements mean that we must limit the number of Soldiers away from their units. Therefore, not all Soldiers will be able to take leave prior to redeployment. Commanders will prioritize participation based primarily on the length of Soldiers' deployment; those that left home first will be the first to go on leave.

The mid-tour program is designed to be executed over a seven-month period. Since we are nearing the seventh month of deployment, we have only a four-month window to get as many Soldiers home as possible. Approximately 21,000 of the 27,000 Soldiers assigned to Task Force Ironhorse are with us for the full one-year tour and are eligible to take leave.

Despite only having four months to work with, we estimate that 60% of all Soldiers who deployed in April or before will be able to take advantage of this program.

Commanders must balance the mission with Soldiers' welfare, and will select participants fairly and equitably taking into consideration all mission and personal factors.

All flights from theater will be routed through Frankfurt, Germany, for Europe-based Soldiers, and will terminate in Baltimore-Washington International airport (BWI).

Soldiers will pay for round trip transportation from BWI to their leave location. Soldiers will purchase their tickets prior to departure from Kuwait to provide as much notice as possible to families preparing for the arrival.

This is a tremendous opportunity for our Soldiers. It is unfortunate that not everyone will be able to participate, but I am confident that leaders will take care of their Soldiers and manage the program fairly. I have tremendous faith in the Soldiers and families of Task Force Ironhorse, and I trust this program will run as smoothly as possible. Like all other missions, our Soldiers will complete this one in exceptional fashion.

Steadfast and Loyal.
Raymond T. Odierno
MG, Commanding

23 September - A Letter to the FRGs from 4ID Commanding General

Dear Friends and Family of Task Force IRONHORSE Soldiers,

Your loved ones here in Task Force IRONHORSE continue to serve their country and fellow Soldiers in an exceptional manner. I want to express the tremendous pride I feel in the sacrifices they make each day to help the Iraqi people. I know that you are extremely proud of them too.

Task Force IRONHORSE Soldiers are contributing to the security, reconstruction and democratization of Iraq across a multitude of critical areas that impact the daily lives of Iraqis. We are establishing representative governments, renovating hospitals and clinics, repairing the critical infrastructure of power, water and sewerage and opening banks to energize the business community to generate jobs. Hardly any aspect of Iraqi life is not being improved in some manner by the efforts of Task Force IRONHORSE Soldiers.

One of our top priorities is the rehabilitation of the Iraq Public Education system. Under Saddam Hussein, Iraqi schools suffered severe neglect and stagnation. All of the schools require some level of repair and renovation, and many lack desks, chalkboards and school supplies for effective teaching. In order to address these needs, TF IRONHORSE has initiated renovations on over one hundred eighty schools within our area. We are also purchasing over $250,000 worth of chalkboards and desks for distribution to local schools.

As part of this effort, we will conduct a Division operation in late September called "Operation Pencil Box". Task Force IRONHORSE subordinate Battalions will 'adopt' local schools to assist them in preparing for the new school year. Task Force IRONHORSE Soldiers will work alongside the parents and teachers of these schools to remove debris, install furnishings and make minor repairs. These 'adopted' relationships will continue into the upcoming school year with frequent delivery of supplies.

The Fort Hood Family Resource Group is currently holding a school supplies drive to receive donated supplies and forward them to Task Force IRONHORSE for distribution to our adopted schools. For those family and friends who are interested, we welcome your participation in this program. Feel free to share this letter with those who may be interested in contributing and ask them to forward any donated supplies to the following address:

Operation Pencil Box
C/O HHC DISCOM
Ft. Hood, TX 76543

Steadfast and Loyal,
Raymond T. Odierno,
MG, Commanding

24 September - Always Our Babies

I received word from my son, B CO, 299 EN, early this morning that he would be home on his mid-tour leave sometime between 25th and 27th. I am ecstatic. I must go to the grocery store immediately and stock up on his favorite foods.

I am so happy that he gets to come home and meet his son who was born June 29th, but I also know the good-bye this time will be even harder. I will do a lot of praying between now and then and try not to become a blubbering idiot. They never stop being our babies. So, for now my cup runneth over. Pray our Soldiers' sight is acute, their aim is true and that as many come home as can be spared.

25 September - Thank You!

I hope you can find room for this thank you note in your newsletter. I bet he (General Odierno) doesn't get many thanks, and gets an earful of complaints. I know this probably isn't 'proper etiquette,' but the leadership needs to know how much this is doing for the morale of family members everywhere:

Dear General Odierno and the senior staff of the 4ID,

Thank you! Thank you for temporarily giving us back our husbands, sons, wives and daughters. Thank you for giving us a dose of normalcy, even if only for fourteen days. Thank you for giving us unlimited access to our best friends. Thank you for reiterating the concept that the army takes care of its own. Thank you for putting a smile on my face today. Thank you for showing the nay-sayers that the top leadership in today's army not only listens to the concerns of Soldier's families, but does something to address those concerns. Thank you for showing Soldiers all over Iraq that you appreciate the sacrifices they are making. Thank you for acknowledging the hardships endured by military families, and giving us something to make the stress and challenges a little more bearable. I thank you for the priceless gift of fourteen unexpected days with my husband.

26 September - More Praise

From a reader, to the authorities who approved mid-tour leave:

I'm sure that you have received thousands of e-mails from people asking tons of questions about mid-tour leave and complaining and hopefully praising. I would like to add to the praise. I think it's the most wonderful idea for morale that I have heard. My Soldier will not be eligible for mid-tour leave, but seeing what the Army is doing for the Soldiers and families has heightened morale phenomenally. I want to send my thanks on behalf of my Soldier and our families for instituting this system.

27 September - He's Part of the Family

I just wanted let everyone know how thankful I am for the great doctors I work for. They have been so supportive since my brother with 3-29 FA was deployed back in April. Yesterday, we bought about $200.00 worth of candy, Halloween gag gifts, and Trick or Treat bags to make about one-hundred fifty trick or treat goody bags for the guys in my brother's group and for the adopted Soldier that my office got. We worked all day putting them together so we can get them mailed out by next week. Our adopted Soldier is with 2nd BCT RECON. He has called us about five times over the last two months and has become part of our family.

29 September - Rock-A-Bye My Baby

Our son who is with B Company, 3-66 AR is home on leave now. He arrived Saturday the 27. He and his wife had a baby girl on September 15. My daughter-in-law said that she heard our son rocking and singing lullabies to his baby girl this morning. We will enjoy each day we have with him; it's a beautiful gift.

Nikki Theriot - Wife of SSG Steven Theriot - HHB DIVARTY

We have been in the army for fourteen years. Steve used to be a fuel handler, but about three years ago, he became a Career Counselor. He loves being in the Army and helping other Soldiers to accomplish their goals in their careers. Steven and I were high school sweethearts. He was seventeen and I was fifteen.

Shortly after we became engaged, we got pregnant, so our parents encouraged us to get married. Most of the people in our families said we would not last past a year. He joined the army two months after we got married. Here we are; we made it to fourteen years on the 12th of August, and we are still happy with each other. I feel blessed to have such a wonderful man in my life. I quite often feel like I don't deserve such a good one. We now have our thirteen-year-old son Nicholas Steven, our eleven-year-old son Blake Alexander, and finally our nine-year-old daughter Victoria Elizabeth.

Our children are happy, healthy, well mannered, beautiful, super intelligent, and proud of the sacrifices their father has made so they may have a wonderful and better future than our parents provided for us. I personally, am the happiest I have ever been. We have had some hard times in our marriage, but it was all worth it to have experienced all of it with my best friend, my husband Steve. I knew being an army wife wasn't going to be easy, but I really had no idea how hard it would truly be when it came down to seeing my husband deploy; either pregnant or with little ones that needed their father.

My husband has been to Korea twice, NTC at least eight times, PLDC, BNOC, Desert Storm, Career Counselor school, a few more places somewhere in between, and now Operation Iraqi Freedom for the last six months. We have been separated quite a bit in fourteen-years of marriage. His family says they could never be so strong. I tell them that they would if they loved their spouse. They ask me how I do it with the kids and all the things that come up in life without my husband here to share the responsibilities. I tell them I try not to think about it that way. The way I see it, he does his job and I'm doing mine as his life partner and the mother of his children. There is no other way for me to think about it. To me there are no options because I can't help but love a man that could raise his hand and promise to die for the people and reputation of this country. He believes that this is what God put him here to do—to serve others.

Me being his wife, I can't help but love and serve him through thick and thin. I look up to him because I believe he is wonderful. He is a man of God, a good husband, a wonderful father and an awesome Soldier. We miss him terribly, but we know God is protecting him so he can come back home to us. When I am having a difficult time with things I says these three little sayings to myself: "God won't give me anything that I can't handle." "That which doesn't kill us will make us stronger" And the serenity prayer: "God, grant me the serenity to accept the things I cannot change, the courage to change what I can, and the wisdom to know the difference." Then I take three deep breaths, one for my children, one for me and one for Steve. I know I can overcome.

29 September - Lot's of Kids
The 'tears on my pillow' comment started my drive for pillows for B BTRY, 6-27 FA, in Balad. The hospital that I work at has agreed to let me hold the drive there. If we exceed the number of pillows needed for my son's unit, we will start collecting for another unit that is represented by members of our small community. In just a couple of days, we have received twenty-five pillows! We will be collecting pillowcases and washing them so they smell great of Downy. I'll keep you posted on how we do.

I threatened to send my son a body pillow and a pillowcase with my picture on it, but he said he would rather have one with his girlfriend on it! I don't understand why!

Anyway, it was great to hear his sense of humor and the laughter in his voice. He also said that with six more months to go, I had better send new socks and underwear! He also gave me the names of a couple of Soldiers that have not received much since they got there; he's been sharing his stuff. He warned me that I now have two more adopted sons. So off to Wal-Mart I go to get stuff for all of them. ....always wanted more kids! If anyone is feeling down, just start a drive of some sort for the troops and your energy level goes really upbeat. Just got to figure out how to get it all shipped/ ...might have to have another fundraiser!

30 September - Soldier Says it All
My husband, 1-66 AR, called at about 2:30 this morning. We did a three-way call with his parents; a close family member passed away over the weekend. It was a short call and a sad one, but he said that although things, according to the news, were getting more

heated in some areas, where he is it has actually calmed down some the last week or so. He said he'd seen a news report with people blasting the President and the continued presence of the US over there and I thought it would be nice to pass that on:

"Those people have no clue! After spending a rotation in Kuwait three years ago and a rotation in Kosovo last year, I know that those people had mansions compared to what most of these Iraqis are in! If they could just see what it was like before we got here and how much it has improved since then! They need to walk a mile in these Army boots before they even think of opening their mouths." And... I think that about says it all!

Heidi Hennigan - Wife of SPC Ryan Hennigan - HHB 1-44 ADA

Many people say that they cannot comprehend what it is like to be a military wife. What it could be like to have your loved one so far away and not know when or if you are going to hear from them again. But I can truly say that I am proud to be a military wife. One of my husband's dreams was to serve his country and he is accomplishing that. People ask, "Aren't you scared and worried?" I say, "Yes... but it is in God's hands now and I trust him to do the best for our family." And if something were to happen to him, I have this feeling that I would know already, and I do not have that feeling. He is going to come home. Stay positive about life, it makes the days go by so much faster.

Task Force Ironhorse - September 2003 Casualties

SGT Anthony O. Thompson, 26, of Orangeburg, South Carolina, **SPC Richard S. Arriaga**, 20, of Ganado, Texas, and **SPC James C. Wright**, 27, of Morgan, Texas were killed in an ambush by small arms fire and rocket propelled grenades, on September 18 in Tikrit, Iraq. The three Soldiers were assigned to Headquarters and Headquarters Battery, 4th Battalion, 42nd Field Artillery Regiment, Fort Hood, Texas.

CPT Brian R. Faunce, 28, of Philadelphia, Pennsylvania, died on September 18 in Al Asad, Iraq. Cpt Faunce was moving in a Bradley fighting vehicle when his vehicle crossed under some low laying power lines. The Soldier reached up and grabbed the lines and was fatally injured. He was assigned to Headquarters and Headquarters Company, 3rd Brigade Combat Team, Fort Carson, Colorado.

CPT Robert L. Lucero, 34, of Casper, Wyoming, was killed on September 25, 2003, in Tikrit, Iraq. Captain Lucero died and another Soldier was injured when they were struck by an improvised explosive device. Captain Lucero was assigned to the 4th Infantry Division Rear Area Operation Center, U.S. Army National Guard from Casper, Wyoming.

SPC Kyle G. Thomas, 23, of Topeka, Kansas, was killed on September 25, 2003, in Tikrit, Iraq. Specialist Thomas was on patrol when an improvised explosive device exploded. He died of injuries sustained in the explosion. Specialist Thomas was assigned to 2nd Battalion, 503rd Infantry Regiment, 173rd Airborne Brigade, based in Fort Ederle, Italy.

SSG Steven Theriot, Nikki Theriot and Children

SPC Armando Rodriquez, Son of Valerie Pugh

SEVEN

October - 2003
Halfway Home

182 days and a wake-up until April 1, 2004...

*O*ur Soldiers' living conditions were about as varied as they could be. From living in their fighting vehicles to a palace compound in Tikrit, the Task Force carried on with the mission given to them. We looked up the towns of Bayji, Baqubah, and Tikrit on maps. An Iraqi Battalion graduated from a nine week Basic Course.

Those of us back home continued to plan, purchase, and mail holiday supplies to our Soldiers. The deadline to send holiday items was announced, so we got busy. Donald Rumsfeld wrote an open letter setting the record straight on what our Soldiers were accomplishing, while the media generally focused on explosions and death. We heard stories from families who were able to participate in the Mid-Tour leave program. We were at the halfway mark, and those of us at home had gotten into our 'battle rhythm'.

1 October - Help Iraq to Help Itself
By Donald H. Rumsfeld
If you are like most Americans, the news you see on television and read in the press from Iraq seems grim—stories of firefights, car bombs, battles with terrorists. It is true that Coalition troops are serving in difficult and dangerous circumstances. But what is also true, and seems to be much less often reported, is that the Coalition has, in less than five months, racked up a series of achievements in both security and civil reconstruction that may be without precedent.

I recently visited our forces in Tikrit, Mosul, Baghdad and Babylon. Their spirits are good, because they know their mission is important and they know they are making progress. Many recently got access to satellite television from the U.S., and their first glimpse of the news coverage back home. Some expressed amazement at how few of their accomplishments are reflected in the news on Iraq. As one Soldier we met in Baghdad put it, "We rebuild a lot of bridges and it's not news, but one bridge gets blown up, and it's a front-page story." Their successes deserve to be told. Consider just a few of their accomplishments:

—Today, in Iraq, virtually all major hospitals and universities have been reopened, and hundreds of secondary schools, until a few months ago used as weapon's caches, have been rebuilt and were ready for the start of the fall semester.

—Fifty-six thousand Iraqis have been armed and trained in just a few months, and are contributing to the security and defense of their country. Today, a new Iraqi Army is being trained and more than forty-thousand Iraqi police are conducting joint patrols with Coalition forces. By contrast, it took fourteen-months to establish a police force in postwar Germany, and ten years to begin training a new German Army.

—As security improves, so does commerce: five thousand small businesses have opened since liberation on May 1. An independent Iraqi Central Bank was established and a new currency announced in just two months—accomplishments that took three years in postwar Germany.

—The Iraqi Governing Council has been formed and has appointed a cabinet of ministers—something that took fourteen months in Germany—In major cities and most towns and villages, municipal councils have been formed and are making decisions about local matters—something that took eight months in Germany.

—The Coalition has completed six-thousand civil affairs projects with many more under way.

All this, and more, has taken place in less than five months. The speed and breadth of what Ambassador Paul Bremer (and his predecessor Gen. Jay Garner), Gen. John Abizaid and Gen. Rick Sanchez, and the Coalition team, both military and civilian, have accomplished is more than impressive—It may be without historical parallel. Yet much of the world does not know about this progress, because the focus remains on the security situation, which is difficult, but improving. Baath remnants and foreign terrorists are opposing the Coalition, to be sure. But the Coalition is dealing with them.

This does not mean dangers don't exist. The road ahead will not be smooth. There will be setbacks. Regime loyalists and foreign terrorists are working against the Coalition. Increasingly they do so by targeting Coalition successes. Yet the Iraqi people are providing intelligence for our forces every day. Division commanders consistently report an increase in the number of Iraqis coming forward with actionable intelligence. With Iraqi help, the Coalition has now captured or killed forty-three of Iraq's fifty-five most wanted, as well as thousands of other Baath loyalists and terrorists, and seized large caches of weapons. As Iraqis see Coalition forces act, their confidence grows, and they are providing more information.

In Baghdad, a reporter asked why we don't just 'flood the zone'—double or treble the number of American troops in the country? We could do that, but it would be a mistake.

First, as Generals Abizaid and Sanchez have stated, they do not believe they need more American troops. If they did, they would ask, and they would get them. The division commanders in Iraq have said that, far from needing more forces, additional troops could complicate their mission because it would require more force protection, more combat support, and create pressure to adopt a defensive posture (guarding buildings, power lines, etc.), when their intention is to remain on the offense against the terrorists and Baath party remnants.

That is why, at the end of May, Gen. Jim Mattis, the Marine division commander in the south central area, decided to send home 15,000 of his 23,000 troops. As he recently explained: "If at any point I had needed more troops, I could have asked for them. But I have not needed them. The enemy over there, once we get the intelligence on them, [is] remarkably easy to destroy. My way of thinking: If we needed more people on our side, enlist more Iraqis."

That is precisely what Coalition forces are doing—training tens of thousands of Iraqis to serve as police, border guards, a new facilities protection service, a new Iraqi National Army, and an Iraqi Civil Defense Corps. Iraqis are eager to participate in their own security. The commanders in Iraq report that they are exceeding recruitment goals for these forces. The Coalition is not in Iraq to stay. Our goal is to help Iraqis so they can take responsibility for the governance and security of their country, and foreign forces can leave. That is why the president has asked for $20 billion to help the Iraqis get on a path to self-government and self-reliance. He's requested $15 billion to speed repairs to Iraq's dilapidated infrastructure so Iraq can begin generating income through oil production and foreign investments. And he's requested another $5 billion to help the Iraqis assume the responsibility for the security of their own country.

The goal is not for the U.S. to rebuild Iraq. Rather, it is to help the Iraqis get on a path where they can pay to rebuild their own country. The money the president is requesting is a critical element in the Coalition's exit strategy. Because the sooner we help Iraqis to defend their own people, the faster Coalition forces can leave, and they can get about the task of fashioning truly Iraqi solutions to their future.

In Baghdad, I met with members of the Governing Council. One message came through loud and clear: They are grateful for what Coalition forces are doing for their country, but they do not want more American troops. They want to take on more responsibility for security and governance of the country. The goal is to help them do so.

Those advocating sending more Americans forces, against the expressed wishes of both our military commanders and Iraq's interim leaders, need to consider whether doing so would truly advance our objective of transferring governing responsibility to the Iraqi people.

Iraqis will have to overcome the physical and psychological effects of living three decades under a Stalinist system. But the ingredients for success are there. Iraq has oil, water and vast wheat and barley fields. It has biblical sites, and great potential for tourism. It has an educated, intelligent and industrious population. We should resist the urge to do for the Iraqis what would be better done by the Iraqis. We can help, but only if we balance the size of our presence to meet the military challenge, while putting increasing responsibility in Iraqi hands.

2 October - Love Conquers All

Had to share my joy! My Soldier asked me to marry him Monday! I am having fun now trying to plan a wedding around a 'tentative date!' He is a lucky man: Since I am an Army Brat, I have the patience for this! Besides I feel like the happiest girl on the planet.

Life is ironic: We had our first blind date set up by my best friend whose hubby works with him. But, our first date started about fifteen minutes before he got his deployment orders. After time spent together, we decided that the bond we felt was worth pursuing and that this deployment would not break what we shared. It is quite the contrary. I feel as though I have known him forever. I know that in a way, for us, this deployment has helped two people find what true love really is. Doesn't God work in mysterious ways? Like I said earlier, I just wanted to share my joy!

3 October - Good Advice

I heard from my husband yesterday; he's part of 1-10 CAV, 4ID. He sounded good but tired. I miss him, and I can't believe it's already halfway over. And to the woman who got proposed to, congratulations. I myself am an army brat of a retired Airborne Ranger father so you can imagine how used to this separation I am. I hope you and your soon-to-be hubby are always filled with love and happiness as we should all be with our loved ones over there. Congratulations.

And for all the wives and girlfriends and soon to be wives, if you don't already know, go to www.cinchouse.com, they have wonderful stuff to get you through the military life as a spouse. I highly recommend the book, *Married in the Military*. It tells you everything you need to know and more.

5 October - Hi Honey!

I was able to IM (Instant Message) my husband, HHC, 3-67 AR yesterday morning. We had a web cam up and running, and he was able to see our baby girl for the first time since he left in April. She was eight days old when he was deployed. I've sent lots of pictures, but he actually got to see her. Happy Birthday goes out to him tomorrow! He was very excited and thought that was a wonderful birthday present. Mid-tour leave is probably not in the picture for us, but I'm happy for the rest of you!

6 October - They Did Not Die in Vain

My son called this morning. He is with the 4ID band. He sounded good and stated he just got back from a ceremony for the new Iraq Soldiers and told how they wanted to take pictures with our band guys. He sounded so excited that the Iraqis really were happy they were there. He even said he joked around with some.

"Mom, for the most part, these people want us here, and I only hope we finish the job here that we started, so that those who have lost their lives for Iraq, ours and the Iraqis, will not have been in vain. I am proud to be an American doing what we are doing here. Let people know, Mom, that there is more good than bad going on here."

I worry for my son and all our troops daily, but when I hear my son talk like he does, it makes me feel so proud of them all. I only wish as a nation we all could unite more. We must continue to lift up our troops' morale and let them know we in the States have not nor will we forget what they are doing and why. God Bless them all.

6 October - Coming Home on Wednesday!

My husband, HHC 2-8 IN, called me Friday morning with good news. For the first time since he left Ft. Hood, he saw clouds! He also told me that his mid tour leave had been approved! He will be flying into BWI sometime this upcoming weekend. He leaves the unit Wednesday! I could hardly believe it. I am very excited and so is he. I am flying to meet him. Due to another deployment before leaving for Iraq, my husband and I have only lived together six weeks in the past year. I will cherish these fifteen days. Thanks CENTCOM and DOD for approving this program!

6 October - Tough as Steel

From one of our family members:

I want to personally express my extreme respect and admiration to many of the families that contribute to your e-mail. To the countless mothers who have endured pregnancies and deliveries without their husbands, you are tough as steel. You are the women that hold our country together. Our men and Soldiers protect our way of life and our country with their strong women.

To mothers, fathers, sisters, brothers who do all they can for their loved one and for others: Like the lady who wrote in that her son so unselfishly offered his place on the list so a married man could see his wife and child. I am incredibly proud of these exemplary Americans. As long as we have people like this in our country, we will always prevail. It helps to strengthen my spirits and puts hope in my heart for another day. God bless you all, and may every American Soldier make it safely home! God bless America!

7 October - Support Them Always

My son now has e-mail, and we e-mail each other on a regular basis. He said on his birthday he was able to get a good bath and some sleep. My son said he can't wait to get home and get a good home cooked meal and sleep for a week. He is also excited about the birth of his son, Kris, who is to be born this month. We are a little sorry he will not be here for the birth.

He said the guys are hanging in there but can't wait to get home to their families. I want to say to every family out there I send my love and prayers for our children and all the men and women out there fighting for our freedom. Remember, when they return home, don't stop supporting them, and continue to support them throughout their military life. Our men and women have put their lives on the line for us.

7 October - It's a Soldier Thing

We heard from our son, B Company, 299 EN, out of Fort Hood. He was preparing to leave for four days to Qatar for some R&R. He said he is looking forward to wearing some civilian clothes for a couple of days. Needless to say his spirits are very good. He might get home for mid-tour in December. At this point, we are all hoping his grandfather's remaining vision will last at least until then.

My dad, a retired Sergeant Major, 82nd Airborne Ranger, is all but blind, yet so proud of this kid. I really hope he has the chance to 'see' him just once more before he loses all of his vision. I guess it is a Soldier thing. I am so proud that he lived to 'pass the torch of freedom' to another generation.

Our other son, also in Iraq, is attached to the 1st Infantry Division. We have no idea where he is, right now. We believe that we will find out when the mail catches up, and until then... no news is good news.

8 October - Told Her What it's Like

My husband is with B Troop, 1-10 CAV. I have had the chance to see a couple of the guys that have come back for ETS, (Enlisted Time Served) PCS, (Permanent Change of Station) and one for R&R. I just want to say thank you to them because they have shed a little light as to what is going on with our husbands, and what they are doing. I know that they can't tell us everything they are doing, but they have let me know that they are all doing good. They have told me stories to make me laugh, and some that scare the hell out of me, but all in all the stories have been good. Seeing them and talking to them has helped me prepare for when my husband comes home. That way maybe I won't expect too much from him.

9 October - Ramen, Ramen... Sure Taste Great

We got a phone call from my son who is with the 1-12 IN, Fort Carson, Colorado. His little nine-year-old 'sissy' answered when he called at 3:30 this afternoon, our time. He was so shocked to hear her innocent voice. He said when I got to the phone, "that is what it is all about, Mom, the innocent ones." He can make my chest puff up with pride and my heart melt without even trying.

He said it is much cooler and sometimes even cold at night. He loves to sleep in the cold, so he is sleeping well, that is, when he gets to sleep. They are getting one hot meal a day. He loves his little hot pot to heat ramen noodles and other things his grandmother and I are sending them to eat. He asked for some magazines for someone who does not get mail, so 'army mom' to the rescue. It is so wonderful to see how much they all care for one another. Bless them all.

9 October - What's For Dinner?

Here are some suggestions based on the feedback that I received from my son, 1-44 ADA: Campbell's chunky soups, fruit cups & applesauce, instant mashed potatoes, cereal with Parmalat milk, Pepperidge Farm cinnamon swirl bread, flour tortillas (he makes tuna, turkey and chicken wraps with them), and Bisquick shake and pour pancake mix. Surprisingly enough, the tortillas and bread were not only still edible by the time they got to him, but they were also a tremendous hit.

I just sent him some biscuits that I purchased from Wal-Mart and country style gravy in a can. We'll see how that goes over. I sent my son a camp stove, hot plate, and now a griddle is in the mail. He really likes going to his buddies' room and cooking up pancakes for all of them.

9 October - Little Miracle
From proud grandparents:
I thought I would share some good news with everybody. My son's son was born tonight at 9:16, weighing in at nine pounds sixteen ounces, and his name is Kristopher Seth.

10 October - Understatement
We received an eleven-page letter from our son, A Company, 1-67 AR. The letter was so wonderful. His letter consisted of two days in the life of our Soldier. He went into detail on raids and how his unit was involved in a firefight (I can't believe I'm writing that in association with my son!), and what they do in their down time. And what we never hear from the media—all the good our Soldiers do helping the children and the surrounding community.

His work consists of helping to rebuilding a school, cleaning a field for kids to play on or just being there to prevent fighting. It was so amazing; I made copies and sent it to family, his friends, and shared it with co-workers.

He is doing well, is happy, healthy, and waiting for the next care package. Proud is an understated word for how I feel about my son and his guys. I pray for their safety. May God continue to bless them all.

10 October - An Old Army Wife and Mother
Dear Proud Grandparents, I am so happy for you and and your new grandson, Kristopher Seth. It made me cry. We army wives have children, and sometimes they don't know their father for a long time because of situations like Iraq. I had my children during Viet Nam, and now my son is in Iraq.

When he was born, I cried because I thought I didn't want him ever to be in the military, and see where he is now. Those were my thoughts then, but now I am very proud of him. I am still terrified and worry about him, but I just pray to God that he and all our Soldiers be kept safe so they will be able to come home and hug their children and wives.

10 October - Just Walked In...

Today, I got the surprise of my life: My Soldier with B Co, 299th EN BN walked in for his mid-tour leave. He always has loved to surprise me, and I sure can't chastise him this time! He looks wonderful, although he has lost some weight. He is very confident and self-assured and unfaltering in his support for his mission. He is particularly glad to be home for the big game this week—that would be Texas vs. OU.

God bless our troops, and I pray that each one of you gets to hug your Soldier really soon.

11 October - Talking to Superheroes

I spoke with my brother this afternoon. It was a wonderful surprise when my cell phone rang. He is with Task Force Ironhorse, 4ID. He sounded great. We both talked so fast we could hardly hear each other's answers. He said they're working hard and getting a lot done. No specifics of course. He let me know the guys want a Polaroid camera to send photos home. I told him I was on it!

The coolest thing was that he talked about fifteen minutes and had to get ready to roll out to a long mission. He had to get his gear on and he had five minutes left on the phone card. He handed the phone off to his Soldiers, and I was able to talk to about four of the guys from his platoon. It was so neat to talk to his gunner and his driver. I was even able to speak with his captain. Today I was able to talk to some real life superheroes!! More than I bargained for!!

14 October - Because I'm Your Mother...

Our son, B Company, 1-22 IN, who has been deployed since the first of February, recently called home every day during a two week stay in Tikrit. Until now, communication has been 'hit or miss.' He sounded tired but terrific: loves his job, is proud of his unit, and loves being a Soldier.

He told us that he misses us like he's never missed us before. He's overwhelmed with the support he's received from everyone back home, and wanted to know how I know what to send before he knows what to ask for.

I told him that I have special 'connections' (meaning Mr. Bob Babcock and all the great folks who contribute to this website), and I'm his mother and that he should never forget that mothers have special powers. He laughed and told me to thank everyone for their support.

I told him, 'Consider it done.' This is our family's first real experience as a military family, and I have to say that I've never been more proud to be an American in my life. God bless our Soldiers, their families, and their mission.

14 October - Does My Heart Good

Bob, heard from my son today; they lost two more Soldiers—one in Bayjai, and one in Tikrit. The one in Tikrit he took care of; he said it's very hard to see a fallen Soldier. My husband and I just came back from Ft. Hood, where we visited his wife and our grandchildren. The whole town of Killeen, Texas, supports their Soldiers. Everywhere we went and in all the stores they have things up on their windows supporting the Soldiers; it did my heart good.

I met a young girl there about fourteen or so. She asked me if I had someone in Iraq, and I said, "Yes my son." She asked me to tell him thanks for protecting America. Now wasn't that great?

15 October - Frustrating

Our son, who is with Charlie Company, 1-22 IN, 4ID, called early this morning to assure us he was not the one killed last night in Tikrit, but it was one of his buddies, and the entire unit is very saddened. It is very frustrating to chase an army that can hide among civilians, attack from a distance, and then melt back into the background. His unit goes out daily on raids looking for Saddam, or they work to keep demonstrations from turning into riots, all the while watching out for opportunities for Saddam loyalists to attack. They do a good job and feel they're making progress, but it is very hard work. And when one of their own falls to an ambush, it's hard to take.

Our hearts go out to the family and loved ones of the Soldier killed last night. Please know that his comrades thought very highly of him. We all pray that this insanity will be over soon, and they can all come home.

15 October - Surprise!

My husband is with B Company, 3-66 AR. On the night of September 27, there was a knock at my front door. It was my husband! His parents were there, and his dad had a video camera in hand. I had no idea that he was coming home for mid-tour leave; he surprised me. Our first child, a daughter, was born on September 15. He got to see our little girl for the very first time. He had to leave to go back to Iraq this past Sunday, our first wedding anniversary. It was a wonderful two weeks and an answer to our prayers. I can't wait to see him again when he comes home to stay.

17 October - Progress
It is 3:00 in the morning and the phone rings. I know who it is because I have been willing him to call. He is with Charlie BTRY, 6-27 FA, out of Ft. Sill. He was very upbeat and we got to talk for a long time before the phone went bad. We talked a lot about what we see in the media vs. what he sees. His exact words were, "I'm amazed at the progress that has been made since I've been here."

He says the kids are playing on a soccer field the army built for them, and the women are dipping water from a well the army dug for them. They are working together with the Iraqi people; so much so that they have become familiar with each other and it is not unusual to greet each other by name as they pass by. It is also not unusual to have the Iraqi people show them scars or tell them stories of family members executed by Saddam. They are all joyous at his loss of power.

The Air Force has moved in to their base, and the facilities are crowded right now, but he laughingly said, "they will bring their money, too, so we should get some amenities."

He was thrilled that the chow hall now has ice cream. He has received all my many packages and says he is in need of nothing, only more homemade cookies as some of his buddies have offered to pay me to make them. I will continue to send enough to share.

The days are cooler and the nights very comfortable. The satellite is working, and they get to keep up on the current news. He sent fourteen rolls of film, and I got to see him and he looks great. Prayers go out for all.

18 October - Just Camping With the Guys
...Finally heard from my husband Wednesday. He is with B Company, 3-66 AR. The connection was kind of bad; you had to wait for the other person to hear what you said. It was a true

Godsend because I had not heard from him in over six weeks. It was pretty nerve wracking with 4th ID fatalities being announced so often.

He sent me pictures of his trailer; they are nicely renovated large Conex trailers, with windows and doors cut in. He has air conditioning and a dorm fridge with microwave. He says it has really helped morale.

He also said he sent me pictures of a hedgehog that runs wild there. It is surreal talking to him sometimes; you would think he was camping with the guys. He is always upbeat. He turned down the mid-tour leave; I am really disappointed but will deal with it.

19 October - The Face of War

Bob, I received a letter from our Soldier son. I hesitated to even share any of it here, since it is very clear that these guys are not out on a camping trip, but in an ugly war. Nonetheless, here you are. Use it if you like. I know the community service side is by far the more popular news folks seem to want to hear, but here is war as it is. This is in a Soldier's own words. I cleaned the language up a little; he used the same Infantry language I used in Vietnam; probably not suitable for a general audience.

"Well, they say we're going into a bad area called Samarra. Rocket propelled grenades and remote controlled mines are almost nightly events there. It's going to be B-CO, 1-8 IN's job to show these bad guys who's wearing the 'daddy-pants' out here. I've been all over this damned country, and they're saying this will be the toughest of all we've faced to date. So far I've survived an ambush and a mortar attack, as did all my comrades, but I'm a little scared. I tell you what, I hope we can kill us some terrorists.

"Yesterday, we heard mortar rounds going off about one hundred fifty meters away and as we were running out of the 'Brads' (yelling and hollering like cowboys), we could see the rounds impacting right in the backyard of some Iraqi home. These bad guys do not care who they hit. They don't care if they hit their own people. It's frustrating because we have a hard time finding these punks conducting these attacks. I pray to God we can kill us some bad guys. It's a stressful cat and mouse game.

"Every day out here, I try to make everyone back there proud. I want to come out of this a square-jawed individual, and that's that. This conflict will end for us someday soon. So keep praying for us. We aim to be tigers in this vast wasteland of terrorism. Tigers are ferocious and powerful and when they get hold of their prey they show no mercy or remorse for what they've done. We are eagles, tigers, wolves... all out to kill the elusive prey and foul of Iraq. I love you Mom and Dad."

These are the words of our square-jawed, tenderhearted Soldier. Go Eagles, Tigers and Wolves. And God bless and keep you in your hunt.

20 October - Not So Easy to Say Good-bye

My husband left on the 17th of October to go back to Iraq. He is with 204th FSB. For the families that await your loved one's R&R, be prepared for the heartache of watching them leave a second time. It's not easy to say goodbye, but we have to remember that it's a countdown until they return now. It was wonderful to see my husband and watch him with our one-month-old baby girl. Let's none of us stop praying for our Soldiers. They all need us!

Ann-Marie Morefield - Sister of PVT Jason Morefield - Co C 1-66 AR

I am the sister of one of our brave Soldiers in Iraq. I would say that the hardest obstacle is of the constant worry. He is my baby brother, and has been the light of my life from the day he was born. I love and want to protect him as I do my daughter. Even through my teen years, when I was mad at the world, he was my light, and he could make my heart melt! Because of the age difference, I helped care for him from the day he was born. I remember crying because I had wanted a sister. Yet from the second I saw him at the hospital, I loved him more than life itself. I guess I can explain this because I feel like sometimes people forget about the bonds between siblings. We love and protect each other. We were each other's first comrades in life. In good and bad times, we stuck together. I would fight with my other siblings but never with Jason—mi Vida.

I was also blessed because I didn't have to be the disciplinarian (but then again he never needed disciplining because he was always a good kid—an exceptionally awesome child and teenager and really smart too.) Even though it was never a question of "if" but "when," that didn't make that phone call (I am being deployed to Iraq) easier. It is a bittersweet flow of emotions from love and pride to despair and helplessness that reaches your toes. The realization is that he, and his unit, and all of our Soldiers are in God's hands and there is nothing we can do to protect them, comfort them, laugh with them or just shoot the breeze. I miss just being able to pick up the phone and talk about everything and anything.

There was a long time where I was letting the fear and anxiety eat at me. I did not go out with my friends or really do anything special. How could I live when my brother is in harm's way and risking his life for others? My husband and friends would try to get me out, but I had isolated myself. I actually found that I was kind of angry at them for trying to drag me out of my safe place (locked inside myself). I thought I had to be strong for everyone, and I could not show weakness. In my mind, if I came out of isolation, then they would all see my weakness and my pain, and I didn't want that. I needed to be a rock for my parents and brother. Especially since I did not want my brother to worry about us and lose focus because of worry.

My close friends and husband saw right through me. In the beginning I was good about asking for help—just someone to talk to. I talked to our Family Readiness Group (FRG) about concerns and fears, and a couple times to rear detachment with technical questions. Eventually, I stopped calling when I needed someone to talk to. That was the biggest mistake I made. I finally broke and made myself physically ill from the stress and worry and outright panic every time I saw something horrible happen in the vicinity of where my brother's unit was located. I knew that I had to somehow control the flood of emotions when months into his deployment I was still waking up sick everyday, and now, I was having horrible nightmares at night.

I was okay at work, but outside of work I was not functioning and became more listless and sad. I can't pin down the exact turning point for me. I believe that it was a long and slow process of learning from each new experience and anxiety attack. I was always raised to put my faith in God, and he will take care of everything. I always thought my faith was stronger. I take that back, my faith is strong, but I wasn't sure if God's will was something I might want to face. Again it goes back to the fear of the unknown. I believe that causes more emotions than imaginable, and then the mish-mush of emotions created stuff I never experienced.

Through a lot of prayer, talking about my feelings again, and releasing myself from my own isolation, I started dealing with the situation better. Don't get me wrong, the worry, anxiety and missing your loved one does not go away. It is still there, and sometimes it rears itself, and it hurts. But the bad days are not the norm anymore. I know there are still days when I go home from work and cry, whether it is from fear or sadness, because we have lost another selfless Soldier, or because I just plain miss my kid brother. To be frank, I have not gotten a full night's sleep since Jason was deployed, but I accept this as normal and I am not fighting it, but using it as a learning experience. I accept what I am feeling and know that it is okay. We all deal in different ways, and it is never easy to find comfort and peace while the one you love is in harm's way. You have the exuberant feeling of being so full of pride and love, and the rock bottom feeling of fear, sadness, and anxiety all at the same time.

The biggest help was talking, making packages filled with goodies, a lot of prayers, gardening, and actually spending time with my friends again. Other great helps were our FRGs Ann, Lachelle, Janet, Juana, Faye and Bob Babcock for his daily updates.

My brother was transferred from one unit to another, so we are blessed in having awesome FRGs from both units!

Try to find your peace! It's not easy (you lose it and then find it) and trust that God will grant you the comfort you need. That has helped me immensely. I need to be strong, so I can properly support my brother, my parents, my daughter and my husband. Especially to support my brother; I miss him and love him so much. It is always the little things you miss the most. I look forward to the day when we can call each other on our cell phones and spend hours talking with no time limits, even if we just talk about nothing! Most of all I can't wait to see his sweet face, give him a big hug, and maybe a noogy on the head!

20 October - Made My Day
My Soldier isn't in 4th ID. He's with A Company, 15th MI over there in Iraq, and I thought you and your readers might like to hear about my husband's and my very special few minutes today.

166

My friend and I went to the PX here at Ft. Hood for a Lonestar mini concert and autographing. The concert was great; they sang eight songs, four more than we thought they were going to. But it was at the signing that the event occurred that made my husband's and my day.

My husband called me just before it was my turn to get my autograph, so I told him what I was doing. He thought that was cool. But when I got there, I told the lead singer, Richie, that I was on the phone with my husband and that he's in Iraq. He thrust his hand out for my phone, so I gave it to him, and he talked to my husband!

He said, "I'm Richie from Lonestar. I just want to thank you for what you're doing over there. You're doing a great job, keep it up and come home safe."

I don't think my husband knew what to say. When I asked him, he said, "I just said you're welcome, and thank you."

When I told him it made my day, he laughed and said, "It made *your* day?"

I'm so happy he got to be a part of that and have someone like Richie tell him how much he's appreciated. He needed it. Thank you, and God bless our Soldiers!

21 October - Felt Like a Rock Star

My son, who is with B Company, 299 EN BN was among the first ones to come home on the mid-term leave, and he went back October 12. It's been hard the second time around, but well worth him getting to meet his new baby boy. He was taken aback at what the sight of him in his desert fatigues did to people. He said he felt like a "rock star."

When he arrived in Baltimore initially, Maryland police officers bought beer for him and a couple of his buddies in a bar at the airport. That totally shocked him. He couldn't seem to figure out what all the fuss was about, but I made darn sure I told him to be accepting of people's thanks and gratitude and always be humble and gracious. He was. His reply mostly was, "Thank you for your support, and I'm just doing my job."

The day he left, his last stop before the airport was our small-town hospital where he went to kiss his hospitalized grandmother goodbye. He was in uniform carrying his new baby, walking with his wife, and she told me they drew a crowd around them in the hospital and he was a little embarrassed. I never thought he would be the shy type.

He even made our hometown newspaper along with photo of him, his wife and the baby, which was great! I am overjoyed at the love and support complete strangers gave him. He expected it from family and friends but not strangers. I feel sure he's spreading the word of the welcome they should expect to his unit back in Tikrit. I pray every Soldier gets such a warm and loving welcome and goodbye upon their return. Many blessings to all our Soldiers and their families.

22 October - Family Section Pulls Her Through

My husband joined HHC, 1-12 IN, 3BCT, 4ID, at Ft. Carson in July; his first duty station. After relocating away from family and friends, we were told he'd be going to Iraq. We were both scared, but he was eager to do his part and be with his fellow Soldiers.

Being new to the military, I had no idea how a deployment works. When he called and told me he was in Iraq and safe, I felt relieved. Then I didn't hear anything for over three weeks. I nearly went crazy. Other wives from the unit were getting calls, but I wasn't. Another wife suggested maybe he didn't want to call me. I began to have doubts and really got stressed out. However, it was the family section of the 4th ID updates that got me through. I would read them and hear about families not hearing things for weeks. I knew then that I wasn't alone and reading their stories comforted me and got me through difficult nights.

This past Saturday I received a letter. It was full of him explaining he was okay and doing fine and that they have been moving and had no phones available. He talked about the places he wants to take me when he returns. He was so upbeat and dedicated to his job (even when he said that they'd lost two Soldiers and another was wounded).

He says they all work together, and he is glad he is doing his share. He couldn't believe I'd thought he wouldn't call. He said that calling home, letters from loved ones, and goody packages are the best and that they all look forward to them. He couldn't think of anything special he wanted except for me to send extra goodies for him to share. I am so proud of my husband, his unit and the other Soldiers. Go 3rd BCT!

23 October - What it Means to be the Mother of a Soldier

From PVT Miller's Mom:

The article about 'Being a Soldier's Wife' inspired me to write about being a Soldier's mom.

The alarm goes off at 6:30 am as it does every day. The radio announcer is reporting the current local news and traffic reports. On the worst days, the newsman says, 'outside of Ba'quabah...' That's a hard way for a mom to start off the day.

At the office, everyone says good morning and asks how she is. But, it's just a passing question not really intended for a lengthy conversation about how she has not had a decent night's sleep all this week.

It's hard to concentrate when the conversations are about such mundane things as concerts and lunch plans. She has worn the red, white and blue ribbon with a yellow rose in it for over six months now. It's a little bent up from the seatbelt, but she wears it every day, just the same.

Going to the grocery store has a whole new meaning. She doesn't buy her son's favorite cereal and milk; it sure lasts a lot longer. Instead she looks for things that are easy to store, stay fresh for a long time, and might have some semblance of nutrition. She wonders if his favorite (although weird) snack—ranch dressing and tuna fish—might be running low. So she picks up a small bottle and some of the new foil packages of tuna. There is a special spot in the dining room where she stores goodies for him to send out in the next box.

When she goes to the post office, only the postal workers know why she is there. Everyone else is there for normal postal needs like stamps, returning a book they don't want, or picking up the mail they received while on vacation. She wishes she could share with them all how special this box is because she made her son a special 'iron-on' on the computer for a tee-shirt that is just for him. She wonders if her son ever notices the snowman stamps that she saved from last winter just to put on his letters.

In the beginning, her ribbon used to elicit comments and "thank you's". Now it seems to go unnoticed. Her co-workers and friends used to ask if she had heard from her son, but interests have waned and the answer seems to be the same anyway, "not lately" or "nothing really new."

She remembers when he was home. She thinks of how excited he was to get his car and how nice it is and how well it suits him. She remembers worrying about him driving too fast with the radio blasting and reminding him to be safe and to drive defensively. Now she worries about him driving on roads that aren't safe even without any traffic. She remembers what a sweet boy he was and how he always liked babies and small children. Now she worries if he has seen children hurt or living in terrible conditions.

But she can't let these things get to her or dwell on them for long because she has another child at home who needs her attention. It's her first year in high school, and things are so exciting for her. There is marching band practice and getting ready for her performances and competitions. She has tests to take and drills to learn. Her sixteenth birthday came and went, and all she wanted was a phone call from her brother. She got flowers instead and declared them the best birthday present she had ever received.

No one has any idea how hard it is for her to play the national anthem at the beginning of the home football games. Luckily for her band mates, the director insists that they stand at attention without fidgeting when they are the visiting team. Her wrath at anyone even suspected of being unpatriotic is well known among her friends. Her brother is her hero.

This mom was lucky enough to be able to be present when the company reported for deployment; many weren't able to be there. It took up the whole day, what with packing and cleaning up the rooms in the barracks—having them inspected and cleared. Then there was more waiting as the bags were loaded and Soldiers were accounted for. Pictures were taken and stories were told in the same way these things happen at most family gatherings.

When the weapons were issued, it was the first time this mom had seen a gun in her son's hands. But she gritted her teeth and pasted the smile on her face and silently reaffirmed the vow to herself that she would not cry in front of her kids.

She remembered the first time she saw her son in his uniform at his basic training graduation just a few months earlier and how grown up he looked. She was desperately trying to forget that the young son she was about to put on the bus would not be the same grown man that would come home.

When the order came to form up at the gym, she felt her resolve and strength start to give way. But when she looked into his eyes, she saw he needed her one more time to be strong and confident while he got on the bus. She was. He gave her a picture perfect smile and an OKAY sign as he stepped into the doorway. As he found his seat, he looked out the tinted windows and mouthed the words, "I'll write soon, I love you, mom" and waved goodbye. She waved back and said the same and turned to the parking lot, looking for the privacy of her car. If there were tears, no one saw them but her husband. If there were sobs, those sounds were muffled by his strong arms around her.

As the clock begins to tick towards the day her Soldier son returns, a mother remembers how fast the time has already passed. Wasn't it only last month he was saying his first words? And just last week he was bursting thru the door with excitement to share the news of his latest accomplishment at school. And surely it was only a few days ago that he was learning to drive.

So she consoles herself that in a lot less time he will be back in her living room, leaving his shoes in the middle of the floor, not rinsing out his milk glass, or calling to say he can't come to visit next weekend because he has plans with his buddies.

This is what it means to be the mother of a Soldier.

24 October - Another Mom's Reply

I just had to respond to 'What it means to be the Mother of a Soldier.' People still ask about my son all the time—most of the time they have no idea how much I worry. Sometimes I wake up in the middle of the night, sit outside and talk to my son via the moon. I miss him so much, and PVT Miller's mom has pretty much described my son. We are all proud of our Soldiers and pray God will bring them home safely. Another Soldier's mom

25 October - A Soldier Says, "I Love You."

Bob, my wife has been forwarding your Iraqi News Updates to me for the last few weeks. I appreciate your efforts (and the efforts of the rest of the contributors) in keeping the families up to date with the nation's effort to restore this region to peace.

When I read the section, 'What Our Families Are Hearing From Our Soldiers in Iraq,' it brings memories to the surface that brings tears of joy and misery to my eyes. The tears of joy are because of the love and support that is shown; the tears of misery for the separation of loved ones. I have a small request of you.

Could you please include my journal entry in your newsletter as a measure of devotion and love to my bride of twenty-two years? Thanks you for your support.

24 October - HHC 4FSB - 1st Bde 4ID - Tikrit South - FOB Packhorse

Twenty-two years ago we had a dinner for two at the Old Spaghetti Factory. Nineteen years ago my company commander came up to me while I was standing guard during a field exercise. "How are you doing this morning?" was his question.

It was wet and rainy. I had just bailed ten gallons of water out of the foxholeand more water was trickling in from some runoff. In other words, it was not a good morning. I looked up at him and said in an even tone, "Well sir, considering that I just bailed out this hole, and I am already ankle deep in water, the coffee from the chow hall is cold, and today is my third wedding anniversary I can think of lots of other places I'd rather be..."

Well, it's not wet and rainy. I do, however, walk through some ankle deep dust every now and then. Coffee is normally hot around here. But I can still think of another place I'd rather be.

The living room at Mom's house was emptied of all the furniture to hold the reception. Three hours earlier I had been rooted in a spot next to the organ at St. Michael's. I could not move those final five or six steps on cue. I was stunned at the glow on her face. We started our life together as husband and wife. Every time I think of that day, and those since, tears of loneliness seem to creep into the corner of my eyes.

I checked my e-mail early today. From her: "Hi Honey, I just wanted to wish you a happy anniversary. Can you believe it has been twenty-two years together through so much? I wish you were here to spend it with me. I don't know what I am going to do without you, but maybe cry... both of us... And I had spaghetti for dinner tonight, alone."

28 October - Just Another Mom of an Infantry Soldier

My son is in A-Co, 1-8 IN, 3BCT from Fort Carson, Colorado. He is serving in Iraq, but had a fifteen-day leave, so this is the seventh month now that he's been there. Yes, it's hard, but we are very proud of him, although we miss him deeply. Sometimes you wonder why someone would choose to do such a job. Being an infantry Soldier, I think, has a downside. Let's face it!

But while my son was home we went to DC to visit the Smithsonian. In one of the museums they had the flag that had hung on the Pentagon on 9/11, and a plaque that told you some reasons our sons or loved ones are those infantry Soldiers. I must say, I had to walk away because the tears were beginning to be to hard to control. But my son came up from behind me and said, "It's all about that."

As hard as it is to be separated from our Soldiers, we must remind ourselves what an honor it is to be a parent, or girlfriend or family member to these wonderful guys! Love them, respect them, and pray for them to come home safe soon.

Thanks again.

29 October - E-mail From A Soldier - 299 EN BN
To his Dad:

Hey Dad, I have no clue what I am doing. I doubt this will even get to you. Anyway, we got in this morning at 6:00 a.m. I slept until noon, and then just sat around the rest of the time. I saw WSU won yesterday; they are sure doing well. I just wish I could catch one of their games.

It was good talking to you last night. I have so much more to say, not about anything in particular, just stuff. There are many things I have taken for granted in my life, and I'm going to try my hardest to enjoy all those things when I get home. I miss talking to you and mom, I miss the garage (not getting anything accomplished and being totally happy about that). I miss dinners together, to make a long story short, I miss a lot of stuff.

We all know things will never be the way they were before I left, but that's a good thing because that means I am growing up. It's time for me to start my life and go through the good and bad times on my own, just like you and Mom have. I'm excited about it. I just want you and Mom to know, this is as far away as I will ever be from Spokane! Whatever I end up doing in life I'm sure I will succeed because I was raised to succeed, we all were.

You guys have done a great job in raising three hell-raisers. I just hope I can do the same for my kids. Well, Dad, I'm going to go... love you.

29 October - Excerpts of the Dad's Reply to His Son

You have made my day, my week, my life! To come to work on a typical Monday morning, log on my computer and the first thing I get is your message. How can anything be any better!

It's always good talking with you. at times. I have a hard time hearing you, but I'll make it—it's that damn microphone that is on my hearing aid that I have to always have the phone at, and it's hard sometimes finding the right spot. I can talk to you about 'stuff' any time you want to. I am especially looking forward to all the talking we can do when you come home.

You hit the nail on the head with what you say about the garage. My term is 'shop.' Isn't it great? The only thing that is terribly frustrating about it is that you're not there doing your thing while I'm doing my thing. I think about it all the time.Yes, We are excited about your return also. You have no idea of the magnitude. We know the 'great man' that you are and will be at your side as you conquer life to the fullest.

I Love You... Dad.

Tami Motley - Wife of CW2 David Motley - 1-10 CAV

At first some days seemed to pass by in seconds not hours. I remember the way I felt driving home from the drop-off point. It was like I was in a daze. I had cried all I could days before. Just the look on my husband's face was burned into my memory. I looked in my rear view mirror at our four children. I remember the somber looks on all their faces. Our older teenagers looked like they were deep in thought. Our six and two year olds wanted to know how long Daddy would be in the field.

This was six months ago. Yet it seems like yesterday. Where does all the time go? I knew it was my time to step up and do the job of two. Before we got home that afternoon, I knew it was going to be a long, long haul but as time goes on, days turn into weeks.

I watched the news and tracked the progress of the 4th Infantry Division, always looking for the 1-10 CAV E troop guys. I remember watching as our guys were interviewed from Kuwait. I looked closely for my husband's face but did not see him. At least I knew he might be in the crowd. That somehow gave me relief. After several weeks his first letter arrived one month after deployment. I read it over and over. Once he made the jump from

174

Kuwait to Iraq the letters almost stopped. I felt a real sense of being alone.

I remember I wrote thirty letters in thirty days. My best friend was away, and I had a lot to share with him. Our children wrote to Daddy as well, telling him all about school, birthdays, and swimming. Our extended family wrote to my husband, and then the care packages began to flow to Iraq. We had many people praying for us and asking what they could do for my trooper while he was serving in Iraq. Our local church called to pray with me, and I began to write a family newsletter to all our family. My husband's letters lifted me up. I was like a schoolgirl waiting for that special love letter at the mailbox. Our postman got to know me pretty well. My husband's letters told of many flying missions and some of the dangers he faced everyday. But he always said I know we are making a difference every day.

His positive attitude about being deployed strengthened me. I could tell he didn't want me to worry and I also never complained about the children. I felt it more important to support him than weigh him down with little things he could do nothing about from Iraq. It is amazing how strong we can be when we have no choice. I was proud of me.

It is also magnificent how our husbands can serve our country with such bravery. Even though time apart has been hard for both of us and our children, I know the deployment has changed the world, the future of America and our children's future. I am proud of that, and I am proud of my husband. I know when he lays his head down at night, his thoughts travel home where he is loved and missed. When I lay on our bed alone my thoughts travel to him, and through my heart, I let him know how much he is loved, missed, and appreciated. Now we e-mail, and he calls when he can. We write, and I send care packages. We still get support from family and friends. But as time goes on, my love deepens for my husband in a way I never thought it could. He has come to realize how much we mean to him in a much different way than before.

I know God has heard many prayers spoken from the desert, and He will listen until every trooper is home in the arms of their family and Iraqi freedom is complete. My heart and prayers are with the families of our troopers who gave their lives. I truly believe they look down upon and protect the ones they left behind. I know deep bonds and lifelong friendships are forming within

E troop that time will not wash away. Our love in our home has deepened within our marriage and with our children. I am proud to be an army wife serving with my husband in Iraqi Freedom.

29 October - From a Vietnam Vet

Thirty-four years ago, my dear mother would bake brownies to send to me in Vietnam. She used a coffee can to cut the cooled brownies, then wrapped each large, round brownie individually in cellophane. Next, she filled the coffee can with brownies (I'm sure there were extra layers of wrapping) and taped up the lid on the end real well. When that coffee can arrived, my squad in 3rd platoon, 2d BN (MECH), 22d INF Regiment were all my best buddies, and the rest of the platoon was circling our track, too.

In those days, when I was still a new guy, Mom's care packages helped me get accepted among the combat veterans. She may well have saved my life with her love and devotion. All those who express admiration for my efforts to look after her now, as she deteriorates in a nursing home with Alzheimer's, don't realize I could never do enough for her.

Cynthia Louck - Wife of SPC Paul Louck - B Troop 1/10 CAV

I would first like to express my appreciation for all the troops overseas. I am very proud of my husband Paul. He left on March 30, 2003. Just three and a half months after we were married, I found out I was two months pregnant. Paul was upset about having to leave me here pregnant, but he also knew God was watching over me. It is hard only to have contact with him once a month if that. I was very depressed after he left but, I knew I had to be strong not only for our relationship but, also for the baby. I love Paul with all my heart. He has now been gone for almost seven months now and I know the faster the days go by, the faster I get to see him. I am due any day now and I just want him to know I am very proud of him. He is a big inspiration to me. I truly can't wait to see him and most of all to see his newborn son.

Jolene K. Boykin - Wife of SGT Boykin - Co A 2-20 FA

I have been blessed to have a husband who is very poetic and loves to write home.

A Find
By SGT Boykin

There is a light in the distance, it must be her.
I am lost, she will find me.
I am alone with my memories.
Pictures of the past get me through the sunrise and the sunset.
But she will be there until the end.
She will find me.
I'm alone, but travel in numbers.
With the might and force of a thousand armies of old,
yet I'm weak.
I have a lack of love, of comfort that I once had.
Of being safe within her grasp, in her arms
But she will find me.
Though my travels are long and far about
I will return. I will be there upon the wings of angels.
To her I will fly.
She will again find me, for I have found her.
She is my one true love.
The pillar that I lean upon
She will find me.
I am gone for now, in a world I must travel.
With time against me and on my side
I have only hope to carry me by, for the months will come
and they will go.
But she will find me.
I stop only to pause for a moment for her memories
to wash over me.
They cleanse me for a while.
Until they are needed again
She has found me.
At last I will be able to rest
But until then I will walk with my memories
and pause for a picture.
Until she will find me again

Task Force Ironhorse - October 2003 Casualties

CSM James D. Blankenbecler, 40, of Alexandria, Virginia, was killed on October 1 in Samarra, Iraq. CSM Blankenbecler was in a convoy that was hit by an improvised explosive device and rocket propelled grenades. He was assigned to 1st Battalion, 44th Air Defense Artillery Regiment, Fort Hood, Texas.

PFC Analaura Esparza-Gutierrez, 21, of Houston, Texas, was killed on October 1 in Tikrit, Iraq. PFC Esparza-Gutierrez was in a convoy that was hit by an improvised explosive device and rocket propelled grenades. She was assigned to A Company, 4th Forward Support Battalion, Fort Hood, Texas.

CPL James H. Pirtle, 27, of La Mesa, New Mexico, was killed October 4 in Assadah, Iraq. CPL Pirtle was in a Bradley Fighting Vehicle when a rocket propelled grenade struck his vehicle. He was assigned to C Company, 2nd Battalion, 8th Infantry Regiment, 4th Infantry Division, Fort Hood, Texas.

CPL Joseph C. Norquist, 26, of San Antonio, Texas, was killed on October 9 in Baqubah, Iraq, while supporting Operation Iraqi Freedom. CPL Norquist was in a convoy that came under attack from rocket propelled grenades and small arms fire. He was assigned to the 588th Engineer Battalion, 2nd BCT, 4ID, Fort Hood, Texas.

SPC James E. Powell, 26, of Radcliff, Kentucky, was killed on October 12 in Baji, Iraq. SPC Powell was killed when his M2/A2 Bradley Fighting Vehicle struck an enemy anti-tank mine. He was assigned to B Company, 1st Battalion, 22nd Infantry Regiment, 4th Infantry Division, based in Fort Hood, Texas.

CPL Donald L. Wheeler, 22, of Concord, Michigan, was killed on October 13 in Tikrit, Iraq. CPL Wheeler was searching for a possible improvised explosive device when his unit came under attack from a rocket propelled grenade. He was assigned to C Company, 1st Battalion, 22nd Infantry Regiment, 4th Infantry Division, Fort Hood, Texas.

PFC Stephen E. Wyatt, 19, of Kilgore, Texas, was killed on October 13 in Balad, Iraq. PFC Wyatt was in a convoy that was hit by an improvised explosive device and small arms fire. He was assigned to C Battery, 1st Battalion, 17th Field Artillery Regiment, Fort Sill, Oklahoma.

1LT David R. Bernstein, 24, of Phoenixville, Pennsylvania, and **PFC John D, Hart**, 20, of Bedford, Massachusetts, were killed in action on October 18 in Taza, Iraq, when enemy forces ambushed their patrol using rocket propelled grenades and small arms fire. The Soldiers were assigned to 1st Battalion (Airborne), 508th Infantry Battalion, 173rd Infantry Brigade, Camp Ederle, Italy.

CPT John R. Teal, 31, of Mechanicsville, Virginia, was killed on October 23 in Baqubah, Iraq. CPT Teal was in a convoy when an improvised explosive device exploded. He was assigned to 2nd Brigade, 4th Infantry Division, Fort Hood, Texas.

SPC Artimus D. Brassfield, 22, of Flint, Michigan, died of wounds received from an enemy mortar attack on October 24 in Samarra, Iraq. He was assigned to B Company, 1st Battalion, 66th Armored Regiment, 4th Infantry Division, based in Ft. Hood, Texas.

SPC Jose L. Mora, 26, of Bell Gardens, California, died of wounds received from an enemy mortar attack while supporting Operation Iraqi Freedom on October 24 in Samarra, Iraq. He was assigned to C Company, 1st Battalion, 12th Infantry Regiment, 4th Infantry Division, based in Ft. Carson, Colorado.

PFC Steven Acosta, 19, of Calexico, California, died on October 26 in Baqubah, Iraq. PFC Acosta died from a non-hostile gunshot wound. He was assigned to C Company, 3rd Battalion, 67th Armored Regiment, 4th Infantry Division, Fort Hood, Texas.

SGT Michael Paul Barrera, 26, of Von Ormy, Texas, was killed on October 28 in Ba'quabah, Iraq. SGT Barrera was fatally injured when his tank was hit with an improvised explosive device. He was assigned to the 3rd Battalion, 67th Armor Regiment, Fort Hood, Texas.

SPC Isaac Campoy, 21, of Douglas, Arizona was killed on October 28 in Baqubah, Iraq. SPC Campoy was fatally injured when his tank was hit with an improvised explosive device. He was assigned to the 3rd Battalion, 67th Armor Regiment, Fort Hood, Texas.

EIGHT

NOVEMBER - 2003
Thanksgiving in Iraq

151 days and a wake-up until April 1, 2004...

Our Soldiers conducted more raids and patrols and retained individuals during Operations Ivy Cyclone I and Raider justice. They also had to delicately balance being in a combat situation (staying aggressive and lethal) and working with the Iraqis to rebuild their infrastructure.

Back home we worked in earnest to get holiday packages sent off. Chaplain Brewer continued to help families and friends by getting our holiday packages sent to Iraq from Ft. Hood. We found out the 1st Armored Division would replace the 4th Infantry Division in a massive troop rotation in the spring. We also learned about body armor and that soft-shell Humvees are going to lose the battle with an IED.

Thanksgiving in Tikrit was celebrated with a turkey run, turkey, and a concert. Our Commander in Chief made a surprise visit to Baghdad International Airport and served Thanksgiving dinner to 600 troops. While he did not make it north to Tikrit, the visit meant so much to the Soldiers and their families. One of our young 4ID Soldiers said it best what we were all feeling. 'I didn't get to see him, but what matters is that he cares enough to come and visit.'

3 November - Feels Closer to Him
I just heard from my husband (HHC 1-12th IN) who told me that he had given his slot for R&R up for the good of another Soldier. Even though I was upset with him, I know he did it because it was the right thing to do. He will be home in February for thirty days,

180

and then he leaves for school right after that. It was so hard to tell our children that Dad is not coming home for mid-tour after all, but I was proud to tell them why.

I believe this shows us that our guys are looking out for each other and are trying to take care of each other. I know that they will return home safely and be with their families soon. For all of the guys who do not get to return home my thoughts go out to their families. Let everyone know that their family member is being watched out for even when they are away. Thank you for all your updates. It helps me feel a little closer to my husband.

Submitted by Amanda Durham - Wife of a 4ID Soldier
You asked for things that made us step up to the challenges of being a military wife. We were married only two weeks before he was deployed, so this deployment has been a great challenge for me. The support of the other wives and forums like the 4th infantry.org has helped me get through this and become a great army wife.

I Love a Soldier

I love a Soldier with all my heart.
I see him almost never; we are always apart
We may not be together, but love does not give in.
To let something like this go would be such a sin.
He is courageous, and he is a man
He protects his country as best as he can.
The last time I saw him? Seven months past.
But I feel his love for me, and I know it will last.
Perhaps there will be peace, perhaps there will not
I hold onto the hope; it's all I've got.
My love for him grows; it's stronger each day.
The distance between us can't hold it at bay.
He calls, I write,
We both hold on with all our might.
I cry often, I will not lie.
Sometimes smiling is hard, but I sure do try.
I love, I hope, I dream, I cope.
His heart is strong, his feelings are true,
He loves me, and I love him too.
Yes, I love a Soldier, and though we're apart,
We're always together-together at heart.

4 November - Gone Fishing

My son, B CO, 1-22 IN, in Bayji called us three times while on R&R in Qatar, and, among other things, relayed a relatively amusing story. Bayji is on the Tigris River north of Tikrit. My son's unit was patrolling in a brushy area near the riverbank when they heard an explosion coming from the river. Everyone hit the dirt and prepared for an attack through the brush, which screened them from the river, but no further shots or explosions ensued. They sent a couple of guys to scout out the situation.

The scouts spied a lone unarmed Iraqi standing by the river, looking intently at the water. They rushed through the foliage with their rifles up and by gesture and sign language, demanded that the guy explain the explosions. He immediately raised his hands and tried to make them understand. It seems he'd just been fishing—with a hand grenade! There is so much loose ordnance lying around Iraq that it's easier to find grenades than fishing gear. It may not be sporting, but it's really efficient, as long as you don't mind an occasional piece of shrapnel in your fish fillet.

5 November - Counting the Days

147 Days and a Wake-up! I love the count down and anticipation of my husband returning. My 'Welcome Home Banner' is getting longer by the day. This time is very exciting for me, but it is also exciting for my friends and family around me. We must remember that many wonderful people have stepped up to support our Soldiers while they have been overseas, and although they should not expect anything in return (which I am sure they don't), let us not forget to share the joy of the returns and GOOD things with them too.

Just as we are to share each other's burdens and mourn together, we are also called to share each other's joy and rejoice together! So take the time to share some of the good stuff and pass it around, because although we continue to have losses, we also continue to have a lot of gains... plus, they are coming home! How many more days and a wake-up?

6 November - A Proven Pioneer wife

My Soldier, 4ID, 1st Brigade, 299th ENG, came home recently, and I just wanted to give a bit of info to those spouses and families waiting for their heroes to come home for R&R.

Like most wives, I had my vision of how our time would be spent together. Reality never truly measures up to fantasies. After a few days, I was honestly feeling a bit upset. I had to step back and realize that I have had all the luxuries of home throughout this deployment, but he hasn't. So as we military spouses have to do, I 'sucked it up' and calmed down and didn't get upset that he just wanted to spend Sunday afternoon in front of the TV, remote control in hand, flipping from one game to another.

As he said to me, just relaxing, no worries, hanging out in our home, listening to the sound of the dish washer and clothes dryer running, the air conditioning blowing cool air and just watching his family go about our day, bear hugging and tickling any one of us who walked by him, was heaven to him. We did spend lots of family time and couple time together. It was great!!!

Just remember to give them room to relax and have fun, don't get bogged down by how you imagined the time would be, just enjoy the time together!

6 November - A Lump in My Throat
I've been debating whether or not to even say this, and you can include it or not. This incident happened a couple of weeks ago, and the wife involved probably doesn't even know how it affected me. A word to all of you whose Soldier, husband, son, brother, etc., comes home on mid-tour leave: not everyone is coming back. I am truly happy for all of you and have not fallen into the 'what about me' trap. I have three kids and would love to see my husband, but it is not going to happen. I accept that, but some days I get a lump in my throat wishing that he would get to come home, too.

On one of those days, a wife bounced up to me and said, 'I just wanted you to meet my husband!' Then in the next ten minutes, I had about five other people ask me, 'When is your husband coming back for his two weeks?'

I was cordial and smiling, but I got my kids and just about ran back to my car before I started crying. I don't think anyone saw me. I hope no one did. Please have a little consideration for the rest of us. We are keeping it together, but sometimes just barely.

6 November - Take a Break From the News
I would just like to thank you for these updates. They keep me going through the day. My husband, who is with A Company,

183

1-66 Armor, over in Samarra, got a break. He has been in Kuwait for over a month now. I guess it is like R&R, their tanks are over there for maintenance. It is nice to talk to him every day and get e-mails and not have to watch the news every day.

Sometimes you have to take a break from watching the news, or you would have a nervous breakdown. I still cry every time someone gets hurt or dies, knowing that that Soldier is someone else's son, daughter, dad, mom, brother or sister. It is not always easy to present a brave front to the world, but we have to. God bless our troops!

6 November - No Longer a Child

Our son, A Company, 3-67 AR, arrived home yesterday by way of Kuwait to Ireland to Atlanta to Mobile, for his two week leave. He got to meet his son for the first time yesterday. The baby was born two days after he deployed from Ft. Hood. I've never been so proud to be an American as I was yesterday seeing that boy in that desert uniform. His youth, his manners, his love for home, family, and country just seemed to radiate from the way he walked through the airport terminal to meet us. No one could have doubted he was one of America's finest.

The difficulty of war, the loss of friends only a week ago in the M1 tank attack, reflect in his demeanor. There is no longer a child's heart in my son, but the braver heart of a man who has shouldered the responsibilities of being with and protecting comrades in war. He is a man I've never known before, but oh God, I'm so proud of the man he has become.

6 November - Lights are Coming Back On

I Received a much needed phone call from my husband yesterday. He is a Kiowa pilot with E troop, 1-10 CAV. We talked a little about the Chinook tragedy. He was extremely mad about it and could tell that I was very nervous for him. They are flying so many hours, but he feels that what he is doing is preventing more attacks on our ground guys and is helping the Iraqi people. He said that every week he sees more and more lights as he flies over; the area he is patrolling was completely blacked out not so long ago.

I asked him if the weather was much colder and he explained how they drilled holes in the water tanks and put heating elements in for hot showers! Our Soldiers are pretty inventive and can make the best out of practically nothing. I am so proud of my Soldier and all the men and women he serves with!

7 November - A Great Sense of Humor

Hi! ...just wanted to tell everyone a funny story. My son is a medic with 1-22 IN, 4ID in Tikrit. Their aid station is at Saddam's main palace. The medics have to pull guard tower duty because they are short of help. One night last week he was in the tower and they radioed him, telling him to be on the lookout for some Iraqis who had lost their cow and didn't want to be shot looking for it. Well, my son kept looking and finally he saw them. He kept calling down to them, 'cow,' 'cow'. Not understanding English, they didn't know what he was asking them. So finally he yelled, 'moo,' 'moo' to them, and they said yes, they found the cow right by the guard tower. My son called back to the base and said, 'I got cow.' Everyone laughed. I thought it was funny. I can see my son doing that; it is good to know he still has a sense of humor. Hoorah!

God bless our Soldiers.

7 November - Two Years Alone

When I read the update today and saw that story from the mother of three whose husband isn't coming home, it made me cry! That could have been me writing that. My husband is in B CO, 1-68 AR, and he isn't coming home. He has been gone for almost two years now. He left in December 2001 for Korea, came back for leave in June 2002, came home from Korea December 2002, went to school January 2003, and came to Ft. Carson in March 2003.

I was in Washington State about to have our third child. He came to Washington two days after I had the baby and brought us all to Colorado. His unit left that week, but they let him stay until a later date. He left for Iraq, May 21. He doesn't fit into any of the categories to come home. He didn't just get back from Korea, he didn't get to Iraq until two months after everyone else and even though we have a new baby (well, he is almost eight months old now) he saw him for the first two months. He was at the very bottom of the list. He gave up his slot, because if he had stayed on the list, he wouldn't have been able to go to Qatar for R&R.

I too, understand how that woman is so happy for the others,

185

but at the same time so envious! We would love to see him, but it would be so hard to say goodbye after our time together.

7 November – Incoming...

I heard from my Soldier son with the 223rd ENG BN (Mississippi National Guard), at Camp Warhorse in Baqubah. He called at a time when I was feeling low, and I choked up when I heard his voice. We assured each other, though, that we were okay.

They were watching a movie and he was a little distracted. He said he was fine and didn't need anything. Then I heard a lot of noise, and he commented that he hated it when that happened. He said there were mortars coming in. I asked if they have any warning. He said 'Yeah, when they go boom.'

He always is quick with the humor. Or is it Mom with the silly questions? They were running to the bunkers and he said he would lose me when he got in there and would call me back. Of course, I had a good cry while waiting for him to call back, which he did pretty quickly. He said that it was not mortars, but they had found an IED on the side of the road and had exploded it.

I had to try to clear those emotions out of my head with humor, too, so I asked him if they paused their movie. He laughed and said they usually didn't bother with that. Sorry, this sounds so gloomy; it's just one of those days for me. I know I'm not the only one, but at times I feel like if I don't get my hands on him soon, I'm going to explode!

May God be with me and the rest of us especially at these low times. God, please grant them all protection and give comfort to those who have lost loved ones.

Latorial Faison - Wife of CPT Carl J. Faison - 502 PSB

For Veterans Day 2003 - by Latorial Faison
Many Mighty Brave Soldiers

Many dwell among us
Many laid down their lives
Many are what sustain us
Many bring tears to our eyes
Mighty are the men who sleep in harm's way
Mighty are the women who stand for us today

Mighty are the Soldiers who fought to their deaths for life
Mighty are the souls who have perished
for the cause of right
Brave for every wound and shot
Brave for every cadence and cot
Brave for the red, white and blue
Brave for people just like you.
Soldiers standing proud and strong
Soldiers facing the enemy all day long
Soldiers dedicated to the upward way.
Soldiers who stand with pride for the USA
Veterans because of humility
Veterans because of loyalty
Veterans because of unity
Veterans because of duty

11 November - MG Odierno's Veterans' Day Message

As we honor the veterans of past conflicts and the current global war on terrorism, I would like to thank you, the Soldiers of Task Force Ironhorse. And, just as important, I would like to thank your families for the sacrifices and contributions you both have made to this war.

You face danger and hardship every day as you conduct combat operations to defeat the enemies of democracy in Iraq. Just as the veterans of the 4th Infantry Division did in the Meuse-Argonne, we are making a stand against forces that would like to see the liberties we enjoy destroyed.

Our fathers and grandfathers made history on Utah Beach and in the Central Highlands of Vietnam; the spirit of these heroes is alive in Task Force Ironhorse and you continue the tradition of the Ivy Division in every mission you perform.

No challenge has ever stood in the way of the Ironhorse, and we will complete our task and free the Iraqi people from their history of tyranny and we will destroy terrorist's forces here before they can bring the fight to American shores and threaten our families.

On this Veterans' Day we need to reflect on the legacy of our predecessors and remember those who gave their hearts and their lives to our nation's defense. Many have made that sacrifice here; we will never forget our brethren from this or past wars. Their loss is a loss to all of us, but their contribution to preserving the lives and liberties of America will be remembered and appreciated by our nation and all of us who fight together in Task Force Ironhorse.

We will continue to fight for our families, for our country, and for each other. God bless the Soldiers and families of Task Force Ironhorse and God bless America.
Steadfast and Loyal
Raymond T. Odierno
MG, Commanding

11 November - Mom Buys a Christmas Tree

I pulled up my bootstraps and went shopping today for a Christmas tree to send to my son in Iraq. I wandered up and down the aisles looking for just the best stuff. The tree couldn't be too big. (He is in a container now, and I know he doesn't have much room.) I picked out cute little ornaments and some footballs and things I knew he would put on a tree that he was decorating for himself.

I struggled looking at each ornament wondering what he would be thinking as he got them and wondering if he knew how much love and thought went into every item I picked. Because this is our first Christmas apart in twenty-one years, it will be tough for all of us. As I was standing in the store, my mind kept wandering to Christmas morning, and I won't hear him telling his little sister to, "go back to bed, it's only four in the morning. Santa probably hasn't even been here yet." Hearing her saying, "come on, Dus, hurry, get up."

I finally decided on the right size of tree and some of those silky looking ornaments so they wouldn't get smashed. I got the colored lights; he doesn't like just one color. I did really well until I got to the checkout stand; the girls there know that my son is in Iraq. I rarely let anyone forget, but they know and asked me how he was, is this going over to him?

I stood there, not even being able to answer and started to cry. Not for myself, but knowing that they all are going to be there without us. Have we sent them enough to have a Christmas remotely as nice as the one we'll have here without them? Did we get enough names of the Soldiers who aren't getting anything and will they have something? I shouldn't be allowed out in public,

I tell ya. Anyway, remember to get the stuff off before the 13th is what they are saying now. Love you guys and thanks for all the prayers and support.

11 November – It Has Brought Us Closer

I am grateful that I hear from my husband, with 4-42 FA, quite often (at least once a week). Hearing his voice feels great and is comforting, and it carries me through until the next time, to know he is all right. Just as I do, he has his ups & downs, good and bad days, but overall seems to be doing okay. Mail is the key word here. He writes me every days—says it's his therapy. (I think the Oreos are therapy too!)

I have a big box under our bed full of letters and pictures from Iraq. Someday we will enjoy going through them all. I make sure that he also gets a steady flow of letters and packages from me. As crazy as it may sound, I feel we have bonded even closer through all of this. We have definitely decided that we will no longer take for granted the simple, small things in life and our relationship with each other. I miss him dearly and pray daily for his and the others' safe return home. He's the hero in my life, and I'm so proud of him and the job they are doing over there. Hooah Highlanders!

11 November - Twelve Days of Christmas

Here is what a friend and I are doing for Christmas presents. We are doing our version of the twelve days of Christmas—one picture CD, three calling cards, five magazines, seven books for reading, nine candy canes, ten pictures of myself, eleven sticks of beef jerky, twelve flavored coffees/cocoas are some of what we came up with. I am sending one through six in a box and the other six in a separate box.

All presents are wrapped individually, decorated with a tag on the outside with a number on it so he knows what order to go in. Be creative and fit the items to what your Soldier enjoys! I also bought a few other items such as football shaped summer sausage that he can open on Christmas day. I'm sending a stocking of things that will all be wrapped, too. Even wrapping every item you send and every package for the month of December can be fun for them. My husband is going to be showered with presents if he can't be home for Christmas.

Jackie Maglio - Wife of Chaplain (MAJ) Steven Maglio - 4th ID DIVARTY

I have always been the kind of person with plans, short term and long term. I like to track how I complete each goal and the successes or lessons learned along the way. During a deployment I have learned the best plan I can have is to live one day at a time. I was given a bracelet with 'one day at a time' inscribed on it, and I wear it every day during a deployment. Many times tasks will not be completed, the house will not get cleaned, the laundry will not get done, or all the errands completed, but I will celebrate because we made it through another day. There is always a tomorrow to complete those tasks.

I have learned to celebrate the little things and let go of the things I cannot control. Live one day at a time, and no matter how tired you are at the end of the day, go to sleep thankful that you made it through another day. Tomorrow will come soon enough.

12 November - The Least I Can Do...

My husband is in the 2nd Brigade Recon Troop and I wanted to share with you a heartwarming story. This past week I stopped off at a small town post office in Jarrell, Texas, to mail three Christmas trees and three boxes of decorations to the Soldiers in our company. I stopped off at the small post office because I figured it would be easy to just run in and run out. There was a gentleman behind me in line who overheard me and the postman talking about the items I was mailing. He asked if I was sending the items over to the troops, and I told him I was.

A few minutes later, with tears in his eyes, he asked if it would be okay if he paid for the cost of the postage for my Christmas items. He said it was the least he could do for all the sacrifices being made by the Soldiers everyday over in Iraq. The total came to $66.00, and I asked him if he was sure he wanted to pay for it all, and he said yes!

I asked him for his name and address so I could write him a thank you card and thank him properly for his contribution, but he didn't want to give it to me. He just wanted it to be an anonymous donation. I have a feeling he might have been a Vietnam veteran, but I will never know. Nevertheless, he was just a kind stranger doing what small part he could to help boost the morale of our troops over in Iraq. So thank you, kind stranger.

You touched my heart and renewed my faith in the American people! The families and the Soldiers of our company thank you!

12 November - Faith Sustains Him

I heard from my son, 4ID Band at Tikrit. He received the six-foot tree I sent him for the unit. Said that it made them sad knowing they won't be home for the holidays, but they loved it and were going to make ornaments to hang on it.

We talked a bit, and then he informed me things have gotten a bit tough, but they're hanging in. My son said, "You know Jesus was born for all mankind, Mom, even the people in Iraq, and knowing that will be what gets me through these holidays. That is all about what we are doing as his servants here. If it weren't for my faith, I think it would make it harder on me being here and not at home."

As always, I told him how proud I am of him and all our troops. To do your best give 110 percent and never give up in what you believe. God bless each of them over there and may we all learn from them what it truly means to be an American.

13 November - He's a Vet Now

Yesterday morning did not start out a joyful day for me. I was another year older! But with friends and family giving me their birthday wishes, it did get better. Then I got a call about 1:30 in the afternoon from my son, 223rd ENG BN, Camp Warhorse in Ba'qubah. He said "Happy Birthday," and my day was brighter still. We got to talk for thirty to forty minutes.

He immediately told me that if I heard a loud boom, not to worry. They were firing a tank. He was not sure if they had a target. About that time I heard it. He said that was about the ninth one. He said they were watching a movie when the first one went off. He had his flip flops on, and when it went off, he said, "I just curled my toes and ran!" We had a good laugh.

They had been busy that day moving, cleaning, and taking down some tents. He and others had moved into the trailers. They also had a bad night the day before when a lot of wind came through and blew down some tents. He was excited still about the Ole Miss win over Auburn, stayed up in the early Sunday morning hours to watch it. I told him Happy Veteran's Day, and he said, "Yeah, I guess I'm a vet now." He said they had steak and lobster for supper that night. God bless the ones serving now, and the ones that are no longer with us.

13 November - Father Daughter Bond is Affected

My husband is with HHC, 1-8 IN, and we had a wonderful R&R time together (he went back yesterday). I did want to share that our two-year-old daughter had a very difficult time adjusting to his visit, and it wasn't until the last few days that she was completely at ease with him. I could see that it broke his heart that he was no longer able to comfort her by just picking her up.

The two of us are able to deal with the separation through letters and late night phone calls, but their bond has definitely been affected by this. Just as she got back into the routines with him, he had to leave, and she was up all night crying for her daddy. I can't imagine being in his shoes, coming home as a stranger to his own child.

He came home really skinny, but I managed to send him back with a little more meat on his bones. We had a great time just sitting and talking, although I didn't press him to share stories of his experience.

Saying goodbye was extremely difficult, but it will only be a few months now. I escorted him to the gate by asking for a pass from the ticket agent. I believe you can ask to be there during arrivals as well. Just a few extra moments can mean so much. I'm sure my daughter will be fine, and I will stop crying in a day or so, but he needed the break so badly, and it was great to see him asleep in his easy chair while football was on. So I would definitely say it was well worth it, and I wish everyone could experience a homecoming, no matter how short it may be.

13 November - First Class for This Soldier

Just wanted to let you know that my husband, Company A, 404 ASB, made it back to Camp Speicher on Monday, after having spent his two week R&R with me back here in the states. He called to let me know he made it back safe and sound. He also told me that on his flight from Charlotte to Baltimore, he had a gentleman in first class ask him to exchange seats with him. My husband was floored by the offer, and accepted graciously. He told me he was amazed by how thankful the gentleman was about his serving over in Iraq.

I also want to take this chance to thank that gentleman, whoever he is, for lifting up my husband's spirits. Throughout his visit home, he felt as though no one cared that he was serving over in Iraq, and then out of the blue this man went out of his way to thank him for his service.

14 November - Why We Hope - By Chaplain (CPT) Kenneth Sharpe, HHS 2-20 FA

What does hope do for mankind? Let's answer that question because 'hope' is a powerful word that can change individual lives if not a whole nation.

Hope shines brightest when the hour is darkest.
Hope motivates when discouragement comes.
Hope energizes when the body is tired.
Hope sweetens while bitterness bites.
Hope sings when all melodies are gone.
Hope believes when evidence is eliminated.
Hope listens for answers when no one is talking.
Hope climbs over obstacles when no one is helping.
Hope endures hardship when no one is caring.
Hope smiles confidently when no one is laughing.
Hope reaches for answers when no one is asking.
Hope presses toward victory when no one is encouraging.
Hope dares to give when no one is sharing.
Hope brings the victory when no one is winning.

So, don't lose hope for it is your strength to carry on even when the future is questionable. Americans must hope. Blessings....

14 November - Tacos to Go, Please

Just thought I'd let you know that several times I've been able to talk to my son and asked him what it is he misses in Iraq. His response was "Taco Bell."

Lo and behold, last week I was shopping at the local Wal-Mart, and they now have vacuum packed precooked taco filling located where the vacuum packed tuna is. So I was able to buy him several packages of Taco Bell, soft taco shells in the box with sauce, and I went by Taco Bell and asked for wrappers to send in the box to him. After they heard this, they were very happy to give me several wrappers to send to him so he could have his very own 'Taco Bell' for him and his unit. Just thought your readers may want to know. My son is with 1-12 IN out of Fort Carson. His unit is gonna' love his fast food.

14 November - Others Are Not So Fortunate
Thanksgiving is almost here. Today, I want to take the time to thank you and my fellow readers for the updates I receive. I realize the families in other units do not have the advantage of updates of this caliber. I have a son in a National Guard unit deployed, and there are no regular updates such as these. The historical background, along with the current reports from the media and my fellow Task Force Ironhorse family members makes me all the more proud to be an American and the mother of three American Soldiers. I am thankful to all of the families who write in with hints and tips. I wish you the most blessed Thanksgiving.

Michelle Frye - Mother of CPL Lawrence Frye - 1-67 AR
We are not a religious family. We don't go to church on Sunday, but we believe in living a morally correct life and treating people fairly. But as they always say, "There are no Atheists in foxholes." I have a little prayer that I have said every morning upon waking up since my son has been in Iraq.

"Dear God, Please watch over our son. Give him the strength and courage to face the things that he must face. Wrap your arms around him and guard him and protect him and bring him home safe and sound and sane. Amen."

It was said as much for his safety as it was for my sanity. But in one of his letters he described an incident while on patrol. He was in the back of a Humvee on the machine gun. His vehicle had passed by and the truck behind him had, when an IED blew up the engine. The men in the truck were OK. Shrapnel flew all around him, but nothing hit him. When I read this, I felt such a rush because I knew that he was being watched over and God would keep him safe.

18 November - Bob Babcock
The following note from one of our wives brought this topic home to me. When we have a KIA, our thoughts and prayers go out to the families of the Soldier who was killed. However, I know that

I don't spend enough time focused on those who have been wounded, either from hostile action or from accidents.

Let us not forget that we have many 4ID and TF Ironhorse Soldiers who have been wounded, some with life altering wounds that will be with them always and others who will return to normal with the benefit of time.

In the interest of privacy, DOD does not name the Soldiers who have been wounded, and I won't either. The following is one of many that we want to remember in our daily prayers:

"I just wanted to let you know I received a heartbreaking phone call from my husband, who's with 299 Engineers in Tikrit. The other day, a close friend of his was in a horrific accident in which he was very badly burned all over his body. From what I could understand, there was an explosion in an ammunition bunker as he was driving past, and somehow due to the explosion, he drove his vehicle into the bunker, and then jumped out of it.

"I don't know if you can do this, using his name or whatever, but I was wondering if you can include him on your update so that everyone can pray for this Soldier and his family and friends. My husband heard that he's in really bad shape. He's in Germany now, and he heard they may try to get him to a good burn center in San Antonio soon. Let us all remember our wounded Soldiers in our daily prayers."

18 November - Top 15 Ways We've Spent Our Husband's Combat Pay:

Don't get me wrong, we have definitely gotten good at spending your combat pay, but we couldn't talk about all of those presents we bought for you!

The Top 15:

15. More new furniture (I may need to buy a bigger house for it all soon.)

14. Lots of take out dinners and dinners out!

13. 20/20 vision by Dr. Wright—A girl has to be able to see her husband when he comes home!

12. Packages, packages, packages (but they are all worth it!)

11. Extra activities at school for the kids (cause they are worth every penny, too!)

10. New clothes, shoes and accessories because we don't have enough (and here's the good news: some of them don't fit anymore

because we are getting so much smaller and smaller! Believe it!)

9. Paying off credit card debt—you know, the debt we created right before you left and on the packages we keep sending.

8. Vacation planning for when you come back and we know not to include sand, heat or camels in the trip!!!

7. Cable TV, videos, the movies (although they aren't the same without you) and stocking up on DVDs for your return!

6. Diapers and let me tell you, you have your share to change!

5. Pampered Chef, Longaberger, Creative Memories, Stampin' Up, Tupperware, Party Lite, Mary Kay, Usborne Books—You know, all of those home parties we make you leave the house for!

4. A horse, and of course a saddle and all the other accessories a cowgirl needs.

3. Numerous Elmo videos because mommy needs a break!

2. Starbucks—caffeine we've been on since the day you left

And, the number one place we are spending your extra combat pay at is Victoria's Secret. You know you guys are coming home sooner than later, and it's been a long time!

The Top 15 Presents we would like to send to Iraq:

15. Central air and heat, and of course, indoor plumbing!

14. Snow

13. All of my holiday cheer!

12. A tele-transporter so we can just beam each other back and forth until this is over.

11. Lots of hugs, kisses and love so you can use them for whenever you need them!

10. "A long winter's nap!"

9. A first class ticket out of there!

8. My yummy turkey dinner!

7. A tanning bed—so you can get rid of those horrible tan lines before you come home!

6. A Select Comfort bed with me in it!

5. The kids—I need a break...

4. My mother—like I said, I need a break.

3. Your mother—enough said.

2. Me with a big red bow (no really, just me and a red bow!)

And, the number one present we would like to send to Iraq is PEACE IN THE MIDDLE EAST, so you can all come home!

18 November - Be Patient With Him

Just a few words from a Soldier that was in 3-16 FA at Ba'quabah. I have just returned home and wanted to let everyone know that everything there was pretty good. Good food, good living accommodations, and really good friends. But the best part is when mail comes and a Soldier receives a package or letter from friends or family.

When your Soldier returns home, please be patient since he will be getting up at all hours of the night for some time. I would tell you for how long, but I do not know because I am still going through some changes myself. I know everyone over there would like to call more, but the phone situation is frustrating. When you do get through after waiting in line and repeated dialing, the connection is often filled with static. Soldiers have learned to deal with it just to hear the voice of the ones they love.

Every Soldier there really appreciates the love and support that has been given during this deployment.

Thank you all very much.

19 November - Land of the Free

I experienced the most wonderful two weeks of my life followed by the hardest two days of my life. My husband left Saturday afternoon after his mid-tour leave. He got to meet our two-month-old daughter and actually arrived the night before our son's second birthday. The two weeks we spent together was time that we will never forget. I thank all those who have made this possible and God bless you.

As expected and warned by all, saying goodbye the second time was no easier than the first. It was harder the second time, to be quite honest. I was strong for my Soldier, who no more wanted to leave than I wanted him to leave, but he knows what he has to do and believes in it. I broke down by the end; I am only human and I love that man with everything that I have.

Holding his two babies, I watched him board the first plane on his journey back to fight the war. I listened to a two-year-old boy cry out for his daddy and tried to hold him as he ran from window to window crying out and watching his daddy leave on that plane. Looking at our infant daughter in my arms, I realized once again he will come home to a new family.

I wish that all of the American people could see what their

military men and women sacrifice in order to keep a country's freedom, a country that seems to have forgotten that freedom does not come free. It is a 'Land of the Free, Because of the Brave.'

I love my husband and I want him home with our children, but if he and all the men serving with him aren't willing to fight for us, then who would? God bless our troops and all who support them.

Families need huge thanks. God bless each and every wife, raising our children alone, spending countless sleepless nights wondering if we'll be doing this alone for the rest of our lives, hearts pounding at the knock on the door of any unexpected visitors, living life without the man we are supposed to wake up next to every morning and share in raising our children with. Keep strong, God bless, and thank you.

Renee TenEyck - Wife of SFC Christopher TenEyck 4 EN BN 3rd BCT

Here's the editorial I sent to several papers and other sources. I get through the deployment because I believe in what we're doing there.

What can we do to counter a media that claims to operate in the best interest of America, but clearly cannot stand one of the most essential elements of American society?

I was fortunate to be invited to attend the Fort Carson Town Hall Meeting, which was hosted and facilitated by Secretary of Defense Rumsfeld on October 8th, 2003. Defense Secretary Rumsfeld spoke off the cuff, answering questions, and even though he did not have specific answers to all questions, he tried to shed light on the factors affecting a particular issue. He was humorous and sincere, and most everyone left feeling positive.

I found, within hours of the meeting, an Associated Press (AP) article, which completely misrepresented what was communicated that day. When I asked what checks are in place to ensure that what reporters write truly represents what was communicated, a man at the Denver bureau of the AP stated that reporters are "on their honor" and assumed by their superiors to be writing ethical and actual representations of the facts. In other words, much of what we are seeing in the media today is based on the perception and opinion, and, probably the mood of the writer. Unfortunately, many news sources use AP reports.

Amazing things are happening in Iraq: schools, hospitals, clinics, EMS systems, and representative government operations have improved a hundredfold since Coalition Forces entered Iraq. The 1-12 Infantry Battalion under the 4th Infantry Division has renovated more than 100 schools. The media is quick to persecute the military and this administration for its flaws, but refuses to acknowledge our incredible accomplishments. Does this profession not have a code of ethics?

I have become painfully aware that many media writers (no names, but the vast majority that bother me are associated with AP) not only misconstrue and misrepresent what is communicated by politicians, military figures, military families, and service members, but they are also focusing only on the negative: the poor families and poor Soldiers, and the negative aspects of the situation.

These writers completely ignore the fact that military families are among the strongest in this nation. I am a Soldier, a mother, an army wife, and a Family Readiness Group leader. I try to focus on the positive aspects of being a military family. Our Soldiers are warriors. They are knights. They accept the sacrifices and dangers that accompany their membership in this dynamic institution. The families accept this as well. This is a time of renewal for Iraq, and renewal does not come without conflict in any nation. Our mission there is critical. Does that logic mean I do not feel the sacrifice? Absolutely not. But I will not subscribe to, nor will I propagate the negative, melancholy and depressive attitude these media writers force on Americans. Things are not totally bad. The media should be the tool to uplift and inspire the American people and its military through this time of separation. Where are the reports of our accomplishments? Several government figures have gone to see for themselves all that has become realized in Iraq. Representative Bob Beauprez (R-CO) stated in November that "...it is amazing what some American ingenuity can do to improve a neglected nation..." a nation where "evidence has proven that Saddam funded his madness and excess while perpetrating economic and cultural terrorism on his own people and nation."

Defense Secretary Rumsfeld quoted a Soldier in an editorial in September: "We rebuild a lot of bridges and it's not news, but one bridge gets blown up and it's a front-page story." Secretary

Rumsfeld further stated, "Their [Coalition Forces] successes deserve to be told.

Representative Jim Marshall (D-GA) said "But there will be more Blumbergs killed in action, many more. So it is worth doing only if we have a reasonable chance of success. And we do, but I'm afraid the news media are hurting our chances. They are dwelling upon the mistakes, the ambushes, the Soldiers killed, the wounded, the Blumbergs. Fair enough. But it is not balancing the bad news with the 'rest of the story,' the progress made daily, the good news. The falsely bleak picture weakens our national resolve, discourages Iraqi cooperation, and emboldens our enemy."

In a letter to his church, a 4th Infantry Division major said, "The United States and our allies, especially Great Britain, are doing a very noble thing here. We stuck our necks out on the world's chopping block to free an entire people from the grip of a horrible terror that was beyond belief. This country was one big conventional weapons ammo dump anyway. We have probably destroyed more weapons and ammo in the last 30 days than the U.S. Army has ever fired in the last 30 years (remember, this is a country the size of Texas), so drop the WMD argument as the reason we came here."

Where are the human-interest stories? Where are the stories of inspiring personal interactions between service members and Iraqi citizens? They are out there. Service members constantly communicate home, telling of small, seemingly insignificant interactions they have experienced. Let it be known: Our warriors will be remembered for generations to come in Iraq. Our warriors have influenced and affected Iraqi citizens in ways the rest of us will never comprehend. Just ask a Dachau survivor how he feels about his liberator.

As a Soldier and an army spouse, I know that deployments depend on the mission, not on whether it is convenient for my knight to be gone. In a commentary published by the Army News Service, Beau Whittington stated, "Reporters find it easier to sell fear than to build hope through actions."

I challenge reporters to find ways to support our military by gathering and presenting all the facts, rather than just those that suit the concept you would prefer to broadcast. I further challenge media editors and supervisors to hold your writers ethically accountable, to factually represent all aspects of a given situation.

Honor those who serve their country and their families. The sacrifice and separation would be a lot easier if our warriors and families were not surrounded by the paradox of evil and profit.

19 November - What is Truly Important

I heard from my husband a few days ago. He is with C Battery, 4-42 FA near Tikrit. When he left last March, our daughter was just four months old. He is really concerned that she won't know who he is when he comes back home. I put together a little 'Daddy photo album' for her. She looks at it constantly and smiles and says, "Dada" but I could never get her to say it when he was on the phone.

I've even tried taping her, but you know how they never do what you want them to when you want them to do it! She had her first birthday last week, and my husband was really sorry that he wasn't here for the big day. But when he called on Saturday, she gave him a great gift; he got to hear her say, "Dada" for the first time! When I got back on the phone with him to ask if he'd heard her, I could tell he was a bit choked up. It almost made me cry knowing how much that meant to him! Then our five year old son got on the phone with him and offered to come to Iraq to help them find and defeat "the evil Saddam," so that Daddy could come home. He is always great for some comic relief!

I think this deployment has changed most of our opinions about what is truly important in our lives. It has definitely put a lot of things into perspective! I thank God everyday that He has kept my husband safe from harm. And I can't wait for the day when he gets to come home and to see the look in his eyes when he gets to hear his little girl say, "Dada" in person for the first time. Then he'll wind up on the floor wrestling around with our son and playing all of their special games together. Those are the little things that life is all about!

20 November - Can't Wait for Christmas

Thank you, Bob, for the updates. Today's just made me cry reading all the letters from the families. My son called us several times this past week; seems he is on the range, and has access to a phone. He says he is sleeping in a shack in his sleeping bag, different from the palace accommodations; also he sounded very cold.

His dad told him to go and put on something warm; well, the next time he called he had his winter wear on. I asked him where he was having Thanksgiving Dinner. He said out of his truck and most likely Christmas would be the same. But he was okay when he said this to us. I told him we sent off his presents and that he had to wait until Christmas to open them, but his dad stepped in and said, "No, he does not have to wait!!" And of course, he said: "I wasn't going to wait anyway, Mom."

Anyway, he says he is on the range with about twenty troops and that they would be there for about three weeks. His last words on the phone were, "Keep the cookies coming!"

20 November - Thanks to All Veterans

My son is in the 173rd ABN BDE assigned to 4ID Headquarters. I hear from him more than most (for which I'm truly thankful), and my heart goes out to those who don't (the worry doesn't change). I was in the post office mailing packages to three Soldiers, and one gentleman stopped by and said to tell my son that another veteran captain from the 4ID said to keep up the good work. The way he said it clearly gave me the impression that he was in the Vietnam War. It sort of startled me, but I thanked him kindly and went about my business.

In a flash it hit me. I have had my blinders on thinking about my son being at war and what was happening in Iraq, and not giving the credit to all veterans for their contribution to our freedom. His mother must've been praying daily, as I do for my son, for him to come home safely. Before he left, I made sure I thanked him for his service to our country. A lesson learned.

My son says they are doing a lot of good that is never written about in the newspapers, but they know it, and the people of Iraq know it. He says he's gotten mail, packages and e-mail from friends of friends and strangers and wanted me to let everyone know how much they appreciate the support from home.

21 November - What Kind of Men Are These?

I am the mom of a Delta 2-20 FA Soldier. I want to share a story from our battery. Like the rest of the batteries in Iraq, Delta has its share of new dads who haven't seen baby sons and daughters who were born after they deployed. Last week at our monthly FRG meeting, we met one of those new dads who was home on mid-tour leave, holding his child in his arms. He stood and asked if there were any family members of two other Soldiers who are still in Iraq, and one mom identified herself. The SGT looked her in the face and thanked her for the sacrifice her son made because he had given his mid-tour leave slot to the SGT to come home and see his wife and new baby. Giving away his week of leave was a sacrifice, but that was not the whole story.

During the week that Soldier would have been home if he had not given his leave away, he was in a Humvee convoy that was ambushed. Not only was he injured in the explosion of an RPG, but he is also credited with helping save the life of another Delta Soldier who was badly injured in the blast as he immediately jumped out to where the injured Soldier lay in the sand and applied compression bandages to his wounds.

What kind of man would do such things? There is a name for it, and the name is US Army Soldier. We have a lot of heroes in Delta battery. We have those who serve day after day in dangerous conditions; those who have been wounded in action; those who have risked their own safety in protection or defense of their fellow Soldiers, and those who will return their new babies to their mamas' arms and board a flight back into harm's way in defense of freedom. God speed to each and every Soldier of the 4th ID serving in the war against terrorism.

23 November - She Shares Her Happiness

I just wanted to share my good news. My husband is with HHC 104th MI BN from Fort Hood, Texas. My husband had just got back from a year tour in Korea in February when we moved to Texas. He left for Iraq right after getting there. That was hard at first, but I know that is his job, so I adjusted to it quickly. It was especially hard after finding out this would also be a year tour, which meant we would be apart two years in all. He was told that he would most likely not be able to take the two weeks R and R because he went to Qatar for four days.

Then things were changed, and they said that did not matter; since he was in Korea, he ended up being able to be one of the first ones home. He called and told me that he would be home October 15 for two weeks. Well, that was a big surprise to me; I was adjusting to him not coming home until April.

All went well while he was home. Things were really great.

Ladies of the Ironhorse

In fact, I just got news that he left me a great surprise when he left. We are now expecting baby number four. We have three boys already, so I hope this is a girl. The funny thing is that we have a Bosnia surprise already, and now we have an Iraqi surprise. I just wanted to share my happiness.

23 November - A father writes from Kenya

My son, 'Kenya' is serving somewhere in the Sunni Triangle with the 1-66 AR BN. I am working in the middle of a tribal African game reserve in the remotest part of Kenya, East Africa. There is no phone, post, telegram or Internet service between here and anywhere, just a solitary HF radio link by which I can send very slow 'radio e-mails' and occasionally, text messages by mobile phone, depending on conditions.

Things are tough and tense for all our troops in Iraq, and the 4th ID is in the worst part of it. I wish to send my best to all parents of US service members and especially our infantry and armor, the pride and spear of the Army. Most of all to the 4th ID, 1-66 AR BN and to anyone who knows my son, I send thoughts, best wishes and prayers.

It is odd being so utterly remote from communications, though we do have a satellite TV down here. So, the bad news gets through, and until I joined this site, little of the good.

How does someone from Kenya end up fighting in Iraq? My son is a US citizen, born and brought up in Kenya, and fluent in Swahili and English. As you know, Kenya suffered devastating Al Qaeda attacks in 1998, with the equivalent (adjusted for US size of population) of 2500 killed and 50,000 wounded in a single attack, had it been in a country the size of the USA. As it was, 250 killed and 5000 wounded in one attack was bad enough. There have been some other attacks. These made a deep impression on my son at the time.

He decided, after 9/11, and as he was now old enough, to join up even though he had spent very little actual time in the USA and was schooled entirely abroad. He always felt a pull for the USA. As a Dad, I was surprised he would really jump in the deep end and enlist. He is probably one of the very few Soldiers in the US Army without a US home address or relatives apart from cousins he had met once! But he did, and he passed basic. He spent quite some time among wild animals on safari, and we hope

204

his bush skills will help in keeping safe. The Swahili that he speaks has many Arabic words in it, though one doubts he has time to learn more, with all the action.

His mother is British, and so it is a joyful thing that Britain has so strongly supported the USA in Operation Iraqi Freedom. The Prime Minister of Britain has a crystal clear vision of the new threats to democracy and we must always be grateful for the British war effort and the Churchillian courage of Tony Blair.

Well, this little posting is not to boast, because every single Soldier in the struggle in Iraq is a unique person who has made sacrifices: Every story is interesting and different. It's perhaps a little off the regular, and mums will forgive me for a 'Dad's story.'

I have not spoken to my son for nine months, but I get regular letters from Iraq, except it seems he can't buy US postage stamps, and they are hard to come by. I would have thought combat Soldiers in a fighting Army should be handed out stamps or pre-stamped envelopes like bubble-gum, free. I'd like to send him some phone cards, but what kinds work in Iraq and are best, can anyone post some ideas? (AT&T seems to always work.)

Being a parent, mother or father, is nerve wracking at a time like this. I can't express my feelings for those who have lost Soldiers to fatalities or even casualties of wounds. The words won't come out, because we all know the shudder when the TV announces another casualty in Iraq, and the dread of the area or town being one a son or daughter is in. Sympathy would have to be as deep as an ocean to express my thoughts sometimes.

The 4th ID may have many other interesting backgrounds and even nationalities who have come to join up. Tonight a fierce tropical storm rages around me, in this remote and beautiful part of Africa, inhabited by proud Maasai tribesmen with spears and not a few lions. I also know Iraq is temporarily inhabited by proud warriors from the Ironhorse tribe with guns, and, they are all lions.

25 November - Soldier Praises His Wife

Hello, it is 10:30 at night and I can't sleep. I really miss you so very much. Not a day goes by that I am not thinking of you and how wonderful you are. I can't wait for this to be over and then I can return home to you. I am careful every day to ensure my safety and that of my Soldiers so we can all go home to what is truly important—our families.

It is with your support and caring nature that I am able to do what I do; yet I am the one who gets the awards and medals, when they should go to you. You have the hardest job in the Army, and I want you to know that I realize all that you do and go through every day, and I am forever thankful and grateful to you for all that you do. If I haven't said it enough, let me say now I appreciate everything you do. I know these are difficult times, yet you continue on being the best wife and making it all seem easy.

When I get home, I want to pamper you and give you some time off so you can relax and go to a spa or whatever. I will take care of the house for you and you can get a break. Just as you have made my life better since I have been here, I want to do the same for you. I love you.

26 November - Unusual Thanks
This is an e-mail from a 588th Engineer Battalion Soldier to his family, written the day before Thanksgiving:

I spent my time today wondering about Thanksgiving, and I have come to the conclusion that this will be both my first true Thanksgiving and not a Thanksgiving at all but simply Thursday. First, I am truly thankful this year. I have been able to think of things to be thankful for in the past, but this year it is literally all around me.

I am thankful that a car bomb attack on the local police station is a shock and horror for me.

I am thankful that all of the attacks and security precautions are not just part of my hometown.

I am thankful that when all of this is over that I will be able to go home. I wish that these people could know a fraction of the security and freedom we have and take for granted.

I wish the kids will never have to worry about getting shot in a street fight, or worry about going home to a bombed out building.

In other ways tomorrow will just be Thursday. The difference between tomorrow and a week from tomorrow will be that tomorrow I will be serving a slightly better meal to my Soldiers. Other than that, we will still be running our missions and doing the same job we have been doing for the last two hundred thirty-four days.

Have a great day, I will be thinking about all of you. Take pictures, I will.

26 November - Thank You Mr. President

I was one of the fortunate ones to be able to go and to listen to President Bush speak yesterday at Ft. Carson. It was really a great thing to see the leader of our country concerned with how we, the military families, are doing. He expressed gratitude to us all and commended us on a job well done. Of course he can't bring our Soldiers home right now, but he does appreciate all that they do for us. He came at a time when our post has been suffering from so many casualties that it was like a shot in the arm for us. It uplifted our spirits and gave us something to hope for. Thank you, Mr. President!

26 November - Thanksgiving Message from MG Raymond Odierno

I would like to extend a Happy Thanksgiving to all of our great Soldiers, and your families and loved ones at home. Today we celebrate America's founders who fled religious persecution to establish a nation where all people could worship freely. As we are thankful for our many blessings, Iraqis are also thankful today that we successfully liberated them and they are able to worship and celebrate freely. Years from now, when we reflect back on this Thanksgiving, we will remember celebrating this great American tradition in a country that is just beginning to develop some of the freedoms we enjoy. Every Soldier in Task Force Ironhorse should be proud of their tremendous contribution to Operation Iraqi Freedom and the positive impact they are having on this nation and this part of the world.

We give thanks today for the tremendous support we receive daily from our families and friends across the United States and the world. We would rather be with them enjoying our own unique family traditions today, but we understand our mission and will see it through. As you celebrate Thanksgiving, I ask you to consider three things: First, remember those who have given their lives for their country and their families. Next, reflect upon the freedom we cherish and the liberty we enjoy; this is what all nations strive to achieve. Finally, and most importantly, think about the vital role you are playing to ensure this country never returns to the horribly cruel dictatorship of the past.

America is saying a thankful prayer today for all the Soldiers, sailors, airmen, and marines placing their lives in harm's way. Our nation's resolve and your uncommon sacrifice are the pillars for our way of life and the principles we hold so dear as a civil society. Along with our nation's gratitude, you have my personal appreciation for your courage, dedication, and hard work. Happy Thanksgiving, and God bless you and your families.
Steadfast and Loyal,
Raymond T. Odierno
MG, Commanding

Submitted by Linda Odierno - Wife of MG Raymond Odierno - Commanding General

A Thanksgiving poem by Linda Ellis:
Who Will Carve the Turkey?

My daddy has always carved the turkey
As far back as I can remember,
For it's his very favorite job
That happens each November.
He stands at the head of our table
With his freshly-sharpened knives
And leads us in a prayer of thanks
For the blessings in our lives.
He cuts each piece with loving care
So nice...and neat...and straight
And puts everybody's favorite part
Upon each empty plate.
And each year he asks my mom to make
Her special Mac 'n cheese,
But I don't think she'll make it this year...
'Cause my dad is overseas.
She told me he can't make it home
And secretly wiped away a tear
And I wondered, who would carve the turkey
Like he does so well each year?
I told her not to worry
Because I'd watched his steady hand

And if I were to cut the turkey this year,
I just know he'd understand.
As he hugged me before he left he said,
It's MY freedom, he'll fight to preserve
Because he loves me AND this country
That he's so very proud to serve.
Then he handed me an American Flag
Just about ten inches tall,
Which now hangs right above my bed
'Cause I pinned it to the wall.
"My dad is away protecting my future,"
As I slice the turkey, I will brag
And at the head of the table, in his seat,
I will place that American Flag.
And when I put upon his empty plate,
His favorite slice of turkey breast,
I'll thank God for my dad AND my country
Because they're both the best.

28 November - A Soldier Reflects on Thanksgiving

It is the day after Thanksgiving here in Iraq, and I have time to reflect on yesterday. Many would wonder what I as a Soldier have to be thankful for. True, the separation from my wife and two beautiful daughters is rough, but it is something I chose to do a little over eleven years ago. You see I am thankful that I can be a part of something bigger than myself, that I can volunteer to ensure that a terrorist, who believes his ideology should be violently imposed on all peoples around the world, will never see his goal. I am thankful that I was given the opportunity to raise my right hand and pledge my life in my nation's defense.

I am very thankful that I have a wife and children that support what I do. They have endured having their lives uprooted, shook up and interrupted. They watch the news with dread hoping not to see any negative news from my corner of the world. Yet they never waver in their commitment to me. My Wife and my children are my heroes, and I am thankful beyond everything else for their support.

I am thankful for the Soldiers around me, going through the same thing I am going through. I feel a kinship with my fellow Soldiers here and feel a responsibility to them. I honestly feel that I did spend my Thanksgiving with a large part of my family, here in Iraq. Over the past eight months we have developed a bond that can never really be explained to someone that hasn't been through what we have been through. We have been through many attacks, many problems, some tragedies, and many victories together. Through it all we have stood side by side, ready to give our lives in each other's defense.

Regardless of what I hear on the news, regardless of the political spin put on the everyday occurrences here, I am convinced we have done the right thing. I have seen the opulent palaces Saddam constructed while his people suffered. I have seen the effects of Saddam skimming funds off the top of the Oil for Food Program and thirty-five years of abuse the people of Iraq endured. I am more convinced now that we did the right thing.

You see I chose this life over eleven years ago. I had the freedom to decide if I wanted to commit to this life, I have had many chances to enter civilian life, but I chose to remain. I feel that I am part of something more important than myself, something that needs to be done and I believe that if I don't do it, then who will.

Recently I participated in the Rest and Recuperation leave program that is being offered to as many troops as possible over here. While I was home, I was exposed to very little positive press reporting from Iraq, there were no stories of the advances we have made rebuilding schools, reestablishing the electrical system, and bringing water plants back to life so they treat more water than before the war. I grew so frustrated with the news reports that my wife actually banned me from watching the news.

A few days before Thanksgiving, Fox news sent a crew up here that included LTC Oliver North. He reported on some positive advances we have made here and that was refreshing. He was here when we first deployed and found the advances we had made in this corner of Iraq truly a success story. LTC North was here as we were invited to share in three days of traditional feasts called Eid-Al-Fitr with our Iraqi friends at the end of Ramadan. If the Iraqis opposed us being here, they never would have invited us to participate with them in Eid-Al-Fitr.

Yes, a few terrorists who believe they can bring a defunct regime back to power still attack us. These terrorists have everything to lose now that Saddam isn't in power. They will not win; they will only sacrifice their lives for no reason. Saddam's regime is dead and gone, blown away by the wind. I have been told by several Iraqis that Saddam will never return, that if they ever saw him, they would kill him themselves for what he had done to their nation and denied them for so long.

You see, it is hard to explain why we choose to be Soldiers; we know that at anytime we could be faced with life or death situations, we know the risks, we were not drafted into service, we chose this mantel of responsibility freely. I am proud to be a Soldier in Iraq. I am proud to serve my nation, earn my battle stripes defending my nation, and ensure the freedom we enjoy with my life. I could have followed a different path; those of you that knew me in high school remember a longhaired kid that really expressed no interest in the military. In fact I was probably believed to be the least likely to join the military.

I am thankful for so many things, some of them here in this letter, some of them deep within my heart. I hope you can understand now that I am thankful for every experience, every problem I have encountered, and every freedom that we enjoy. I am thankful I have been given the opportunity to represent my country, and ensure that you have the freedom you deserve. I hope this sheds some light on why, even through this holiday season, I am not depressed, and I do not feel like I am in the wrong place. I know that this is where I need to be, to do my duty.

Remember us in your prayers, remember that we are out here, but also remember that this is the life we chose. We will be home soon.

Task Force Ironhorse - November 2003 Casualties

PFC Rayshawn S. Johnson, 20, of Brooklyn, New York, was killed on November 3, 2003, in Tikrit, Iraq. PFC Johnson was on patrol when his vehicle hit a landmine. The Soldier died as a result of his injuries. PFC Johnson was assigned to Company C, 299th Engineer Battalion, 4th Infantry Division (Mech), based in Fort Hood, Texas.

SPC Genaro Acosta, 26, of Fair Oaks, California, was killed on November 11 in Taji, Iraq. SPC Acosta was on patrol when his Bradley vehicle hit and detonated two improvised explosive devices. SPC Acosta died of his injuries. He was assigned to 1st Battalion, 44th Air Defense Artillery Regiment, 4th Infantry Division (Mech), Fort Hood, Texas.

PFC Jacob S. Fletcher, 28, of Bay Shore, New York, was killed on November 13 in Samara, Iraq. PFC Fletcher was riding on a bus when an improvised explosive device exploded. PFC Fletcher died of his injuries. He was assigned to Company C, 2nd Battalion (Airborne), 503rd Infantry Regiment, 173rd Airborne Brigade, Camp Ederle, Italy (part of Task Force Ironhorse).

SGT Joseph Minucci, II, 23, was killed by an improvised explosive device on 13 November in Samara, Iraq. SGT Minucci was assigned to Company C, 2nd Battalion (Airborne) 503rd Infantry Regiment

CWO Alexander S. Coulter, 35, of Tennessee, was killed on November 17 in Baqubah, Iraq. CWO Coulter was in a convoy traveling to Tikrit when his vehicle ran over an improvised explosive device. CWO Coulter died of his injuries. He was assigned to Headquarters and Headquarters Company, 124th Signal Battalion, 4th Infantry Division (Mech), Fort Hood, Texas.

Mr. Brent A. McJennett, 40, was killed on 17 November in Iraq. Mr. McJennett was an employee of Proactive Communication Inc., and assigned to Task Force Ironhorse.

SSG Dale A. Panchot, 26, of Northome, Minnesota, was killed on November 17 south of Balad, Iraq. SSG Panchot was on patrol when he was fatally injured by enemy fire. SSG Panchot was assigned to B Company, 1st Battalion, 8th Infantry Regiment, 3rd Brigade Combat Team, 4th Infantry Division (Mech), Fort Carson, Colorado.

PVT Scott M. Tyrrell, 21, of Sterling, Illinois, died on November 20 at Brook Army Medical Center, in San Antonio, Texas, of wounds received on Nov. 14 in Tikrit, Iraq. PVT Tyrrell was at an ammunition point when it caught on fire. PVT Tyrrell was assigned to C Company, 299th Engineer Battalion, 4th Infantry Division (Mech), based in Fort Hood, Texas.

CPT George A. Wood, 33, of New York, New York, was killed on November 20 in Baqubah, Iraq. CPT Wood was on patrol when his tank rolled over an improvised explosive device. CPT Wood was assigned to B Company, 1st Battalion, 67th Armor Regiment, 2nd Brigade, 4th Infantry Division (Mech), based in Fort Hood, Texas.

CPL Gary B. Coleman, 24, of Pikeville, Kentucky, was killed on November 21 in Balad, Iraq. CPL Coleman was on patrol when the vehicle he was driving flipped over into a canal trapping him inside the vehicle. CPL Coleman was assigned to B Company, 1st Battalion, 68th Armored Regiment, 3rd Brigade, 4th Infantry Division (Mech), based in Fort Carson, Colorado.

SSG Eddie E. Menyweather, 35, of Los Angeles, California, was killed on November 23 in Baqubah, Iraq. SSG Menyweather died of his injuries after an improvised explosive device hit his vehicle. SSG Menyweather was assigned to Company C, 588th Engineer Battalion, 4th Infantry Division (Mech), based in Fort Hood, Texas.

CPT Carl J. and Latorial Faison and Children

Sammi Thompson, Daughter of SSG Patrick Thompson

NINE

DECEMBER - 2003
Christmas and The Capture of Saddam

121 days and a wake-up until April 1, 2004...

When December began we were busy preparing for Christmas. We sent packages, put up trees, and tried to decide how to celebrate our holiday without our Soldiers. But Sunday, December 14th, the message came through—WE GOT HIM!

Many of us have our 'Where were you when they got Saddam stories?' We were proud jubilant, and let's face it, we thought that the 4th Infantry Division and Task Force Ironhorse was the best division in the army; they are not—they are just a part of the best military in the world working as a team, but for us families this was our Rocky-Balboa-on the-steps-moment. We had turned the corner in the war.

The operation was named Red Dawn. Once they found Saddam in his hole, he was whisked off within the hour, but we knew that this was an important part of the Iraqi War for Freedom, and our children and grandchildren would read about Sadaam's capture in their history books. Later that month *Time Magazine* named The American Soldier person of the year. We were reading reports of spontaneous acts of kindness shown to our Soldiers as they traveled home for mid-tour leave. The people of our country not only remembered our Soldiers, they honored them for what they were doing.

Through the highs and lows of December our families rose to the challenge. And that countdown to April 1st dropped from three digits to two.

1 December - Bob Babcock

To the best of my knowledge, we only have one Vietnam era 4ID veteran currently serving in uniform in a combat zone. The following note from a colonel in the Rhode Island National Guard shows the pride that still exists in our two-war Soldiers. Though not serving now in the 4ID, he is very proud of his 4ID combat patch and is representing us well in Afghanistan:

"Bob, Happy Thanksgiving to you also. I will be celebrating here in Kabul, Afghanistan, with my new friends and comrades. The last time I celebrated Thanksgiving in a foreign country was in the hospital with malaria in Cam Rahn Bay, Vietnam, in 1969. I thought what we were doing then was right, and I feel the same way this time. Danger here is not as constant or intense as Vietnam or Iraq, but it is still there to remind you once in a while. Like the rocket attack on the hotel downtown the other night or the shooting of several demonstrators a few blocks away.

"I always wear my vest when out of the compound and carry my 9mm all the time, even in the compound. I really miss the family and friends, but I feel it is worth the short time investment I will put in here. Once a grunt always a grunt, as they told me at Benning thirty-four years ago. I am still trying to set the example.

"Some folks seeing my 4ID right shoulder patch thought I had just come from Iraq. Guess it's hard to believe some of us old timers are still around. I am proud to wear the patch again. Will keep in touch, more from this front later."

1 December - President Pays Tribute

From a family member of an HHC, 1-67 AR Soldier

God bless President Bush! I am so impressed with his surprise visit to the troops in Baghdad to carry the message of our support and thanks for the job they are doing. No matter what your political affiliation, you must admit it was a very heroic act on his part. Hope everyone enjoyed their holiday and all our guys and girls got some turkey!

2 December - 520 Pounds of Christmas

In a conversation with my son (555 14th EN BN from Fort Lewis) last month he relayed the concern that many Soldiers were apprehensive about the upcoming holidays. He said some don't receive much from home and that the holidays would be especially hard on them. This sparked an idea in the hearts of a local ABWA (American Business Women's Association) group, and we went into action based on the list in your updates. Along with other community supporters we sent lots of holiday cheer to my son's unit and other local Pocatello, Idaho Soldiers in six locations.

The amount of supplies and gifts donated were amazing; soaps and lotions from hotels, razors, batteries, socks, candy canes, beef jerky, Powerade, sunflower seeds, pillows, etc. along with four artificial trees complete with decorations for them all. Letters and cards were sent from local elementary schools and a note from our group wishing them all a speedy journey home in the new year. Packages were stuffed into large holiday burlap bags that resembled potato bags, straight from Idaho. My son thinks we'll be sending a few extra boxes and will be very surprised when over twenty-seven show up!

After it was all boxed and taken to the USPS, even I was stunned: five hundred twenty pounds of goodies, and it's all on its way! Thanks for the suggestion list and of course the Soldier's updates. Happy Holidays to everyone, we're especially thankful this year for our own angel, Bob Babcock. From a proud and hopeful Mom! Stay safe, work together to get through the holidays and hurry back, 4th ID!

5 December - Sights are Breathtaking

We finally got an e-mail from our son who is a medic in the 1-10 CAV, 4ID. They are outside the Tikrit area, and he said they have been busy running raids. He said he has seen more things than he cares to talk about. But on the good side, he said there were three things that were absolutely beautiful over there. He had gone into Tikrit to one of the palaces where the headquarters is, and looking out from the palace window over the Tigris, he said was absolutely breathtaking.

Another is the sunrises and the sunsets. The last and most phenomenal are the stars at night. Because there are no big city lights to dilute the darkness, he said the stars "twinkle and sing" from one horizon to the other. He said he had no idea they were that bright. It has caused me to stop and think, and to be grateful for the beauty of the creation God has given us and to be thankful, yet another day, for the safety of all of our Soldiers.

8 December - Old Glory Stands Tall

My son (3-29 FA Charlie BTRY) is currently near Samarra where some of the recent conflicts have occurred. I have gotten some e-mail and one call from him this past week. He received a box I mailed within two weeks. He sounds very positive and getting into the Christmas spirit. He even asked me to send some Christmas music so they could sing Christmas songs. Also I received a newsletter yesterday that he had dated November 10.

He described a storm that had occurred there with strong winds that were blowing some of their tents down. He described some of the effects of the wind and included some pictures of their area after the storm. He ended, however, with this, which I want to share with everyone: "But if you look close, you can see something that didn't fall during the storm, the American flag. Coincidence? Luck? Not to me. It was truly amazing to see it still standing there this morning amidst the destruction. It gave me hope that we really are doing the right thing here and despite the storms, we won't fall." Of course I was crying after reading this. God bless all our troops and keep them safe.

8 December - Selfless Service

I have been so blessed because my husband (Alpha Co, 1-22 IN is in a different location in Iraq now and has better access to the phones. I have been getting a phone call every other day, and we get to talk as long as we want. Yesterday when he called, I was telling him how one of the new guys who is running for president said that if we vote for him he will bring all the troops home. My husband told me that would be the wrong thing to do. He said the Iraqi people need us, and we can't just leave them. That no matter what we hear on TV that we are making a difference, and yes, some of them don't want us there, but a lot do.

He said he sees women and children walking the streets now, and schools and businesses going up. He said he met a man that thanked him for being there because when Saddam was there, he got caught drunk and for punishment they cut his right arm off.

My husband said we cannot be selfish, and even though he does want to come home, he knows he is needed elsewhere. I am so proud of him! He is across the world and missing all the holidays and will miss the birth of our first child, and he is thinking of someone else! What a man!

9 December - Humpin' and Whoopin' Aggie Fan

My brother, who is with HHB 3-29FA, is on his way back to Samarra after being home for his two week mid-tour leave. When he arrived here in Houston, we had about seventeen family members at the airport with signs and flags to meet him. As he walked into the terminal wearing his fatigues, I watched my Mom and Dad well up with pride and joy. There were three other Soldiers coming off the plane too, and we shook their hands as well. In the time he spent at home, we went to the Texas A&M game, and even though they lost, he had the best time "humpin'" it and "whooping" with all the other Aggies.

We then went to the University of Houston game the next day, and the cheerleaders walked up in the stadium and brought him down on the field! He wore his desert fatigues, so it was obvious he was home on leave. What a blast he had, and what a great Thanksgiving it was for all of us to have him home. I will say that it was just as difficult to watch him go back again, maybe even a little harder this time, but we're grateful for his visit.

10 December - A Traveler Meets America's Finest

Yesterday I was sitting on the second-tier floor at the Denver airport awaiting a return flight to Houston. Below me on the ticketing floor was a young woman standing near the exit from whence passengers from newly arrived aircraft could finally meet their loved ones. She wore a T-Shirt emblazoned with 'I love my Soldier boy.' She was a girl with the wholesomeness of mid-America that some of us remember. She stood there patiently for some time until finally arriving passengers streamed through. And then a smile brightened her face, and she ran with absolute abandon into the arms of a skinny kid wearing desert BDUs. They hugged, and they kissed, oblivious to everything, and I am sure that I was not the only person there with a constricted throat and moist eyes.

Eventually, they pulled away from each other and walked hand-in-hand toward the exits. And then a middle-aged woman approached them. She put her arms around the young Soldier and hugged him for extended moments, and then stood back to look at him. Then she turned to the young woman and shook her hand, and then walked away. I had thought she was the mother of one of these fine young people. She was, in fact, a member of a grateful country welcoming a Soldier home with extreme gratitude. I kicked myself for not having extended my own thanks. Then again, I was on an upper-floor with no ability to get to them before they would disappear into the netherlands of the Denver airport. Shortly thereafter, I saw more Soldiers in BDUs, including what appeared to be a proud father holding the hand of an equally proud toddler, striding together through an admiring throng.

Finally, my own plane arrived, and I made my journey to Houston. Once there, I rushed to my final flight from George Bush Intercontinental to Ellington Field. I had only five minutes to spare. And then I saw another young Soldier. He was alone, and dressed in battle-gear. And I remembered the woman in Denver and her wonderful gesture. And so I walked up to the young Soldier. He was a friendly buck-sergeant, and I thanked him for his service and dedication to our country. He was married, and had two kids waiting for him in Baton Rouge when his own flight arrived there. He had been in Iraq through the entire battle, and then in Baghdad. He had received OSOT packages including the neck-cooler, and said they were much appreciated. He said to tell anyone who would listen that he was proud to have been there, that the mission was being accomplished, that the news on the ground was not what was being reported in the press, and that, as badly as he missed his family, he was ready to go back and do his duty—just before Christmas. To paraphrase someone famous, "where do we get these guys?"

I felt humbled, proud, and could scarcely contain my own emotion as he spoke about his family. He could have been the quiet teenager next door that the 'popular' crowd thought to be a geek. He might have been Mr. Wizard on the basketball court. It did not matter. To me he was a genuine American hero, one deserving of our concern and our gratitude. And then a remarkable thing happened. As we spoke, I mentioned my son at West Point and my other one at the prep school. Just then, my flight was announced and I had to leave. The young Soldier said something to me, which I could not hear. "I'm sorry, what was that again?" I asked.

He reached for my hand. "God bless you," he said, "and God bless your sons."

With examples of duty like that, priorities fall into place. Where do we get these Soldiers?

10 December - A New Mom

My Soldier is 1-44 ADA 4th ID out of Ft. Hood, stationed in Tikrit. He is home for two weeks R & R. Originally he was supposed to come home, December 15, but got 'bumped' up and came home on December 2. We were expecting our first child on December 24. The baby decided to come early. He was born today. Dad is on cloud nine. He will have to return to Iraq on December 18, but thank God and the US Government he got to come home in time to see his son born. Our newborn will probably be crawling by the time Dad sees him again.

My heart goes out to the families and Soldiers that won't get to come home, but I am grateful that mine did. We married on January 18, this year, and he deployed March 30. We have been married almost a year now and have only been together for about a month of that time. Sorry about rambling, but this is the third happiest day of my life.

12 December - Reply to New Mom

I would like to welcome the new mom to the website. I would be the first to say because of Bob's website I have felt close to what is going on with 4th ID. So I say to you, hold your head high and remember to pray. I too, am a first time military mom, and it does get lonesome, and we feel blue, but it brings a smile to my heart knowing my son and all the other men and women are doing a great job to keep us all safe. Again welcome. When you feel down drop us an e-mail, and we can share the tears or joy together.

Gel Detrick - Wife of MAJ Tom Detrick - HHD 704 DSB

The War Is Over
By Gel Detrick

The war is over, or so we're told.
So where's my Soldier for me to hold?
Where's my hero to hug and cheer?
Why is he still there and not with me here?
The war is over, the job is done,
To all intents and purposes we have won.
Yet Soldiers are still dying every day.
America's finest, still in harm's way.
The war is over, get back to ordinary life.

Yet I'm still waiting, a deployment wife.
The media's moved on, the reporters come home.
But the battles and skirmishes, they still go on.
The war is over, but there's no peace in sight.
Our peacekeeping military still has to fight.
Their loved ones at home still living in fear,
Just wishing and praying that they were all here.
The war is over, don't you believe it!
There are brave men and women who every day lives it.
The war is not over 'til they are all back
In the arms of their loved ones and not under attack.
The war is not over and peace can't be found
'Til there's not one more tear shed,
no more blood on the ground.
When my husband is with me in peaceful accord.
Until then there is war, and I pray to the Lord.

11 December - Advice From a Wife and Mom

This particular message was about how hard it was for those whose Soldiers were not coming home on the R & R program to read in the updates each day the stories of those families who were able to take advantage of time together.

I share the lady's pain in the fact that many of us have to accept that some of the Soldiers aren't going to make the rotation for the R&R, but I would also offer some suggestions. My husband is a 1SG in 1-4 Aviation Regiment, 4th BDE, 4ID. We were married just shortly before he became an NCO, so I've had sixteen years of marriage to get used to the 'selfless service' way of life. Even before the R&R was approved, and the list was created, I had accepted the fact that my husband would not take R&R until all his Soldiers had the opportunity. I can tell you though; it is really hard to explain 'selfless service' to our nine-year-old little boy who hears his friends at school talking about their daddies coming home.

Even though I am supposed to be one of the strong wives, it hurts sometimes to read about the R&Rs. It is a double-edged sword. My heart aches for the Soldiers who have missed the births of their children, and tears fill my eyes when I read about those sweet reunions. Just as the people who are writing are exercising the freedom of speech, I also have the right to exercise my freedom of choice and can skip some of the updates on the R&R experiences. Bob, your daily updates have brought me so much comfort, and they serve as a daily reminder that I'm not the only one experiencing pain in my heart from the absence of my Soldier. I am so grateful for what you do for all of us every day.

But if I could make a suggestion for an improvement to your daily update, since in reality the R&R accounts aren't actually *What Our Families Are Hearing From Our Soldiers in Iraq.* Would it be too much to ask that maybe you separate the postings into two categories, one being: *What Our Families Are Hearing From Our Soldiers in Iraq* and one possibly, *Families Sharing R&R Moments.* This could help those folks who want to exercise the freedom of choice make the choice.

12 December - Understanding Wife

My husband isn't coming home for mid-tour leave either, but I don't mind reading about others who are getting to enjoy it. When they make me cry it's because I'm happy for them even if I am a little jealous. Oh well, that's just the way things go. But I do like to hear about their happiness and experiences because I think we're all in this together. I just don't think they should have to feel ashamed because they got to see their loved ones, and if anything, it's given me insight into what to expect when my hubby gets home. Other than that, I do not have a whole lot to say.

I haven't heard from my husband in 299 EN in almost two weeks. I was getting spoiled with the two phone calls a week I was getting for awhile. Last time I spoke with him he did tell me he'd gotten his Christmas box nine days after I'd sent it!

13 December - Bob Babcock

This essay was sent by the sister of one of our 2nd Brigade Combat Team Soldiers in Iraq. She has done a great job of expressing what many of us think.

As our nation finds itself in the midst of a lingering war, the news has become a part of our family and everyday life. The media is enjoying some of the highest ratings in history because of the war. You can walk into almost any home in America and find the news on the television at some point in the day. However, more and more families are discovering the daily news may not be the best source of information on the war in Iraq. There are many

American families with loved ones currently deployed in Operation Iraqi Freedom. These families reside all across this great nation from the coast of California to New York. The families have frequent contact with their deployed loved ones and other servicemen. Americans are sending care packages and letters and are receiving letters from the Soldiers on the front lines every day. These letters provide a direct insight into what is really occurring in the heart of the war zone because they are from the best source possible, the Soldier serving in Operation Iraqi Freedom.

It is apparent that a great amount of high interest information is being sent directly from Iraq, where the war on terror is presently being fought, a country getting its first taste of freedom because of the diligent efforts of our American military. Or is it? With the media coverage not showing both sides, most Americans are uncertain about the reality of this war. That is, unless you are receiving those prized letters from the front lines of Iraq.

The same thread of hope and assurance runs through each of these prized letters: "We are making a difference; We are giving these people the freedom and the life they deserve; We are making incredible progress every single day."

The letters are words of Soldiers written with no regard to the media, informing their families about their daily life in Iraq in support of Operation Iraqi Freedom.

It is evident that there is a great deal more humanitarian progress being achieved than our national media is willing to share. We should ask ourselves, why is this? What could we possibly lose by sharing these wonderful accomplishments? There is so much to gain by bringing the good news of such grand successes in Iraq. Successes such as schools being opened for the Iraqi children, schools which promise to provide them with an education that they could never have experienced under Saddam's regime. Hospitals are also being restored and serving their cities again. Police forces are on patrol rebuilding relationships with their communities. Where are these stories and why is the media failing to show the accomplishments of our military?

Many ask about the Soldiers. Where are they in all of this? The letters tell it all. Are they homesick? Absolutely. Do they miss their families? Indeed they do. But they have a job to do. They have a mission set before them. That mission is being accomplished every hour of the day, and the Soldiers accomplish that mission with pride in their country and in hope that the Iraqi people will some day experience the gift of freedom that Americans sometimes take for granted.

If only these letters could be read by the American people, it might even change the face of this war forever and provide them with the same assurance that these military families have because they have the best source possible. The best source is found in the letters from the Soldiers serving proudly in Operation Iraqi Freedom. These Soldiers deserve to be heard. Their thoughts and their words do matter. America is truly the greatest nation in the world. If only the media would take these reports from the front lines of the war, we could be reminded of that once again.

14 December - Bob Babcock - Saddam Captured!

"Babe, we got him!" That's the phone call to the wife of one of our Raider Brigade (1BCT) 4ID Soldiers (a platoon sergeant) this morning after the official announcement of the capture of Saddam Hussein.

As you can guess, this is a special edition relaying the outstanding news that we have all been waiting to hear since March. This is a day that will change the future for the Iraqi people and the world. And equally as good news is that our own 4th Infantry Division was the unit that captured him. Our Soldiers today have written a great new chapter in the long history of the 4th Infantry Division.

I'm sure most of you have already heard the news since it broke at about 7:10 EST this Sunday morning. But in case you haven't, here are some of the early news releases as of 8:30 EST on Sunday morning. More will be coming as the day progresses. Next update will be tomorrow unless today's events indicate I should send out another update later today.

The smile on the face of General Sanchez during the news conference this morning was the brightest thing I've seen in months. Let's all go to church and thank God that Saddam is in custody and that none of our Soldiers were hurt in the raid. This is a great day for the proud and dedicated Soldiers of the 4ID. I think history will record the capture of Saddam as one of the most significant events of the modern era and certainly as a seminal event in the Middle East.

14 December - A Wife Gets the Good News
My husband told me yesterday around 1:00 in the afternoon Texas time that he thought they had got him, meaning Saddam. He is an AH-64D Longbow Apache driver with 1-4 AVN REGT at Camp Speicher in Tikrit. His and another aircraft were both flying during the time of capture. He said, "All hell broke loose on the radios, and everyone was excited saying, "Jackpot, Jackpot."

He said he was in the air and he couldn't get confirmation. He hadn't been to his briefing yet for the night, but he was pretty sure that Saddam was either caught or dead. He couldn't tell me Saddam's name over the phone, so he called him Elvis. My husband had told me to watch the news, but nothing came out until this morning. It is amazing that there was a wrap on this for that long. I think it's great that both military and media seem to be doing a good job reporting this.

14 December - Huge Neighborhood Party
I heard the news this morning in a phone call from Nebraska from a friend who heard it on the radio. Believe you me; I was up and at 'em early today! I was glued to the TV. I had to call the neighbors; all of us wives put on the coffee and watched it together. This is what we needed to hear! This makes all the waiting worthwhile! Shows our 4th ID Soldiers are wonderful and if anyone was going to do it, it would be them—and they did! We're so very proud. Our neighborhood was like a huge party this morning. Everyone was awake, even the kids. We were all watching the news together. It's a wonderful feeling to know our Soldiers here at Ft. Hood made history today, and we'll pass this along for generations! Congratulations to all the Soldiers!!

15 December - Early Christmas Present
My son is with the 4th ID, 3BCT, in Balad. Today in church at Cornerstone Church in Madison, Tennessee, our pastor started his sermon with "It's the Christmas season and Baghdad got their Christmas present early!"

The congregation went wild! Over two thousand people were up on their feet clapping, whistling and cheering. The pastor has said repeatedly that he believed President Bush was the right man for the right job at the right time and he felt it was God's doing. I would like to go a step further and say I believe God put the right

Soldiers in the right place at the right time! God bless our Soldiers! I love the 4th ID!

16 December - Restores Her Faith

I'm searching for words on how this capture has made me feel. The amount of pride I feel for our Soldiers in 4ID right now is overpowering. My husband is 4ID 1BCT 299 EN. I hope so much that he was one of the six hundred who got to take part, so that he can have that story to tell our children when he returns and our grandchildren years down the road. I don't care if he was just there helping to secure an area, to be part of history like that is so awesome. But even if he wasn't, they're ALL part of history and ALL deserving of this overwhelming pride.

Also, I am very appreciative for what his capture has done for me because although I've always been a vocal supporter of this war and believer in this country, the last few months the violence I've seen towards the Soldiers I admire so much had taken a serious toll on keeping my positive outlook on all this. This enormous accomplishment has restored that for me and has filled me with the strength to keep positive until our Soldiers come home. This was the best Christmas present God could have ever sent us. God bless 4ID!

16 December - An Observer Speaks Out

As I read these updates I have noticed one very important item that seems to not be said enough. On behalf of those of us that do not have any family active in the military right now, I would like to thank every military family for the sacrifices they make so that their loved one can help to protect our country.

I read these updates and it makes me feel good to in some ways stay connected so that I know what the families are going through. I cannot imagine not being able to communicate with my husband, sisters, parents etc. on a daily basis. I truly have a much greater appreciation of our Soldiers and their families now. The support they give the Soldiers is unreal and should be recognized. Every military wife, husband, mother, father, sibling, and significant other should pat themselves on the back because you are all special and very significant in making the world a safer place as well. Thank you to all of you from the bottom of my heart. Merry Christmas and God bless all of you!

17 December - Lucky Young Man

My son, Ryan, was one of the lucky young men to be interviewed on 'Good Morning, America' yesterday. In an e-mail he sent to his wife, Bryanne, the day before, he certainly didn't single himself out as being instrumental in Saddam's capture, and I'm quite sure he still wouldn't. In fact, the e-mail was very vague. I'm sure they wouldn't mind if I share it with you:

"Dear Bryanne, I had a very big night last night. I just had a nice shower, and I have the next two days off to relax and calm down for a job well done. I can't specify right now what the big event was, but the details will be in the mail. As you know, we moved up north recently. Well, night before last, we were rushed back down to Tikrit for a very important mission.

"All I can say about it at this point is the news is right, and I was there doing my job when it happened. Once you know what I mean, then you will understand how good G-Troop (10th CAV) is feeling today. I need to get some rest now. I've been up for two days. I love you. I love Aubrie. (His seventeen-month-old daughter.) Take care."

Since Ryan rarely has the opportunity to e-mail, Bryanne didn't read it until after Ryan mentioned it on Good Morning, America. We were genuinely shocked when the phone rang at 4:50 in the morning and we were told that he would be on the show and that we would have the opportunity to talk to him. Seeing him on that screen filled us with such pride and relief. I'm sure everyone reading this will understand completely my reference to relief. Each time we get a phone call, the two weeks we had him home in November on leave, the rare e-mail, all create moments that we can breathe a sigh of relief, for we know he is safe right then.

I think everyone watching that show swallowed hard when Ryan started to choke up as he heard Bryanne say she loved him. I hope we don't wear out that videotape before he gets home and has a chance to see it! Unfortunately, we lost the phone connection and have not been able to talk to him since our brief greetings on the air. Needless to say, we have a thousand unanswered questions. Two local TV stations came to do interviews yesterday and both did very nice short pieces for the five and ten o'clock news.

In one of them, they were filming Bryanne, Aubrie, and me watching the Good Morning, America piece and Aubrie reached

---

her hand toward the screen and said, "Daddy." He will treasure that tape for the rest of his life.

I have always been proud of Ryan. For being so young (he was twenty-one in October), he has a strong sense of duty and a great love for his family and his country. I am happy that through the permanent record of pictures and video he has been afforded a small place in history. I have no idea yet why Ryan's unit was rushed back to Tikrit to be a part of this operation, but I know he will be forever grateful that he was allowed to participate.

17 December - Lessons Learned

There has been a great deal of commentary about Saddam's limited abilities as a military and political leader. And there has been some mention of his folly in attempting to kill the senior Bush. If there is one lesson that history has taught in Saddam's neighborhood and elsewhere, it is that you do not cut down the head of a powerful family without accounting for the sons in ascendancy. I believe the Romans had a proverb that addresses this issue. Noli me tangere. In English, it translates today as, 'Don't mess with Texas.'

19 December - He Gets It, Now

I heard from my son today. He is with the 720th MPs, and it had been a long time since I last heard his voice. It was music to this mother's ears! I hung up on him the first time after saying, "Hello, Hello, Hello" with no response, but thank God he called right back.

I must admit that my feelings were getting hurt, and I must also admit that there was some anger from not hearing from him in such long a time. There was a period when he called weekly like clockwork. I asked him how he was: He sounded tired, and he said although it was 60 degrees, it felt really cold since they had been used to the 130 degrees plus.

I asked if he needed anything and what could I send for Christmas. His response to me was, "I don't need anything for Christmas. Every time I get a package from you it's been a Christmas present for me."

Like many of our young Soldiers, he graduated from high school and off he went to basic training, and then after a brief visit home, he was off to Iraq. I forget that although he is so far away from home he has created a life. He is trying to maintain a relationship with the girl left behind. Both of them are so very young and caught up in the romance and emotion, having never given a thought to what truly lay ahead. The lonely nights, being on their own for the first time, and when the reality hits, neither are there for the other, and perhaps they both make mistakes.

I was used to never seeing my child while he lived at home; I only knew he existed because his dirty clothes would pile up in his room. Sometimes he'd be home for dinner, but only the nights I didn't cook enough to feed him. There were the fights over taking out the trash, feeding 'his' dog, making his bed, etc. However, he was in my home.

I wasn't prepared for my firstborn to leave the nest. I remember wishing he would many times after heated arguments, but nobody told me the loneliness that comes when the first departs. To make it worse, he went to a place where I was denied access. The Army set the rules—when or if he could call. When I saw him after sixteen weeks, I saw what a wonderful job they had done with my son, and now I wanted him back. He had become the fine young gentleman I always knew he could be. He was polite; he told me, "I used to think your house was hell, but I've been to hell, and it wasn't your home." I knew at that moment he got it. All the lessons I had tried to teach him, he knew. I wanted him home.

Instead he left for what has become his home. These young men are living a life, trying to build a relationship with a girl back home and trying to fight loneliness, boredom and fear. They too, had to adjust to the separation of leaving home. I thought of my child in Iraq, and today I realized that my 'child' isn't in Iraq. He has become a man and I can't wait to have him visit me.

I wish to say to all the girlfriends or new brides, give us moms a day with our sons when they return, and we will give you a lifetime of loyalty and support. Too soon they departed, and I know for the longest time my arms ached to hold that baby one more time. Bear with us, for someday you will also experience what we are going through.

19 December – Good Humored Soldier

Hi everyone! We don't have any snow in Iraq, but there's plenty of mud. Perhaps during Christmas we'll make a mud-man or mud-angels. The Iraqis are trying to get in the spirit by throwing snowballs, but again, there's no snow, so they throw rocks. It is the thought that counts, I'm sure. To spread the cheer we often carry these improvised snowballs and return the gesture.

One of the most enjoyable jobs I have is working with the interpreters. I'm sure it was lost in the interpretation, but instead of spreading the Christmas spirit, we searched his bag and found some Christmas spirits. He was bringing in champagne and beer for the Soldiers, so he got a pink slip to wrap around the lump of coal Santa will put in his stocking. It's too bad, he was the one offering to be my personal bodyguard and assassinate anyone I asked him too. Good help seems hard to find these days. His buddies are trying to make up for his shortcomings by offering to bring in a huge Christmas tree. They woefully explain that there is no way to bring it in; however, so again it'll have to be the thought that counts.

Still training the Iraqi Civil Defense Corps. In the spirit of friendship, certain ICDC are given American sounding names. They seem rather grateful to receive the honorific titles such as Dracula, Tuna and Elvis. They give us Arabic sounding names like infidel. It's quite a cozy relationship....

The communications are good enough that I get to call Laurie five times in a single day—just to say hello. I mean literally, it takes five calls to string together enough airtime to get that one word out. The silver lining is that hey, she and I do get to talk. It's rather nice though, now I'm broken into this type of interrupted communication. I imagine ordering our first meal at home will be quite an adventure. The pizza shop will probably think I'm a prank caller the first few dozen times I call. It should get better by the next day, however.

That's it for now, thanks to everyone for the support. It's been fantastic and there is never a doubt in anyone's mind that America's support is directly behind the troops. My gratitude goes out to everyone on behalf of your boys in the muddy boots. Take care!

19 December - Leaders Take Care of Their Soldiers
A Soldier's e-mail to his wife:
Yes, it makes me a little bitter and jealous (not coming home for R & R), but we're only human, and many who will not get to go home are feeling that way over here right now. Yesterday I was

talking with a fellow officer, and like me, he is towards the bottom of his list as well. He reminded me of the reason why I put myself on the list where I did—because leaders take care of their Soldiers.

I know you are probably gritting your teeth right now, but that is what it means to take care of one's Soldiers. It's just like putting the needs of my family before myself, and right now, being over here and making this country a better and safer place, so the world can be more secure in the future, is part of taking care of you guys. Years ahead, we can hold our heads high and say we made sacrifices, as did those who came before us, to a cause bigger than we are and feel good about it. We will get through this and be stronger for it.

Cindy Richardson - Wife of LTC Gil Richardson - HHC DIV Chaplain

I have been helping a member of Gil's unit, Kim, whose spouse is an E-4 in Iraq and is herself a Soldier. She just moved here with seven-month-old twins and all got the flu. She will sign in to HHC 4ID in one week.

On December 22, I got a call from Mary, another chaplain's wife, who asked me to watch her three small kids while she went to help Kim unpack. Kim had moved less than one week ago from San Antonio, and now her seven-month-old twins had RSV, and she had the flu.

The Family Readiness Group leader and Mary helped her unpack some boxes and hold sick babies, but there were few people willing to help as RSV is so contagious and can be deadly. Plus, the ER didn't give Kim much information, and she was feeding the babies formula, perpetuating the diarrhea. Anyway, I went over that evening with humidifier and Pedialyte popsicles, and unexpectedly ended up spending the night, as Kim was too sick to take care of both kids. I asked the Family Readiness Group to get more help for her next day, but there were few volunteers because it was Christmas Eve.

I received a call at church that the babies were worse and dehydrated, so the FRG leader and I and Gracie brought them all to the ER that evening. They were not sick enough to admit, but they changed their meds and gave more advice. I told Kim to call if she needed me to help again. I got a call on Christmas day while we were eating supper at a friend's house with other families of deployed chaplains. Grace and I went over to Kim's at 1900 hrs. and spent the night rocking babies. I know that RSV is contagious, but I just told Grace to wash her hands. Grace and I had received flu shots, plus I'm a nurse and would have been dead by now if I'd have caught everything. The next morning the babies looked much better and Kim finally got almost a whole night's sleep. The babies did sleep some, although they were still not taking much Pedialyte.

Her folks will be coming in from Minnesota on December 29 and will stay for one month so that Kim can go back to work. She is a nice person and was pretty desperate, but is looking better. I told Gracie that that is more of what Christmas is about—not getting presents and shopping, but giving of ourselves.

20 December - Proud Friend of a Vietnam Veteran

Bob, one of the most moving reactions to Saddam's capture was from one of our friends who is a Vietnam veteran. Not only is he a Vietnam vet, but he was cut off from his platoon and wandered alone in the jungles over there for over ninety days! He was listed as an MIA and was presumed dead. Here are his thoughts:

"Those boys and girls hunkered down over there and caught that bad boy! I guess the thing that makes me the happiest is that it is easy to see that America is supporting her troops in Iraq. Sure would have been easier for us that went to 'Nam if we had been supported like that. But that's okay, you tell that little blond haired girl of yours how proud this old man is of her and all the others over there and for them to take names and kick ass!"

This comes from a man I have heard probably speak only five words at one given time in a complete conversation.

From a proud mom of a 4ID Soldier and a prouder friend of a real-life American hero that paid his dues in Vietnam nearly forty years ago! HOOAH!

22 December - My Soldier Left Again...

Well, my Soldier (B CO 299 EN BN) left for Iraq this morning. Yes, there were tears, but more importantly, pride in the strength of character, integrity, and honor our Soldiers possess. As he said, "There is work left to be done."

My favorite memory of his visit happened on this past Sunday as he, my husband, and I had the chance to watch a New England

Patriots football game together, the first one we have seen together in a couple of years. Seeing him sprawled on the couch (just like the old days) completely relaxed and exchanging commentary with his dad and me brought tears to my eyes. Of course, there were many other wonderful moments with him the past couple of weeks, but I want to keep this relatively short. We will miss him, and continue to count down the days, write letters, and send care packages. By the way, he was very impressed that I knew how many days until 1 April.

Rhonda Eggleston - Wife of LTC Kirk Eggleston - Division Surgeon

Excerpt of the 2003 Christmas card sent by the Eggleston family.
"This year is different for our family in many ways. Most of the differences center on the fact that Kirk is deployed to Iraq. While our family does not like being apart, we are focusing on how greatly God has blessed us. We usually try to put a family picture in our card, but since Kirk could not be in it, that was just something we were not interested in doing. The picture included is of our Christmas tree. It is not one that you would find in a department store window, but every ornament on our tree has been a gift to one of us from family and friends.

"The tree itself has a special story. The Oregon Tree Growers Association got together and delivered 1,000 trees with stands to Ft. Hood to be given to the families of deployed Soldiers. The truck driver for the Association brought a Santa suit and played Santa for the young children when we went to pick up the trees. My brother Brad was with us when we picked up the tree and helped a young mother who had her two young children with her. She said she was expecting a 'Charlie Brown' tree, and to be honest, so was I. But then I was given a fresh six-foot Douglas Fir. It is probably one of the nicest trees we have ever had.

"There was a sweet atmosphere when it was our turn to pick out our tree. No pushing or shoving or yelling, just everyone helping one another. I will never forget seeing Eddie carry our tree across the parking lot and thinking how proud Kirk would be of him. This tree is special to us this year because it is one more thing that has been a special blessing to us. Our tree represents so many of you who have called to check up on us, you who have mailed Kirk packages, you who have e-mailed inspiring stories to us, and all the many kindnesses and love you have shown us.

"This tree represents a country that is grateful for the Soldiers and understands that what they are doing is vital not only for Iraq, but also for our country. And when you appreciate our Soldiers, you help those of us at home who are being Mom and Dad and you help our children to be strong while their parent is away. Each time I look at our tree, I am so thankful. We have a Soldier who is doing his duty with all he has. We have family and friends who love us. We live in a country that is not spitting on our Soldiers when they come home, but rather have been giving them standing ovations at air terminals.

"After we take down our tree, put the ornaments away, and when Kirk gets home, we will look back on this year, we will remember all of you, and be thankful. As I finished putting up the decorations around the house, I thought it was ironic that Kirk is apart from his family because of depraved people. God chose to separate himself from His Son because of depraved and sinful people. The difference is Kirk's separation from us falls under the heading of 'wars and rumors of wars', and any solution the U.S. comes up with is only temporary. God choosing to separate Himself from His Son while Christ was here on earth is the only permanent solution, and we are thankful for the hope and reassurance this gives. Have a wonderful Christmas season."

23 December - Pictures of His Boots

While my son was home for two weeks, his uniform was hanging mixed with his civilian clothes in the closet and his dusty boots were sitting in the hallway. After I walked by his uniform and boots several times, I decided to take pictures of his uniform hanging in the closet and of his empty boots on the floor. I knew my family would think I had lost it, but when I got the pictures back, it seemed like everyone understood. I noticed (which I didn't when I took the picture) that I could see my son's (last) name on the inside of his boots. Seeing his name made me even prouder of him. These pictures will be used in the scrapbook I am putting together for him and his future family.

Also the night before he had to leave, I washed his uniform and my husband asked if we should put Downey softener in the wash, and I said, "Yes, of course". My husband thought his uniform would smell "too good," but I told him at least for a day or two, he could be reminded of home when he smelled the Downey on his uniform. We made sure it was wrinkle free, hung and ready to go back on the man who was ready to go back and finish his job.

I have a lot of respect for all the men and women who proudly wear their uniforms and commend *Time* magazine for recognizing our Soldiers and naming them People of the Year!

23 December - Spirit of Love

I just spent three wonderful days visiting with my son who's home on Christmas R & R leave from Iraq. My son is a medic with the 1-68 AR stationed around Balad. He hadn't planned on coming home, as lower ranked Soldiers were a higher priority on the list. Thanks to the generosity of two very selfless, single Soldiers, my son is spending Christmas with a grateful wife and two beautiful daughters (ages six and four).

These two young Soldiers gave up the opportunity to come home for Christmas so that my son could be with his family. They opted instead for a four-day R & R in Quatar. My family will forever be indebted to these men. They truly reflect the spirit of love found within the hearts of our American troops. God bless them and God Bless America.

A proud dad of a 4th ID, 1-68 AR Soldier.

Karen Holt - by Daughter Courtney Holt - Wife and Daughter of 1SG Carter Holt - D CO 1-4 AVN

There once was a boy
Who didn't want any toy,
But on his Christmas List
He wrote down the one thing he missed
And he wrote a letter
Saying that Santa had better
Bring his Soldier back
In that big ole red sack.
And on Christmas Day
A Soldier rode on that sleigh
And the little boy got his Soldier back
Who was all the way in Iraq.

24 December - 99 days and a wake-up until April 1, 2004

When I first started receiving your updates from my brother's FRG leader (Fox Troop 10th CAV), I would look at the 'days and a wake-up' and wonder to myself why in the world you included the number of days until our Soldier returns. It just served as a reminder as to how long Jonathan would be in Iraq. Well, as you can imagine the past few weeks have brought whole new meaning to the 'days and a wakeup'. When I opened this morning's update and saw ninety-nine days I couldn't stop the tears. Now, it does seem like April really will get here. With a twelve-year age difference, my own child might as well be in Iraq. I'm certain that you realize how hard it is to find the balance between pride and fear.

I'm so short I may be able to sleep again after all!

Submitted by Linda Odierno - Wife of MG Raymond Odierno - Commanding General

'Twas the night before Christmas, he lived all alone,
In a one-bedroom house made of plaster and stone.
I had come down the chimney with presents to give,
And to see just who in this home did live.
I looked all about, a strange sight I did see,
No tinsel, no presents, not even a tree.
No stocking by mantle, just boots filled with sand,
On the wall hung pictures of far distant lands;
With medals and badges, awards of all kinds,
A sober thought came through my mind.
For this house was different, it was dark and dreary,
I found the home of a Soldier, once I could see clearly.
The Soldier lay sleeping, silent, alone,
Curled up on the floor in this one bedroom home;
The face was so gentle, the room in such disorder,
Not how I pictured a United States Soldier.
Was this the hero of whom I'd just read?
Curled up on a poncho, the floor for a bed?
I realized the families that I saw this night,
Owed their lives to these Soldiers who were willing to fight;
Soon round the world, the children would play,

And grownups would celebrate a bright Christmas day.
They all enjoyed freedom each month of the year,
Because of the Soldiers, like the one lying here.
I couldn't help wonder how many lay alone,
On a cold Christmas Eve in a land far from home;
The very thought brought a tear to my eye,
I dropped to my knees and started to cry.
The Soldier awakened and I heard a rough voice;
"Santa don't cry, this life is my choice."
"I fight for freedom, I don't ask for more,
My life is my God, My Country, My Corps".
The Soldier rolled over and drifted to sleep,
I couldn't control it, I continued to weep.
I kept watch for hours, so silent and still,
And we both shivered from the cold night's chill.
I didn't want to leave on that cold, dark night.
This guardian of honor so willing to fight;
Then the Soldier rolled over, with a voice soft and pure,
Whispered, "Carry on Santa, it's Christmas Day, all is secure.
One look at my watch, and I knew he was right.
Merry Christmas, my friend, and too all a good night!

24 December - My Army Sergeant Daughter

A short word about my daughter in the Army Reserves attached to the 4th ID when she went over in April. She is with the 705th Transportation unit. They were extended for a year; she has been very homesick, and at times she wants no more of it. Then others times she is more positive about staying in the Army. While being in Iraq, she has decided to go on for her sergeant stripes. She discussed this with me, and of course, I told her I would stand behind her whatever decision she made. The mother in me was asking, "how much longer you will have to do this?"

She is the first grandchild on both sides and everyone's favorite—the one that makes everyone laugh—so there is a huge void here without her. Just this last week, on her return from a mission, she was promoted to Sergeant. I don't have to tell you how proud I am right now! The holidays are difficult; I miss her so much, but I try to remain strong as she has asked me to. After all, I still have all my freedoms here, while she is there doing what she was trained to do, so this is the least I can do for her.

Watching her and hearing the stories of others she is serving with amazes me at the resolve and pride that all our Soldiers have. No matter what your personal or political opinions are, they are the best America has to offer. They deserve complete support and respect! Thank you again, Proud Mom.

25 December - From the Babcock Family to All...

Merry Christmas. Santa Claus was good to us, and we are enjoying this time together. Fortunately, all four of our grown kids and our two five-year-old grandkids are in town. Jan and I understand how fortunate we are that none of our sons or daughters are in harm's way on this Christmas and are spending this special day with us. Two of my WWII 4ID friends have already called me today, and before the evening is over, I expect to talk to several more of my WWII and Vietnam veteran buddies. It always makes me feel good to know that the best friends are those veterans you have a common bond with.

Michelle Sneed - 4th ID Mother

Tears flow this Blessed Day as I think of you Son, far away
Even though you are there, and I am here, our spirits join as one.
The Mighty One Son of God was born this Blessed Day.
As friends will gather here to pray for all who are far away,
Let it be known our hearts are filled with pride and joy
For you my son on this Blessed Day,
May the Lord heal our hearts this Blessed Day
For he was born for you and all, my son,
Who are over there so far away.
My tears that flowed now have stopped
For God has given me peace of heart.
So, my son, on this Blessed Day knows we are one.
On this Blessed Day the Holy One came for all of us.

Submitted by Ann Campbell - Wife of COL Donald Campbell - Chief of Staff - *4ID - HOOAH!!*

T'was two weeks before Christmas, and all through Iraq,
The people still worried that Saddam would be back.
The Soldiers went out on their nightly patrol,
Capturing the bad guys was always their goal!
With raids seeming endless in the triangle Sunni,

We hoped that not all of Iraq was so loony!
We gathered the tribe of Saddam, in Tikrit,
And suddenly now they all started to snit!
They told of a farm where Hussein just might be
Odierno then called on our boys from the great 4th ID!
More rapid than Baathists our Soldiers they came,
And he whistled and shouted and called them by name
Now Delta, Now Rangers, Now Cavalry too!
On Green Hats, on Pilots, I need all of you!
Go to that farm and secure it right now!
Capture his ass—you guys know how!
Off went our Soldiers under cover of night,
So stealthy, so quiet with no trace of light.
While we back at home were eating our lunches,
Our boys on the ground were following hunches!
And then it was time for the raid to begin.
The first target came up—empty within!
Could it be our Intel was wrong once again?
No! Somewhere nearby is the wolf in his den!
And then, in a twinkling, camouflage torn away
In a hole in the ground did their quarry lay
Dazed and confused, right at them he looked,
Did the stupid old fool know his goose was now cooked?
He was dressed all in rags from his toes to his head,
And his beard was as matted as twelve day-old bread!
How the mighty had fallen, could this be Hussein?
One look in his eyes was to know he's insane!
Our boys got their man—how proud we all are!
The relief in our country is felt near and far.
A bath he has had now—yet he'll never be clean—
Forever tainted with mass torture and his Fedayeen.
To our Soldiers we give our undying respect,
You always give more than we ever expect.
We hope you can have now a night with some fun
Your loved ones back home say—JOB DAMN WELL DONE!

26 December - Best Present Ever

This is the first time I have written but I got the best Christmas present ever this morning at 7:17, December 25. My son (4th MP CO, 5th PLT) called to wish us all a Merry Christmas. I personally

240

haven't talked with him since August, though he has called and talked to his dad at work. We talked for about forty-five minutes on a speakerphone. We put incoming calls on hold during the entire conversation. His brother and sister didn't even seem to mind.

He said everything has been good, and he has received a ton of boxes for Christmas. He said that it was good because they would crowd around the people who got boxes and share the stuff with each other. I plan on sending many more boxes to help him celebrate his twentieth birthday next month.

26 December - Santa Visits Soldiers

This has been a great week as we have heard from our daughter almost every day, either by phone, e-mail and finally Instant Messenger. She even had access to a web-cam and we got to see her great smile, which we have missed for so long. It is such a blessing to see her looking so good. We received an e-mail today, and I just wanted to share a small part of what she said.

"Merry Christmas! It's 11:00 Christmas morning here. We all found presents under the tree for us this morning. Not knowing where they came from, we ripped them open. I guess Santa visits Soldiers too."

So, I guess if some people don't think Santa Claus exists, they will just have to argue that point with the whole US Army. Our many thanks go out to whoever is responsible for these acts of kindness and seeing that our Soldiers had gifts to open on Christmas morning.

She also sent our family a fresh flower arrangement with a candle enclosed in a glass chimney. She had them tie a yellow ribbon and bow on the chimney. I placed it at her seat at the table and lit the candle during dinner. Our daughter is a medic with HHC 1-4 AVN, stationed in Tikrit.

26 December - Friends Become a Family

With our husbands in Iraq (3-66 AR, Bayji), a few of us decided to spend Christmas with each other, marking the special occasion with friends that have become family. We had a lot of fun watching the kids play, watching movies, eating great food, and playing games. We have come to cherish the bonds of friendship that have formed due to this deployment. Prior to the guys leaving, some of us had only met briefly and a couple of us, not at all. We know we are blessed, even if we don't always feel like we are.

We have so much to look forward to in the coming year, and reveling in the excitement of our warriors returning home will be the highlight. Merry Christmas and a very Happy New Year 2004! I'm happy to report that we have all heard from our dear husbands within the last two days!

29 December - Overjoyed
We got a wonderful Christmas morning phone call from our son in Ba'quabah. We have received only four or five phone calls since he got there in April, and he e-mails us about every seven to twenty days. He e-mailed us on the twenty-third, that he would call on Christmas! He told us he would have ten minutes. We didn't get to discuss much in those few minutes, but the whole family got a chance to say "Hi." His younger brothers and sister haven't heard his voice since March! We were overjoyed! The news this morning brought us down hard. They were shelled ten minutes after we hung up. So now we wait, we pray. If our Soldier is safe, then we shed tears for those who are not, their comrades and their families.

29 December - Patriot Santa
Just wanted to share our own Santa experience with you all. My little girl is nine and her brother has been in Iraq since March. (HHC 1-67, Ba'quabah) They are pretty close, so she misses him a lot. Well, we went to the mall so she could sit on Santa's lap and tell him what she wanted for Christmas.

When we got there the line was so long that I was thinking in my head of all the bribes I could use to avoid the line this year. I asked her if we could just write him and go ahead on up to the toy store, but she gave a horrific look. So we stood there. After an hour and a half we got up to Santa and he called her by name, which thrilled her.

She went and sat on his lap, and I went and stood by the photographer. She proceeded to ask for 'GO-GO My Walking Pup' and for her brother to come home from Iraq. And Santa looked at me and at my blue star pin that holds my yellow ribbon next to my heart and smiled and proceeded to tell my little girl what an important job her brother was doing and how the children in Iraq will soon be enjoying the same things that she enjoys here because of her brother and the other Soldiers there with him.

He talked to her for about ten minutes, which was nine minutes more than I had seen him spend with most of the other kids. Then she got up and gave him a big hug, and he gave her a coloring book. She said thank you and walked to the exit, and I looked at him to tell him thank you for making her feel so important and that the time away from her brother will be worth it. He was looking at me with tears in his eyes and said, "Please tell your son thanks."

Trust me, I felt very guilty about my thoughts during the wait in line. Thank you Santa...

29 December - Santa Came Early

My son is in 4th ID, 1-22 Infantry in Iraq, and my daughter-in-law gave birth to their first child on Christmas day. He came six weeks early but is a strong little guy just like his daddy! When my daughter-in-law talked with my son and told him about the baby, he cried. How proud this new Gramma' is! Not only of my new grandbaby, but also of my son who missed out on such a blessed event because he knows his job is in Iraq at this time and also for my daughter-in-law who has had to go through the entire pregnancy and birth without her husband. I hope and pray my son will be home soon to enjoy his new son.
Proud Mom (and now Gramma)!

Alisa Bubela - Wife of Matt Bubela - 2nd CHEM BN 46 CHEM CO

I have been an Army wife for two and a half years now, which is ironic since I had always said I would never marry into the military because of the risks and unstable lives they lead. I let my guard down and I began dating my husband, Kallen "Matt" Bubela, in February 2001. Soon after, I became pregnant. I graduated from high school on May 26, and a week later I married my husband. We moved up to Ft. Hood and been married three months when September 11 occurred. I remember that day like it was yesterday. My husband called saying the United States had been attacked and the whole post was on lockdown.

From that day on I knew we wouldn't be the same. I prayed that they wouldn't send my husband to Afghanistan. I forgot to mention Iraq, too. Well, a year passed, and once again everything was fine. Our little girl, Krysta Renee, was about to turn one-year-old in December, and we had just found out we were pregnant with our second child.

As issues started heating up with Iraq, my husband told me that if a war began, there was a great chance that he would go since he was in a chemical unit (2nd Chemical Battalion, 46th Chemical Company), and it was their turn for rotation.

We went home for a four-day weekend in January. While we were there, Matt took a call from his sergeant, and with no explanation he said, "Let's go!" I got our daughter, told my mom bye, and we got in the car to leave. I was puzzled for a second; then it sank in. They got orders; that was the only explanation. They would never call them in on a holiday unless it was important. My worst fears were unfolding right in front of me. I realized that I would be giving birth to our second child without him and began to cry.

We moved all of our things back home, and I got an apartment. The whole battalion was going, so they had to load all their vehicles on eighteen-wheelers, but Matt drives an '88', which is like the one they used in Baghdad to knock down the Saddam statue. It was too heavy for the eighteen-wheelers so it had to be loaded on a train. After the vehicles were shipped off, the battalion waited around until they got word to leave. He left the first week of April. His parents and I came down the night before and we spent the morning with him. They had to take the Soldiers to Abrams gym to manifest. He had to tell me to let go and pulled my arms away because they were lining up to head out.

We waited for the Soldiers to come out and load the buses. There was a sergeant of some sort out there telling us not to cry, to clap for our Soldiers and cheer them on. I couldn't... I stayed in tears as they came out, and then here came Matt. I wanted to just grab him and run. He looked at me gave me, a quick smile, and kept trotting along. We tried to see where he was, but couldn't see in the buses because of the dark tint. We could only wave bye to a bus instead of Matt.

He called late that night; he was in Germany on a layover. When he called me the next day, he was in Kuwait. It was a few days later that they moved into Iraq. That's when I became scared. Every day I dreaded getting an unwanted phone call.

About two weeks later he called and said that they were all okay. I tried to write as much as I could, and I waited anxiously by the phone every day for him to call, but he rarely had the chance.

On my twenty-first birthday, July eighteenth, I was at my in-laws when a florist delivered twenty-one roses from my husband. Matt called and asked me what I got for my birthday, and I told him that he knew what I got. He just laughed and told me he had made arrangements with his dad before he left to send me twenty-one roses on my birthday. I thought how lucky I am to have him. He was getting ready for war and still thought months ahead about my birthday. He had to let me go and said he'd try to call soon.

My pregnancy was coming to an end at that time so he got to use the phone more. He called at least three to four times a week in August to see how I was doing. The doctor induced me on August 22nd. I went in at six in the morning and had Ty (my husband named him) at 11:37 that same morning. My husband had to go out to the range that day, and they let him take a satellite phone to call and check in every hour. He called me before I hit the hard stages of labor and told me that he would be thinking of me all night, and that although he couldn't be there physically, he was there spiritually. A few days before I went in to deliver, I had a picture of him put on a pillowcase so he could be there with me. After I had Ty, I showed him the pillowcase so he could see his daddy. Matt called at noon asking, "Have you had that kid, yet?"

I told him, "yes," and he said, "You did? That was quick!" I could hear relief in his voice. He said that he had been trying to call for half an hour, but the phone wasn't picking up signal. The guys brought him in so he could call. I told him if he had gotten through that he would have heard the baby's first cry. Darn satellite phones!

I held up pretty good during labor; I cried one time and held in the rest so I wouldn't stress the baby. Now the first night I was home was a different story. I felt so bad for him because our kids mean the world to Matt, and he doesn't want Ty to hold the fact that he wasn't here for his birth against him. I wished he were here and could see the life that we created and hold his baby boy. Instead, he was over there alone with no one to share his inner feelings while waiting on the DVD we recorded of me delivering Ty. I would have given anything to be there with him to comfort him.

245

Matt called every day for about a week. He wanted to make sure we were okay. Then one day he called and said that he was getting R&R, he just didn't know when. When Matt called back, he said he wanted to surprise me and wasn't going to tell me and made me promise not to question his mom since she was going to be his accomplice. I agreed because I knew they couldn't pull it off. When we talked again, he gave me a hint as to when he would be in, and I was expecting him the last days of November or first days of December.

On November 2nd his mom called me up and asked me if I wanted to go see a movie later that day. When I got to her house, she sent me in to the den to check my e-mail. I heard someone call my name and I turned around; there was my husband walking towards me. I couldn't believe what I was seeing. I started to drop to my knees crying, and he kneeled down to hold me. It was the first time in a long time that I felt relieved, and I didn't want it to ever end.

My daughter took a few minutes to realize that Daddy was an actual person and not just a picture on the wall. She attached to him quickly. I was glad, because he was worried that she would be scared since she was only fourteen months when he left. Then he held his baby boy and didn't say anything; he just smiled and looked into Ty's eyes. That was priceless! We were a complete and normal family for the first time. We enjoyed each other's company, and we didn't argue over little things like we used to. Our love for each other grew so much, and we could both see that. That's the only good thing the deployment has done.

We had a great time while he was here. We bought a computer so I can e-mail him letters and pictures every day. We went out and took family pictures, which came out great. It actually felt good being home with nothing to do and for once no worries in the world, even if it was for a few days. We went gambling and lost money, but we had a ball.

Before we knew it, he had to leave us again. He was flying out of Austin to Dallas. His aunt was going to watch the kids so we could take him to the airport. After we left them and got back into the car Matt cried. He didn't want to leave his 'little princess' again. She had grown so much since he had been gone and Matt didn't want to miss out on anything else. He felt bad for having to leave us again. I didn't care; I was happy he was here.

I promised him I wouldn't cry as much, and I stuck to my word, almost. I had watery eyes, and when he came to hug me and tell me bye, I could see he had started to cry. I had to cry with him because I hate to see him hurt. Matt went through the metal detectors and turned around one last time, gave me his smile, blew me a kiss, and walked away. It was then that I broke down. I was alone again. Except this time I had four months to go rather then a year. I got home with the kids and held them.

Matt called me a few times on his way back to Iraq. He struggled with being away from us the first few days of being back in Iraq. He is ready to come back home. Now it's the holiday season and all we're waiting on now is redeployment orders. When that'll come no one knows. I just pray that it is soon.

He calls at least twice a week and always asks how we are doing. I put up the Christmas tree by myself. I really didn't want to, but I promised him I would for the kids. The tree is red, white and blue.

The holidays will be hard with him not here, but he counts on me to make the most of it for the kids. He feels that they shouldn't be punished because of him. So with all that I got, I have to suck it up and smile and try to enjoy Christmas for the kids. The only thing that keeps me going is knowing that as the days go by, this torturous year will soon end. Matt will be home, and we'll go through with our plans of marrying in the church. I have taken classes while he's been gone, and I'll be a full Catholic soon.

He told me he was proud of me, and marrying through the church is permanent, nothing can come between us. When we married two and a half years ago, it was by a justice of the peace. I can't wait, because that strengthens our marriage. Matt and I have loved each other up close and personal since the day we fell in love, and now we have learned to love from a distance.

I am thankful I didn't stick to my word about not marrying into the military. I wouldn't know love like I do now, even if it does bring pain, loneliness, fear and lots of tears. Through all the emotional up and downs, I have learned to appreciate what I have in my husband, and I will never have any regrets, only pride, in carrying the title of ARMY WIFE.

31 December - A Great Way to Start the New Year

Happy Holidays! I heard from my daughter this morning at 4:00 a.m. She is with 21st CSH in Balad. She got to see her husband who is in B Co, 2-8 AR yesterday. She said his unit had to go get some supplies, and they let him visit with her for a couple hours and picked him up on the way back. She said he looked really good. They hadn't seen each other since early October when he got his R&R and went home to Ft Hood to see their newborn son.

She said her unit set her up good by telling her that a Colonel was outside the operating room wanting to talk to her and was really mad. She wasn't sure what was going on until she got outside the tent and saw him and a friend standing there. Glad to see that they still have their sense of humor. And, what a great way to start the new year! Still hoping that they both return on schedule and come get their son and begin being a family. As always, our thoughts and prayers are with all of them.

Just sign me "a proud mother and mother-in-law."

31 December - Daughter's Reply

Note: This is the daughter's view of the story her mother told above—great that they could get together after all those months.
Dear Bob, I don't know if you remember me, but I had written to you a while ago telling you that my husband is in B Co, 2-8IN, and that I am in the 21st Combat Support Hospital. Well, my husband has been over here as of last April, and I have just returned to my unit after the birth of my now four-month old son.

I got to Iraq on Christmas night after a long journey and a week stay in Kuwait. Well, to my surprise, Monday afternoon when I had just finished my last case (I work in the OR where I am a surgical Tech), I went to put my supplies away and one of the nurses came and got me because my husband was here! I can't even begin to tell you how happy I was! He only got to stay for about two hours, but it was the best. Isn't it funny how going all the way around the world can bring part of your family back together! Till we all come home God bless our Soldiers!

31 December - What a Surprise

My son is in the 2nd Brigade Recon and surprised me two weeks before Christmas by coming home! What a surprise: He had told me he wasn't able to get leave! We had a great visit. He was able to visit with his daughter and all the family. His uncles couldn't get over how much of a man he had become since he had left.

He was also invited to speak to a couple of classes at a school nearby. It shocked me that he did it because he never liked speaking in front of a group of people. I also have a son in the Navy who had not spoken to or seen his brother in a year; he was out on a mini-cruise when we were surprised with my son's visit. As it turned out, my Navy son got in the day before his brother was to leave. We were able to have our Christmas early with everyone present. What a treat! I do feel he was ready to go back. He was well rested and tired of not working.

Task Force Ironhorse - December 2003 Casualties

SPC Raphael S. Davis, 24, of Tutwiler, Mississippi, was killed December 2 along MSR Tampa, in Iraq. SPC Davis died of injuries suffered when his vehicle was hit by an improvised explosive device. SPC Davis was assigned to B Company, 223rd Engineer Battalion, Army National Guard, based in Calhoun City, Mississippi.

Chief Warrant Officer Clarence E. Boone, 50, of Fort Worth, Texas, died on December 2 in Kuwait City, Kuwait. Boone died as a result of a non-combat related injury. Boone was assigned to Headquarters and Headquarters Company, 4th Infantry Division, based in Fort Hood, Texas.

SSG Steven H. Bridges, 33, of Tracy, California, **SPC Joseph M. Blickenstaff**, 23, of Corvallis, Oregon, and **SPC Christopher J. Rivera Wesley**, 26, of Portland, Oregon, were killed December 8 in Ad Duluiyah, Iraq, when their vehicle flipped into a canal. All three of these Soldiers were assigned to the 1st Battalion, 23rd Infantry Regiment, 3rd Brigade Combat Team, 2nd Infantry Division, Fort Lewis, Washington.

SPC Charles E. Bush Jr., 43, of Buffalo, N.Y., was killed Dec.19 in Balad, Iraq. Bush was in a convoy when his vehicle was hit by an improvised explosive device. Bush was assigned to the 402nd Civil Affairs Battalion, 354th Civil Affairs Brigade, 352nd Civil Affairs Command, U.S. Army Reserve, Riverdale Park, Md.

MAJ Christopher J. Splinter, 43, of Platteville, Wisconsin, **CPT Christopher F. Soelzer**, 26, of South Dakota, and **SGT Benjamin W. Biskie**, 27, of Vermilion, Ohio, were killed on December 24 when their vehicle struck an improvised explosive device on Highway One near Samarra, Iraq. The Soldiers were assigned to the 5th Engineer Battalion, 1st Engineer Brigade, based in Fort Leonard Wood, Missouri.

SGT Michael E. Yashinski, 24, of Monument, Colorado, died on December 24 in Kirkuk, Iraq. SGT Yashinski died of injuries sustained while running a communication wire. SGT Yashinski was assigned to the 501st Forward Support Company, 173rd Airborne Brigade, based in Vicenza, Italy.

SSG Thomas W. Christensen, 42, of Atlantic Mine, Michigan, and **SSG Stephen C. Hattamer**, 43, of Gwinn, Michigan, were killed on December 25 in Baqubah, Iraq, when their living area came under mortar attack. The Soldiers were assigned to the 652nd Engineer Battalion, U.S. Army Reserve, based in Ellsworth, Wisconsin.

SPC Charles G. Haight, 23, of Jacksonville, Alabama, was killed on December 26 in Iraq. SPC Haight was in a convoy vehicle, which struck an improvised explosive device. SPC Haight was assigned to the 14th Engineer Battalion, 555th Engineer Group, based in Fort Lewis, Washington.

SGT Curt E. Jordan, Jr., 25, of Green Acres, Washington, died on December 28 near Bayji, Iraq. SGT Jordan died of non-combat injuries. SGT Jordan was assigned to the 14th Combat Engineer Battalion (Corps) (Wheeled), 555th Combat Engineer Group, based in Fort Lewis, Washington.

SSG Michael J. Sutter, 28, of Tinley Park, Ill., was killed Dec. 26 in Baqubah, Iraq. Sutter was attempting to render safe an improved explosive device when it detonated. Sutter was assigned to the 745th Ordnance Company, 79th Ordnance Battalion, Army National Guard, based in Grayling, Michigan.

Matt, Alisa, Krysta and Ty Bubela

Soldiers Say "Thanks" for the Christmas Presents

Major Tom Detrick (Right) lining up for Holiday Parade

Early Christmas Present for
the 4ID and the World

TEN

JANUARY - 2004
End in Sight

90 days and a wake-up until April 1, 2004...

*A*fter the holidays the end was in sight. Once the 101st Airborne started to re-deploy we knew it was just a matter of time before our Soldiers returned. The largest troop rotation since World War II was beginning. SSG Womack was invited to be Mrs. Bush's guest for the President's State of the Union address. He was representing the unit that had captured Saddam. It was the beginning of the end for the Task Force's deployment, so we started planning welcome home celebrations.

We survived and flourished in 2003. A year ago at this time, twenty-five million Iraqi people were enslaved by Saddam, and now they're started on the slow road to recovery, freedom, and self government. 2004 is going to be an even better year. We're down to the final three months of our Task Force Ironhorse deployment. All in all, things are positive as we start 2004

1 January - Let Me Go
I have to tell you that I had been a little down these past few days, because I had not been able to talk to my husband in a while. He's in 2/20th FA, 4th ID. It seemed like I was missing him every time I got online. Well last night, just as I was about to sign off, he sent me an instant message. I was so thrilled, I almost cried.

He told me he was doing well and that he had been logging on almost every day, but I guess we were missing each other. We talked for about forty-minutes. He said they were going to see some boxing matches around five o'clock, one of the events they had scheduled for New Year's Eve. Toward the end of our conversation, when we were talking about the New Year, he got a little choked up and decided to sign off because he said, in his own words, "Let me go, before I lose it right here."

It hurt me to know he was feeling so down. We miss him terribly and wish he could be here for the New Year's Eve celebration. But like he always does, he put himself back together and said he was O.K. and that he loved me and would talk to me soon. After we signed off, I had a good cry. Well, it's almost over. God willing, they'll all be back soon. God bless our Soldiers. A proud Army wife

1 January - Miracles

My son-in-law left tonight (31st of December) to go back to Iraq. He is with the 1-67AR. He was able to be home at Fort Hood with his family. He was able to be at the hospital for the birth of his son. He also has three daughters. Everybody is doing fine. My wife and I are heading in the morning from Ohio to Fort Hood to help out for a couple of weeks. Just an extra note, my daughter said that she was praying and expecting two miracles: 1. That her husband would get to come home. 2. That he would be there for the birth of their son. Both of these miracles happened. Having faith in God does have its reward. Her husband is the chaplain for the 1-67th AR.

2 January - A Little Remorse

Our holidays were wonderful but bittersweet. Our son, who returned from Iraq to get out of the army last fall, is doing much better. We have put the 20 pounds he lost back on, but he was visibly upset. I know he feels like he shouldn't be so happy when his friends and battle buddies are still in harm's way.

Of course he wanted to be there when we finally got the rat (Saddam) in his hole, but I reminded him how he was instrumental in the capture of #4 and without his time there and his dedication to duty, things may not have worked out as they had.

I know that you have a lot of parents writing to you concerned about their Soldiers. I ask you to please tell them that the Soldiers who have come home have not forgotten their battle buddies and neither have their families. I keep all the members of the military, both ours and the rest of the coalition, in my thoughts and prayers daily. But, as always, the 4th ID is closest to my heart. We will

254

never forget what they have done and continue to do for us and the newly freed people of Iraq.

Note from Bob: For those who have Soldiers who return before the rest of the 4ID and TF Ironhorse returns, you need to know that this is not an uncommon feeling. Be aware that your recently returned Soldier has real feelings of remorse and guilt about leaving his buddies in harm's way while he is safely home. It takes time to get over those feelings so just be aware and sensitive to them.

Christina Petersen - Wife of CW2 Cory J. Petersen - E Troop 1-10 CAV

When the war started I was still new to military life. I was from what I considered the 'real world.' I connected my self-worth with my job and was less than thrilled at the idea of being just a wife. Looking back, I couldn't possibly have known what it really meant to be an army wife. It wasn't one single monumental moment that made the skies part. It was the subtle show of character and dedication in the women around me over the months that has brought me to a better understanding.

On Mother's day, I was feeling very sorry for myself. I missed the usual flowers and trip out to dinner to show that I was appreciated. My husband had recently deployed to Iraq and I felt very overwhelmed with three kids to care for on my own. I decided to take them for a walk. As we went through our neighborhood, I noticed all of the houses with one car in the driveway and the other car covered. I noticed the moms at the park with their kids and the moms out washing their cars. It was strange, like the Twilight Zone, a neighborhood full of moms and no dads. I realized that I wasn't alone in this.

Then I noticed the mom that had just moved in. She probably hadn't even met her neighbors yet. She was keeping an eye on her two-year-old, telling her to stay put on the porch so she wouldn't get hurt while mommy was mowing the lawn. I hadn't thought of how much harder it would be if we had just moved here and didn't even know anyone. The mom next door to her had a baby on her back in a backpack, one child helping her put up a tent, and two others running around playing. I was stressed out with three kids, and here she was on her own smiling from ear to ear with four.

In the 'real world', "it's not in my job description" is a very popular phrase to get out of doing the little things that you don't really want to do. These are women that take over every single facet of running a home when their husbands are sent away. It's not in my job description is not in their vocabulary.

I remember the Family Readiness Group meeting about a month after the guys left. Our Family Readiness Group leader was so sick she could hardly speak. She had a throat infection and a temperature, but there she was, with her three children sitting outside, giving us the specifics on how to mail packages to our husbands and who to contact in case of an emergency. About halfway through the meeting a couple of tears rolled down her cheek. She regained her composure; apologized, and continued as if nothing had happened.

I think it was a combination of things. Stress over the war, things going on in the troop, and just being sick without someone to take the kids so that she could catch a few seconds of sleep. I was in awe of her strength—to just keep going and do what the families needed her to do. In the 'real world' you can call in sick because you are often given monthly 'sick time' by your employer. Her job doesn't allow for that.

Another time, I spoke with a new friend about the emotional stresses of deployment. I just didn't understand how she made it look so easy. She said, "Oh, I haven't told you my secret? You are allowed to cry all you need to in the shower. You have fifteen minutes to let it all out, then you dry off, get dressed, and you go take care of your family."

I realized these are not just ordinary wives. These are extraordinary women, tried and true just like their husbands. They are both Mommy and temporary fill-in for Daddy when need be. They push through when things are tough and they keep going. Although not a minute goes by that they aren't thinking of their husbands, life does not stop. They keep a home for their children and a home for their Soldier to come back to. They take great pride in their responsibilities.

I want to put up signs all over that say "THANK YOU for being the kind of women that you are, and THANK YOU for everything that you do. THANK YOU from all of America"! I am so proud to be one of you! Although you don't wear medals on your chest to show your accomplishments and your missions don't make the headlines like your husband's do, you are heroes to us. In THIS world you set the bar high for the rest of us. I have a new pride in calling myself an Army wife.

January 2 - Captain "P"

On Friday, in Iraq, Bravo Company 4th Engineer Battalion lost their leader, Captain Eric Paliwoda. CPT "P" took command of "the beast" a couple of months after they were in Iraq. I remember sitting here at home, worrying, thinking about how my husband as well as the rest of the troops would have to get used to this new commander. I was wrong to worry. They quickly grew to admire and respect him, and more importantly, to trust him. I know this to be true. I know this from my own Soldier who frequently spoke about his genius, his humor, his genuine respect and concern for the men under his command.

I know this from the friends I've made in the Bravo family, friends who come together to get through this deployment one day at a time. I've heard stories of CPT P writing to wives who were having a hard time. I've even heard stories of him personally calling family members of deployed Soldiers. I've heard stories about how he personally took care of Soldiers' problems. He even sent us pictures of our Soldiers and a note for Christmas. I know that he not only cared for his Soldiers, he cared for the families of his Soldiers who were waiting here at home.

I want his family to know, I want his fiancée, the woman he loved, to know that we will never, ever forget him. I want them to know how deeply we feel their tremendous loss. I want them to know that what he did, who he was, how he lived, made a difference to the people in Iraq, to the men under his command, and to their loved ones here at home.

4 January - From the Mom of a CPT Paliwoda Soldier

I am writing because unfortunately, the mortar attack on Friday hit close to home. CPT Eric Paliwoda was my son's captain. When my son came home for R&R, he talked of how his captain was one that the guys could all talk to. He was a commander who was involved and really cared for his men. I pray that his family would hear that he was a great captain and that his men really cared for him and were proud to serve under him. My prayers and thoughts are with them thru this ordeal.

5 January - From the Wife of an Officer Who Served With CPT Paliwoda

On behalf of my husband and me, we give our thoughts, prayers and hugs to Captain Paliwoda's parents and his fiancée. My husband is a platoon leader who has worked hand-in-hand with Captain Paliwoda. In all my conversations with my husband on the phone, he has always commented on what a strong, devoted and sincere leader Captain Paliwoda was. That he always put the needs of not only his Soldiers, but also their families, in the forefront of his mind. I am forever grateful that your loved one was one of the ones that has led my husband through this war. To you all and to Captain Paliwoda, I am forever grateful.

5 January - From CPT Paliwoda's Driver's Fiancée

As a member of Captain Paliwoda's Bravo Company "family," I never had the pleasure of meeting him. However, I understood how important his entire family was to him, the Soldiers and their families. My fiancé was his driver, and I knew from him that he held Captain "P" in the highest esteem. He admired his intelligence, his compassion, his leadership, and, very importantly in a battle environment, his sense of humor. I know this has deeply affected not just the Soldiers under his command, but the families who entrusted their Soldiers to him. He will be sorely missed by all. Our prayers and thoughts go out to his family and fiancé.

When through one man, a little more love and goodness, a little more light and truth comes into the world, then that man's life has had meaning. ...Alfred Step

5 January - Don't Be Shy

Traveling to be with my daughter-in-law and her family over Christmas brought us time to be together and lift some of the constant worry. My son is a SSG with B CO, 1-22 INF BN. While visiting my in-laws, their daughter, a SGT with HHC 3-66 AR, was able to call and talk to all of us, especially her two-year-old boy and eleven-month-old girl. She got to hear all of the noise and confusion that goes with opening presents, including the crying of children who are so young that they don't understand that there are many presents to open, and they cry when you try to take one present away so that they can open up the next one!

I didn't get to hear from my son that day, but he knows that our hearts were with him over there in Bayji. On the way back home waiting for my luggage to appear on the carousel, I saw a young Soldier with his wife and took the time to inquire which direction he was traveling. He had just arrived home for his two-week leave. I welcomed him back and let him know that I have a son over there. It was good to chat with him and be one of those letting him know just how proud we are of our men and women who serve their country. So if you happen to see a Soldier, don't be shy, go speak to them and let them know how we care for them and pray for their safe return! Happy New Year!

6 January - He Mattered
Mr. Babcock, we lost our captain, Sir: This Friday when their base in Balad came under mortar attack. Once his family was notified, we all were as well. Sir, when DOD releases his name, if you have room, will you please put this in your newsletter? All of us in the Bravo family receive it, and I think his family gets it. I'd like them to know that he mattered. Thanks.

8 January - Cheered and Applauded
My husband is in C 1/10 CAV. Last weekend I was in Galveston with some friends, including my 'battle buddy' and her husband who has recently returned from Iraq for a Permanent Change of Station (PCS). We were having a last hurrah before we have to go through that part of military life that I will never get used to, saying goodbye to dear friends.

We went to eat dinner at Joe's Crab Shack on the Seawall and had an experience that gave us all that warm, fuzzy feeling, so I thought I would share it in the hopes that the feeling would be contagious!

My friend's husband was wearing an 'Operation Iraqi Freedom' t-shirt, and after we had been there for a little while, our server approached and told him that another patron wanted to buy him the drink of his choice as a thank you for his service. He went to thank the person, and found out his benefactor was a Soldier himself, recently out of flight school, and 'PCS-ing' to Fort Hood to be a part of the 1st CAV. Shortly after that, our server asked them both to stand up and announced to the restaurant that there were two special patrons she wanted to recognize, one who had recently returned from Iraq and one who would be going over soon. Both were cheered and applauded by the other diners in the crowded restaurant. You could tell they were somewhat embarrassed, but also gratified that their efforts were appreciated.

When everything settled down and the time came for us to pay our bill, our server brought it over and told us that one of their regular patrons, who wished to remain anonymous, had left $100 to put toward our bill! It was truly a moving experience as we realized that complete strangers were so appreciative of what our Soldiers do for our country. Several people came over to our table to thank my friend's husband, and we all received hugs and thanks from another man who was teary-eyed as he recalled his father's service in WWII.

It was one of those moments that we will always remember, and I hope others feel comfort and pride when they realize how much the effort of our family members and friends mean to those for whom they are fighting.

8 January - The Baby Business

I am an Army Nurse midwife stationed at Fort Hood. I am amazed at the number of babies born to our Soldiers and their families at this place. I will say, however, that we have hit a low in the numbers now that it has been more than nine months since the 4th left. We in the 'Baby Business' are calling this the calm before the storm! I love my patients and strive to bring them the best birth experience they can get.

I know it is difficult to go through labor and birth without your spouse. Birth is a beautiful experience and if I could have one wish, it would be that all my moms have their loved ones present; but that is not something within my control. I would, however, like to commend all the women who have been so brave and endured labor during this last year of deployment. Also, to the fathers coming home to see their children for the first time, remember that it does not make you a daddy just because you were there for the delivery; you are a daddy when you are there for everything that comes after that. Enjoy your babies, guys!

8 January - My Hero

I just returned from Ft. Hood yesterday afternoon. My brother is home on R&R. He is with the 2nd Brigade. He looks fantastic, and he kept me laughing the whole time I was there. First, I want to thank my wonderful sister-in-law for sharing him with us for a few days in the middle of his R&R. It meant the world to my mom and me to see him. It is sure to help these next few months go by a little faster.

It is the coolest thing I have ever experienced as a sister. As I would sit and listen to him share stories and talk about his Soldiers, I could not help but be consumed by his energy. His passion for doing his job and doing it well is overwhelming. It is obvious he is a great leader. I have the letters from many of his Soldiers confirming that. It was such a privilege to be in his presence for those few days.

I know he is 'just' my brother, but for the first time in my life, I actually saw him as the great hero he really is. No one could possibly understand what these great men and women are going through unless you hear it first hand. I never heard him complain. I only heard him talk about his work and how well his Soldiers performed. I only wish his guys could have heard their sergeant saying such great things about them. He is as proud of them as we are of him.

Poem by Gladys Watson - Mother-in-law of CH (MAJ) Steven Maglio - DIVARTY Chaplain
Where is Iraq?
Daddy and I went shopping.
He said we would go fishing
When he returned from Iraq.
"Where is Iraq?" I asked my brother.
He said it was a place where our Soldiers
Are keeping other children safe.
My big brother said we can be proud
Of all the Soldiers, like daddy,
For such a good job in Iraq.
At night I look at the stars
And talk to God.
Then I ask Him to keep
Daddy and the Soldiers safe.
"Dear God, Where is Iraq?"

9 January - Beyond Description

My husband (1-68 AR, HHC Medics) mailed me a disposable camera, and I just picked up the photographs yesterday. All I can say is, "Wow!" There are pictures of the children waving, of the streets packed with Iraqi people waving and cheering, as their troops moved through! The pictures of the buildings, landscape (well, sand with the occasional tree), the riverbank and the historical buildings were beyond description!

Unfortunately, no pictures of Paul, though. But just to know that he took these pictures and has a thousand stories to go with each one is enough! There was one picture of a sign of Saddam that was all shot up! What a wonderful message! I look forward to developing the next camera he mails home!

He wrote in a letter that he was in the Biblical area of the Garden of Eden where the rivers meet. That is amazing to me! I wish he had taken pictures there! I would love to have this country up and running so as to one day be able to actually visit Iraq and view these sites first hand. God willing, that will be a reality.

10 January - Stand Firm in Your Faith - A Spiritual Reflection from CH (LTC) Brewer

I am sitting at my desk this Saturday morning catching up on some loose ends (seems I am always chasing after something without an end, anyway) and thinking about what lies ahead in this New Year. I had waited all last year for Christmas and New Year's to come and they did, and now I am waiting all over again, but I sure am thankful for making it through last year. I am looking at a desk top plaque given to me by CH (MAJ) Spencer Hardaway for Christmas that simply reads "Stand Firm" James 1:12. The whole verse says, "Blessed is the man who perseveres under trial, because when he has stood the test, he will receive the crown of life that God has promised to those who love him." Another translation of the phrase "perseveres under trial" is "endures temptations" or as I have used it, "who stands firm." Standing firm has been the theme of my reflections to you, as I encourage each of you not to quit or give in to the various temptations we all face in moments of trial.

It is nice to have a reminder on my desk to look at each day that speaks to me again and again about God's promise that I will receive the crown of life if I seek to love and serve Him and others in the work He has given to me to do. I wish at times I had such a visible reminder speaking to me when I face those moments of trials and temptations this life brings my way, something to help me remember to the promise of what waits for me when I stand firm in obedience to God's command. How about you, do you ever feel like giving up or just giving in to the tiredness you feel in the face of all the trials you must endure each day as you wait?

At that very moment I pray the Lord will bring to your mind and heart not only this particular verse as well as many others that speak of His faithfulness, love, and promises to you but also a gracious and encouraging word from someone who loves you and wants to help. It is amazing how many times we find ourselves just at the point of giving up or giving in, and then someone comes along and says just the right word or does something to encourage us to keep going for a bit longer as we wait.

How many of you like to wait on something you really want or need? Not many of us are good at waiting, yet time and time again, God calls us to wait on Him. I am realizing two things about waiting on God. The first is that the Bible tells me God loves me and He wants to do good to me and others. Therefore, to wait on God is to expect something good to happen to me since that is what He wants to do. The second is that while waiting, I am to do what He tells me to do, to walk in step with His Holy Spirit and to be obedient in all areas of my life—pretty simple, huh? I am discovering that the latter part is the most difficult for me in learning to wait on God and the good He has in store for me. I am also discovering that these ideas of 'standing firm' and 'waiting' go together. So I think in the coming year I will seek to learn more about both, and I pray you will seek to do the same. Do not ever give up.

12 January - Still Know Each Other

My husband and I were fortunate enough to be able to spend Christmas and New Year's together! It was great to have him home. Our sixteen-month-old daughter knew exactly who he was, and she was as much a daddy's girl as she was the day he left.

He had a little trouble adjusting, but we only had one stressful day while he was home. It showed me how dedicated he is to the Soldiers that he serves with and how much they are a family.

One day while he was home we saw on the news that some

Soldiers in the city that his unit is in were wounded and killed. He was a nervous wreck until we got the e-mail from Bob saying that the Soldiers were not from his unit. I knew that he cared about his guys and that they were a huge part of his life, but I never realized that these guys would become so close and be so dedicated to each other.

He was telling me that some of the guys who had come home on mid-tour leave were coming back and saying that it wasn't worth it to come home and have to say goodbye again. But as awful as the goodbye was, I have to say if I had the choice to do it again, I certainly would. It helped so much to know that he was okay and that we still know each other.

13 January - Dad Works to Bring it All Back Home
My brother is with HHB, 3-29FA in Samarra. Our dad works on the ships and boats that come through the port of Corpus Christi, so needless to say, it was rough on him last year when my brother got his orders to Iraq because my dad saw hundreds of tanks, missiles, Humvees, etc., come through his dock going to Iraq. Ironically, most of the equipment was from Ft. Carson where my brother is stationed.

I spoke to Dad yesterday, and now he sees transport ships heading out to Iraq to bring back the same equipment and our 4th ID Soldiers. So, to hear him sound excited about working on those ships to make sure they're in tip-top shape to bring it all back home to us just made my day!

14 January - I Saw a Ghost
This is my Christmas story. My family (mom, brothers and sister-in-law) were insisting that I go to Virginia for the holidays so that I would not be alone. They understood that I was feeling really sad that my son would not be here for this time. I went and spent my time with my beautiful nieces. In the back of my mind I was wondering how my son was and if he would be alone for the holidays. I tried not to let on that I was feeling really bad without him.

On the evening of December 26, my brother said he needed to talk to me; he looked very serious. I was scared. We went to the porch (this is where the 'family meetings' are held). I asked him to put the light on because it was pitch black outside. It was so quiet, dark and scary. When he put the lights on, I thought I saw a ghost. My son was standing there very proud, in his uniform. I was screaming so loud and crying that I felt my chest hurting as though I would have a heart attack.

When I went to my son, he said, "Yes, Mom it's really me." As I touched his face in disbelief, he wiped the tears from my face and asked me to sit down. I was a mess. I held on to him and cried like a baby. I did not let anyone near him for a few minutes. Eventually, I had to let go. My mom and son put this surprise together (it took him three days of travel to get to Virginia), and I will forever be grateful. It was the best Christmas present I could have ever received.

We came back to New York and spent the rest of the time with family and friends, eating, crying, and listening to stories that inspired me and filled me with compassion for so many of our men and women. My son continues to show that I did a great job raising him, and I want to thank the Army, his battle buddies, and God for keeping him safe to the best of their ability. Thanks, and God bless.

15 January - We Care

I read your news almost every day, but this is the first time I have written. My only two children (boys) are in the military. My oldest is in the Army (B Co, 1-8 IN), currently in Iraq, and my youngest is in the Marines and was with the first unit entering Baghdad. He came back in May, and his unit is returning to Iraq in February to relieve the current troops. I can truly say this last year has been the longest and proudest year of my life.

I'm truly thankful for the brave men and women who represent the United States in our military. They are all heroes no matter what their job may be. To the families who support them back here in the States, I want to say thank you for supporting your Soldiers while they are away.

I want to say one more thank you: To all the Viet Nam Vets I say, thank you. You were never given the respect and recognition you should have received. Most of you didn't have a choice, but you went and you fought, only to be ignored or hurt when you came home. I'm sorry for that—please know there are those of us who do care and thank you for your military service.

16 January - Touched...

I received a letter from my brother (3-66 AR, Tikrit). It was dated December 25. Three weeks to make it via post! He mentioned that on Christmas Eve, gifts from companies, churches and support organizations from the nation were distributed to our troops. Each Soldier in his unit had five to six gifts to open! They were so touched by the kind words and generosity from so many here in the U.S.

My brother was grateful for a simple pleasure, receiving a box of chocolate turtles and a Whitman sampler amongst his treats. For a split second he said that it felt like home as he always received turtles and Whitman samplers from our parents during the holidays. I am thankful that so many people here in the states find the time and means to support our Soldiers. God bless our Soldiers and those who support them.

19 January - Crossing the Border

The 101ST is arriving in Kuwait! My Soldier is now on safer soil, thank God! It may take weeks for them to clean up, pack up, and get out of there, but I like the location lots better than Iraq. Wouldn't you agree? So all you 4th ID supporters, the dominoes have begun to fall. Soon it will be your turn to enjoy the news that your Soldiers have crossed the border into Kuwait. Next stop, God bless the USA! Amen!

20 January - Technology Rewards

Yesterday during the New England game our son was online with us. He got to listen and watched most of the game with the family through the web-cam. He was able to see and comment about the game and listen as we cheered and then booed, as the Colts went down in defeat.

How different technology has made this war from Vietnam or the Gulf War when we recorded letters on regular and mini-cassettes and thought an instant Polaroid snapshot taken from our Soldier's area of operations was the next best thing to him being home!

21 January - Kind of Mellow Right Now

My husband, who's in 2-20th FA based in Taji, called me this past Saturday, January 17, 2003. He was upset because the three

Soldiers who were killed in the Bradley incident this past week were in his unit. He said he had not been able to call or e-mail me because they had shut down everything when it happened. I've learned that this is procedure after an incident like this. It's done to prevent news leaking out before the families are notified.

Anyway, he said that the Soldiers at the base were pretty down about it and that things were kind of mellow and quiet. My heart went out to him and the others. I felt like nothing I could say could make things better. It hurts to know we've lost more precious lives. My prayers go out to the families.

Every time I read about another casualty, I cry my heart out. My husband and I were just talking on instant messaging and he said they had the ceremony for the fallen Soldiers today. He said it was very emotional. He seemed in better spirits today, but our prayers continue for our Soldiers and those families who have lost loved ones. I just can't wait until all our solders are home.

21 January - What Will He Do With Himself?

I heard from my grandson today. He is with HHC, 2 BDE, 4ID in Ba'quabah. He told me he is not sure when they are leaving to come back to the States, so he didn't know when to tell me to stop mailing packages. He gave me a list of things he needs. He also told me that they are getting things ready for coming home. He told me, "To tell you the truth, I don't know what I'm going to do with myself when I get home."

I'm sure it will be quite an adjustment being back in the States. He had just come back from two years in Korea when he was sent to Iraq. He is really looking forward to coming back. He will still have a couple of years left of the six years he signed up for, so I suppose the Army will keep him busy when he gets back, and then he plans to return to college.

22 January - Sweet Tea

My husband is in HHC, 1-12 Infantry, 3BCT, and the wives around me who also read your updates are always happy to share with others what you have shared with them. The Army family truly is an amazing thing.

When my husband first joined in 1988, he went straight to the Rangers after basic and airborne school. We were married in 1989, and I moved away from home to join him at Ft. Benning.

What a wonderful experience that was—being a part of an Army family. We made memories and friends that will last a lifetime, and I see it happening again for us now, as part of the 4ID family.

The experiences that people have during a time of crisis certainly shape them into who they will be tomorrow. Those experiences leave a lasting impression, sometimes good, sometimes deep and raw, but always worth looking at and learning from.

Also, to let you know, I really miss Georgia! After ten years total time at Ft. Benning, we really felt as though it were home to us. So I love it when you throw in there a little bit about Atlanta or anything southern really! Enjoy a glass of sweet tea for me!

23 January - Letter From the Commanding General
To the Ironhorse Family:

Your husbands and wives are tentatively scheduled to re-deploy from Iraq in March-April 2004. This redeployment will be the culmination of over eighteen months of an incredibly high operational tempo for the Soldiers and families of this great division. You and your Soldier spouses have been through an extraordinary experience that few will ever understand. With that in mind, I have asked the FORSCOM Commander and the Department of the Army to augment Fort Hood and Fort Carson with professional counseling services in addition to the already established redeployment programs.

Initially Soldiers redeploying from OIF 1 will be authorized up to a ninety-six hour pass before beginning the reintegration process. This reintegration process is outlined below and should require about four weeks to complete Phase I and II. Upon completion of this process, Soldiers will be authorized to take up to thirty days block leave. Although Brigade Combat Team will conduct block leave, the entire division should be on block leave by May 17, 2004.

The nation has asked much from the Soldiers and families of the 4th Infantry Division, and we now have a unique opportunity to establish a model reintegration program for the Soldiers returning to their loved ones. This program will leverage current programs and draw on professional counselors and educators to provide seminars to ensure beneficial reintegration to all families of the 4th Infantry Division. I envision this model program to be conducted in three distinct, yet supporting stages. The first stage is the initial reintegration. This consists of medical/dental and support briefings to allow the Soldiers to deal with the first few weeks of returning home. The second stage is the core of the program. It consists of seminars aimed at specific target audiences, which allow families and Soldiers to gain a deeper understanding of the challenges they will face. The last stage is an ongoing process and provides long-term assistance for Soldiers and families. This program would be a test case for the Army. It would allow the Army to collect the data necessary to truly identify the needs of Soldiers and families separated for a year under the stresses of combat.

The Fort Hood and Fort Carson Soldier and family support structures are fundamental to the overall concept of the initial stage of reintegration. They will afford us the opportunity to conduct the mandatory classes as outlined in FORSCOM and III CORPS orders. These include safety classes, healthcare, entitlements, and general information on the normalization of Soldiers after deployments. These classes will establish a foothold from which we can gain the momentum required to move into the next and most critical stage of reintegration.

The Soldiers of the 4th Infantry Division will be redeploying from an environment unlike any the U.S. Army has faced in many years. The uniqueness of this experience presents us with complex challenges in reintegration. Unlike recent deployments, the protracted combat operations have probably taken a toll on both Soldiers and spouses mentally, physically, emotionally, and spiritually. Therefore, the second stage of our reintegration program is where these challenges are met and overcome. Through the use of seminars led by professional counselors, combat veterans, and educators from various institutes, Soldiers and families will come to grips with the changes in their lives.

This program will not only target the Soldier but also the spouse and all family members. I intend to employ these

269

professionals to provide insight and useful tools for our families and Soldiers dealing with post deployment stresses. The concept involves conducting seminars tailored to the unique needs of each Soldier and family. The seminars would be conducted using both on-post and off-post facilities.

This seminar format would involve Soldiers and families attending mandatory seminars organized by demographics to include: married, single, children (by ages), experiences in Iraq, and military leadership by position/rank. The seminars would take place over a period of up to three months. Seminars, workshops, and classes are in small groups, up to no more than thirty personnel. In addition to the mandatory classes, there will be an opportunity to receive assistance both through additional seminars and one-on-one counseling. The end state is Soldiers and families with the ability to recognize, communicate, and overcome the stresses in their lives.

The last stage of reintegration involves the long-term care for the families and Soldiers. The lead for this support would be the garrison organization. Although the Fort Hood and Fort Carson garrisons are capable of handling most issues, I envision a program that would involve the sustained use of professional counselors and experts to provide continual support.

Our tour in Iraq has demonstrated the professionalism, dedication, and selflessness of the 4th Infantry Division Soldiers and families. I intend to pay back that selflessness with a reintegration program that is truly professional and conducted in a first class manner. This nation will never truly understand the debt that is owed to the Soldiers and families of this great Division; however, I intend to quickly do the next best thing by conducting a professional program that thoroughly reintegrates all of us back into the normalcy of life at Fort Hood and Fort Carson.

God bless all the Ironhorse families and God bless all the Soldiers assigned to the 4th Infantry Division.
Steadfast and Loyal
Raymond T. Odierno
MG, Commanding

23 January - The Stuff That Matters Most

My little brother called me last night. (B Co, 1-22 IN, Bayji). He had his R&R from the end of October to November tenth, and this is the first call I've gotten that he didn't sound exhausted. We talked for an hour. It was one of those great calls that didn't have static. We talked about stupid stuff that doesn't even matter, which probably matters the most.

He told me that the hundreds of Ramen noodles that my Aunty Krist sends him on a regular basis are well appreciated by him and his guys. They all know her by name because of her frequent boxes filled with awesome goodies. Because it is almost time for my Soldier to come home, I wanted to thank all you readers for making me feel less alone.

And I also wanted to apologize for my ignorance. Before my brother joined the army, I was your average person. I would always stand at a game for the national anthem but wouldn't give it a second thought to talk to the person next to me or run down to the stand for a Coke. Oh yes, I knew they were out there fighting for my freedom. I would always watch the newest war movie and cry and think how terrible. My great uncle died in the Korean War and my other uncle served in Vietnam. But that was before I was born. So when my brother joined the army, I was proud.

He graduated from his basic training, two days after 9/11. I remember watching the news on that morning, and watching those towers fall to the ground. I could see the future. I saw my brother, a tired, exhausted, dirty, but strong Soldier fighting for his life and the lives of every other American. And I became the most patriotic person I know. And I now stand during the national anthem as erect as a Soldier, tight lipped, with tears streaming down my face. I could tell you every house on my way home from Wal-Mart that has a flag in its yard. If possible, I would write every veteran and currently serving American Soldier a letter of thanks. So this is my letter, to reach out across the world to thank you all. THANK YOU from a big sister.

23 January - One Year Ago Tonight

Today I took that last box I will be sending my son (B Co, 2-20) to the post office to be mailed. What a great day it is. I smiled at the postal clerk and said they wouldn't see me anymore to mail a box to an APO address. It was a year ago tonight that our phone rang and it was our son saying he was leaving on Saturday. My husband and I left for Fort Hood from Tennessee at midnight, driving straight through, wanting to be able to at least hug our child before he left. As we all know, the military can change their minds, and when we got there, our son said his time had been pushed back to Sunday. How wonderful, a whole day together!

We spent that day packing up his apartment and going over financial records etc. That evening we got another reprieve; he wouldn't be going on Sunday either. He questioned closing out his apartment, but I told him we needed to, so that if he walked into work on any given day and was told he was going for certain, all would be ready. We returned to Tennessee on Monday after long hugs. I got a call on February 5th just as he was getting on a plane for Rota, Spain, where he got on a ship and sailed off into the history books.

The postal workers in two or three post offices know my face now and ask how my son is doing. It makes me happy to be able to tell them that he will be home soon and that I will no longer be sending boxes to that APO address.

26 January - Plumb Wore Out

The following is an e-mail I received from my Soldier who is at FOB Warhorse in Ba'quabah (E Co, 204 FSB). That's the one that was hit with mortars the other night. Throughout the past nine months, E Co, 204th FSB has received almost all of the casualties that occur in the area. The news always reports that injuries and casualties were sent to the nearest CSH, but my Soldier and the rest of the company are always the ones that treat, stabilize and see the injured Soldiers first at their aid station before evacuating them to the CSH (if at all). My Soldier can go down the list of KIA from the Ba'quabah area and say, "We saw him," to almost every one of them. His e-mail message:

"...Internet has been down for the last few days due to bad weather and a multitude of other reasons. Don't have much time, so I just wanted to let you all know that I am okay and so are my men and women. It was a terrible night, but we all did what we were trained to do.

"I did see one report on CNN. I have no idea where they got the pictures because they were not even related to this base or what happened, and they only told half the truth when they reported

272

the story. I was one of the first guys on the scene and helped in treating and evacuating one of the guys to my aid station. I ended up with blood all over me, something that I am, unfortunately, getting used to. I thought we were over the hump, but I guess not.

"I thought the beginning of the movie, *Saving Private Ryan,* was pretty close to showing real combat, but now I think it is only moderately close. I guess it is as close as you can get it on film without really experiencing it, but they need to add all of the senses, the smells, and the sounds are totally different. That, and you; don't get the adrenaline rush watching film. I swear I could have lifted that kid all by myself, but I knew if I did I would have caused him more pain than he was already in.

"Bottom line though is that physically I'm okay, but emotionally I am just plumb wore out. Definitely ready to get out of this hole. Love and miss you all..."

26 January - Postman's Tears

Just wanted say how touched I was reading the note from the 'big sister' Thursday, as well as the one from the Mom sending her 'last box' to her son. I too sent my last box to my son (B-CO, 2-8 IN) yesterday. He actually started his basic on 9/11, and my mind shot immediately to the future. I knew he would eventually end up somewhere fighting to protect our freedom.

There are not words to express how very proud I am of my son and all of our military for the sacrifices they have made and will continue to make to preserve our freedom. He has two big sisters also that are beside themselves with joy and anticipation. The people I work with continually ask about my son and were just as excited as I was when he told me that he would be heading out sometime in mid-March.

I am so grateful to you for the tireless work you have done to keep me and the 4th ID family informed of the important news. Having been a Vietnam veteran's wife and now an Iraqi freedom fighter mom, I cry every time I hear the national anthem or any patriotic song, see an American flag or a yellow ribbon, or a Soldier in an airport, and I do not feel embarrassed any more. When I told my postal worker that the box would be the last one to my son, he cried!

29 January - If it Doesn't Kill You...

I found myself shedding a few tears last night as I boxed up the last care package to my husband's platoon. As I filled bags with Valentine treats and cards for his Soldiers, I realized that we were almost at the end of this yearlong bumpy road but the word 'almost' loomed in my mind. The safe exit from Iraq still remains.

Thoughts of the joy (and ordeal) of dealing with issues of the spouses and family members ran though my mind: The memory of the times I've held my breath while I waited to learn of the safety or peril of my husband and his Soldiers; the laughter the spouses and family members have shared at gatherings; bragging; complaining; remembering our Soldier; the friends and 4ID Family I've developed.

This has been a year I said I wanted to forget, but in retrospect, I know I can't. The personal growth, the bonds that have been forged, the memories; just prove the truth of the old saying: What doesn't kill you, makes you stronger!

30 January - Never Had a License

I got a call early this morning from my son in C Btry, 3-16 FA. He is located in a hospital complex about 20 miles north of Baghdad. He sounded in good spirits and we talked for a good half hour before getting disconnected. He told me he had a new job. Instead of gunner for the Paladin Howitzer, he was now the driver. This amazed me because, even though he was eighteen when he joined the Army, he never had a driver's license! When I mentioned that to him, he said it wasn't that big a deal because he has been driving the Humvees around since he got there. He also said he would be getting his license when he got back.

Angela Craft - Associate Member, 22nd Infantry Regiment Society

My story does not begin with the deployment of my Soldiers. It actually begins eleven years ago in a cemetery in southern California. While looking for my mother's grave, I had a most wonderful encounter that would change my life forever.

As I read the names on the headstones, I noticed some ducks ahead of me. When I got to the graves they sat upon, I read the name "Curtis Lamar Duck" on both. For most people, the irony and coincidence that ducks were sitting on the Ducks would simply be a comical thing which they shared with friends over dinner. I, however, took it as a sign. At first I just thought it was two spirits needing company. To my surprise, it was so much more.

In December of 2002, almost ten years after my first meeting with the Ducks, I was prompted to learn more about them. I began researching the life of the younger Duck. He was a member of Alpha Company, 1st Battalion, 22nd Infantry Regiment, Fourth Infantry Division, and Army. He died while serving in Vietnam during Operation Sam Houston. At the time of my research, our great nation began to ready for war. The war happened, was deemed over, and more Soldiers readied to move into Iraq for reconstruction. Among them were the 'Alphagators' of the 1/22.

Because I was a new associate member of the 22nd Infantry Regiment Society, I was given the most wonderful opportunity to serve the Soldiers, none of whom I'd known. I was given instructions on how to address and send a letter to a specific unit, and of course I chose to send my support to the Alphagators in honor of their fallen brother, Curtis Lamar Duck. This is how I became a Lady of the Ironhorse.

I am not a mother, daughter, girlfriend, or wife to a Soldier of the Ironhorse. I am merely a woman who has sent countless letters and packages. I am a woman who has prayed and thought of her Soldiers every single day. I have worried while reading the daily updates, and cringed with sadness and fear as I've opened the DOD e-mail notifications of death. I have smiled with joy as I've opened letters from some of my Soldiers, and have worried when long stretches without any word have passed. And now I am anxiously waiting to see if my family and I can be there when our Gators come home.

What makes me different from the other women who wait for their Soldier's return, is that those women will be able to share hugs, stories, smiles, birthdays, and everything else that family does. They will be able to call and know how their Soldiers are. I, on the other hand, will wonder. Sure, I will hear from a couple here and there. But not a day will go by that I won't think of those men whose name is all I know, or even those whose names I don't know. I will wonder if their re-adjustment went well, if they are happy and their relationships are successful. I will wonder if I've missed any birthdays or anniversaries, or births of new babies. But what I will always have is the irreplaceable experience of

❖   **Ladies of the Ironhorse**   ❖

this last year. Because of my Gators, I have learned so much. Because of them, the world is a better place. This is a poem I wrote for them in November, 2003:

> Gallant and strong are we
> Always completing the mission at hand
> True to the cause for which we fight
> Only men of "Deeds, not Words"
> Regulars, by God. By choice
> Steadfast and Loyal, Forever

Task Force Ironhorse - January 2004 Casualties

Captain Eric T. Paliwoda, 28, of Texas, was killed on January 2 in Balad, Iraq. Paliwoda was in his command post when it came under mortar attack. He died of injuries sustained in the attack. Cpt. Paliwoda was assigned to 4th Engineer Battalion, 3rd Brigade Combat Team, 4th Infantry Division (Mechanized), based in Fort Carson, Colorado.

PFC Cody J. Orr, 21, of Ruskin, Florida; **SPC Larry E. Polley, Jr.**, of Center, Texas; and **SGT Edmond L. Randle,** 26, of Miami, Florida, were killed January 17 north of Taji, Iraq. The three Soldiers died while conducting a surveillance sweep for IEDs north of Baghdad when their Bradley Fighting Vehicle struck an improvised explosive device (IED) and overturned. All three Soldiers were assigned to the 2nd Battalion, 20th Field Artillery Regiment, 4th Infantry Division, Fort Hood, Texas.

SPC Gabriel T. Palacios, 22, of Lynn, Massachusetts, and **PFC James D. Parker**, 20, of Bryan, Texas, were killed in a mortar attack on a forward operating base near Ba'quabah the evening of January 21. Both Soldiers were assigned to the 588th Engineer Battalion (Heavy), 4th Infantry Division, Fort Hood, Texas.

PFC Ervin Dervishi, 21, Fort Worth, Texas, died January 24 in Baji, Iraq, during a combat patrol when a rocket-propelled grenade hit the Bradley Fighting Vehicle in which he was traveling. He was evacuated to the 28th Combat Support Hospital where he

276

later died. PFC Dervishi was assigned the Company B, 1st Battalion, 22nd Infantry Regiment, 4th Infantry Division, based at Fort Hood, Texas.

SGT Eliu A. Mier, 27, of San Clemente, California; **CPL Juan C. Cabral**, 25, of Emporia, Kansas; and **PFC Holly J. McGeogh**, 19, of Taylor, Michigan, were killed when their vehicle was hit on January 31 by an improvised explosive device during convoy operations in Kirkuk, Iraq. The Soldiers were assigned to Company A, 4th Forward Support Battalion, 4th Infantry Division (Mech), Fort Hood, Texas.

ELEVEN

FEBRUARY - 2004
Keeping Busy

59 days and a wake-up until April 1, 2004...

*W*ork continued in Iraq. Saddam's hole was sealed. Our Soldiers continued working to stabilize all aspects of life for the Iraqis. School supplies, updated medical books and journals, and clothes were sent to Iraq for the Iraqi people. Police departments from Fresno and Medera, California donated bulletproof vests, helmets, two-way radios, and various other pieces of equipment to coalition trained police forces in Iraq. The donations came from individuals and businesses, showing that, as a country, we want Iraq's new freedom to be successful, and we wish them the best.

Back home, our mail cut-off dates before redeployment were announced. But we kept busy with redeployment briefings and making plans for welcome home celebrations. General Odierno's goal was to have the bulk of the division home by Easter. We hoped and prayed that it would be so.

Ft. Hood Rear-Detachment worked with local leaders and businesses to prepare for the transition of troops. The support we received from them was phenomenal. Contractors from the area volunteered their services to build the foundation for the beautiful memorial safely stored at the museum after being sent over from Iraq. The target date for completion was April 22, which was also the announced date of the official 4th ID welcome home celebration.

The Memorial, made from the bronze of one of the Saddam statues in Tikrit, is of a Soldier kneeling before a battlefield memorial (an M-16 standing up with a Kevlar helmet balanced on the stock, the bayonet in the ground, and the dead Soldier's boots sitting on the ground in front of the rifle). The Soldier kneeling in front of the battlefield memorial has his head in his hand and a small Iraqi girl is reaching out to put her hand on the Soldier's shoulder. It is a touching tribute to the fallen Soldiers of the Task Force but what makes it especially poignant was that the same artist who first used the bronze to make the Saddam statue asked to be the artist who crafted this tribute. The bronze pieces had to be taken to him secretly because he feared for the safety of his family and himself.

The statue was paid for by Task Force Soldiers and with other donations. The permanent home of the statue is next to the Headquarters' building at Ft. Hood.

2 February - Steak and Rockets

Here is an E-mail from an HHC, 2nd BDE Soldier to his wife:
Had Outback Steakhouse folks here last night, and they cooked a meal for us: steak, shrimp, bloomin' onion, bread, cheesecake, and near-beer. Very good! Had two steaks. We had some contact while they were here: rockets, but they missed. We fired back and conducted a raid on some houses we saw them run to.

...UAV—has a camera in it and we fly it around our camp so we can see what's going on. We blew up their boat with helicopter gun ships. They were using the river to try to get away when we spotted them. They came ashore, and then we shot artillery at them again and watched them run like crazy. They ran into some houses; we went in and got six people. We're not sure if they are the right ones yet or not. Outback people will be telling stories about Ba'quabah for years.

3 February - A Soldier's General

I can't begin to tell you how excited I was to be able to listen to General Tommy R. Franks in Salina, Kansas, on January 29. What an honor! General Franks is the type of man whom you would love to have for your next door neighbor. He is warm, humorous, and exudes the highest degree of patriotism, love for democracy, the United States, family, and especially our Soldiers. Before he spoke, he asked that the American flag be placed at the front of the stage.

My brother and sister-in-law gave up their reception tickets so that my husband and I could meet General Franks. I told him that my son was with the C/1-44 ADA, and his words were, "I love your son." He signed my program with the message, "Cindy, Thank you for your patriotism and your support."

I told General Franks that earlier during my son's deployment, we had had a conversation about him. My son has never met him, but he told me that General Franks is a 'Soldier's General.'

I told General Franks of our conversation, and he replied that this compliment was the highest he could ever be paid. I will always remember this experience as one of the best in my lifetime.

Peggy Ayres - Mother of SPC Jonathan L. Ayres - HHT 1-10 CAV

My son joined the military under the delayed entrance program in high school when he was seventeen-years old. In May he graduated from high school, turned eighteen, and in June we sent him off to basic training. Happily, we traveled to Kentucky to attend his graduation from basic—a proud day for all of us. Two days later (9/11) the planes hit the towers.

In January of 2003 he was called to go to Iraq. When he left in March, I felt a deep anguish. Everything in me was screaming to protect him. As I entered a desperate time of prayer, God spoke to me to read the 91st Psalm. I'd read it many times before, but this time it came alive. When I got down to verse 4, I read, "He will cover you with His feathers and under His wings you will find refuge." These words jumped off the page into my aching heart. The truth was, I wanted to cover him with my feathers and tuck him under my wing. That day, through prayer, I tucked him away under the Father's wings where he would be protected and taken care of by the Father rather than me. This has kept me strong throughout his yearlong tour, and I've had a tremendous peace. I give my Father in Heaven praise for caring for my son perfectly—a thing I cannot do.

3 February – Ready for the Challenge

It was the energy and enthusiasm you hear when a milestone is met and the next one is in view. Our son (555 14th EN BN, Fort Lewis, WA) has spent months taking Soldiers on convoys so that they may travel home to see their loved ones, never taking the opportunity for himself. He called to say that they had completed the last R&R convoy and were looking down the road to the date in February when they'd head out toward Kuwait, and then on to home at long last! At the young age of twenty-two, he'll leave the army as a sergeant. He is totally excited about entering school and pursuing other avenues in life, but he is the first to say that without the structure, training, and drive taught by the military, he wouldn't be ready for the challenge.

3 February - Today Was Not a Good Day

I received E-mail from my son (HHC 1-22 IN) on Saturday afternoon with some bad news. He knew all three Soldiers killed Saturday in the roadside bombing incident. He was a good friend with two of the Soldiers. I ache for these young Soldiers and their families. I have included his e-mail for you. Keep these Soldiers and their families, and all of our Soldiers and their families, in your prayers.

"Dad, well, today was not a good day. The day is still not over, but the first part was very bad. Three of our mechanics died. I can't say the place, but it's probably on the news already, so you can get the details from there. I knew two of the guys very well. For three years they have been fixing my Humvees. Even more than that, I knew them and their families. They each have a wife and kids.

"They were my friends, and I was actually going to stay in touch with them after we got back. I knew the female Soldier also. She was a very good person. Anyway, now they have all gone to heaven. This I know. And why did it have to be them? I don't know. They were not 'combat arms', they were mechanics. It should not have happened to them. But who am I to say what should and should not happen? It happened, and I have to live with it. I will be going to their memorial service on Monday to pay my respects. I hope they rest in peace. I will go on my mission tonight with them in heart and the bad guys in my mind.
Love,
Your Son..."

3 February - Proud Platoon Sergeant

An e-mail note from an A Troop, 1-10 CAV Soldier to his aunt:
Hi, I hope this finds you in good health. ...Just an update here. I am getting very close to leaving Iraq and getting back to

my family. It looks like I will be leaving around the first week of March after a very long year here. I would like to thank any and all who have been praying for me and the Soldiers who have been deployed to Operation Iraqi Freedom. The support we get from those back home has been an enormous help in keeping spirits up, as this has been a very difficult time.

So far, I have managed to avoid injury, but ask everybody to think of those here who will not be coming home. We just lost another Soldier yesterday, and there is now another family who will not be joining us upon our return to Fort Hood, Texas. Keep the families and these Soldiers in your prayers.

While nobody wants to be over here, we do this for so many different reasons. We do this for our country, for the citizens here, for our fellow Soldiers and most important to me, our families. I have been leading Soldiers a long time now, and am proud to serve with them as they work for me. As a platoon sergeant, it gives me a great feeling to be bringing all of my Soldiers home to their families and loved ones. For me, I have three years until I retire from the military, and after two wars and numerous lengthy deployments, I am ready to spend time as a husband and father to what I feel is the most wonderful woman and children in the world.

This has been tough on them all, and I am so proud of how my wife has handled it, and the kids too. She has managed the house and all five kids (and one dog). I am ready to 'spell' her and help out again. Keep us in your prayers, as I will all of you.

4 February - The Future of Iraq

Today my husband e-mailed me a picture of himself with about five Iraqi children. He had one on his lap about the same age as our youngest, eighteen-months or so. Some weren't even wearing shoes, and all were dirty from head to toe with rags for clothes. This picture put it all in perspective for me.

The faces of those children, smiling with a little glimmer of hope in their eyes, said it all. They are the future of that country, and the world for that matter, and what our Soldiers have done for them is remarkable.

If you had asked me a few years ago if I cared for the future of Iraq, I probably would have said I didn't care one way or another. Now that my family and your families have been so affected by the state of their country, I hope and pray that Iraq has a prosperous and democratic future. I hope the children—whom I saw stand so proud next to my husband—who's been away from his three children for so long, never forget the sacrifices our American Soldiers and their families have made for them. I truly hope that they take their newfound opportunities and succeed in life, professionally and morally.

I can stay strong and be patient these remaining months because I know my husband is doing a profound thing for thousands of Iraqi children and all people. I wish you all the best these next couple of months and God bless all our troops!

Jackie Switzer - Mother-in-Law to SGT Christopher Hardt - Alpha Co 3-66 AR

I don't know that I qualify as a 'Lady of the Ironhorse' but will share some insights from a mother-in-law's viewpoint. We love our son-in-law like one of our own children. His uncle-in-law and us kept our Soldier well supplied with weekly packages, with enough to share, during his deployment. We told him before he left that he only had to concentrate on himself and his job while he was gone, and we promised to make sure that his wife and two young children would have our unqualified support. He need have no worries about them that would serve as a distraction.

Of course, I am speaking of our daughter and grandchildren, but we would have done the same for a daughter-in-law. We provided a warm, stable haven for the children when they visited, occasional childcare services for Mom who was under twenty-four hours a day stress, meals and goodies to help with their budget, time management, outings, and anything we felt could make life easier for them. Our granddaughter was deeply touched when she heard her dad's name mentioned during prayers at church. When the children visited with us, we sent them home fed, bathed, and ready for bed so Mom could have a little extra time to herself.

In short, anything that we could do to make life uncomplicated for his family would make life easier for everyone. He could concentrate on his job. He is scheduled to come home soon, and we plan to be there when he arrives. We'll be ensuring the children are under watchful eyes so their mom and dad can concentrate on the homecoming. We are proud to have had an opportunity to serve in these small ways.

4 February - Bad Day at Balad

Our son is in HHT, 1-10 CAV, Camp Anaconda, Balad, and we've had two E-mails from him since the attack on Sunday. The words are his; I edited out the names. Please say a prayer for our Soldiers and their families. Mom of a 1-10 CAV Soldier.

"2/1/04: Mom—I am okay. We had a rocket land in our tents and it killed a guy. Ten people were injured... two tents destroyed. They just set these rockets on the ground and light a fuse much like a bottle rocket. I was quite lucky. I had a piece of metal fly thru the tent within a foot of me. But for the grace of God, there go I. It wasn't much of a good day. I had to use my belt as a tourniquet yesterday. Now I am using my suspenders to hold my pants up. I am waiting for the fog to clear out of my head.

"2/2/04: We were sitting around the tent we live in when we heard a boom. I looked out and saw a Soldier limping and asking for help. I grabbed my helmet and went to help him, along with another Soldier. We did the best we could until a medic got there. By that time there were many people going in and out of the tents where people were hurt. He survived. We then went to the tent where the maintenance guys were. They were the worst hit. I knew it was bad. Everyone was put in an ambulance and taken to the aid station. One died after he got there.

"Everyone else is good. Some are in Landstuhl, Germany, at the big hospital there. It was not until later that I looked at our tent and saw the holes through it. I have a hole through my towel that was about a foot away from me that got hit. We are okay, just a little in shock. I will be fine as will the rest of the people here."

WASHINGTON (Army News Service, Feb. 4, 2004) Some Soldiers Missed Super Bowl - By LTC Andrew Straw

At kickoff, I was touching up the shine on my combat boots. I thought of calling my wife in Charlotte, N.C., but she had already gone across town to a Super Bowl party. As I left Washington for the drive to the airfield, the first half was winding down and the score was still 0-0. I couldn't find the game on the car radio and forgot about football for the next 30 minutes.

I arrived at Davison Army Airfield to find the eight young Soldiers from the Honor Guard, also dressed in camouflage fatigues, sprawled out in the small passenger lounge. They were ogling the halftime show on TV and wisecracking back and forth just like thousands of other groups of young guys across the country at that moment. I learned that the score was 14-10, Panthers behind.

The general arrived five minutes later, just as the pilot stepped in to say the aircraft was ready. Anita called from Charlotte on my cell just as I was walking out the door. "...Can't talk, gotta go..." On the TV behind me, play was just beginning for the second half of the game.

The ten of us followed a sergeant through the darkness from the near-deserted terminal to the waiting helicopter. As we carefully tiptoed across patches of ice on the apron, one of the Honor Guard Soldiers whispered something about Janet Jackson. Another Soldier beamed with adventure as he climbed in, "It reminds me of the first time I rode a tractor!" I was beaming too. It would be my first ride on an Army Blackhawk.

I was warned in advance that Blackhawks had no heaters, and had bundled up with two layers beneath my uniform. The night was clear. We flew to Delaware at low altitude over beautiful snow-covered scenery. We landed at Dover Air Force Base forty-five minutes later and parked near a huge C-141 cargo plane with Air Force Reserve markings. The rear doors and ramp were open, and light spilled from the huge cargo bay.

I followed the general as he was quickly ushered into a small, neat passenger lounge. Coffee? Water? The game was on TV; the score was 22-21. A half dozen others in various uniforms were waiting. I introduced myself to a major from New York City—a forensic dentist in the Army Reserve, called up to help out for a thirty-day tour. A Methodist minister serving as an Air Force chaplain bragged about the support his wife gives him while he is recalled to active duty.

While the general got a briefing on the mission details, an Air Force colonel gathered the rest of us together, and we marched out to the C-141. I followed him up the ladder into the cargo bay. It was empty except for the three oblong boxes in a perfect row down the center. Two Loadmasters were adjusting the ramp in the rear of the aircraft, and several others were carefully arranging U.S. flags over each of the boxes. A congenial major explained the proceedings to follow the way a priest leads a family through a wedding rehearsal.

I line up with the flight crew along the fuselage, facing the caskets. Attention! The Honor Guard marches in silently; wearing white gloves with their camouflage uniforms now. The general marches up the ramp with the Air Force wing commander, a colonel. The chaplain says a prayer with all the right words: fallen warriors ... the Army family ... selfless service ... the price of freedom.

Nobody is thinking about football. Nobody... The young Soldiers from the Old Guard are standing smartly, solemnly, expressionless. No slouching or snickers now, only the serious task at hand. Ready... Down! Ready... Up! Ready... Face! Forward... March! They move to the measured commands with astounding precision.

In the cold dark night, there are fewer than two-dozen of us present. No outsiders are watching, but those young men give a TV-quality performance, as if their burden were a fallen president. Present, Arms! We salute as the first remains are marched off the plane under the watchful gaze of the general. He salutes.

We do it again for the second set and the third. The unmarked, clean, white truck then drives off very slowly with its red, white, and blue-draped cargo. The Honor Detail marches behind it. The general dismisses us.

Back in the small lounge, the game is still on, eight seconds left. I watch the unfolding excitement numbly.

Welcome home, fallen sergeant, corporal, and private first class. You missed the Super Bowl. The Patriots won.
Thank you.

SGT Eliu Miers, 27, CPL Juan Cabral, 25, and PFC Holly McGeogh, 19, of the Army's 4th Infantry Division, died Jan. 31 in Kirkuk, Iraq, when their vehicle hit an improvised explosive device during convoy operations. LTC Andrew Straw is an Army Reserve officer from Charlotte. He has been serving on active duty at the Pentagon with the Army's G3 since October 2002.

7 February - 1ID Mom Shares Her Thoughts

As I write this my son is making final preparations to deploy from Vilseck, Germany, to Iraq with 1st Infantry Division. I know all family and friends, as well as the Soldiers of the 4th Infantry Division are counting the days and minutes until they all get home! Please, Soldiers of the 4th, when my son and all your replacements come to relieve you, please help them with all the advice and preparation you can so that they will survive. I read about the Soldiers of the 4th getting ready to return, and it's bittersweet news, as my own Soldier is about to meet you there, in Iraq.

On another note, I want tell you about a wonderful incident that I witnessed on Christmas Eve. I was at LAX, waiting for my son's flight to get in from Germany. An International flight arrived before my son's, and I passed the time by watching all the arriving travelers come down the escalators and meet their families, etc. I noticed a tall, handsome young Soldier disembark, wearing his desert DCUs. He was met by his family, who all wore USA emblazoned shirts, waving the American flag.

They all cried and hugged and laughed, and you wouldn't believe it; all the people in the whole terminal area (including many people from other countries, in all kinds of different native dress, etc.,) burst into spontaneous applause and cheers. It made me cry, not only because I too, was meeting my Soldier and could empathize—and not only because it was a beautiful incident—but because I remember meeting my Soldier returning in 1971, when he was spit on and sworn at. I'm very thankful that times have changed.

13 February - Excerpts From Newsletter
The wives of 1-68 Armor out of Fort Carson have sent several newsletters to their husbands in Iraq. We've featured some of their top ten articles before and gotten a kick out of them. Here are excerpts from the last newsletter that they sent to Iraq before the troops come home. Enjoy and smile.
We are all anxiously awaiting the phone call we get that says your plane safely landed in this great place we call the U. S. A!!! For now, here are a few of the things we would like to do with you when you get here, listed in no specific order:
   -sit in front of the fireplace and cuddle
   -take you to a nice restaurant
   -have a few beers
   -have a long talk
   -buy you some new clothes
   -talk (without being cut off or without having to say "can you say that again—I didn't hear you!")
   -run errands alone without the baby or the kids—all by myself

-get rid of the kids for the weekend and take you to a spa resort
-fix you a home cooked meal and then take you to McDonald's for a Big Mac
-have sex (like I said—no particular order)
-go to Branson for vacation
-take lots of pictures with the new digital camera
-have our movie and pizza Friday night
-catch up on all of the scary movies we were too chicken to watch without you
-have you carry the groceries
-shave your head
-cuddle
-take a bath together (we tried to keep these clean)
-go get Baskin Robbins banana splits
-hug you, hold you, let you know how much we love you!!
-wake up next to you knowing it isn't a dream
-we want to leave the kids with you for anything and not feel like we are forgetting something
-have some R & R of our own
-cuddle on the couch and spend the whole day watching movies and eating popcorn
-go on vacation—even if it is hot and sandy—at least there will be a swim up bar!
-go to the park, zoo, family fun center, grocery shopping, fishing, ice skating, roller skating, Mickey-D's play land—whatever it is as long as we are with you.
-catch up on all of your favorite Reality TV shows and introduce you to all of the new ones!
-start a family—FINALLY!
-Disappear

Things Husbands SHOULDN'T Say When They Come Home:
-I thought you bought a gym membership.
-What do you mean you are going to happy hour?
-Where's the beer?
-What do you mean you are going out? Can't you get a babysitter?
-I don't remember buying stock in Longaberger, Victoria's Secret, Gymboree, Pampered Chef, the Citadel mall, etc.

-Whose car is that? (pointing to the new one in the driveway.)
-Tax Refund? You said we broke even.
-Did you rearrange the garage—I can't find a thing...
-What, you got a tattoo?
-Did we really need new furniture for the WHOLE house!
-Why are the kid's favorite words "charge it?"
-Where are we going to put the new 60-inch TV?
-What do you mean you didn't tape the Super bowl?
-You threw away my swimsuit edition!!!
-Has my Harley arrived?
-I don't think the vacuum has moved since I left.

Things Husbands SHOULD Say When They Come Home:

-Honey, why don't you go to happy hour tonight!
-I hired you a maid for the next year.
-Honey, we still have ALL the kids!
-NO VISITORS for the next month (including my family).
-The yard looks GREAT!
-Sure—Quit your job!
-I love the new purple car—It is so you!
-I am going to wash all of my clothes myself.
-I am going to send you on a week spa vacation—thanks for doing such a great job!
-Honey, I love your new belly ring and tattoo!
-Your new wardrobe looks great!
-Where would I be without you!
-What can I do for you?

We can think of a million and one things we want to say to you when you come home. We just can't wait until we get to say them in person!

14 February - He Sounds Awesome

I was able to 'instant message' my husband today (3-67 AR in Ba'quabah). He says, "Hey Hon, doing something a little different today, I'm starting to recover my gear."

He sounds awesome. He is really looking forward to the return trip, whenever that may be! I can't wait for him to see the kids. I think each of the boys have grown about six inches since he deployed. Since he didn't come home on mid-tour leave—the last time he held the baby—she was about a week old. I have lost fifty-five pounds—mostly baby weight, but hey, it was there when he left! My job on redeployment is the same as it's been several other times: keep an open mind, listen as much as talk, and most importantly, maintain a sense of humor!

15 February - Until the Last Rose Dies

My husband (C Co, 588 EN BN) totally surprised me for our one-year anniversary. With the helping hand of my father-in-law, he had a beautiful dozen roses delivered to my workplace. On the card it read: "Happy Anniversary! Sending All of My Love From Iraq.P.S. I'll love you until the last rose dies."

At first, I was a little concerned because I knew my beautiful roses would only last a few days, but then I noticed that he sent me eleven real roses and one silk rose. That was the best anniversary gift that I could have received while he was away, and I'll cherish my silk rose for the rest of my life.

Jazlynn Cole - Wife of SPC Ryan Cole - HHT 1-10 CAV

My husband left for Iraq on March 31, and has been gone since. I am used to these deployments because my dad was an Airborne Ranger for the US Army. But when it comes to your husband, it is a different feeling of being scared, and anxious for that homecoming day. I think the one thing that has helped me through this is all the letters he wrote to me, and what helped him is all the letters I wrote back. I also sent him six or seven little photo albums of pictures of me and our son who is now thirteen-months old— Instead of three months when my husband left.

That helped him; he said it was like he was here with us to watch him grow. He did call me every chance he got, but sometimes, some Soldiers do not get to call. I always try to keep myself busy doing something and my infant son does aid in that.

I also bought a book called *Married to the Military: A Survival Guide for Military Wives, Girlfriends, and Women in Uniform*. It is by Meredith Leyva, founder of cinchhouse.com. The book is full of good tips about everything that military wives deal with when it comes to their Soldiers, and the military way of life because we all know that being a military wife is very different than being a wife of a civilian. You endure things most wives

would never and could never handle. There is a reason why we wives were picked to be military wives: We are a different kind of strong.
Forever a Soldier's wife!

15 February - Encouraging Words
Just wanted to let you know that my son (223rd MS NG) is in Kuwait now. We feel such a relief that he is out of Iraq. I told my husband that now maybe we didn't have to watch Fox News all the time. We tried, but it didn't last long, we still have military 'family' over there that we care about. We are so thankful that he will soon be home, and I would like to encourage those that are now leaving for Iraq to keep the faith.

"The Lord is good, a refuge in times of trouble. He cares for those who trust in Him (Nahum 1:7)."

18 February - No Dry Eyes...
I took my four-year old, with infant in tow, to get his haircut over the weekend. While we were there a Soldier asked me how old my baby was, and I told him, "eight-months." He told me that his wife was due in a couple months, but that he would be leaving for Iraq before then.

I told him how my husband had left two months before our son was born and wasn't able to come home for R&R to meet him, and they will meet in the gym the day he returns. We talked a little longer until he had to go. As he was leaving, I told him to stay safe and that I would pray for him.

He said to me, "Thank you and thank you for all that you have sacrificed and done for us so we may go off to war. God bless you."

I couldn't believe that this Soldier was thanking *me,* as he was about to go off to war! I stood up, tears running down my face, and gave him a hug and told him, "No, thank *you* for what you are doing. God bless you and Godspeed."

After we finally let go of each other, I looked around to see that there wasn't a dry eye in that Barbershop as that Soldier left. My four year old broke the silence with his wondering out loud if the lady was going to finish his haircut. That helped us all to dry our eyes and carry on.

Our Soldiers are truly amazing. Not only do they fight for

our freedom and for the world, but even as they head off to war, they thank us. They thank us when it is we who can never pay them back for what they have given and done. I didn't get his name or unit, but he is in my prayers every night! God bless our Soldiers, and thank you for what you will do and have done.

Cindy Richardson - Wife of LTC Gil Richardson - HHC DIV Chaplain

Cindy e-mailed to Gil:
"Hi dear. Wish we could do the instant message thing. I cried for grandma and for missing your folks. Gracie asked why I was crying, and she cried for them too. She also cried because she didn't want to die last. She said that she hated being the youngest because she didn't want to be alone one day. It made me so sad. I tried to comfort her, but the thought must be scary. It's hard for her to imagine getting married and having a family of her own one day."

Gil e-mailed to Cindy:
"Being the youngest, I can identify with her. I will compose a message for her. I love you and miss you, and I miss our three treasures—each a priceless gift from God that he created through our love and marriage—so much. I also miss the animals. I head south in three weeks from today to start my pilgrimage to you. I should start flying Wednesday the twenty-first, and arrive Thursday the twenty-second. Ryan can help drive to DFW. I love you. Gil...""

Gil e-mailed To Grace:
"Gracie, as you know, Sweetie, I am the youngest in my family. Sometimes it seems unfair—I didn't have a little brother or sister, so I was the caboose. I told people yesterday in a sermon that when I was a little boy, I was tired of being the one bossed around, so I asked your Grandma Sally if I could be the "boss of the dog" (we had a very nice dog named 'Taffy.')

"Grandma Sally agreed, but Taffy did not (she still was a nice dog to me). I have stayed very close to family, and I know that they have been close to me. I also know that someday, a very nice, well educated, stable, gentlemanly, Christian boy will fall in love with you, and you with him—and you will want to marry and have a family. You will stay close to Joe and Ryan—they love you very much, and were so happy when they got you as a

baby sister years ago. They will have wives, too, so you will have sisters-in-law, and they will have kiddos (so you will be Aunt Gracie some day). You will have your cousins, just as we see cousins in Indiana, Arizona, and Tennessee (at family reunions) and Virginia (Grandma Sally's side of the family). You will not be alone, as God is always with you, and he sends people into our lives to be our friends. I love you, Little Girl, and I cannot wait to see you in three and a half weeks. Ryan is coming to visit you in a little over two weeks!
Love, Dad."

19 February - More Than Milk and Bread
I had the greatest realization yesterday as I ran my errands, dragging my kids around. I get to go grocery shopping next paycheck for my husband! Never did I think that I would be so excited to go grocery shopping. I haven't been able to shop for him for food that is going to stay in the house (rather then be sent in a package) in 330 days and I can't wait! I, of course, will wait to pick up those 'big, fat' steaks and fresh fruit he has been craving until his arrival day, but come payday, I will be running to get that six-pack of Corona and limes!

I know that the next big trip to the grocery store I will be beaming ear to ear knowing why this trip is more than just 'milk and bread' while I push my kids quickly down the aisles!
See you soon, 4ID!

Nina Vangordan - Wife of SSG Elijah Vangordan - Co B 2-8 IN
What has encouraged me to stay strong through this deployment are our children. We have a three year old and a five year old. I promised my husband I would stay strong not only for myself but for our children's sake and his. I know they don't need to see me all sad, walking around like a zombie. I was, the first two months, and then I started attending a support group here on post called Women Supporting Women. Without having this group or my children I think it would be a lot harder on me. My children are the reason I get up each day.

This is our first deployment as a family; we were married in January of 2003. I had to take on doing a lot of things I didn't think I could do myself without my husband. We moved to a new state, I have no family here other than my husband (when he is home) and our children. I had to move out of our house where we were living and move on post by myself and get our children onto a schedule. I bought my first lawn mower and I actually mow the yard and cook, both of which I hate, but I can do it.

A lot of things have happened while he was away. I had a miscarriage, and I was able to get through it with the help of the group I attend, Women Supporting Women. They've been my family through this whole deployment. If I had sisters, I'd truly like to have them as my sisters.

I also tried to stay busy as much as possible and started a scrapbook of his deployment as a gift for my husband so he could look back on it later. All the pictures he sent me I had developed and placed in there, as well as all the letters family and friends have sent me are in there, pictures of the kids and pictures they drew for daddy, his letters to them and his letters to me and letters I've written him are included in the scrapbook. He has three big binder scrapbooks to come home to and now I'm working on my fourth one. He's been gone almost a year and is suppose to return this year in April 2004.

23 February - Their Loss is Our Loss

This past week has been both an exciting and horrible week. My husband's unit, the 2-20th FA, was heading to Kuwait for redeployment. The convoy would take approximately two days to get there. Our family was both excited and nervous. We had many praying for their safe arrival.

I didn't expect to hear from my husband too soon, because I knew that they would be extremely busy in Kuwait, but on Thursday I received an e-mail from my husband stating that gloriously the Lord had got them to Kuwait safely. I was so happy and excited. My children were elated. I think that this was the first time in a long year that I had truly felt total happiness. I just felt relief that he was in a safer environment and that everyone arrived safely. He said he wouldn't be able to contact me often, because he would be real busy but would try to check in as often as he could.

My joy didn't last but a day. On Friday at noon, I received a phone call from my brother who is in the 1st CAV (due to leave at the end of the month to Iraq), and he informed me that my sister-in-law's father was just killed in Iraq. I cannot tell you how devastated I was. He had had two close calls prior to this, and we thought that he was almost home free.

He had already met retirement status (would retire with twenty-one years) and had less than two-weeks to come home. He never took R&R and had been gone for a whole year. His family was so looking forward to retirement. My brother had a very close relationship with him. He was a father to him. Their family is devastated. They were so close to making it. He was killed on a convoy, possibly on its way back to Kuwait.

Yesterday was very hard to say the least. My house was grand central station with the phone ringing constantly. Our family is very close and many wanted to express their condolences or try to help. Their loss is our loss. I cannot tell you how my heart bleeds for them. I cannot wait until this is all over and our Soldiers are all out of harm's way. Until then, we just have to hang in there and continue praying.

25 February - My Son is Coming Home!
Thoughts from a Task Force Ironhorse Mom:
Sunday night, fifteen-second news item: Bombing in Kirkuk, several dead and injured... My God, that is where my son is! I turned to CNN and found the same fifteen-second news item. Do they really need to report this? My son is scheduled to return home next month. Needless to say my heart aches all night, and once again sleep does not come.

Monday: I heard the sweet sound of my son's voice this morning! He is with the 720th MP BN, 64th Co. Like many moms, I can tell how my child is by the sound of his voice. For the first time in many months, I could tell that he had a smile on his face, and there was laughter in his voice. They will be heading to Kuwait within two weeks and then home! He is one of many, I am sure, that will not be coming home to what he left behind; however, he still has the love of his family and the experience of age and wisdom.

I want to share with you all that the redeployment tip of "make sure they know what awaits them so they can deal with it over there" was the best advice given. If you really think that they are removed from here because they are halfway around the country fighting a war, think again. Letters and phone calls from wives, children, and family fill them in on all the happenings. If they ask you a direct question, you'd best be honest; chances are, they already know the answer and are seeing if you can be trusted to be truthful with them.

They have faced hardship beyond our imagination; they are owed nothing less than the truth! He told me several phone calls ago about the wreckage of his life that awaited him, and the loneliness he faced.

Today, knowing all that, he is coming home and ready to face it and deal with it. The best thing about all of this, I can enjoy his homecoming and not suffer in silence knowing that his world had fallen apart and not bearing to tell him.

He knows that his family is here waiting to help him and support him, something he didn't really understand when he left last year.

I asked him if he wanted me to be at Ft. Hood when he arrived, something I had asked before with very little response. Today I knew he wanted and needed me there, something this ol' mom needed so much to know. He is my first, he made me a mom and he is coming home!

Monday Night: My heart breaks this evening because in my joy that my son is coming home, someone's son may not have survived in Kirkuk yesterday. My son asked me something that he has never asked, "Pray for me, Mom, as we drive to Kuwait; I am in the lead vehicle, and I am scared... so close to coming home but yet so far." And even with this request, there was a smile in his voice knowing that he is coming home!

I have a bag packed and am waiting for the call so I can buy my plane ticket. My son is coming home!

Christine A. Wallace - Wife of SFC Chris R. Wallace - HHB 4-42 FA

This has been a year, to say the least, and I am so very thankful for people such as you who help ease the pain by being such a positive, supporting source. Thanks so very much! As of tomorrow, I will be able to say, "He's coming home next month!" A BIG HOOAH on that one! The following letter started out as being a 'vent' letter, and turned out to be printed along with my photo in the Killeen Daily Herald. It seems I touched quite a few hearts with this one. I hope you like it. God Bless ALL of our

brave men & women, representing this fine country we live in.
UNITED WE STAND

"To all the families, friends, and veterans of all the armed
forces—this is for you. For all the rest of the citizens of the United
States—take note, this is for you also. I want to express my deep
appreciation for all of those who are involved one way or another
with our fight for freedom now and in the past. For those of you
who are not personally affected, but enjoy the everyday freedoms
that you have, or don't realize that you are enjoying them, I hope
by the end of this you are thanking a Soldier of present or past.

"My life as a military wife has become increasingly difficult.
Not only for the obvious reason of my husband's deployment,
but more so of the attitudes of others around me. Being alone is
one thing; I have endured years of that because of divorce. At the
time, it was hard, but looking back it was nothing compared to
being alone because your spouse is fighting for freedom. There is
a constant 'black cloud' of fear and worry that looms over your
everyday tasks, chores, and routines. It starts with the signing of
the wills, not because it's something all families should have, but
because you HAVE to. Most twenty year olds don't think about
these things; or what about the last night together, and you don't
know what to say to each other, so you don't. You just lie there
staring at each other, holding each other, fighting off the feelings
of, "what if this is our last time?"

"There are the constant reminders of news broadcasts,
demonstrations, and President bashings. You have nightmares of
bombs, if and when you finally fall asleep. You hear of Soldiers
being killed, find relief in knowing it wasn't in his area, but then
feel guilty because you know another family is grieving. You carry
a phone with you constantly in hopes that he will call, to hear his
voice, so you know he is all right. You try to smile, to keep things
'normal' for your kids. You hold back tears, because you want to
be strong, but also want to crumble. You spray his cologne on
your pillows to feel close, you talk to his pictures. Everything is
a reminder of his presence. You are alone for anniversaries,
birthdays, and other special occasions. You carry the world on
your shoulders for the both of you, for the whole family. You pray
to God every day as if he was sitting right beside you: "Please
bring him home safe."

"So no, this isn't the average life of a regular citizen. To you, the Soldiers are merely the reason your community exists, or just another GI, the guy in that uniform on TV. I've heard quite often, that they all look alike. Tell a military wife that; we know exactly what their haircut looks like, or they way they walk, the shape of their pants, boots, the way their helmet looks on them, we know and we constantly watch the news in hopes of catching a glance at our Soldier. Those men & women are husbands and wives, sons and daughters, brothers and sisters just like the average citizen. They enjoy football, good food, movies, just hanging out. Yes, they volunteered, and they are doing their job, but let's not forget that that job is for all of us. They don't know most of you from Adam, but are putting their lives on the line for you.

"So don't take for granted the good things in your life. The time spent with loved ones, the restful sleep. Please have more respect and try to put yourself in our shoes. A simple, "'How are you doing, or call me if you need me,'" means the world. We'd love our world to be worry free like yours.

"To all of you military families and friends, thank you, for your understanding, mutual support and being there for me. United we stand. I appreciate you more than words can express."

Katrina Cannon - Wife of CPT Jacob Cannon - HHC 588 EN BN

What a privilege and blessing it is to be an Army wife. Yesterday was my birthday and although some might think it would be 'sad' to celebrate my birthday alone without my husband, currently serving with the 588th EN BN, this has been by far my best birthday ever! And really these memories have only been made possible due to my husband being gone in Iraq.

First, my husband surprised me last week with the delivery of a new digital camera! Thanks to the 'Internet Café' that is now up and running on a much more consistent basis, he was able to get online and order one shipped directly to me from Best Buy. With the Internet access, they also have a great new website for Task Force Ironhorse with lots of pictures of all our Soldiers. As soon as I learn more about my camera, I will be able to send digital photos.

Next, he called me on my actual birthday—bright and early at 4 am! He was definitely the first of the family and friends to call and wish me well. He said he loved me, and just hearing his voice was all the present I wanted! This was only a memory that can be made with a husband in Iraq.

And to top it all off, some of the other officers' wives totally surprised me at work with cake, flowers and balloons personally delivered to my workplace that evening while I was on night shift. My family from out of town had contacted them to get a workplace address for the flower delivery, but these ladies went above and beyond with the personal delivery, which included singing their own rendition of Happy Birthday, live! What a neat group of ladies representing the same kind of character as their spouses serving overseas; always going above and beyond whenever possible!

So as much as I wanted to celebrate the day with him in my arms, the day was blessed in ways only possible in light of our husbands' deployment. And now these memories will be cherished for generations to come. It is such a joy to see how circumstances really can work out for the good, even when they may not appear that way at first.

God bless our Soldiers and God Bless America!

Marta Robles - Wife of MSG Efrain Robles - 2-20 FA

Freedom Has a Cost
We have come a long, long way;
Since that moment we all dreaded;
Soldiers left us on that day;
To foreign land is where they headed.
To a country where they say;
People seem to be in need,
So our Soldiers went away.
To perform their awesome deed,
All the children they must feed.
One dictator overthrown,
Crimes committed, awful greed,
Soften hearts as hard as stone.
Even if it took forever,
Look at all they have achieved.
Pressing on in this endeavor,
For a country so in need,
Can the storm ever grow calm?
Precious lives being lost,

Will this be another Vietnam?
Seeking peace at what cost,
Seems as though it were a dream,
For those who cry and grieve,
Since forever it may seem,
Since they saw their Soldier leave.
Soldiers suffered long ago,
And no one seemed to care,
But our nation had to grow,
Learn the meaning of what's fair.
We now appreciate those lives,
Who fearlessly fight for the weak,
Leaving children, leaving wives,
The right to choose is what they seek.
To those Soldiers we're indebted,
As they made such sacrifice,
Never once have they regretted,
Leaving home to save a life.
As they start to come back home,
We can finally see the light,
Reuniting with their own,
Is their only one delight,
Celebrations left and right,
Having fought the long, hard fight,
No more desert, no more grub,
Lots of hugs and lots of love,
Some in joy, some in strife,
Don't forget that precious life.
Remember always, this we must,
Those who lost their lives for us.

Task Force Ironhorse - February 2004 Casualties

SSG Roger C. Turner Jr., 37, of Parkersburg, West Virginia, died February 1 in Anaconda, Iraq. SSG Turner was in his sleeping quarters when the logistical support area came under mortar attack. He died as a result of his injuries. SSG Turner was assigned to the Headquarters and Headquarters Troop, 1st Squadron, 10th Cavalry Regiment, 4th Infantry Division, Fort Hood, Texas.

SFC Class Henry A. Bacon, 45, of Wagram, North Carolina, died February 20 in Ad Dujayl, Iraq, when he was struck by a recovery vehicle while he was assisting a disabled vehicle. SFC Bacon was assigned to Headquarters and Headquarters Troop, 1st Squadron, 10th Armored Cavalry Regiment, 4th Aviation Brigade, 4th Infantry Division, Fort Hood, Texas.

PFC Nichole M. Frye, 19, of Lena, Wis., died February 16 in Ba'qubah, Iraq, when an improvised explosive device struck her convoy. Frye was assigned to Company A, 415th Civil Affairs Battalion, U.S. Army Reserve, Kalamazoo, Mich.

TWELVE

MARCH - 2004
Coming Home

31 days and a wake-up until April 1, 2004...

From the middle of February until our Soldiers finally landed at home was a time period that could be dubbed, "so close and yet so far." We were still losing Soldiers to terrorist attacks in Iraq so patience was a lesson that had to be learned on a whole new level. The transfer of authority to the 1st Infantry Division took place on March 16. SSG Mack greeted all of our Soldiers and kept families entertained in the gyms at Ft. Hood. As far as I can learn, he attended every welcome home ceremony. He was not able to deploy because of medical issues, but he made the three to four-hour waiting time in the gyms go by more quickly.

Many Soldiers stopped in Bangor, Maine. The Bangor folks exemplify what the 4th stands for: steadfastness and loyalty. Every plane that lands there is greeted by volunteers with cell phones, food, and a smile. What makes this particular group exceptional is that they would end up meeting four-hundred fifty planes by May 2. We can all learn from this group. Patriotism and support of our troops is not just needed when we have a loved one deployed. It is something that is always needed and appreciated.

Homecomings were great! By the end of March, ninety-five percent of our Soldiers were at last home. Re-integrating training was underway to help the transition of Soldiers coming back from a war zone and families used to life without the Soldier. They were almost all home, they had done their job well, and it was time to celebrate! Our joy was somewhat tempered, though, because there were some spouses, sons, daughters, kin, and friends who would not cross the threshold into the gyms with music, smoke, and cheering crowds to the hero's welcome they deserved. There were also physically and emotionally wounded Soldiers who were still learning to live with injuries suffered in a war zone. But we would honor them by living and celebrating a job well done. As a military and a nation, we pledged that our enemies would not demoralize us or destroy our way of life.

3 March - I'm Still Scared
My husband is with HHT, 1-10 CAV, 4th ID and is going to be home this Friday. I'm so excited, but also so scared. We haven't been together for so long, and I got used to being independent (with me and our son, who is now fourteen-months old.) I know they tell us to be patient, but I'm still scared. I know we'll do okay, though. It has been a long year but one that I will never forget. And I especially want to thank you, Mr. Babcock, for all the hard work you've done to help us and keep us families updated.

3 March - Wonderful Ladies at Ft Hood
I have a wonderful grandson in Tikrit, 4th Div. 16th SIG BN. He is 'short' and I look forward to his return to Ft Hood. I was feeling sad I could not be there to greet him when he returns but am feeling much better, thanks to you and two wonderful ladies at Ft Hood. On February 25, 2004, your news of the 4th ID balloon bouquets made my day. I called to ask about having a bouquet delivered to my grandson on his return.

It was explained to me that families pick up the bouquets and greet their Soldiers with them. After visiting with the lady, I thanked her and hung up the phone only to have it ring back in five minutes. The lady told me good news: yes, there was a lady who she called that would greet my grandson and present my balloon bouquet to him for me. That wonderful lady is the colonel's wife. I am overwhelmed with gratitude to all of you.

I now know what being a member of the military family means. It is a family that goes that extra big step to bring tears of happiness to a grandmother's eyes and the family of that precious grandson and brave Soldier who will be greeted with fifteen balloon's presented by a wonderful caring lady at Ft Hood, who takes time from her busy day to honor a Soldier and his grandmother.

Melissa G. Bouldin-Reeves from Tennessee - Letter to a Military Spouse

While I have never had the pleasure of meeting you or your husband, I felt the need to write you and express a very deep feeling that I have in my heart.

I, as a person, am not brave. I do not tackle things head on, as I hate confrontation. I will travel one-hundred miles out of my way just to avoid a conflict. I am an American woman who has no idea what is going on in the military other than what I hear on the news.

I have never had to let go of someone so that they could go fight for people that they didn't know, people that sometimes do not appreciate or understand what they are fighting for. I have never had a sleepless night of worry because of a report that another bomb has exploded, and I still haven't heard from my husband. I have never had to wait for months on end to hold the one that I loved so.

I have never had to tell my children that Daddy wasn't coming home tonight because he was so far away fighting for something that they aren't yet old enough to understand. I have never had to hold my head high and suppress the tears as I hear that it will be at least another six months of separation before my loved one gets to come home. I have never had to deal with a holiday away from the one that I thought I would share every day of my life with. And I have never had to feel the panic raising in my heart at the sound of a ringing phone or knock at the door for fear that it is the news that everyone is terrified of getting.

For the reasons listed above, I cannot tell you that I understand how you feel. I cannot tell you that you must be strong. I cannot say that you shouldn't be angry, because you "knew what you were getting into when you married a military man." I cannot say these things because I have never had to walk in your shoes.

What I can say for certain is that because of your unselfish acts of bravery and your husband's willingness to stand up for those who see him as "just another Soldier"—I will never have to walk in your shoes.

I do understand that as a military wife you are expected to maintain a certain amount of control, but I never understood how you could do it, until now. I have figured out that you are not like other women. You are a special breed. You have a strength within you that holds life together in the darkest of hours, a strength which I will never possess. The faith you have is what makes you stand out in a crowd; it makes you glow with emotion and swell with pride at the mention of The United States of America. You are a special lady, a wonderful partner and a glorious American.

I have more respect for your husband than I could ever tell you, but until recently I never thought much about those that the Soldier leaves at home during deployment.

Until this moment I could never put into words exactly what America meant to me. Until this moment, I had no real reason to... Until I heard of you.

Your husband and his military family hold this nation close, safe from those who wish to hurt us, but you and those like you are the backbone of the American family. You keep the wheels in motion and the hearts alive while most would just break completely down. Military families make this nation what it is today. You give us all hope and you emit a warming light at the end of a long dark tunnel.

Because of you and your family, I am able to be me. I am able to have my family. I am able to walk free in this great land. Because of you and your family, I can look ahead to the future with the knowledge that life is going to be okay. Because of you and your family, I can awake to a new day, every day.

I realize that you are a stronger person than I will ever be because of these things, and I just wanted to take the time today to say thank you to you and your family for allowing me that freedom.

I will never be able to repay this debt to you, as it is unmatchable. However, I hope that you know that no matter where you are, what you are doing, what has happened today, or what will happen tomorrow, your husband will never be "just another Soldier" to me. And you, dear sweet lady, will never be forgotten.

You are all in my prayers every day, and I pray that God will bring you back together with your loved one safely. May God Bless You!

4 March - Back Into Old Routines

My husband, Alpha Company, 1-44 ADA, 2 Platoon, has been home (for good) for a little over a week and it has been just wonderful! He never had the chance to take mid-tour leave, so it had been around eleven-months since we had seen each other. We slipped back into our old routines without much difficulty. He is enjoying things like not having to wear shoes in the shower any more and being able to use the phone without waiting in line.

I am so happy we decided to send him a digital camera during his deployment. He was able to document his experience through hundreds of pictures and movies, something that I'm sure will be very valuable to him in the future and that helped me to understand his experiences.

5 March - Children Adopt Hometown Heroes

Several months ago when our daughter left, the gifted classes at our local elementary school took on a project about the war and decided to adopt our Soldier. The teachers have kept me up to date on the progress they have made. The children undertook this with their hearts in it and have really become attached to their hometown hero. They have written letters and sent goody boxes and pictures and lots of drawings. Some have even sent e-mail and received e-mail back from our daughter. They have sent my family and me letters of reassurance of her safe return.

As I read each and every one, I had to drag out the old Kleenex box because it amazed me how much these fourth graders understood what was going on. Some of them even mentioned they had family members serving in Iraq also, and yet here they were comforting us. They are now so excited that she is coming home and have planned a big surprise celebration for her. When we had an idea of when she might be coming home I mentioned to the teacher that I wanted them to be a special part of her Texas and hometown homecoming, so I asked them to make welcome home posters and banners, some for Texas and some for here. Today I received around thirty-five to forty precious posters and was told that there were more coming.

I was touched at the creativity, excitement and heart that went into each one. Now I have the hard task of deciding just which ones we take to Texas and which ones to use here. This is just a small example of the support that we have received. It's amazing how these little ones have touched our lives. Our daughter is a hero to them, and they will always be touched by this experience. Our Soldier is a medic with HHC, 1-4 AVN Regt based in Ft. Hood and she along with all our heroes will be home soon.

7 March - Crying, Laughing, Dancing and Singing
I went to the homecoming ceremony for a friend of ours from Fort Carson. His family was unable to attend as they live so far away and his arrival was unexpected. Let me just say that the fanfare was unbelievable. This is our first deployment, so I've never seen anything like it! The women and children were everywhere, mommas crying, and children smiling. Just thinking about it gives me the chills. Behind me in the bleachers was a woman in her mid-thirties, with six children. She didn't know whether to cry, laugh, dance, or sing, so she did all of the above, no matter who saw or heard. It warmed my heart to know this woman was so truly dedicated to her man. She was an inspiration for me. When it's my husband's turn, I'll be the one in the bleachers dancing and crying and singing.

7 March - A Man of Experience
Our son was one of many Soldiers greeted in Maine last month. Thanks to those 'Maine Troop Greeters' for their dedication to our troops at any hour! He was impressed and grateful for all the handshakes and cell phone use. He used the cell phone to call us in Ft. Hood while we were waiting on his plane to arrive, three days later then planned, but just a mere inconvenience in the scheme of things!

He had a four-day pass, and we had a great visit in Texas. This morning he came home to Arkansas on his leave. Tonight we are celebrating big time with family and friends! He left a young man fresh out of high school and has returned a man of many experiences he thought would never happen in his lifetime. We are grateful for his safe return and will keep all families of our troops in our prayers until all are home! Proud mom of a US Army Soldier!

7 March - He's a Nut
My husband has been home for three days now, and it is really great. Your e-mails have been a wonderful link to what was his 'world' for the longest time; you will probably never know how grateful I, as well as countless others, are for these updates.

Luckily, redeployment so far hasn't been tough at all; he was a nut before he left, and he's a nut now. I didn't anticipate any problems but was prepared to put on my 'redeployment hat' if needed; so far we're just enjoying being a family again and are now headed away to spend a weekend together with no kids!

On the down side, there are still Soldiers in Iraq (and elsewhere) who aren't home yet, who are just leaving and who haven't or won't make it home. What a seesaw of feelings for everyone. I still look forward to reading my e-mails; the only difference is now I won't be reading them alone.

7 March - Grocery Shopping

I just went and bought groceries today for our whole family! He's not home yet, but he'll be home before I have to buy groceries again. I can't believe something as mundane as grocery shopping can get me so excited! I just had to share that. I'm not close enough to his return to start counting laundry days yet, but I can count grocery-shopping days now.

7 March 2004 - One father's feelings

After almost a year of receiving your newsletter, I felt I needed to write and thank you for providing information the general public is so unlikely to hear. Our son is at the tail end of four years with the Fourth Infantry Division out of Fort Carson. He is a medic, Specialist, twenty-seven years old, a twin, and married one and a half years, with a one-year-old son. I wanted to write to say that this is our family's first experience with a son in the military, let alone a war.

I had always thought of myself as a pretty tough guy, able to handle a lot of stress and challenges on a daily basis. I have found out that with this situation, this is not true. My business associates have come to understand the impact that this has had on me, as my performance has dropped to about thirty-percent. Thank God they do, as they have been great. I am fifty-three years old, have been through every type of business challenge over a period of thirty-four years, start-ups, winners and losers.

I will say right now that this has been by far the toughest year of my life. Most people cannot understand that a man who rides three Harley's, and would kick the ass of anyone who needed it kicked, would sit at his computer daily and shed tears like a baby. I can't imagine what those have gone through and are going through who have lost a family member in this war, or any war for that matter.

When someone asks me about our son, I can only reply, "I just want him home."

I am sure there are fathers out there who have had to deal with this as I have. Hide the fear, hide the tears, be there for everyone else when needed, handle the problems, stop everyone from reading too deep into and analyzing the phone calls we get from him, and hide the calls and e-mails that he tells me not to show Mom or his wife. I cannot count the times when asked, "Do you think he is okay?" that I have said, "Yes, he is fine," when I was not sure if I was going to be made a liar.

Well, all I can say is this: all you other fathers out there, hang in there, take a lot of walks, don't be afraid to talk about it. I guess it took this to realize how much I love my son and the rest of my kids. I am ashamed for this, but better late than never.

When he comes home, I am going to be back on top. All I think about is the times we will spend fishing, riding the bikes and all being together doing all the things I took for granted when he was home. Never again will I take for granted the time I have with my kids.

Anyway, thanks so much, Bob, for everything you have done. And for all the rest of the families, and all the Soldiers: I think about, pray for and am so proud of everyone that has dealt with this either at home or abroad. And oh yeah, I am so glad I am not a mother... just one father hangin' in there for only a couple more weeks.

8 March - The Worst and Perhaps the Best Year
I also am a fifty-three year old father experiencing a son at war for the first time. He is finishing his third year out of Ft Carson (1-12 Infantry). We have, as has everyone with a loved one involved, spent one of the worst, but also one of the best years of our lives. We have worried daily about the safety of our son as he performed one of the most unselfish acts a young man can do at this time in our country.

I couldn't be more proud of the young men and women of our country and never passed up an opportunity to make people aware of my feelings. I also worried about the son of my sister with the 82nd Airborne as he fulfilled his commitment and was so relieved when he returned in February. This morning brought tremendous relief as we heard from my son. We knew he was headed to Kuwait to help with the transition but hadn't heard any confirmation until this morning when he told us he was working at Shuaiba Port, south of Kuwait City. He won't be stateside until all of the 4th ID's equipment and personnel have left the area, but I know that he is a lot safer now. I can only hope the day comes soon when all of our young men and women are out of harm's way.

8 March – Joy, Concern and Sadness

Our son with the 1-10 CAV arrived home at Ft. Hood Friday night. We traveled up there to join in the celebration, and boy, was there a celebration! The gym was packed with people and all kinds of celebration gadgets, banners, flags and balloons. We arrived at the gym at 7:30 a.m., but the Soldiers didn't file in until about 11:00 a.m. So for three hours we watched kids running and playing, families line dancing, Soldiers rocking to the beat of the music, and just in general people having a good time.

The Family Readiness Groups did a superb job at making it a memorable night. There were free sodas, snacks, flags and clappers handed out and a D.J. playing great music. A quite entertaining Soldier kept us informed of the whereabouts of our Soldiers throughout the night and gave us instructions on when to yell, "dismissed." By the time the buses arrived, everyone was fired up. When the Soldiers began to file in, the crowd went wild. What a reception! My heart was filled with joy knowing this is what they deserved, a joyous and grateful welcome home.

We are so overjoyed that our son is home, but part of my heart still lies with the Soldiers that are still there and their families. When we attended church this morning, our pastor announced that our son was back. He received a standing ovation and throughout the morning many people greeted our son to say thank you. While we were in line for communion, a Soldier's wife came over to hug our son, tell him she was glad he was home, and that her husband was still there. After church, I went to meet her and ask about her husband and get his name to put on our weekly prayer list. There is just a deep sense of concern and even sadness knowing what she will be going through. I will still read your daily updates and keep the Soldiers' names coming before our Heavenly Father.

Little did I know that when our son came home, that would

not be the end for me. I'm still aching for those that are still there. The war is not over until they all come home. I am hoping to meet you and some of the wives that were so faithful to keep me abreast of the happenings in our son's unit at the April 22nd celebration. Thanks to all of you who have served and are serving on the home front as well as those that are still fighting this war.

Jennifer Henley-Sweigart - Wife of G Troop 10th CAV 4ID Soldier

I've been meaning to contact you, but as you probably know, time is a very sacred commodity when one's spouse is due to return any day! I've definitely learned that I don't manage my time well; I'm forcing myself to take a second to write you about someone who touched the families as G Troop. To start at the beginning would probably be best.

I'm married to the Executive Officer (XO) of G Troop, a light Reconnaissance unit based in Tikrit. This past September, three of G Troop's Soldiers were killed in action and many of our Soldiers were injured. While the wives and families of our troop all banded together to support each other, we really didn't expect to have anyone else take heed of our situation. A man by the name of Ed Kane of the Back Creek Rocking Horse Company donated rocking horses to the children of our fallen Soldiers. The rocking horses are handmade and have a music box that plays whatever song the child or parent requests. They're really beautiful, and Ed Kane is a wonderful, generous and very patriotic man. The mere fact that he lives in West Virginia and really has no ties to the military, yet spent many hours on this labor of love, is a testament to his character!

Sometimes we, whose lives are so entwined with the military, think that no one else cares that our Soldiers are paying the ultimate price for their freedom. It's so heartwarming and refreshing to know that there are plenty of people out there who are as patriotic as we are, and willing to do whatever is in their power to show it! I'm proud to be an Army wife, and proud to be an American!

8 March - Honk! Honk!

I just wanted to share something that made my heart swell with pride. Saturday, as we were at our Battalion motor pool making welcome-home signs for our soon-to-be-returning Soldiers and attaching them to the fence, there were several passersby honking their horns to show enthusiasm as they passed. It really made me feel good that people took the time to encourage us and share in our celebration. It was wonderful seeing all the ladies who came out to support their husbands and the unit. The welcome home banners and cup designs filled every last bit of space on the fence. The smiles on the children's faces as they painted notes and pictures for their daddies were contagious; we caught it, and we had a wonderful time.

As I drove home it hit me for the first time that this deployment really is nearly over for us, that soon our Soldiers will be back in our arms again. It seems almost surreal. Meanwhile, I hug and comfort friends whose husbands have just begun their tour or are getting ready to go soon. Telling them to keep busy and assuring them that they are stronger than they think and that the time will fly by before they know it. It's a very bittersweet and humbling experience. And I just want to say thank you to all the spouses, children, and family members who have gone through it or are about to. The world may never know the price they pay for freedom, but we do!

9 March - A Sea of Hugs and Kisses

What a great day. Our Fightin' 5th Engineers made it home (Fort Leonard Wood, Missouri) Thursday, March 4. They arrived home with a hero's welcome, escorted through the town outside post by many police cars with lights and then picked up at the gates by our MPs with lights and sirens. The community had lined the street, and local businesses had all changed their bulletin boards to read, "Welcome home 5th Engineers". The FRGs had decorated many posters and signs with love and placed them on the route.

They arrived to a gym fully decorated, with many loved ones, and of course the Army band. It was an amazing sight to see them march through the doors as the gym erupted into screams and applause. The speeches were kept very short, and once they were released, the families poured down from the bleachers to find their Soldier. It was a sea of hugs and kisses on the gym floor. It was an evening that I'm sure none of the Soldiers will ever forget.

We still have approximately thirty-two Soldiers in Kuwait

waiting for the ship to arrive to load equipment. They should arrive shortly though. One more welcome home party, and we should have everyone back home. God bless the ones that have taken their place in Iraq and keep them safe.

10 March - Half My Life is Back to Normal
My son (HHC, 1-12 INF) returned to Ft Carson in the early morning hours of March 8. What a glorious God. I thank him every day! I chose not to fly from Ft. Drum, New York to Ft Carson at this time so he can have that re-bonding with his wife. He called me from his wife's cell phone as soon as he was released. He said he flew into Maine before heading on to Colorado and the VFW greeted them graciously there in Maine, and it was very nice.

Shortly afterward, I talked to my son and knew the Eagle had landed safely. I called my husband's Rear Detachment and asked that they telephone his father and give him the message that his son had arrived home safely. We have a wonderful Rear Detachment group because in less than thirty minutes my husband had me on the line from Afghanistan (10th MTN DIV), wanting the number for our daughter-in-law's cell phone so he could call his son and welcome him home and congratulate him for a job well done.

We'll be going to Ft Carson this summer when our daughter gets out of school for summer break. Half of my life is back to normal, now I just need to get my other half back. Thanks to all Soldiers who serve this country and the ones who gave all (past and present). May God always comfort the hearts of their loved ones and know their Soldiers will never be forgotten
Mom/Wife from Ft Drum, NY.

11 March - Real Family
Thanks for all you have done for us this past year. The thing I appreciate the most is your constant reminder that 'family' isn't just a spouse and/or children. Family includes fiancées, moms, dads, boyfriend, girlfriend, grandparents and anyone else who loves a Soldier in the 4ID. My husband (who has been home about a week) and I were able to help the family of a single Soldier surprise him by being at the gym to welcome him home.

It was a spur of the moment trip, and the Soldier's family

drove straight through from California to make it in time. The single Soldier had no clue his mom, stepfather, brothers and sister would be cheering for him as he entered that gym. He thought the best it was going be was a hug from me. The look on his face was priceless. Not only was he crying, his buddies were in tears as well. My husband told me to always remember that moments like that are why I have spent the last year as a family readiness leader.

Every time I hear someone say something negative about the army, I just have to read through your daily updates to remind myself what family is.

12 March - Memories

My memories from last winter and spring are several. I just could not accept the fact that we were going to war, and my son was on this runaway train. I became involved with a mom's military group. The first meeting there was six of us. The next meeting needed an adjoining banquet room and was packed with mothers and fathers. As each mother introduced herself and showed a picture of what looked like just a boy in uniform, there was not a dry eye. The fear in that room could have been cut with a knife.

I remember feeling like I had become an expert on Turkish Parliament. How I rejoiced when they would not let us in! I thought that we had escaped this war!

Listening to my nineteen-year-old discuss his will with me; the five phone calls a day he made leading up to this deployment, each time swallowing my own fear and just reinforcing what he already knew: He was well trained; he would be fine.

A mother of a college student/reservist called me just overcome with worry. I was able to watch CNN and tell her exactly where her son was and that he was safe.

When I came to Ft. Hood to see my son off, we went to get his picture taken. We had to go to two different stores since they were incredibly busy with all of the Soldiers deploying. At nineteen, he was becoming quite irritated, dressed in his camos', about getting what he saw as such a chore accomplished. In the car he said, "Mom, why do we have to do this now? Can't we wait until I come back?"

I remember staring straight ahead and silent because I could not express my worst fear and tell him why we were really doing this now. He grew silent. And it hit him why. He was very agreeable after that.

Behind us in line was another mother from Alabama with her nineteen-year old son. When our eyes met, we didn't have to say a word, we could each read the other's heart.

My best memory was when we were leaving to come back to Ohio. My son's ride picked him up at the hotel, and he did not want me to come downstairs. I thought he was gone, and I began taking things to the car, tears streaming down my face. Just then my son went by, and the car stopped some ways from me; he hopped out and ran for me and threw his arms around me and said, "Don't cry, Mama. I love you. I'll be fine." Then he grabbed me again and again and again saying each time, "Give me another hug, Mama." Oh, no, now I'm crying....

Yesterday, thanks to you, I got an e-mail from my son's captain's wife. I had a chance to briefly send thanks to her husband for being true to his word and bringing my son home safely. I had called the post last March to ask about guest lodging. I was transferred to Captain Jak. I was very embarrassed at first. I certainly hadn't expected this and did not want to be a bother. This man was so nice to me. I am sure he had more important and desirable things to do than to speak to a distraught mom. I have remembered the things he told me, through this year, when I have felt that fear come back. How confident he was being with this unit. He told me about the tanks, where my son would be in this line of the military machine, and that he would bring my son home. Come to find out, he even let my son experience the cockpit on the ride to Iraq, knowing his fear of flying. This man was the epitome of self-assurance and kindness. Everyone in our family knows who Captain Jak is. He fulfilled every expectation of what an officer and a true leader should be. I will never forget him from that brief conversation and will always be eternally grateful to him.

12 March - Wonderful Call

My son, my hero, serves as a staff sergeant with HHS, 2-20 FA 4ID. He was a master gunner and much more, while serving a very long, dangerous, stressful year of duty in Iraq. He is back in the USA! I just wanted to let you know that my daughter-in-law called at 10:25 a.m. on March 9 with the great news, saying those words that I had prayed to hear: "The planes have landed." At 11:20 a.m. I got the second call from her saying, "The buses are on their way," and at 12:40 a.m. on March 10, my precious daughter-in-law called to tell me my son had gone to pick up his belongings and that he is very glad to be back in the USA. Then the wonderful fourth call came at 12:50 a.m.—the one that I have been waiting for. This call was from my son, my hero. We talked a few short minutes; we will speak again after he gets some much needed rest. I thank God for watching over him and bringing him home safely.

13 March - The Children Applauded

He called me early this morning and we had a good long talk. It was so wonderful to hear his voice. Thank you for keeping him in prayer. God listens.

He is a staff sergeant with 4th ID, 1-22 IN, B CO. They flew straight to Germany from Iraq then on to Bangor, Maine where they were greeted by American veterans who treated them like the heroes our Soldiers are. These vets handed out cell phones for the Soldiers to pass around so they could all call home to let their loved ones know they were safe. I've never been more proud to be an American!

I was at an educators' conference yesterday and one of the presenters let us know that his son was in Baghdad, where there was an incident, and he was worried because he hadn't heard from his son yet. Now that I am an experienced mom at this, I let him know what you always told us, no news is good news, and bad news travels fast. It felt good to lend comfort and advice. I let him know that my son was due back, and I had my cell phone on the table. If it rang, I didn't want him to think I was being rude, but it would be my son or his wife with news of his arrival.

Well, the phone rang and everyone in the room was happy for me. They were wiping their eyes and passing out tissues. How wonderful for total strangers to share the depth of my feelings! In school, I announced on the school speaker system early in the morning to the teachers that my son had returned and people have been stopping by my computer lab hugging me with tears in their eyes. I guess I didn't realize how much they knew the amount of stress I've been dealing with. I thanked them all for their prayers and support.

Then, as each class came to my computer lab, I told them that my son had returned from Iraq and each class of third, fourth, and fifth graders broke out in applause! Wow!

My son still has a sister-in-law and brother-in-law in Iraq. She will be home in April, we think, but her husband just got there in January, so he has a long haul. I'll visit my son and his wife over spring break. I told my son that he will have to understand that I will have to give him a long, big hug. He said he thinks he could handle that! He also thanked me profusely for all of the things I did for him and his unit. How thankful I am in return!

13 March - Touching Lives

I remember flying down to Ft. Hood last February to see my brother off. On the way back from the airport he told me a little about his job and told me a lot about the young Soldiers he was preparing to take to war. He talked about the mothers of some of these eighteen to nineteen year Soldiers that were in complete panic. I told him I would be one of them for sure! He reassured me these young men would be fine. He was unbelievably confident in each of them.

As our visit continued, we ended up sitting in his room talking even more about what he was being asked to do for his country. We talked about where he would sleep, what he would eat, and what he thought the enemy would be like. He laughed a lot when he talked about some of the horribly frightening things he may encounter. I couldn't understand how he could laugh, so I asked him. He said, "Sis, I either laugh or freak. I think I am going to laugh."

The one thing I remember most was how he picked my hand up, and he was holding it as he talked. I honestly don't think he even realized he did that. I asked him if he was afraid.

He said "Hell yeah, who wouldn't be. But I have a job to do that I trained my whole life for. I am ready to go and get this done so I can get back home to my family."

I went home and it was another several weeks before his unit boarded that plane to go off to war. I remember sitting on my couch when my mom called to tell me he was leaving. A feeling of incredible pride and sickening fear rushed over me all at the same time. I will never forget it.

He is almost home now. Through this deployment I have learned wonderful things about my brother that I may have never known. I have received shining letters from his superiors talking about his greatness. I have seen him take time out from his busy day to respond to letters and packages sent from children and adults alike from all over the country. He has allowed so many people to touch his life and him touch theirs.

As horrible as this war has been, I have gained an incredible new understanding of the man my brother really is. It's hard to believe it has been a year since this all began.

15 March - Daddy Busses

This writer signed all her notes this year as "Grumpy Mom."
Patience, flexibility, sense of humor: It has taken all of that. We have come from California to greet our Soldier in B Company 1-22 Infantry. His wife and babies stayed with family out there during the deployment. He thought he was leaving Iraq on the 5th, it didn't happen. We came early to start working on resurrecting their car, which had been in storage for a year. That has been a costly process. The extra time allowed his wife to start working on housing. The Ft. Hood housing people have been very helpful and kind.

The rear detachment commander had more accurate dates for arrival, but even that required almost more patience than we had. We got a call from our delightful FRG leader, saying our Soldier would be home the following night, the tenth. We were so excited and were ready the next day. She had to call us back that afternoon to say he was not on the expected flight, but he was on the manifest for a flight that had just left, and he'd be home the next afternoon. That was the real deal; we got a short message from Germany saying he was on his way home.

His wife got a wake-up call from our son on the 11th saying he was in Maine, had been greeted by those generous folks in Bangor, who passed around cell phones so the troops could make calls. We were jubilant!

From where we were staying, we could see where the troop bus drivers stay. We'd see them gather out front before they left to deliver troops. Several buses will leave, and we knew Soldiers were coming and going. The two-year-old hung at the window watching them. He called them 'Daddy buses' because he knew one would bring his daddy home to him. In the local restaurants, we watched 1st CAV families sadly saying goodbye to their Soldiers as we await the arrival of our 4th ID folks—the yin and yang of military life.

We showed up at the gym as directed. The parking lot was filled with cars; many were decorated with paint and balloons. My favorite saying was, "Get out of my way, my son is coming home today!"

The gym was full of deafening music and hollering, joyous families. Children were dancing out in the middle. We were notified when the plane landed; we cheered when the buses left the airfield: A group scream, when the buses arrived out front, even louder screaming. A captain walked into the gym in his desert BDUs and the place erupted. They turned the smoke machine on (yes, a smoke machine) and the first line of Soldiers strode into the gym. It was total pandemonium! I saw my son in the second row and then he was obscured by a few more rows of Soldiers. We stopped hollering just long enough to sing the national anthem, a very few words were said and then we all got to holler, "DISMISSED!"

It took a few minutes and then our dream happened. Out of the crowd and smoke came our son, our Soldier. He looked so tall and fit. When his wife rushed into his arms and they kissed, I thought our hearts would just explode. The toddler knew him instantly and our son looked with wonder into the face of the son born while he was in Bayji.

It was one of those moments etched in my memory for the rest of my life. In a couple of minutes we were outside the gym in the warm, Texas sunshine heading away from combat and toward family. I was surprised to see the troops in good clothes. They are issued new BDUs in Iraq so they aren't coming back tattered.

I hear the 'daddy buses' warming up this morning, so more troops will be moving in or out very soon. Our joy is tempered by the knowledge that others are saying goodbye.

We're just about to gather up our family and drive out in the country where "the best barbecue in Texas" is alleged to be found. Some assertions must be tested. It is a very good day. "No longer a Grumpy Mom."

By Kaylynne Hatch - Dedicated to Michael E. Hatch

My Hero
You fought a battle,
You were brave, you were strong,
I am glad you are back.
You have been gone for so long,
You have saved the lives of many.
I could be rich, if for each life you saved, I had a penny.
So many trials you have gone through,
I know you always fight for what's true,
You have saved us from an evil threat.
Many enemies you have met.
You have been so brave, and so true
To your country of red, white, and blue;
While you were gone I have grown,
But like a little girl,
I run into your arms,
"My Daddy is finally home!"
When you kiss Mommy on the cheek,
Tears of joy she will weep.
I know that last night she received no sleep-
Her husband was coming home.
In your nice, warm bed you can finally sleep,
You can put ice in every one of your drinks,
You can have a real meal, instead of one of those MREs
Because, you are finally home!

15 March - Just Americans

Just to let you know just how wonderful those folks in Maine are, let me tell you. The day we went to see if we may get a glimpse of our son (if he was even on the flight), there were folks there of all ages. The ones that amazed me though were the older folk. Most of them were in their seventies and some well into their eighties. There were many there that had been there since 0100 hours. This included some who had obvious physical disabilities. And to top it off, they would be back at 0500 hours the next day to welcome more planes loaded with troops.

We don't get to that part of Maine often as it is a couple hours away; however, we know now that we will stop in anytime we are there to see if any flights are on their way in so we can join those wonderful devoted people that are there almost every day. They treated us like gold for the five hours we waited in hopes that our son would be on the next flight. The coffee shop and other stores were opened up when the flight came in. Generally these are closed early, as this is a very small airport.

Yet when the flight came in at 2200 hours they opened it for the troops to use. And yes, they have cell phones for them and a few treats as well. I asked if they were sponsored by any particular veterans group. I was curious because I am the historian for our local American Legion and my husband is a member of the VFW. The reply was that they come from many organizations and some have no affiliation to any organization so they simply call themselves "Americans." It is such a proud and fitting title. Just thought I'd let you know how dedicated these fine Mainers are.

15 March - We Can Handle Two

About the article regarding the troops returning for another rotation. My husband (C Co, 124th Signal BN) has been telling me for the last six months to expect him to go back to Iraq in 2005. So, mentally I have been preparing myself for this possibility. From experience I always hope for the best, but expect the worst with the military. If he does have to go back, we will be prepared and even more so next time since we now have experience. I know that we would be able to make it through another deployment because if we made it through once, we can do it again.

With the support of family and friends and above all, the faithfulness of our Lord, I am confident that if he has to return, then we will make it through! However, for the time being I am going to focus on his return home and what a joyous time this is! He isn't home yet, but I know he will be very soon!

16 March - A Precious Moment

Our son was home on the day he received the call to go to Iraq. He came running into my room breathless, saying he was going to war. I could see the adrenaline surging through him. All his friends were called and came running to see him off. We watched him pack his gear and all eyes were on him for hours. Little did we know that night that it would be another two months before he would leave. The daily anticipation was difficult. Would this be the day? For him it was deflating. He was ready. Finally we received news he would be leaving, so we drove to Ft. Hood to say goodbye. We spent as much time with him as we could. However our two-year old son was very tired and we still had a three-hour drive back home. So my husband said goodbye and headed home in our car.

I stayed behind to drive our son's car home so we could store it for him. He asked me if I would like to see a movie, and of course I said, "Sure." After the movie, we went to get coffee, and at about 1:00 a.m. he said he better get to the barracks. When we parked, he said he would run in to get changed so he could leave his clothes in the car. While he was up there, I felt the sobbing trying to surface. That was the last thing I wanted to leave him with, so I prayed a quick prayer for strength to see him off with support and a smile. As soon as the words left my mouth, I felt a supernatural strength for this motherly job. When he returned to the car, we said our good-byes, and I prayed for him without a tear. I will never forget that precious moment.

Now that he's home, it seems like that night was a million years ago. We are so thankful for God's protection over him and for seeing us through a difficult year.

18 March - The Extremes of Emotions
My husband's unit, (5th Plt, 4th MP, 4ID) along with four other units, arrived back at Fort Hood on Tuesday morning. I just wanted to pay tribute to the wonderful homecoming ceremony the Army had organized at the gym. All the family members were crowded on the bleachers, and when the troops finally ran in, with smoke bombs going off all around, the place went wild! I had trouble seeing my husband among the ranks, but as soon as the order to dismiss was given, he came walking straight towards me with tears running down his face. I think it was the happiest moment of my life.

His parents were there too, having traveled from Alabama to welcome him home from his first combat tour. We've only been married just over a year, but I've decided that no other way of life could provide such extremes of emotion—both good and bad! I must admit that morning in the gym made up for a year of worry. It was truly fantastic!

18 March - Treasure Every Moment

You asked for our thoughts on how we felt one year ago when the Fourth Infantry Division was waiting to be deployed to Iraq, not knowing when or how. Well, here's one mother's story. We had a great Christmas. My son was on leave. He had just come back from a year and a half deployment in Honduras bringing with him his beautiful new wife. We had met her when we went down there for their wedding a few months prior and loved her instantly; however, this vacation we came to know her and love her even more. They would be stationed at Ford Hood, Texas, and we went into the attics and the sheds and the garages putting together household items to ship to Texas so they could set up their apartment. They were starting their new life together finally in the US, and we wished them all the best.

But in the background loomed the threat of war in Iraq, and even though we knew that there was a possibility that my son would be sent to the Middle East, we tried to bury it in the back of our minds and concentrate on our joy.

Vacation ended, and they made their way three quarters of the way across the U.S., secured an apartment, received their shipment, and set up their new home. It was wonderful being able to pick up the phone and talk to them without having to worry about the astronomical charges the calls to Honduras had cost. We talked several times a week.

Then the phone rang one evening as I was watching FOX news. They were reporting on the impending war. My son said, "Mom, I have my orders. I don't know when I'm going to leave, but my unit will be going over to Iraq." My heart skipped a beat, and it felt like someone ripped my stomach out of my body. I was speechless. I knew I had to remain calm, I knew there were decisions to be made: his new wife spoke only a little English; she couldn't be left out there by herself. But all I really wanted to do was fall apart. My son was going to war and he might never come back!

I don't quite remember how I got through the next couple of months. I prayed a lot, I cried a lot, and I hung onto every word of every conversation my son and I had together from the night of that first phone call when he told me he was being deployed to Iraq until the last night before he left. I kept thinking: this could be the last one. Maybe I'll never hear his voice again, maybe I'll never laugh at his unique sense of humor or get annoyed at him because I felt he was being too headstrong. Maybe we'll never share computer tips or writing tips or any of the other special moments that are unique to my son and me.

Then there was the waiting. They were going, now they weren't. They were definitely going, but not this week. They were going next week, no the date was changed. Turkey won't let them in, maybe Turkey will... no they won't. And then the next phone call, "Dad is coming to pick up my wife. I'm leaving in two weeks, not sure exactly which day, but we are definitely leaving." We spoke almost every day until the last day, and then there was no news.

I watched every single news station. I would wake up in the morning and start at Channel two and go right on up to FOX news listening to every report. I would fall asleep at night to the voice of the newscaster: "Blackhawk down, Jessica Lynch, ...numbers killed." I didn't know where he was. I didn't know if he was flying or in a convoy. I did know he was alive, because bad news travels fast.

And then one night I was searching the Internet for news and he signed on to Instant Messenger. My heart rang out. He couldn't talk long, but he was okay. He said he was relatively safe. It was short, but it was enough.

Over the next few months it became a little easier. I still prayed a lot. I sent care packages and e-mails. We talked occasionally. He came home on a two week R & R at Christmas. We had another great time.

If this has taught me anything at all, it's this: Treasure each and every minute you have with your children. You never know what the Lord has in store for you. The little annoying things really don't matter. It's the little moments of joy and laughter and even just everyday conversation that count. Hold on to each and every second.

I've been through many rough times in my life—divorce, sickness, and loss. But I must say that this has been the most difficult year of my life. And it's not over yet; my son still needs to make his way out of Iraq, which I think he is in the process of doing now. I haven't heard from him in a while, and I was told that there would be a communication blackout when they started to move. So I continue to pray, and with God's help, he will be safely on the ground in Texas and reunited with his lovely wife in two or three weeks.

Bob, I can't tell you how much your daily e-mails have helped me through this difficult time. I felt like I was still in touch, and when there was no news about Iraq on the networks, there was your newsletter. When I felt everyone had forgotten about our brave men and women overseas, your network of people reminded me that I was not alone; many were hanging in there with me.

20 March - Time to Wave Again

When the orders came down last January for my husband's unit to deploy, it was anticipated, yet a shock. You see, I was pregnant with our second child. My husband had been in Korea when our son was born, and now it looked like he would be gone again. But we made the most of the time we had before he left. We hadn't even told our families that we were expecting again. Now there was a sense of urgency.

Little did we know that we would have two and a half months to enjoy the time together as a family. We were even fortunate enough to have an ultrasound to find out the sex of the baby. My husband's chest puffed out when he saw that it was a girl! It was only a week later that he actually left Ft. Carson. I thank the Lord for at least giving him that picture of our precious baby girl. It is even harder to believe that she is eight months old today!!

When my husband got the call he was leaving, it was a hurried anxiousness. He is a big procrastinator, so his bags were not even packed. We stayed up the first night packing. Sometimes, I just want to kick him in the backside for waiting. But I was right there watching him pack.

At three o'clock the next morning, another Soldier came to the door to ride in with my husband. I hugged and kissed him. I promised to take wonderful care of our growing family! And I stood in the garage and watched him get into the car with the snow falling. As I shut the door, I realized what was happening. I went back to bed to try and sleep.

I knew that the buses would be pulling out the next morning at a certain time. I was determined to wave them off. So, I bundled up my then fourteen-month-old and myself and drove to post. We waited in the car forever (of course, they were running behind). I finally asked some of the Soldiers guarding the buses if I could stand next to them. They were wonderful to me and my baby. We stood right on the corner where each bus would drive out.

Finally, the Soldiers started to come out. I kept looking for my husband, but in their gear, they all seemed to look alike. Then it happened; the buses started to move. My baby boy and I stood there and waved at each and every bus. My husband was on the first bus, and all the guys were beating on the windows to let me know he was in there. As I waved at the other buses, I watched his bus turn the corner out of sight. That is when the tears came in full stream. After the last bus, I just stood there holding my son and crying. The guard Soldiers just left me alone. They understood what was happening.

When I finally talked with my husband after that, he said that he couldn't thank me enough for being there. So many of the Soldiers had come to him and told him to let me know how much they appreciated my being there to see them off. I told him it was my honor to be able to wave off all the heroes in those buses.

By God's beautiful grace, my husband will be returning shortly as well as those Soldiers I saw leave for a world unknown. After watching the first flight of Soldiers return, I am now beginning to get excited. I just have a little while longer until it is my turn to wave at him again, this time from the bleachers with my son and my daughter!

22 March - Dog Pile
I had to share with you the most unbelievable welcome home I could have imagined. Starker Gym was packed and SSG Mack said, "Welcome back, Task force Ironhorse." The crowd went crazy, screaming so loud that we couldn't hear our own voices within the sound. SSG Mack ran through the fog that was released from a fogger from the rear gym entrance and Soldiers, one after another, came running through after him, and there he was, our Soldier, arms in the air with one giant jump and a fist through the air. We knew it was him; all of our girls yelled, "Daddy!"

We quickly made our way and stood ten feet in front of him with our sign that said, "Jones sent me," which is his favorite saying to our girls and me.

After every Soldier was in formation, the Commander initialized the national anthem, then prayer. We stared at each other the entire time during the national anthem and prayer, and all of us were crying, him included. The families had practiced saying "dismissed" with SSG Mack all morning on cue, so we could release our troops. The time came and the Commander said, "family members on three: One, two, three..." And then the crowd shouted, "Dismissed!"

I ran and jumped right into his arms and our girls latched on (we have six girls). We all went to the ground. Remember 'dog pile' when you were a kid? That is what we looked like. We had a friend at the top of the bleachers who was there for the sole purpose of video taping this beautiful memory.

We are so blessed that he is home and with us tonight. Everything to him right now is a luxury: warm water, a mattress and being outside without a helmet or vest on. Above all we are a family together again, and we do not take it for granted.

He is sleeping now and has no worry of an attack. We know there are Soldiers that are still there and Soldiers that are going to Iraq soon. God speed to each one of them. Make every day count, stay focused and stay safe.

22 March - She Set Me Straight

Patience, flexibility, and sense of humor: These words have been driving me nuts lately. I just want to say, I have had all of these things for the past year! Since my husband's arrival in Kuwait, time has stopped. He is already loaded at the port and is just waiting for a spot on a plane to come back into my arms. I have been told so many dates when he will be back here at Ft Hood, I find myself repeating my new mantra, "patience, flexibility, and sense of humor."

Yesterday was a hard day for me. I was done and wanted my Soldier now! I was crabby most of the day and very jealous of my friends whose husbands were home and of the ones who were on their way to the gym to get their Soldier.

I took my son to one of his activities and was complaining to another wife about all the uncertainty, when another wife I know walked in. I just saw her and knew that I was acting like a fool (to put it mildly). See, she just lost her husband a week ago. She will never see him again and struggles to get through each day without him, and I sit here complaining because now I have to wait another four days before I see mine. I cried just at the thought of how stupid I was being.

Yes, I am lucky. My Soldier is coming home. That wife walked in at just the right time to set me straight without saying a word. Now I want to pass this on to you all. When you think that you are going to lose it if your date changes one more time, because all you want is to have your life back with your Soldier, remember those who will only have that life in memories. Remember that you are getting your Soldier back when so many aren't, and the least you can do is have patience, flexibility, and a sense of humor! Today I am not mad, crabby, jealous, or stressed. I am blessed, and I am lucky, and I will be patient, flexible, and will maintain my sense of humor when my dates change again!

23 March - Real Men Cry!

We arrived at Starker Gym early and knew where to sit so our Soldiers would be facing the beautiful American flag, and we were on that side of the gym! SSG Mack announced when the plane had landed and we all screamed and cheered. Then he told us that they were now returning their weapons. Then he came back and said that they had just left the airfield and were on the buses en route to the gym, and we went crazy just yelling and cheering some more!

Then SSG Mack said that the next time we saw him, he would be running into the gym and behind him would be one hundred eighty-nine of the proudest American Soldiers that we ever saw! SSG Mack was right! The DJ started releasing fog, and soon after that we saw SSG Mack running in, and behind came our brave, proud Soldiers! They ran in, and we raised the roof yelling, cheering and crying happy tears! When we saw our son we kept waving and kept our eyes on him, and I'm sure that when others saw their loved ones, they did the same. When we all sang the national anthem we cried and so did our Soldiers! Real men cry!

Everyone was so excited to hold their loved ones! It was so beautiful to see all these wonderful Soldiers reunited with family and friends that supported, loved and prayed for them through this deployment! One of the most touching moments of all was after all the hugs and kisses from family and friends calmed down. I watched these beautiful, proud, loyal Soldiers go up to other Soldiers and with tears in their eyes, yet a smile on their faces, hug each other with the tightest hug that you could imagine and say to each other "we made it."

These young men and women have grown so much and appreciate life. This has been a very hard year having a son deployed to Iraq, fighting and protecting our country! I'm a very proud mom and I'm very thankful that my son is home in the USA. But I'm here to say that this war is not over until all of our men and women come home!

27 March - It'll Take a While

Our son (1-22 Infantry, B Company), called our townhouse in Florida last week from Killeen, Texas. In the last month he has called us from Iraq, Kuwait, Maine, and Texas. The connections were crystal clear. It was like he was calling from the mall—which he was—when he called from Texas. He sounded very young. He sounded very tired and very, very glad to be home.

I cried when I heard his voice, and he said, "Mom, it's me, Mom, I'm in the state of Maine, in the United States of America." His voice lifted an anvil off my shoulders. Until that weight was gone, I hadn't even realized how heavy it had become. I try to describe the sensation to people, but I just can't. I've quit trying.

Yes, he's fine. Yes, he's gotten some sleep. No, they didn't sleep on the transport plane home. There was no heat, and it was pretty cold. But they're home.

When he called from Texas, he startled me by saying, "Mom, I've got an emergency." At first I panicked, forgetting where he was, thinking he was still in Iraq. It can be disorienting sometimes, because they came home so fast. It's like waking up and not knowing where you are. But then he said, "Mom, do dark green pants go with a light green shirt?" It's been a while since he's worn normal clothes. I took a deep breath and said, "...Depends."

"We're at the mall," he tells me. "We feel invincible. Boy, they love us here in Texas. We're doing our bit to stimulate the economy. It's so good to be home and eat pizza."

He told me a story about shopping with his squad. One member of his team went to make a purchase, and before they realized what they were doing, the rest of the group had fanned out, turned their backs to their buddy, and established a protective perimeter while he bought a movie. It's going to take a while.

No bad dreams so far. He has things he wants to tell me. I told him that I'd listen when he's ready to talk. He's so proud of his unit. The 4ID brought home the big prize. They pulled a vicious murderer out of a hole in the ground and helped free a nation. They adore their Commander In Chief. They are warriors. When they arrested one brutal gun-running bully who had been terrorizing an entire town, the people came out of their homes and cheered the American Soldiers in the street.

"Mom, I've got to go. We're headed to Austin."

"It's so good to hear your voice."

"It's so good to hear yours, too."

"We're so proud of you, we're so happy that you're home."

"Thanks."

"We prayed for you and all the others every day."

"I know."

"We're so happy you're home!"

"I am too... Don't cry, Mom."

"I'm not."

"I love you."

"I love you, too."

28 March - Trigger Happy
From a 4ID vet, the bodyguard for BG Teddy Roosevelt, Jr. who landed in the first wave on D-Day, June 6, 1944:
Must have been some treat to meet those guys as they came back. I sure would have loved to be there too. Hope you gave them the best for me too. Any time you can congratulate them for me do so. I am just an old 84-year old survivor of the first wave in the Normandy beachhead. I'll bet that would surprise them. I enjoy all the good stuff you are doing; it is great reading I still think I would be trigger-happy were I in on some of their doings.

29 March - Worst Day is the Best Day
Well, it has finally happened! Our son is back from Iraq! We left last Monday from Ohio and 'drove like the wind' to get to Killeen before him. At that time we were told he'd be there "sometime late Tuesday or Wednesday."

After fifty-four hours of traveling (their plane had to be repaired twice during their trip) our son finally arrived at Ft. Hood on Thursday morning! The gym was packed! SSG Mack and all of the others there were wonderful! It was certainly one of the most emotional and memorable experiences of my life. I am so very thankful to have been able to be there to welcome my son and the other Soldiers home. It's hard to believe that this long, difficult year is finally over for us. As I complained about the misty rain in Texas the next day, from my son came these most humbling words: "Mom, the worst day here is still a million times better than the best day in Iraq".

Sure makes you glad to be in America!

30 March - Ground Zero

My son (1-66th AR) returned home last week. He just left for Ft. Hood after spending his ninety-six hour pass at home with us. He was truly overwhelmed by the gratitude of everyone he saw. Everywhere we went people young and old came up to him and said, "Thank you!"

One of the most meaningful 'thank-you's' came today at church from a member who lost her mother on September 11th. Her mother was on one of the flights that were flown into the World Trade Center that day. This church member came up to my son, gave him a big hug, and with tears streaming down her face presented him with an envelope. When he opened it, inside was the American flag pin and ribbon she had been given at Ground Zero at the memorial service in honor of those who lost their lives 9/11.

She wrote a beautiful thank you note and said she wanted him to have the pin as a thank you for his service in the war on terrorism. My son was so moved he said, "I don't know what to say." To which she responded, "You don't have to say anything, I wanted you to have it as my thank you."

Needless to say, there were not many dry eyes around! For my son, it made the whole deployment worth every minute of it.

31 March - Won't Put That Pin Away

Although my son, with B Co, 1-8IN, 3BCT, 4ID, arrived safely at Ft. Carson about a week and a half ago, I continued to wear a yellow ribbon with American flag lapel pin. I had been wearing it every day since he deployed to Iraq in April, 2003. I wore the lapel pin to the office on workdays as well as on weekends and holidays. When he arrived safely at Ft Carson, we were as thankful as any parents, but I couldn't stop wearing that pin. It just didn't seem right to put it away with all the other Soldiers still over there.

This past Sunday, we were eating out in a recently opened

local restaurant here in northern Virginia, and our waitress saw the lapel pin and asked where she could get one. She explained that both her brother and boyfriend were now in Kuwait, destined for duty in Iraq with their Army National Guard unit. I immediately removed the lapel pin from my shirt, explained its history, and gave it to her to wear. I told her to wear it every day, and just maybe she would have the same good fortune as us in having her loved ones return safely. Her eyes lit up like you wouldn't believe as she nervously accepted the lapel pin.

Later, during the meal, she came by and explained that her mom was at a table in another part of her section. When she told her mom what had just transpired, her mom was brought to tears.

Redeployment Tips

In the midst of preparing for our Soldiers to return home, Bob started a section in his updates titled 'Re-Deployment Tips.' We all get preconceived ideas about a perfect reunion, but reality sets in eventually. These are examples of redeployment tips:

Before my husband came home from Desert Storm, the one thing I remember a Vietnam vet's wife telling me was let my husband take the lead in what he wants to talk about; things he did; things he saw, etc. Don't push it. Let him make the decision on this, and don't be hurt if he chooses to talk to someone else who may understand better than I ever could what he went through. This is what I plan on doing this time as well. He knows he can talk to me, but he also knows I understand if he doesn't want to.

I think first and foremost that everyone should remember to take it slow and keep the lines of communication open. Both the Soldier and the spouse have to be willing to accept the fact that we will all have changed and grown in some way over the deployment year.

In my research for redeployment advice, I remember one thing I read that cautioned against getting into a contest with your Soldier as to who suffered most during the deployment. We all suffered through this in different ways, but it will be in the past. So don't dwell on it; it won't matter any more, move forward; count your blessings and be thankful your Soldier is home safe. Just like having a baby, once you lay eyes on that sweet face all the pain of labor is erased from your mind.

From a Vietnam veteran:

After my last yearlong deployment, I had to realize when I got home that my wife had been the one taking care of everything while I was gone. She had to make all the decisions, be Mom and Dad, bill payer, handyman, and all the little things you just take for granted when you are home. You can't come back after being gone for a year or longer and expect to step back into the same role you were doing before you left. Take things slow and gradually work back into doing the things you were before.

The biggest burden on my wife was the bill paying, so I took that over. Making decisions about how to handle things is something else you have to work back into doing. Make joint decisions; discuss the matter, then you both decide. Keep open communications; that is the strongest piece of advice you can give to someone coming home. Relax and discuss things openly. There will be things you won't want to talk about, and you need to let them know. Just keep an open mind and communicate with each other.

From a wife who has been through three long deployments:

My advice is that when the Soldiers come home, and you reunite, do not have a lot of things planned. Go slowly. It is a time of readjustment. It's important not to have any unreal expectations. Do the simple things you used to enjoy doing together, like sitting on the porch talking, taking the kids to the park, watching a favorite movie on TV, go out to eat or for an ice cream, go to the movies, or take a long walk together, hand in hand. Keep communications open. Understand that your Soldier may be tired when he/she gets back. Be proud of each other and all that you both have accomplished during the deployment.

The Soldier should compliment his spouse on how well he/she did while he/she was deployed. Be proud that your spouse may have become more independent, and be proud that your spouse has handled things well while you were deployed. If you have children, give them time to also adjust and expect them to test you. The Soldier should try to spend alone time with each child when he/she can. Try to keep your routine with the children's activities and school. Be sure to stick to your budget and not go on big shopping sprees.

As a preteen, my dad deployed during Desert Storm. He took a month of leave when he came home and was around all the time. After seven months of 'freedom' while he was gone, it was hard to adjust to his stricter rules when he came back. Now, as a Soldier looking forward to going home, I can understand the desire to be home a lot and recreate a niche for myself. But it is very important for Soldiers to understand that families are not used to them being there and have had a year to create a new routine. Much like leaders arriving at new units, service members should spend some time observing the new family routines before trying to change things. And family members should remember that they aren't the only ones making adjustments.

My mother-in-law wanted me to send along this tip. If you are extended family (parents, siblings, grandparents) please understand that your son/daughter needs to spend some time alone with his or her spouse and kids. It isn't that they don't want to see you but they need that adjustment time first before the big family reunion.

From a single Soldier, veteran of six deployments:
For many of our single Soldiers (including officers) this is their first deployment. All of our Soldiers who live in the barracks put their belongings in storage, and those of us renting turned in our house and put our belongings in storage as well. Vehicles have been sitting in storage for over a year, and it is very likely we will be facing lots of dead batteries and flat tires.

I'd like to take this opportunity to ask the family members to remember those Soldiers who will be returning to no hugs and kisses of loved ones at the gym and an empty room and fridge, and offer some suggestions on how to give them a hero's welcome as well.

Talk to your Soldier. See if they can give you one or two names of single Soldiers in the unit you can adopt for a few days after deployment. Make a welcome home sign with their name on it to wave at the gym. Even though they know they don't have family in the stands, they will still be eagerly scanning the bleachers for a familiar face. One of the hardest moments of redeploying is watching families reunite while you're standing by yourself waiting for the call to load the bus.

Make a little goody bag to give to single Soldiers (along with a hug or two before they get on the bus to go to their barracks or hotel room) with some fruit, chips, a sandwich or two, a drink, and a phone card so they'll have something to snack on when they get to their rooms and they will be able to call their families to let them know they are home. All of our phones were turned off before we left. They will not have a car for a few days to run to the shoppette, and for those arriving after hours, it could be a long wait between meals before the dining facility opens.

I've noticed in the updates that many family members of single Soldiers are worried about their loved ones immediate needs after their return. I don't know specifics, but maybe this will be of some comfort to them. The command structure will not fail your sons or daughters. They will make sure that they have a place to stay; plenty of barracks are being cleaned up and repaired as we speak. They will have enough food. True, it may not be home cooking, but it isn't food that has had to travel hundreds of miles before it was prepared either.

There are several fast food places on post and a bunch of restaurants that are only a taxi ride away. When they get off the planes there will be a welcome home ceremony where everyone will make your Soldier feel welcome and appreciated. Our battalion's FRG (1-66 AR , Semper in Hostes, Iron Knights) made goody bags for our returning Soldiers and passed them out to the single Soldiers returning from Iraq for ETS and PCS prior to the stop-loss and stop-movement orders. I went to almost every flight that had our Soldiers on it to pass out the bags and to thank them. We made signs and yelled like crazy at the ceremony ... great fun, even though it wasn't our husbands or relatives. I was very impressed by the amount of attention given to those flights and ceremonies, so I can imagine what will be done for welcoming home an entire outfit.

Many FRG's are running around like mad to raise funds for these welcome home events. This is in addition to what the Army, itself, provides. If your son (sorry gals, we're a combat battalion) is in our battalion, 1-66 AR BN, we are going to have a goody bag that has some good old fashioned American munchies and personal hygiene items in them and a few extras we've been working on for months in each room. We are working with the 'powers that be' to see if they will let us go in and make the beds. We are also working to coordinate transportation to take the Soldiers to the PX, etc. for the first couple of days. Your sons have done so much for the world, there is no way we would let them down! Iron Knights!

From another Army wife on the same topic:
As for the single Soldiers returning home, please let your readers know that FRG groups are making plans that definitely include the single Soldiers! We will make sure everyone is taken care of! Ft. Hood is one big family!

Be ready to listen. I know guys get hit with the notion of being bad listeners, and frankly most of us are, but this is going to be a time when your wife is going to need an ear. Also invest in tissues, lots of them, because if anyone's wife is like mine, she has a lot of crying pent up because as she puts it, "It doesn't do my Soldier any good to see me cry."

Plan an escape. If you can't afford a real trip away or have to wait a while for block leave, lock the doors, find a sitter (or parents/in-laws), take the phones off the hook and just enjoy the time together.

Get your house in order. My Soldier told me none of those things mattered to him and not to kill myself cleaning and organizing before he got home, but it did matter. Within seven days, the 'honeymoon was over' and he began moving things around, sorting through what to keep or toss, and complaining about the clutter in the garage. I wanted to kick myself for believing he would just be happy to be home. Have a garage sale, solicit help from friends, or splurge on a cleaning service, but for goodness sake, get your house in order. The extra work or expense will be well worth it and save you many arguments in the long run.

I recently spoke with a friend of mine who is a veteran of many 'global hot spots' such as Operation Enduring Freedom and Operation Iraqi Freedom, and asked him if he had any advice to give about the redeployment. He told me (as we have heard many times) not to question the Soldiers, but to let them come to you about what has gone on in their deployment. He said that when they do come to you listen with a big ear and a closed mouth, because they do not necessarily want you to comment.

Also, the same story may be told fifteen different times, but told with different emotions each time. Maybe one time, pride; another, sorrow or remorse, and this is what makes it not the same old story, but different because of the emotion behind it.

He said not to say, "'I have heard this ten times already!'" but rather keep listening. He also told me not to get too upset with my Soldier if he wants to go play golf with the guys that he just saw for the last year. I have not seen him in a year and may think to myself, *Hey, you have been with them, not me! Why do you need to go off with them?* But those guys understand in ways that I never will. No matter how understanding I may try to be, many times they will be able to help him more than I because they were there with him through it and saw it first hand.

He said that war buddies have an understanding and that sometimes you just need to be with them and maybe talk about it and maybe not, but many times things will be better when your Soldier returns home from that game of golf. My friend speaks from experience, so I will listen!

One invaluable lesson I learned after our last long deployment was to take the time to enjoy him coming home. By the time he came back, we had family and friends lined up insisting we had to come see them all. Trying to be kind and trying to let him see everyone, his family and I had a long schedule jam-packed with visiting as soon as he got the okay to take leave. Not only did this exhaust all of us, but with all the traveling, it made a very hard readjustment to our own home schedule. Not only were the kids dealing with Daddy coming home, but also being carted around to several different relatives in a very short amount of time. We had no down time. He didn't get to get used to his own bed, couch, or refrigerator. Please, remember, your Soldier and your family need to be the priority.

If extended family and friends have waited a year, they can wait a couple more weeks (be sure and keep in touch with them on the phone though) so you can enjoy a little down time with just your Soldier and your immediate family.

This is the second war I have had to deal with and the repeated stories are something I noticed that does occur. At first it was something he was not wanting to be mentioned. Now it's easier to talk about something that has happened more than one time. If they do talk to you about it, that is because of that feeling they have at that time. Some will never express themselves to you. Just be patient with them. Be loving and not pushy.

I totally agree with listening. If you are a talker, you had better learn how to just listen. They love you and miss you, and what they need is your support and love even after they come home. So remember when you see them for the first time in a year, they look to you to give them that understanding and patience. Let them plan at their own pace. I have learned to be a person that can be leaned upon at all times and not to be the judge of their emotions and feelings. I cannot wait for all the men to return home. Remember, let them plan their days. I'm sure you will be able to do all the things you plan after a while. I'm proud to be a US Army Soldier's wife of 4ID in Fort Hood, Texas. God bless them all and bless you with patience.

I have been reading the Redeployment Tips daily. Great Stuff! Just read the ones from today's update and it made me think about my uncle. He fought in World War II and never discussed one detail of the action he saw with anyone until the late 1980s. What patience my aunt must have had to not push him for details!

After I joined the army, however, he began asking me questions about what types of equipment, units, etc., were in the army's inventory. About one year after he began asking me questions, he located some of the guys that were in his unit way back then, and not only did he start talking about his experiences during the war, but started attending the annual reunion with his buddies. It not only had a tremendous healing effect on him, but also on my aunt, as she was now able to share in that part of his life. Those reunions turned into some of their most memorable, fun loving, and sharing times.

So whether it takes three months or forty years for our soon-to-be returning husbands to open up, keep your patience and support them in every way possible (easier said than done some days). The payoff will be worth the wait.

Thanks.

I offer a gentle reminder to those spouses whose Soldiers have returned. In the midst of all your excitement and turmoil, please don't forget the friends you have made in this long year whose Soldiers have not yet returned. They do not begrudge you any of your joy, but they do still need your friendship, perhaps even more so, until they also have that great day to celebrate their own Soldier's homecoming. (Mother of a Soldier in Iraq, watching her daughter-in-law's silent loneliness as all her friends' husbands are home, but not hers.)

Bob, just wondering if anyone else is getting the same request from their Soldier that we are. He has asked that everyone NOT come when he comes back to Fort Carson. He has consented to have his dad and me (his mom) there for the homecoming day, along with his wife of course, but has asked that we stay only one day. He says he doesn't want us to see 'the war me, only the real me.'

His siblings (ages seven to twenty-two) are having a hard time with that idea, but I think we've been able to convince them that he has earned the right to have his wishes respected on this. Do you have any thoughts on this? God bless our troops, 4th ID and the USA!

Bob's Reply:
Yes, I do have thoughts on this. Several have commented on this topic and I have addressed it up until now, but think it's now time to do so. Here's what one wife wrote:

When my hubby came home for mid-tour, leave his family came and stayed. We had no private time to readjust. I know that the first few days for him were very overwhelming, trying to get used to the kids, the time change, and just simply being in a non-hostile environment. So my tip for redeployment would be to ask family members to hold off on their visits until your Soldier can settle in. In our case we have a new child, and they need time to get acquainted. Hopefully our family members are reading!

Another wife wrote:
After our first deployment, my Soldier just wanted to be at home with us for the first three to four days. He slept in. We were all bums with him. He didn't want to see anyone and only took a

339

few phone calls from close family and friends. Then we took a little vacation as a family. I think it's important (if you can financially), to get away and reconnect away from your home. Somehow it's less pressure because you are all experiencing something new together.

When we got back, he was ready to see and deal with other people. We did not have a welcome home party for him last time because he just wanted to come home quietly. This time he is open to the idea of a party because he received so much support that he wants to thank everybody.

I know you don't want to spend time on the issue of who should be there for the return of Soldiers, but as I read about Soldiers only wanting spouses there and no parents. I just thought, Wow! I am a wife of a Soldier, and I will never exclude his parents. All of the parents have gone through this emotional year just as well as the spouses. Some have even helped the spouses pull through some hard times. Like the lady said, there is only one mother in that Soldier's life and she has shed her share of tears as well.

From a Rear Detachment Commander:
Look at insurance policies and restore original coverage if you decreased the amounts during the deployment. I would use a date around 1 April (sooner or later based on individual expected return dates) to start the coverage back up. Check plates and registrations. Check your Texas state inspection. Check post stickers and renew. These are ankle-biters that will make your spouses return far less stressful.

Redeployment Tip from a teacher's point of view:
I am an army spouse who has never gone through redeployment, and I do not have my own children yet. However, I have eighteen energetic students in a classroom. From a teacher's perspective, please do not forget about your children and the emotions that they have had this past year. I have read about not expecting too much when your spouse gets back. Please, also discuss these things with your children. Let them know what to expect.

In their minds, they are expecting the same person that left to come back (from the perspective of a school-age child, not an infant). They may be thinking that everything will be perfect when Mom or Dad comes back. Don't burst their bubble, but let them know that you may have things to work out. Tell them about your feelings and how you will handle them if you get disappointed. These kids are going to be so excited that a lot of this may not make sense to them but please make the effort.

I hate to put a damper on everyone's excitement about our guys coming home. My eldest son is in Kindergarten this year. The dad of one of his classmates just came home and surprised his child at school. Several children just had their dads leave. And several others (like my son) were totally heartbroken. I had to take my son out of the building in tears, because he wanted his daddy too. I know my husband is returning soon, and my son's reunion isn't far away, but he doesn't understand that. The best place for the surprise may be when the children walk into their own home. Just an idea.

An excellent tip from a wise woman:
I really appreciate your 4ID updates. I am a seventy-four year old mother of a son in Iraq. I am also the wife of fifty-two years to a Vietnam and Korean veteran. Some of these redeployment tips are not only tips for redeployment, but are tips for everyday life, if you expect to make marriage a lifetime commitment.

Task Force Ironhorse - March 2004 Casualties

PFC Bert. E. Hoyer, 23, of Ellsworth, Wisconsin, died March 10 in Ba'quabah, Iraq, when an improvised explosive device hit his convoy. PFC Hoyer was assigned to the 625th Engineer Company, U.S. Army Reserve, Ellsworth, Wisconsin.

THIRTEEN

APRIL - 2004
Homecoming Celebrations

April was not all celebrating. PFC German Antonio Sierra-Aguilar was our first Soldier killed after arriving home. He had survived the war, but he, his mother, stepfather, and two others were killed by a drunk driver in New Mexico just a few days after arriving home.

Throughout the month, first pitches were thrown at Major League Baseball games. General Odierno was on *Fox and Friends*, and President Bush dropped in for Easter Services at Ft. Hood. The last of our Soldiers came home. Even PFC Hammer, a little kitten born in Iraq, made it back to the states when his unit did not have the heart to leave him behind.

The Welcome Home Celebration was a great way to end the yearlong deployment. Randy Travis, Tracey Byrd, Lynyrd Skynyrd, Steve Austin, and Drew Carey were just a few of the entertainers who came to Ft. Hood for the celebration that approximately sixty-thousand attended. The uncasing of the colors started off the day. The Memorial for our fallen Soldiers was in place, and is beautiful. Two stages with concerts going on throughout the day and into the night entertained, and the entertainers thanked all the Soldiers for their service. It was a memorable day, and there is no way to give credit to all the businesses, artists, Soldiers, and individual volunteers who spent hours upon hours organizing this huge event. It was a great success, and that is all that can be said.

April 1 - We Made It!
It has been quite a year. We went almost two months between the last call from Kuwait and the next call we got from him, which was a response to a Red Cross message. We very nearly lost my

342

father after surgery. From that point on, calls became more regular, even though he and the platoon he was with were living in the desert with no buildings, no amenities, nothing. His determination over the last year only compounded what I already knew. Twelve years ago, I married the most amazing and selfless man in the world. He has sacrificed so much for the good of so many others, most of whom he will never meet. He made sure to send the children AAFES coin pogs in his letters to them and carried their drawings and letters in his wallet throughout a country he never wants them to visit.

His unit returned early Saturday morning. Everything went well. Many of the families exclaimed at the excitement of the event, but it wasn't exciting to me. Seeing the plane land and watching the formation march into the deployment center at Fort Bliss meant that my life could once again return to normal. I could take my home phone off forwarding to my cell phone. I would no longer have to check my e-mail fifteen times a day. And the dreaded call from a military official would go away.

He is home now. Things are so good. We don't do a lot of balloons and signs, no big parties yet. Now I have a chance to make a real dinner every night, while he helps take the kids to karate and violin, and better yet, he gets to make dinner too, while I take the kids. The little ones are smiling more, even though they are adjusting to having another body in the house and another authority figure. I have to relearn how to sleep with someone next to me, which isn't going so well, but I will not complain. I am grateful for the Diet Coke he brought me last night when we were watching TV. I like having him make the bed sometimes, and now I don't have to look at a full trash can and wonder when I will feel compelled to take it out. Life is good. I am thankful.

1 April - Where is My Soldier?
My husband's unit made it home yesterday, except for my husband and seven other guys. They need to stay behind to make sure the vehicles get on the boat. He said it is slow over there, and it could be as late as April 10 before he makes it back home.

2 April - 70 Year Mark
We have finally reached April 1st with ninety-five percent of our Soldiers of the 4ID and TF Ironhorse home. What a welcome relief! I also, remember when you first started using the date of

April 1st counting the days until my seventieth birthday. It has arrived with one hundred percent. Tomorrow is the 25th Birthday of my grandson who is with the 4th ID at Fort Carson. So, since he is home and I have hit the seventieth mark, everything is well.

2 April - Worrying For at Least Another Year
My brother, A Company, 1-22 IN, came home a couple of weeks ago! He is with the 4ID at Fort Hood. I haven't had a chance to see him yet, but I will be flying to Texas in mid-April. I am so excited to see him and am grateful that he came home. He says it's tough adjusting, but he is taking it day by day. After worrying for a year about my younger brother, I will be worrying for at least another year.

My older brother, with the A Troop, 1-7 CAV (I think I got that right) in Baghdad, also out of Fort Hood, left a few weeks ago. Again, I am so excited that the troops are home and safe; however, let's not forget those that are still out there. Keep praying for their safe return!

Florence Ables - Mother of SPC Owen Thomas - 4ID 1-10 CAV
My son was called home from Iraq for the death of my husband on March 6, 2004. But while he was still there, I got on the Internet, and started asking companies for help. Hershey sent me candy, gum, and a case of mixed chips for the cookies I made. Pioneer Sugar donated 100-pounds of sugar; Neco Wafers donated a case of candy; Sunkist donated candy; Michigan Sugar Company gave brown sugar, white sugar and powdered sugar. The company that makes Atomic Fire Balls donated 50-pounds of fireballs; the Green Bay Packers sent him a box of things; and Charlie Daniels sent a CD. I have stuff left and am now sending to my son's best friend in the Marines who is back over in Iraq for the second time. I make boxes of cookies and send those too,
PROUD MOM OF AMERICAN SOLDIER

Gina Sanford - Wife of SGT Sanford - 1-10 CAV
My husband has returned home from Iraq, and is on the way to Warrant Officer Candidate Course and then flight school. I can't tell you how wonderful it is to have him home. The rest of his troop are in our thoughts and prayers daily that they will return

344

home safe and soon. I have to say that my biggest inspiration through all of this is my husband and children. I gain strength by being supportive to my husband, and caring for my three small children (ages six, three, and two). My husband and I have been together since we were fourteen and sixteen years old. We are the epitome of 'high school sweethearts.'

At the young age of twenty-five, I have been married for seven years to the man of my dreams. After getting into the typical married rituals it is easy to forget how much love is there. It seems that daily routines, bills to be paid, and chores around the house drowned out the feelings that you have for your spouse.

My husband, deployed on March 31, 2003, to Iraq, kept a daily journal. From the moment he left our home he wrote his thoughts, feelings, and events down in his little beat up green army book. He wanted to have something to bring home to me that would explain his experiences in Iraq, and to let me know how much he thinks about the children and me. This journal is amazing! It is written in simple everyday language from the perspective of a very hard working Soldier.

As a military spouse it is very easy to feel like your accomplishments go unnoticed. All the things we have to overcome when our spouse is deployed. We are faced with experiences that we thought we could never accomplish on our own. It is easy to feel like our deployed spouse doesn't understand what we are going through, and that they don't think it could possibly be as bad as what they are facing. The journal my husband kept for me put everything into perspective. He expressed his undying love for me; his fears, and his worries. He let me know how proud he is of me, and how much he respects my role as his wife and mother of his children. He also let me in on a little of what it is like to be a Soldier and face unfathomable circumstances. This helped me gain respect for what he has been through. It has given me the inspiration to be the best military spouse I can be.

Yes, I too have been through 'hell' during his deployment. Deaths in the family, sicknesses, neighborhood problems, and a trip on my own from Texas to Montana and back with three children and two dogs. Nothing could make me feel as proud as knowing that my husband is thankful to have me, loves me, and respects me for what I have been through, too.

3 April - 4ID Homecoming - 1-17 FA - Fort Sill, OK

Our daughter-in-law called on Sunday saying that our son would be home at 2:30 p.m. on the 31st of March. This was the best news I could receive; our son had been gone for over a year and had not been able to get the two week R&R. The next call came Tuesday evening; the plane would arrive an hour later than they first thought. My thoughts were, *I have waited over a year, I can accept this, and we all know things can change.*

Wednesday morning the next call came saying they have "run into bad weather, and it will be 5:00 p.m. before the plane lands." This is still okay, I am the happiest mother in the world at this time and then I hear the news, five more troops have been killed. Talk about mixed emotions; I am happy for our family but so sad for five other families.

We all gather at my son and daughter-in-law's house and begin to help our daughter-in-law hang the last of her signs. The outside of the house is covered with welcome home signs, their fence and the neighbors' fence are covered; then we start putting signs on the neighbor's house. My daughter-in-law has written all over her car windows and on my son's truck windows. Next the signs are put on my son's truck. One of the neighbors calls the newspaper, and they come take pictures. We get in the cars to go to the hanger to welcome home the 1-17th FA (six cars). I start to wonder if this is going to be too many people for my son to handle.

We arrive at the hanger and wait what seems forever. My cell phone vibrates, I answer it, and it is our youngest son (he had to drive one of the National Guard trucks to Ft. Sill and is going to the field for five days, and he so wanted to be there to welcome his big brother home). He says, "Mom, I have been dismissed until six o'clock tomorrow morning, can you come get me?" My car is blocked; I cannot leave so I call him back and he tells me he will be there one way or the other. Sure enough, he makes it.

They tell us they are going to open the hanger doors, and we can see the plane fly over. Next, the plane has landed; our Soldier is on the bus; the bus is leaving the airport; our Soldier is in the next hanger; we look out the hanger door, and we can see our Soldiers coming this way. The 1/17th from Ft. Sill march in, and when they are dismissed, the crowd goes wild. I wonder how my daughter-in-law and grandson are going to find the love of their lives, but they do. The most wonderful sight was the hugs, kisses and love in the eyes of three people that I love so much.

My wonderful daughter-in-law backed off and let everyone else have their hugs before the three of them drove off toward home to start their lives as a family again. We told them when they were ready, to call, and we would see them then.

5 April - With Dad on the Farm

Like many families, I'm happy to report that my husband came in to Ft. Hood yesterday. I would like to thank everyone for all the tips on how to deal with the Soldiers coming home. I would not have had a clue what to do when my husband walked through the house and grabbed four sets of clothes and said he was headed to Oklahoma alone, that he needed space. He just needed to spend time with his dad on the farm. So I did nothing but ask him to be careful and to have a good trip. I feel this is something he needs to do to clear his head.

To any other men or women out there, please let them choose what to do to help them feel better; just a tip from someone whose husband has been in the army for twenty-three years. Thank you all for all your prayers, and please don't forget there are still so many more Soldiers that they still need all our prayers.

5 April - Thanks, FRG Leaders

One week ago today my husband and I were blessed to be in Starker Gym when our son arrived home from Iraq. As I sat and waited for him I reflected on all that the past year has meant to us. I want to thank the FRG leaders for all that they have done. The information they provided and the support have been outstanding.

From experience, I can say that the 4th ID FRG sets a standard that should be applied to all deployed units. I am nearly as proud of their hard work and dedication as I am of the work done by our Soldiers. As we drove around Ft. Hood, I recognized many of the places and road names that I had read about in the various e-mails. In some ways this made the post much less intimidating. I just wanted everyone to know how fortunate we are to be a part of such a wonderful group.

5 April - Birthday to Remember

Yesterday was our son's (1-10 CAV, C Troop) twenty-first birthday. He is back at Ft. Hood and he and his buddies went to

Austin to celebrate. Last year, he spent his twentieth birthday in Kuwait, wearing a gas mask while waiting out a possible scud attack. One birthday he'll never forget and one birthday he may not want to remember! We feel so fortunate that he is back in the United States, and we pray for the families that have Soldiers away from home.

7 April - Angel Ladies

Hello, Bob. I am sorry to be this long in sharing the return of my grandson with the 16 Signal BN to Ft Hood. What an exciting welcome he received! We received a most welcome phone call from a wonderful lady with FRG letting us know that my grandson would arrive at Ft Hood the next day, at approximately 8:00 p.m. At three o'clock on the morning of the 23rd, we received a call from him saying he was in Ireland and on his way home. The next call was from Bangor, Maine. He was overwhelmed, excited and happy. He said they were surrounded by veterans from all the wars, who were shaking their hands, hugging them, offering them cell phones to call home, and asking what they could do for them. What a special memory he will carry through life of his welcome by so many heroes from the military family that he is now a part of.

Now for his welcome to Ft Hood. As I wrote in a past newsletter, due to caring for my Mother who is eighty-nine years old, I was not able to be there to greet him, but three wonderful ladies met him for me. They graciously did this out of the goodness of their hearts. I will be indebted forever to them. What a grand job they did! When he ran into the gym, they met him with a banner with his name on it. The Colonel's wife presented him with the huge balloon bouquet I bought for him, and the other ladies took pictures for me and sent them shortly after, so I could see his face and share in this wonderful homecoming.

The 'angel ladies' walk around Ft Hood. I thank them for caring and making a precious memory for our hero and his family. Bob, I want to thank you for making this possible. Your newsletter was how I found the ladies. The updates helped keep me going, knowing how many were sharing the same emotions I had every day. I continue to read the letter every day. My love and prayers go out to all the families who won't be greeting their Soldiers in this life. I cry and grieve for each lost hero! My prayers will

continue until all our heroes come home. My prayers for all the Soldiers and their families will continue. Thank You.
A Grandma in Seattle

9 April - Anything Homemade
From the mother of a TF Ironhorse Soldier who is also the wife of a 1st CAV officer:
It's been a week of contrast. My daughter was going to fly straight from Kuwait to Ft. Lewis with a group from the 14th EN, but her journey landed her on the ground here at Ft. Hood for a few hours!

After I got the call, I picked up my daughter and the rest of her traveling companions and brought them to the house for a shower and "anything homemade." They enjoyed washing the desert off immensely. They liked feeling water between their toes and the smell of the fresh towels. They especially liked walking down the hall for a twenty-minute extended bath, rather than hiking a mile for two-minute shower.

They changed into civilian clothes, but I noticed they were still moving in a group. All in the kitchen, then all in the living room, then all on the carport to check their gear, then all to the backyard to smell the fresh air. Over the next few hours, they seemed to visibly relax; one went to the TV room, one to send an e-mail of his arrival, another outside to call his wife.

I must say, I've never seen such an appreciative group of guests! The big hit was BLTs. We had eggs, toast, donuts and steak biscuits, lots of fresh coffee with real cream. One Soldier just wanted to sit on the floor. She stroked the carpet and remarked how much she missed carpets. Another wanted to play ping-pong and a little football with my son.

After a few hours they got their plane tickets, and we had about another hour before they had to leave. I asked if anyone knew the workings of a charcoal grill. I'd had my husband get one for me, but hadn't had success working it. This became a major project! There was much discussion of technique, airflow, etc. They worked it like a field problem. The fire set, we all gathered to watch. We must have spent thirty-minutes watching the coals go from black to gray with very few words. Each was clearly lost in thought.

I went to the kitchen and returned with some hot dogs and the ceremony began. Dogs carefully placed, discussions about how good they were going to taste, the smell of the grill reminding them of camping trips of years gone by. That was the best hot dog I ever ate! They grabbed some soda in bottles out of the aluminum washtub where I had them iced down, and a great time was had by all.

The doorbell rang, and it was time for them to "do the duffle drill" and get to the airport. It was hard letting go of my daughter, but she chose to return to her unit rather than sign in here at Hood. She'll be back in a few days and I'll count all her toes again, just like I did when she was born twenty-three years ago.

This week also brought the news of several casualties and many, many wounded to my husband's unit, 1st CAV. The news of the attacks came just before her arrival. It was as though the war was captured in a snapshot. It's that odd mixture we family members know well: dread and pride. Yes, a week in contrast indeed. Continue prayers for those down range, and give thanks for those who've made it back.

9 April - So Sad
Just got a call this morning at 4:30 from our son, in the 1st Armor Division. He has just been told that he has to put in up to another one-hundred, twenty days in Iraq. He had just gotten to Kuwait. We are so sad. Now he will not make the wedding of his sister, his only sibling, not to mention another full summer of heat, worry, and stress. He says that he personally will not be going back to Central Baghdad, but he couldn't tell us where he and his tank would be going. It doesn't sound like he will get to have communication with home for a long time again. We would appreciate your prayers.

9 April - Now Others Must Wait
I can't agree with you more about continuing to support the troops who are now in Iraq. My brother just returned to Ft Carson two weeks ago, and even though the weight has been lifted off our family's shoulders, there is still that sick feeling in my stomach every time I hear that another Soldier has died.

They say yesterday was the deadliest for our troops since President Bush declared major battle over. Thank God my Soldier is home, but how many sisters, wives, parents, etc., have to now deal with the worries and wonders and waiting for a phone call to say that they are okay, just like we just did for the past year.

I have really become more appreciative of our military and so much more aware of what they do for us since my brother was sent to war. You're right, we should not question and criticize the efforts in Iraq, just because our loved ones are safe and back home.

12 April - Readjustment

The last few weeks have been filled with yard work, movie rentals, and lots of yummy food. It hasn't all been completely blissful, though, as we both have had to work at the readjustment phase of his return. Part of the problem was I spent the last few months of his tour romanticizing how things would be when he got home—big mistake! When things weren't as 'romantic' or 'fabulous' as I'd dreamed they'd be at every moment, I was let down, sort of like that feeling you get right after all the presents have been opened on Christmas Day.

You know, when you think to yourself, *Okay, I've been preparing for this for the last few months. Now it's here, the big moment is over. Where do I go from here?*

My husband is a wonderful man, loving father, compassionate partner, the whole nine-yards. But once the honeymoon of his first few days at home had ended, I began to see the emotional toll this whole experience has taken on him. He was less patient, had a hard time relaxing or just sitting still, and wasn't as good a listener as he had always been with me.

Knowing that our reintegration counseling wouldn't begin for several weeks, I did the only thing I knew to do: talk. I sat him down, told him how much I love him, and asked him to please listen to everything I had to say. After much discussion, I was able to determine that he had been accustomed to being with the guys for so long that he needed to be reminded that I'm not one of his buddies in the field. He told me to please keep him in check and not let things go that bother me or hurt my feelings.

I urge all your readers to recognize the importance of communication during the initial reintegration period. Don't rely solely on the reunion counseling services to get you through the hard times. Chances are you'll experience some before the classes even start. Suppressing your emotions will only add to the stresses that are already upon you.

Melissa L. Thompson - Wife of SSG Patrick Andrew Thompson - 1st Brigade
This past year that my husband has been in Iraq has been a very hard and trying one but I'm very happy to be a Soldier's wife. As people's loved ones are sent over to Iraq to serve our country and to protect our freedom, I just want them to know that getting involved in the Family Readiness Group really helped me get through this past year, because I got to see first-hand that I wasn't the only one missing a spouse, and it comforted me in knowing that other people cared. Being part of a military family is truly one of the hardest things that I've had to do in my life, and it's been hard. But from my lips to God's ears, my husband should be returning safely by the end of this month. I'd like to share a poem I wrote when I learned he was leaving to go to Iraq.

On the day when I heard that you were leaving,
My heart began hurting and I started grieving.
How could I manage without you here?
When I was so used to having you near,
Your loving smile I'd long to see.
Because you wouldn't be here with me,
But I told myself that you were needed there;
To protect our country and do your share.
With loving memories and my faith in you,
The year will pass by, and God will see it through.
So, I'd like to say thank you for being who you are
Fighting for and protecting our country has made you my star.

Keep your memories of your loved one close to heart, and whenever you get the chance to tell that special someone what they truly mean to you, don't hesitate. Always let your Soldier know that this world is a better place because he's in it defending our freedom and protecting our country.

14 April - If Gratitude and Love Could be Bottled
We had a welcome home open house for our son this past Saturday so his relatives could see and hug him and our church friends could welcome him home after praying for him all year. It was really great. It may have been a little tiring for him and probably hard to answer some of the questions, but he and his wife handled

it very well. (I am so proud of him and her for so many reasons.)

I wanted to tell you about the reactions we got as we put up signs and flags in our front yard. People stopped in their cars and asked who was coming home, and they all said to tell him, "Thank you for serving our country." Those that came to the open house all told him that too. I wish those kind expressions of gratitude and love could be bottled and sent to the Soldiers still over there who so desperately need to know they are doing a good, good thing. But we can let them know through correspondence, and we all need to keep praying.

Thank you to all our returning troops for a job well done!! And thank you to all our troops bravely stationed all over the world. May God richly bless you all.

14 April - Insurmountable Pride

Hi, Bob. I still enjoy getting your newsletters, even though my son, who is with the 4ID, 1-12 IN from Fort Carson, has been home for just over a month now. He, his wife, and eight-month-old daughter were here for Easter. It was our first holiday together since he deployed in April 2003. It was wonderful to have him home. The irony is this: one day I asked him if he missed anything about Iraq, any of the people, or anything at all. He emphatically said, "No."

Hours later he was watching Fox News Channel when they showed the Japanese civilians being held hostage at gun and knife point. He then said, "Now, I want to go back."

As bad as I want him to stay home (and thankful it isn't his choice), the pride I felt for my son at that moment was insurmountable. I told my husband last night that if he were again deployed to Iraq, they would have to take him away from me screaming and kicking, but then realized that that wouldn't do my son any good. So, if he has a job to do, I'll let it get done and let him do it. As it's been said, "Freedom isn't free!" And I'm proud to be the mother of a United States Soldier!

Lynette Dobbs - Mother of Sgt Michael Dobbs - A Troop 1-10 CAV

My gratitude needs to go out to three different sources of hope, encouragement and information over the last year. They are the ladies of the Family Readiness Group of 1/10 CAV, the troop greeters of Bangor, Maine and of course, Bob Babcock for his daily updates. It was a blessing to have them all in my corner

Shortly after my son left in March, we realized we needed a POA. Rear Detachment got word to the unit in Iraq and that was taken care of. But they did more; they connected me with the FRG group. These ladies were wonderful. I don't want to mention names for fear that I would forget one, but they became a lifeline. My husband and I are both Vietnam era veterans. My husband served in Desert Storm as well. So we are not at all new to the realities of deployment. I can remember moving to Germany not knowing whether or not I would get to see him before he left for Saudi Arabia. I did, but only for three jet-lagged days. People thought I was crazy to go under those circumstances with four kids in tow. However, I knew the importance of being close to the unit. I knew it would be much harder to stay at home where everyone worried, no one understood, and there would be no information. The FRG from my son's unit was fantastic. They kept me informed, and whenever I had questions, they were sure to help me find the answers. One poor Sergeant got stuck with getting a huge hug from me as he came through the Bangor Airport. The hug was to take back to his wife who had done so much for us.

The second group is the fine folks at Bangor International Airport. When we heard the unit would be back to Fort Hood the next day, I called the airport to find out if there were any flights from Kuwait City to Killeen, TX. I was told there was one at 1750 hrs. That was the only one they knew of. I picked my son up at school and my mother from a neighboring town, and headed out. It is two and a half hours from my mother's to the airport. We got there at 1645 hrs. and headed straight to passenger information. We were then told that the flight would be postponed until the next day. How could that be! I was devastated. As I started to leave, knowing I could not return the next day, the attendant came back and told us there would be another flight at 2150 hrs. We decided to stay, even though we were well aware of the fact that he might not be on the flight and might not even come through Bangor at all. Mind you, I had not seen my son in almost two years so there were many emotions going through me at his time.

We did leave for a short time but spent the majority of time there with the troop greeters. They had us sign a book and showed us all the pictures of guys that had come through. They had newspaper photos of those who would never return. Many had units scribbled next to their picture—undoubtedly from comrades that had returned. There were coins, patches, and other things Soldiers had donated on display. Lining one wall were cell phones galore for Soldiers passing through to use to connect with family. We had been greeted by an eighty-two year old man that had only missed a couple of flights during the past year. This included outgoing as well as incoming Soldiers to and from various hot spots around the world. He spent so much time helping us stay occupied and feel welcome. He knew we could be like a family who had been there earlier that day, only to leave disappointed when their child did not come in.

When the troops came, the music played and everyone lined up to meet them. At the end of them coming in, there was a steady cadence of clapping that truly brought tears to my eyes. As they left, there was music again and again the cadence of claps. My son was on this flight, and that was wonderful, but those folks were fantastic. They come out for every flight to greet the troops. Remember, this is Maine, and as I write at the end of March, it is snowing outside. Many of these greeters are WWII veterans. Some were Vietnam, Desert Storm, and Korean War veterans and some weren't veterans at all. But all come out. One woman was in a wheel chair. She had been there from 0100 hrs. to 2315 hrs. and was returning in the morning for a 0500 hrs. flight. These people are definitely heroes in my mind. It's important to know that our troops are welcomed in such a way. Especially since many of us can remember the unwelcome response many Soldiers received upon return from Vietnam.

Lastly, but probably most important is Bob Babcock. The FRG got me connected to this source. What a relief to come in from work each day and be able to check out the newsletter. If it had not been for the work he did, I doubt I would have made it through the year ,half as well as I did. I would have been glued to the TV, and I would have been a nervous wreck trying to get just a glimpse of my son. He provided such an important link to those of us who are not able to be a part of FRGs or other forms of support that can be found on post.

When my husband was in Desert Storm I, I could go to ACS

and e-mail or fax him. Calls would come in regularly and wives were notified when the guys would call. There were other people around who knew exactly what you were going through because they were in the same situation, and the 1st Sergeant's wife made sure we were all aware of important things like moves, etc. None of this was available to us. Bob's newsletters gave me security, information, a feeling of connectedness and a peace of mind that I thought were impossible to have as a parent, especially one so far away from the unit.

My gratitude goes out to all three of these very important people and organizations. May God bless them and help them to continue to support all of those who have come to value them and all of those that will value them in the future. Their love, faithfulness, dedication, and kindness have touched many people

If I Could Go Back

If I could go back in time and do it all again,
Knowing what I know now,
I wouldn't change a thing,
I'd marry you again.
And all the sleepless nights we spent at reenlistment time,
Choosing to stand by your side,
I wouldn't trade for all the dimes.
Although it's been a scary ride,
I want you to know
I will follow you my soldier no matter where you go.
I will pack up our family and move from here to there
As long as the army lets me, I'll follow you anywhere.
And when there's danger, and you are at war
I promise to be here like all times before.
My heart breaks at the thought of you
Being in harm's way.
It makes me blue,
That's why I pray,
I pray that you are safe
And that you're all right and that when this war is over,
you will be home to hold me tight.
I Love You SSG Horne.

SGT Christopher Hardt, Wife
Korin, and their children,
Emily and Abbie

Abbie, Korin, and Emily Hardt

Abbie,
Christopher,
and Emily Hardt

Melissa and SSG Patrick Thompson

Welcome Home in Bangor, Maine
Louise Guilleter (Grandmother) James Dobbs, (youngest brother)
SGT Michael Dobbs and Lynette Dobbs (Mother)

SSG Patrick Thompson and Daughter Sammi

SFC Chris and Christine Wallace

SPC Owen Thomas, Son of Florence Ables

**In Memory of the Task Force Ironhorse Soldiers
Who Gave Their Lives for Their Country**

I Would Not Trade This Year

It is now time to say good-bye. This week we will say good-bye to Linda Odierno and Ann Campbell. Changes of command are close together on the calendar. The Thurman's are here at Ft. Hood and ready to take command of the 4th Infantry Division.

They will prepare the division for deployment back to Iraq, beginning in August 2005. As families, what can we take away from this deployment? Have we grown? I would not trade this year, as hard as it has been, for anything. I am proud to have done my small part to support my Soldier and be a part of something as great as giving the Iraqi people a glimmer of hope for freedom. Will they be able to keep it? Only time will tell. But to the families across this great country and around the world who have supported our Soldiers with prayer, packages, letters, and e-mail—job well done.

Bob Babcock, you stepped up and did a job that was a labor of love. By stepping up, you equipped, encouraged, and enabled all of us to stay steady and stay the course. To Linda, Ann, Stephanie, Janet and the rest of the Ivy League, it has been my privilege to have served with you. I will miss you, my friends. I am convinced that God brought all of us together for a season to do a particular work and now that we have done it, it is time to move on. Never once in serving with the leadership of Ivy League did I hear an unkind remark spoken about anyone; never was a problem too large. I am proud to be part of the 4th ID family, but that is now history. There is still a War on Terror being fought. Are we up to the challenge? I will pray for strength for our country, our leaders, and our families of the Ironhorse.

—Rhonda Eggleston

Acknowledgments

My thanks to:
Polly Pat who used her dreaded red pen on this manuscript and did a fine job.

My special church lady friends who encouraged me to stay the course and complete this project.

Bob Babcock who saw a need within the families and took the job on. No one else has even tried to do what you did; your service to the families was invaluable.

My sister and friend, Deb—you have listened to me at my worst and still love me—that is a blessing I hope I return to you.

The Division Family Readiness Group leadership. You are steadfast and loyal Ladies of the Ironhorse. You led by example as you worked tirelessly before, during, and after the deployment. It was an honor and privilege to serve with you.

Linda Odierno and Ann Campbell, you set the standard for Division Family Readiness Group leadership. You were inspired by God to lead us.

Rebekah, Regan, Kala, and Eddie, my children, who let me have the computer more than my fair share and never once felt sorry for yourselves when you missed your Dad so much.

Kirk, my husband, my special Soldier hero.

And finally, to the God I try to serve each day. If there is anything creative or good in this book it is because of His inspiration and to His glory.

1BCT: 1st Brigade Combat Team
1ID: First Infantry Division
1LT: First Lieutenant
1SG: First Sergeant
2BCT: 2nd Brigade Combat Team
2LT: Second Lieutenant
3BCT: 3rd Brigade Combat Team
4BCT: 4th Brigade Combat Team
4ID: Fourth Infantry Division
AAFES: Army and Air Force Exchange System
ABN: Airborne
ACR: Armored Cavalry Regiment
ADA: Air Defense Artillery
AFN: Armed Forces Network
AG: Adjutant General
AHR: Attack Helicopter Regiment
AH-64: Model of helicopter
AIT: Advanced Individual Training
AO: Area of Operations
APC: Armored Personnel Carriers
APO: American Post Office
AR: Armor
ASB: Aviation Support Battalion
ASOG: Army Special Operations Group
AT: Antitank
AVN: Aviation
BCT: Brigade Combat Team
BDE: Brigade
BDU: Battle Dress Uniform
BG: Brigadier General (One star)
BN: Battalion
BNOC: Basic Non-Commissioned Officers Course
BRT: Brigade Reconnaissance Troop
BTRY: Battery (Artillery)
CA: Civilian Affairs
CAV: Cavalry
CENTCOM: Central Command
CG: Commanding General
CH: Chaplain
CHEM BN: Chemical Battalion
CO: Commanding Officer
Coalition: The United States and our Allies in Iraq
COL: Colonel
CNN: Cable News Network

CONUS: Continental United States
CP: Command Post
CPL: Corporal
CPT: Captain
CSB: Corps Support Battalion
CSG: Corps Support Group
CSM: Command Sergeant Major
CWO: Chief Warrant Officer (Expressed as CW1 through CW5)
DASB: Division Support Battalion
DCU: Desert Camouflage Uniforms
DISCOM: Division Support Command
DIVARTY: Division Artillery
DOD: Department of Defense
DSB: Division Support Battalion
EN: Engineer (Sometimes written as ENG)
EN GRP: Engineer Group
EMS: Emergency Medical Service
EOD: Explosives, Ordnance, Demolition
ETS: Enlisted Time Served
FA: Field Artillery
FOB: Forward Operating Base
FORSCOM: Forces Command
FRG: Family Readiness Group
FSB: Forward Support Battalion
FSC: Fire Support Center
FSE: Fire Support Element
G-6: Signal Officer, Division level
HF: High Frequency
HHB: Headquarters and Headquarters Battery
HHC: Headquarters and Headquarters Company
HHS/B: Headquarters and Headquarters Service Battery
HHT: Headquarters and Headquarters Troop
Hooah: Army expression meaning many positive things: yes, awesome, tough, etc.
Humvee: HMMWV, High Mobility Multi-Wheeled Vehicle, also called Hummer
ID: Infantry Division, as in 4ID for 4th Infantry Division
IED: Improvised explosive device
IN: Infantry (Sometimes written as INF)
Ironhorse: nickname for the 4ID and attached units
Kevlar: Protective helmet worn by American Soldiers
KIA: Killed In Action
KIOWA: Type of helicopter
LT: Lieutenant
LTC: Lieutenant Colonel
LTG: Lieutenant General (Three Stars)

M1 Abrams tank: Main battle tank of US Army
M113: Model of armored personnel carrier
MAJ: Major
MECH: Mechanized
MED: Medical
MG: Major General (Two Stars)
MI: Military Intelligence
MIA: Missing In Action
MOS: Military Occupation Specialty
MRE: Meal, Ready to Eat
MSG: Master Sergeant
MSR: Military Supply Route
MTN: Mountain (Referring to the 10th Mountain Division)
NCO: Non-Commissioned Officer
NTC: National Training Center
NVG: Night Vision Goggles
NG: National Guard
PCS: Permanent Change of Station
PFC: Private First Class
PLDC: Platoon Leader Development Course
PLT: Platoon
PT: Physical Training
QRF: Quick Reaction Force
R&R: Rest and Recuperation
Regulars: Nickname of 22nd Infantry Regiment
RGT: Regiment (Sometimes written as REGT)
ROTC: Reserve Officer Training Corp
SFC: Sergeant First Class
SGM: Sergeant Major
SIG: Signal
SPC: Specialist
SSG: Staff Sergeant
TF: Task Force
TF Ironhorse: Name for all units working together under a single command
TOC: Tactical Operations Center
TRP: Troop
UAV: Unmanned Aerial Vehicle
WMDs: Weapons of Mass Destruction
XO: Executive Officer